complicities

PHILOSOPHY AND POSTCOLONIALITY

A series edited by Valentin Mudimbe

and Bogumil Jewsiewicki

complicities

the intellectual and apartheid

MARK SANDERS

DUKE UNIVERSITY PRESS

Durham and London

2002

© 2002 Duke University Press
All rights reserved
Printed in the United States of America on acid-free paper
Designed by Amy Ruth Buchanan
Typeset in Carter & Cone Galliard by Keystone Typesetting, Inc.
Library of Congress Cataloging-in-Publication Data appear
on the last printed page of this book.

Parts of certain chapters have appeared in different versions and are reprinted by permission: "Towards a Genealogy of Intellectual Life: Olive
Schreiner's *The Story of an African Farm*," in *NOVEL: A Forum on Fiction*
34, no. 1 (2000), copyright NOVEL Corp © 2000 (chapter 1); "'Problems
of Europe': N. P. van Wyk Louw, the Intellectual and Apartheid," *Journal of
Southern African Studies* 25, no. 4 (1999), copyright Taylor & Francis Ltd.
⟨http://www.tandf.co.uk⟩ (chapter 2); "Responding to the 'Situation' of
Modisane's *Blame Me on History:* Towards an Ethics of Reading in South
Africa," *Research in African Literatures* 25, no. 4 (1994), © Indiana Univer-
sity Press (chapter 3). The epigraph in chapter 1 from Olive Schreiner's
"Journal: Rattel's Hoek" appears by kind permission of the Harry Ransom
Humanities Research Center, the University of Texas at Austin.

Solomon Sanders (1922–2000)

contents

preface

This book began with the idea of writing a literary history with an emphasis on cultural politics, but it developed into the more difficult project of setting out a theory of intellectual responsibility. As South Africa underwent the momentous changes of the 1990s, the shape of my project also changed. Early in that decade notions of resistance, subversion, and the building of alternative grassroots structures were still the order of the day in anti-apartheid politics and, in turn, set the agenda for left literary and cultural studies. But with the negotiations to end apartheid, the nonracial election of April 1994, and the Truth and Reconciliation Commission, which began its work in 1996, what emerged at the forefront of public discourse was the question of *complicity*. The role of intellectuals after apartheid had become a matter of urgent debate, and it became clear that, like the legacy of apartheid thinking, the activities of intellectuals during the apartheid era would have to be scrupulously examined.

By the mid-1990s I had been in the United States for several years and had followed the polemics in the *New York Review of Books* and elsewhere on the complicity of European intellectuals in Nazism. Sensationalism dominated, and the level of debate, on the whole, was not high. Although some commentators endeavored, with mixed results, to establish deeper links between a given writer's thoughts and deeds, accusers were typically content to identify glaring instances of collaboration or accommodation on the part of their antagonists: Martin Heidegger, Paul de Man, even Jean-Paul Sartre. Defenders, for their part, would adduce instances of resistance or opposition.

Until recently, there has been no full-scale philosophical exposition of complicity on which to draw. I attempted to develop, from incidental remarks in the responses of Jacques Derrida and others, a conception of complicity that would make it possible to think of resistance and collaboration as interrelated and to explore the problem of complicity without either simply accusing or excusing the parties involved. My project became — without relinquishing the pejorative force of the word *complicity* or, indeed, the more positive force, for many, of such terms as *loyalty* and *solidarity* — to mount a conceptual generalization of complicity as the very basis for responsibly entering into, maintaining, or breaking off a given affiliation or attachment. Returning to the South African material, I began to see that complicity was a problem not exclusively for supporters of the apartheid regime and its policies but also for opponents. At another level, in order to resist, victims needed to be aware of and overcome an intimacy of psychic colonization that led them to collaborate with the oppressor.

As a generator of otherness in language and of the self, the literary work, understood broadly, emerged as the place where intellectuals grappled imaginatively with complicity. Autobiographical and testimonial narrative of various kinds formed a hinge between history and fiction as its authors figured the greater complicity or foldedness in human being that stands as the condition of possibility for any opposition to a system that constantly denies it. As I came to see it, apartheid, though by no means unique, was exemplary as a venue for the intellectual as a figure assuming responsibility in complicity.

When making acknowledgments, it is common to speak of debt as if borrowed sums could be repaid, or perhaps to suggest that in the sphere of mind and thought repayment is out of the question. The latter is the sense I would like to convey. However, the language of debt is inadequate for what is due to Gayatri Chakravorty Spivak, who, it is no exaggeration to say, provided the conditions of possibility for this book. Without the space of thought she provided, this book would have been inconceivable. A gift has been made and accepted. Now it is time for thanks.

My book has been a labor in which many people have helped in invaluable ways. Special mention must go to André Brink, who from the outset guided me in the nuances of Afrikaans literary and intellectual history. The warm generosity of his careful and critical commentary gave direction to my first and subsequent investigations, enriching not only my knowledge of the subject but also my sense of the possibilities of translating N. P. van Wyk Louw's sometimes idiosyncratic Afrikaans prose.

Derek Attridge played a vital part, as critical reader and correspondent, in helping me to conceive and set out the implications of my arguments beyond South Africa and apartheid. His deep occupation with literature and ethics and his drawing me into dialogue on the subject in ways that demonstrate far more than an abstract commitment to it were a constant and motivating source of energy.

Parts of this book were first formulated as verbal presentations. Special thanks go to Rita Barnard for inviting me to join Ngũgĩ wa Thiong'o in a roundtable on his prison memoir at the University of Pennsylvania; to Andrew Libby, who asked me to address the graduate Comparative Literature colloquium at CUNY Graduate Center; and to Bogumil Jewsiewicki for finding me a place at a conference on memory, which he helped to organize at the University of Cape Town. These were all occasions that prompted me to develop my thoughts on the intellectual. In this connection my thanks also go to Edwin Frank for providing me with the opportunity, at a difficult time, to review works that, in the end, became key reference points in my book.

It takes time to write a book. A year spent as a fellow at the Society for the Humanities at Cornell University in 1999–2000 was the crucial time for bringing this one to completion. For the opportunity to be at this haven for tranquil study, my thanks go to Dominick LaCapra and Timothy Murray; and for their friendly assistance during my year at Cornell, I am most grateful to Mary Ahl and Lisa Patti. My thanks go to William Flesch and Robin Feuer Miller at Brandeis University for arranging my leave to take up the fellowship.

The critical comments and suggestions for revision made in the thorough reports of the two anonymous readers for Duke University Press improved this book immeasurably. Many other people read parts of it at various stages, offering insights that, even when not verifiably incorporated, became part of the final work. In this respect I would like to express especial thanks to Isabel Balseiro, Taylor Carman, Eric Cheyfitz, Neville Hoad, Andreas Huyssen, Neil Levi, Rob Nixon, and Gerrit Olivier. Conversations with Lisa Estreich, beginning with the slow dissection of Heidegger's *Sein und Zeit,* have, in profound if intangible ways, made this book what it is.

I am thankful to Johan Degenaar for generously giving me an afternoon of his time at his home in Stellenbosch. To Rustum Kozain in Cape Town go my deep thanks for mailing me, at short notice, materials not available in the United States. Archival research for this project was done at several libraries in South Africa. In this regard I thank Hanna Botha and the late Marianne van der Merwe at the Document Centre at the J. S. Gericke Library at Stellenbosch University, and Peter Midgley and the other staff members at the National English Literary Museum in Grahamstown. Janine Dunlop of the Manuscripts and Archives Division of the University of Cape Town libraries kindly assisted me with a last-minute query. I wish also to acknowledge the warm hospitality of Kirsten Stanton, who opened her house to me at the times I visited Cape Town to undertake archival research.

My gratitude goes to the Harry Ransom Humanities Center Library at the University of Texas, Austin, for providing me with access to Olive Schreiner's manuscripts. Tom Keenan stimulated my interest in Kwere Kwere; and Lalou Meltzer, curator of the William Fehr Collection at the Cape Town Castle, helped me learn more. I would like to mention the kindness of Petra Broomans, who, when I was making my final revisions, dispatched me her and Wiveca Jongeneel's Dutch translation of Thomas von Vegesack's excellent book on the intellectuals, a copy of which I could not find in North America.

Without the enthusiasm of Ken Wissoker at Duke University Press, my book would not be seeing the light of day. In this connection, I would also like to thank V. Y. Mudimbe for his constant encouragement and support for my project. Readers of my book will be indebted to the imagination and judgment of Leigh Anne Couch, my managing editor at Duke, and to the scrupulous copyediting of Elizabeth Yoder.

To William Kentridge, who so generously allowed me to incorporate an image from his work on the cover of my book, I wish to express my deepest gratitude.

For so many things — for love, for being a keenly incisive and at times skeptical reader — Louise Kuhn is, as always, the one whom I can imagine no possible way of adequately thanking. In fact, in order to make the acknowledgment that is called for, the language of thanks is itself inadequate. Another will have to be invented.

introduction
complicity, the intellectual, apartheid

Even if all forms of complicity are not equivalent, they are *irreducible.*
—JACQUES DERRIDA, *Of Spirit: Heidegger and the Question*

After apartheid, the question of complicity is unavoidable—not simply because it is necessary to know whose resources gave apartheid life, nourished and defended it, but also because apartheid, by its very nature, occasions a questioning of and thinking about complicity itself. As a variegated set of policies and practices, apartheid may have been and may still be, exemplary for provoking a response from the intellectual that could not simply be of opposition. This idea is twofold. If apartheid was a system of enforced social separation, its proponents were never able to realize the essential apartness they proclaimed as their brain-child's *archē* and *télos,* its originary law and ultimate end.[1] When, in diverse ways, its opponents affirmed an essential human joinedness against apartheid, they thus proclaimed not only the evil of this thinking but also its untruth. At the same time, like its dissenting adherents, opponents found themselves implicated willy-nilly in its thinking and practices and shaped their responsibility accordingly. Thus, beyond its local existence, the obsession of apartheid with separateness may be exemplary for causing the intellectual to emerge as a figure whose responsibility emerges not only from a promise of joinedness but also from a disquieting sense of complicity in what threatens the realization of that promise.

Complicity and Responsibility

In South Africa the Truth and Reconciliation Commission has done a great deal to bring the question of complicity to public discussion. The commission was mandated by the Promotion of National Unity and Reconciliation Act (1995) to "establish . . . as complete a picture as possible of the nature, causes and extent of gross violations of human rights" at the height of the apartheid era and its immediate aftermath (1960–94). It has produced a report that, employing a vocabulary of complicity, does not limit itself to establishing the culpability of specific agents, but seeks to produce an account of complicity that generalizes ethico-political responsibility.

The main lines of the commission's discussion of complicity are to be found in volume 4 of its report in chapters on the "institutional hearings," which sought to measure the culpability of specific sectors of the state and civil society: "the media, business, prisons, the faith community, the legal system and the health sector." Although typically not as directly implicated in gross human rights violations as the police and armed forces, "all these sectors had, over the years, come under attack for what was seen as their complicity with the apartheid system" (*Truth* 4:2).[2] The commission's investigation and findings on these institutional sectors are grounded in a juridical notion of complicity whereby agents in these sectors were usually not the principal perpetrators of the violations investigated but were accomplices or accessories after the fact. Their actions and omissions ranged from creating favorable ideological conditions for apartheid (media, faith community), to materially aiding systematic repression of political activity (prisons), to knowingly profiting from apartheid (business), to not challenging racism in their own professions (legal system, health sector, media), and to falsifying medical reports and death certificates of detainees (health sector). Registering signs of "self-analysis, a mood of introspection," the report notes the acknowledgment on the part of certain sectors (most religious denominations, as well as instances within the legal profession) of complicity in apartheid (*Truth* 4:2, 91–92, 100).

Another notion of complicity and its relationship to responsibility is set out in the chapter on concepts and principles in volume 1 of the Truth Commission's report. Under the heading, "Responsibility and Reconciliation," the report advocates fostering a "moral responsibility" that "goes deeper than legal and political responsibility." In a series of self-critical paragraphs, it puts forward two reasons why the commission failed to focus sufficiently on the dimension of moral responsibility. First, drawing the attention of the public to the deeds of the exceptional perpetrator led to a "fail[ure] to recognise the 'little perpetrator' in each of us"; whereas "it is only by recognising the potential for evil in each one of us that we can take full responsibility for ensuring that such evil will never be repeated."[3]

The second reason given for a lack of attention to moral responsibility assumes a complex network of sympathetic identification that can be realized through narrative and through the imaginative projection of the "little perpetrator" into a quasi-fictive situation where he or she is violating (though not necessarily grossly) another's human rights. This, it is implied, is why it is important that the commission "fail[ed] fully to grasp the significance of individual victims' testimony." These stories, which tell not only of "gross violations of human rights" but of "everyday life under apartheid," must be used by the nation to "sharpen its moral conscience . . . to a point where personal responsibility is [never again] abdicated" (*Truth* 1:133). By actively assuming a role in a moral drama, one is making sure that one does not unwittingly become an instrument of someone else's agenda. Contemplating an intricate play of perpetrator-figures, which transports responsibility into the realm of the literary, the assumptions informing the report's argument go against the intuition that in order to combat evil one must be, or proclaim oneself to be, untouched by it. In this fable, as in all fables, one identifies in order to disidentify.[4]

The Truth Commission's report has learned a great deal from the disasters of the twentieth century and their interpretation by theologians and philosophers. Borrowing Hannah Arendt's notion of the "banality of evil," the report in effect argues for a heightening of personal responsibility, which, paradoxically, would mean not washing one's hands but actively affirming a complicity, or potential complicity, in the "outrageous deeds" of others. Once cultivated, this sense of responsibility would, in the best of possible worlds, make one act to stop or prevent those deeds: "Only in this way can South Africans ensure that they do not again become complicit in the banality that leads, step by step, to the kinds of outrageous deeds that have left South Africans feeling that they can never be expected, even indirectly, to accept responsibility for them" (*Truth* 1:131–33).

If an acknowledgment of actual deeds by perpetrators and their accomplices in sectors of civil society is a moving drama of expiation that can sometimes also satisfy the demand for historical clarification, such an acknowledgment remains, statistically speaking, an exceptional performance. The projection of complicity through an owning of the "little perpetrator" is, however, the ethico-political response available to anyone.

The Intellectual and Complicity

The history of this response is coeval with that of the intellectual.[5] The act of affirming one's complicity in order to assume responsibility for what is done in one's name without simply distancing oneself from the deed can be traced back to Émile Zola's "J'accuse" (1898), an open letter to the President of France on behalf of Alfred Dreyfus, the Jewish artillery officer falsely accused and convicted of treason. "I shall tell the truth," Zola wrote. "It is my duty to speak up; I will not be an accessory to the fact" (*Dreyfus* 43) ("La vérité, je la dirai. . . . Mon devoir est de parler, je ne veux pas être complice" ["Lettre" 97–98]). Zola's letter was followed the next day by a "Manifesto of the Intellectuals" calling for the revision of the Dreyfus verdict, signed by a diverse group of "academics, writers, scientists, artists and poets" (Bredin 276). This was met by attacks in the nationalist and anti-Semitic press led by Maurice Barrès of the Action Française, for whom "intellectual" was already well established as a pejorative label for "men of thought who gave their opinion on public issues" — those whom Foucault later called "universal intellectuals" (Bredin 276; Habermas 72–73, 75–76).

As Dietz Bering has shown, the figure of the intellectual in the twentieth-century sense emerged, in France and Germany at least, amid an intense anti-intellectualism coincident with anti-Dreyfusard agitation. This polarization at the origin helps us to draw out the force of Zola's declaration. The duty to speak out is linked with a will or desire not to be an accomplice. Responsibility unites with a will not to be complicit in an injustice. It thus emerges from a sense of complicity —

not the criminal complicity of the French generals who, having knowingly concealed the truth, are "accomplices [complices] to th[e] . . . crime" (Zola, *Dreyfus* 52), but the actively assumed complicity of one whose silence could allow their crime to go undiscovered.

The second thing to note about this assumption of complicity is that it takes place *on behalf of another* — an other whose otherness is scripted by racism. As in his "A Plea for the Jews" (1896), complicity is assumed by Zola in response to a racism directed against a people abhorred by the Jew-hater who, for want of a better reason, appeals to "the repulsion of one race for another," and "'feel[s] how different and other they are'" (Zola, *Dreyfus* 2). One can thus add to Jürgen Habermas's sense that the universal intellectual "intervene[s] on behalf of rights that have been violated and truths that have been suppressed, reforms that are overdue and progress that has been delayed" (73), a history of responsibility assumed for, and on behalf of, determinate others — as is particularly apparent, for instance, when Zola's gesture is deployed by Sol T. Plaatje in colonial South Africa. In this sense, "J'accuse" is first and foremost a work of advocacy. For Zola to want not to be complicit in racism is, at least tacitly, to accept and affirm a larger complicity — etymologically, a folded-together-ness (*com-plic-ity*) — in human-being (or the being of being human). When Zola writes against the authority of nationalist loyalty and militarist "esprit de corps," he does so "in the name of humanity" [au nom de l'humanité] (*Dreyfus* 52–53, trans. modified).

When Julien Benda, who had also supported Dreyfus,[6] writes in *The Treason of the Intellectuals* [La Trahison des clercs] (1928) of a betrayal by the "clerks" of the spirit in the name of action, Zola's advocacy of Dreyfus is his example — along with Gerson, Spinoza, and Voltaire — of fidelity to their calling: "When Zola and Duclaux came forward to take part in a celebrated lawsuit (Dreyfus affair) . . . these 'clerks' were carrying out their functions as 'clerks' in the fullest and noblest manner. They were the officiants of abstract justice and were sullied with no passion for a worldly object" (*Treason* 50–51). Even as Benda calls for a strict avoidance by the intellectual of practical aims, particularly those pursued in the name of race and nation, his example remains a series of concrete instances of advocacy. When the "clerk" adopts the language and practices of law, the office of "abstract justice" is, inevitably, also the pursuit of a "worldly object."

Read against the grain, as several interpreters observe (Schalk 34–35;

Walzer 34–38; Von Vegesack 103, 293 n.1), Benda's restriction of the duty of the intellectual to a call for justice in the abstract thus entails in all rigor a joining of abstract and empirical, universal and contingent. Benda is not against engagement, even "tak[ing] the part of a race or nation," when "the cause of that race or nation coincide[s] . . . with the cause of abstract justice" (*Treason* 51 n.1; see also *Trahison* 64 n.1). Behind his constraints on the "clerk" lies, however, a more profound intuition. Injustice is, as Benda views it, the outcome of the contamination of abstract and empirical, as he makes clear in an appendix to the preface of the 1946 edition of *The Treason of the Intellectuals:* "Justice is a disinterested value, and thus eminently clerical, for a reason that the majority of its fervent devotees do not see and which they would not want me to divulge here. Justice is a school of eternity, it is not a principle of action; it is static, not dynamic; regulative not creative. All that is done in practice in history is done in injustice" (*Trahison* 93–94).[7] When Benda's procedure transgresses his own stated strictures, we have not merely an unacknowledged contradiction in the writings of a single author[8] but, more generally, a laying out of an aporia of responsibility. It is not simply a question of a cause coinciding or not coinciding with justice. Whenever justice is invoked, as it always is, in the name of a specific cause, there will be the risk of doing injustice.

This aporia imposes itself not only when the intellectual assumes a notional complicity with the perpetrator of crimes but also when he or she affirms a "foldedness" in human-being when particular loyalties threaten to bar the general realization of that foldedness. These elements combine in Karl Jaspers's notion of "metaphysical guilt"; that is, his idea, set forth in *The Question of German Guilt* (1946), that "there exists a solidarity among men as human beings that makes each co-responsible for every wrong and every injustice in the world, especially for crimes committed in his presence or with his knowledge" (32). When solidarity in human-being conditions a radicalizing of "co-responsibility" as self-declared perpetratorship, what matters for the intellectual is not merely a complicity in deeds, of which he or she may or may not be aware, but the generalization of complicity in human-being that gives moral significance to those deeds. As Hannah Arendt observed, Jaspers's notion of "metaphysical guilt" is inseparable from the Dreyfus case.[9] Each concrete "case" produces its own openings and limits of universalization—as we see, for instance, when the powerful formulation that

Jaspers made his own (and that can be traced to a saying of Father Zosima in Dostoyevsky's *The Brothers Karamazov* [190]), is disseminated by figures as divergent in their commitments as Frantz Fanon, and, in South Africa, N.P. van Wyk Louw, Steve Biko, and Nadine Gordimer.

The question of universalization is at the heart of Antonio Gramsci's brief remarks on "The Intellectuals" (1932) in the *Prison Notebooks*. There Gramsci writes that "all men are intellectuals . . . but not all men have in society the function of intellectuals" (9). If all human beings are capable of thought, Gramsci implies, what it means to be an intellectual can be separated from the specific activities that restrict the social function of intellectuals ("the man of letters, the philosopher, the artist" [9]) to activities linked to particular "social groups." Gramsci, however, derives his blueprint for the working-class "organic intellectual" from an account of how, historically, intellectuals have been bound to the feudal aristocracy and capitalist bourgeoisie. Having stated, for example, that the "traditional intellectuals" such as the "ecclesiastics can be considered the category of intellectuals organically bound [legata] to the landed aristocracy" (*Prison Notebooks* 7), he prescribes a state of being bound for intellectuals in the revolutionary party: "An intellectual who joins the political party of a particular social group is merged with the organic intellectuals of the group itself, and is linked tightly [lega strettamente] with the group" (*Prison Notebooks* 16; see also 10, 14). It is plausible to interpret Gramsci's notion of "the humanistic conception of history" (*Prison Notebooks* 10; perhaps phrased in the "Aesopian" language he developed to evade the prison censor) as putting historical materialism forward as agent of the history of human-being in general. There remains the risk, though, that as in Lenin, whose tirade against "freedom of criticism" in *What Is to Be Done?* (1902) (74–77) is a notorious example, the intellectual will be required to submit to the discipline of the party that claims a monopoly over the interests of humankind as a whole. The difficulty recurs in Jean-Paul Sartre's "A Plea for Intellectuals" (1965), where the "technician of practical knowledge" becomes an "intellectual" by rejecting the subordination of his or her "universal" expertise to ruling class interests and aligning him- or herself with the working class in its "effort . . . to achieve universalization" (232, 260).[10]

Although Gramsci and Sartre usefully question the idea that intellectuals constitute an autonomous social group, the solution they offer runs the risk of repeating the problem by privileging particular affiliations. Their solution brings the danger of disqualifying universalist criticism, say, in the name of the "rights of man" or human rights, made from other quarters (for which Gramsci sets the stage when he presents the Dreyfus case as the final battle between the French capitalist bourgeoisie, and clerical and military interests [*Prison Notebooks* 22]). If the goal of the intellectual, by accepting a complicity in human-being as such, is to affirm complicity in a general sense when the loyalties that constitute complicities in the narrow sense threaten the project of human folded-together-ness,[11] it follows that any theory of the intellectual and responsibility that privileges commitment or loyalty to a particular party or cause is a one-sided interpretation of an original impulse that regards such affiliation as a problem. Stated briefly, this is because the actors in question ultimately accept responsibility only in front of their own.

Theories of *engagement* risk merely reproducing, as a norm for revolutionary praxis, a mechanistic view of the social function of the intelligentsia as allied to a ruling class whose hegemony it helps to sustain. It also follows that, whatever the strategic exigencies are, just as critical independence can only be a regulative ideal because of the implication of the mental worker in institutions and policies, any theory that privileges oppositionality or resistance is an incomplete account of responsibility. To have any meaning, responsibility requires a motivated acknowledgment of one's complicity in injustice.[12] Without in any way negating the history of opposition and resistance to apartheid, when it asks readers of its report to acknowledge the "little perpetrator" lodged inside of them, the Truth and Reconciliation Commission situates such an acknowledgment at the heart of its conception and setting to work of responsibility. "Little perpetrator" reminds us that any profession of responsibility — be it in the name of justice, resistance to injustice, or merely in the cause of solidarity — entertains the possibility of *doing* injustice.

I will conclude my short genealogy of the intellectual as a figure of responsibility-in-complicity with Jacques Derrida's *Of Spirit: Heidegger and the Question* (1987). There Derrida tracks the textuality of "spirit" [Geist] in Martin Heidegger's philosophical works and in the texts dating from his period as rector at Freiburg University in 1933–34. These latter works endeavor, philosophically and rhetorically, to align the university with the National Socialist movement.[13] Although Derrida never makes an explicit link between his discussion of Heidegger's complicity and Zola's declaration, and although the vocabulary of *Geist* [geistiger Mensch, die Geistigen] was preferred in Germany over the pejorative *Intellektuellen* [intellectuals] (Bering 33ff; Habermas 76), Derrida's discussion, which has profound implications for the intellectual and responsibility, appears to operate with "J'accuse" in the background.[14] With Heidegger, as it were, its *bad* example, *Of Spirit* can be read as an examination, for the benefit of all European intellectuals opposing Nazism in the name of "the freedom of spirit" (Derrida, *Points* 186), of the openings and limits of the statement "*Je ne veux pas être complice.*" The strategy of *Of Spirit* is to separate, and to track the contamination of, general and narrow senses of complicity. In a general sense, complicity — the foldedness or "contamination" of oppositional pairs — has been a key concern of deconstruction from the beginning, in *Of Grammatology* (1967) and even in Derrida's early *Le problème de la genèse dans la philosophie de Husserl* (1953/4). The most striking departure of *Of Spirit* is to bring the deconstructive motif of complicity into proximity with an ethico-political discourse on complicity — claims and counterclaims swirling, in this case with renewed intensity, around the political career of Heidegger and his complicity with the National Socialist movement or, as some would argue, *in* National Socialism itself.

In a meticulous reading of Heidegger's rectoral address, "The Self-Assertion of the German University" (1933), in which he attempts to avoid the reductive linkage of Heidegger's philosophy and National Socialist ideology by Pierre Bourdieu and others,[15] Derrida identifies a strategy whereby Heidegger attempts to demarcate Geist from its racial-biologistic inscriptions by National Socialism. Without accepting at face value Heidegger's postwar claims to have undertaken, from within the Nazi Party, a "resistance of the spirit" [geistiger Widerstand] ("Heidegger's Letter" 267), we can see that his strategy, though deeply compromised, is nevertheless an oppositional one. When opposition takes the form of a demarcation *from* something, it cannot, it follows, be untouched by that to which it opposes itself. Opposition takes its first steps from a footing of complicity.

This is also the basic structure underlying Zola's declaration. A major difference between the impulse informing "J'accuse" and other interventions of its kind, and the analysis of Heidegger put forward in *Of Spirit*, lies in the will. The force of Zola's voluntarist "I will not be complicitous" [Je ne veux pas être complice] may also be its undoing. This doubt, which an analysis of Heidegger's strategy will not allow to disappear, compels a questioning:

What is the price of this strategy? Why does it fatally turn back against its "subject" — if one can use this word, as one must, in fact? Because one cannot demarcate oneself from biologism, from naturalism, from racism in its genetic form, one cannot be *opposed* to them except by reinscribing spirit in an oppositional determination, by once again making it a unilaterality of subjectity, even if in its voluntarist form. . . . All the pitfalls of the strategy of establishing demarcations belong to this program, whatever place one occupies in it. The only choice is between the terrifying contaminations it assigns. Even if all forms of complicity are not equivalent, they are *irreducible*. (Derrida, *Of Spirit* 39–40)

To "reinscrib[e] spirit in an oppositional determination" is to engage a voluntarism that deploys spirit "unilaterally," as if an act of "subjective" will can overcome the basic condition of its possibility, namely, that it is parasitic on that to which it opposes itself. As the condition of possibility for oppositionality, this parasitism can be characterized as a complicity in the general sense. Specific acts of opposition (in the narrow sense)[16] remain complicit in what they oppose. Dependent on a generalized complicity that is irreducible, such complicities in the narrow sense cannot be avoided. All that can be done is attempt to avoid the worst: "The only choice is between the terrifying contaminations it assigns. Even if all forms of complicity are not equivalent, they are *irreducible*." When opposition does not free one from complicity, but depends on it as its condition of possibility, responsibility is sharpened. No longer can the intellectual, the agent of Geist, simply proclaim his or her opposition. Complicity is to be acknowledged, and, when a strategy of demarcation is adopted, responsibility assumed for choosing "between . . . terrifying contaminations."

Derrida's protocols in *Of Spirit* do not excuse Heidegger's disastrous choice, but they allow us to learn from his exceptional case. Each moment of opposition or resistance depends on complicity. Separating complicity in the general sense from complicities in the narrow sense enables us to distinguish complicities such as Heidegger's alignment with Nazism — which are open to judgment,[17] whether critical or juridical — from a complicity which, being the condition of possibility of such complicities, is not. It makes it possible for us to speak, in the realm of action at least, of complicity in an "extra-moral sense."[18]

Having as its main thrust an analysis of the act — Heidegger's "pragmatic signs" and "practical, 'pragmatic' treatment of the concept and lexicon of spirit" (*Of Spirit* 133 n.5; *Points* 184) — Derrida's account of complicity in *Of Spirit* does not explicitly broach the horizon of value, evaluation, and judgment presupposed by its proviso that "all forms of complicity are not equivalent." It is here that distinctions can be made among Derrida's account of Heidegger and Nazism; the Truth Commission's insistence on a virtual and generalizable assumption of complicity with the perpetrator, which it seeks to actualize quasi-juridically; and the genealogy of the intellectual that comes down from Zola's "J'accuse." Whereas complicity in the general sense with which Derrida is concerned in this text has to do mainly with the ramifications of supposedly unilateral acts, other accounts point at what makes those acts subject to judgment.

It may be worth distinguishing, as interrelated conditions of possibility, between an acting-in-complicity and a responsibility-in-complicity. If the former involves acts subject to a system of accountability, the latter, being the place occupied by the other before whom the "little perpetrator" is responsible, stands as the condition of possibility for any such system.[19] Although the ethics guiding the Truth Commission, with its reliance on the possibility of sympathetic identification in its setting to work, is to be sharply distinguished from Derrida's project of reading, the commission's basic concepts converge with complicity as a deconstructive motif when it is a question of thinking the intellectual as a figure of responsibility-in-complicity.

Complicity, in this convergence of act and responsibility, is thus at one with the basic folded-together-ness of being, of human-being, of self and other. Such foldedness is the condition of possibility of all particular affiliations, loyalties, and commitments. In the absence of an *acknowledgment* of complicity in a wider sense of foldedness with the other, whether welcomed or not, there would have been no opposition to apartheid. The history of the intellectual and apartheid — whether of support, accommodation, or resistance — can, in these terms, be deciphered, not by fixing on apartness alone, but by tracking interventions, marked by degrees of affirmation and disavowal, in a continuum of foldedness or responsibility-in-complicity. What makes apartheid exemplary for a study of the intellectual and complicity is the paradox that, while supporters disavowed or sought to limit foldedness with the other, opponents, though striving to minimize acting-in-complicity with the agents of apartheid and its policies, tended to acknowledge, affirm, and generalize responsibility-in-complicity.

Intellectual History and the Intellectual and Apartheid

An intellectual history of the apartheid era would document the role of various institutions in shaping and regulating South African intellectual life. In order to provide a complete picture, such a history would take into account not only the privilege offered to Afrikaans and white Anglo–South African intellectuals by the universities and through access to the mainstream press and broadcast media but also the complicated fracturing effects of the legacy of colonialism on the emergence of an African intelligentsia. Drafting an intellectual "history of the present" is held to be central to initiatives in post-apartheid reconstruction.

In his programmatic essay, "There Can Be No African Renaissance without an Africa-focused Intelligentsia" (1999), Mahmood Mamdani includes one possible outline for such a history. According to Mamdani, when apartheid, which he views as continuous with the "indirect rule" that prevailed in British equatorial Africa, supplants nineteenth-century "direct rule," the project of "creating a westernised intelligentsia, clones who would lead the assimilationist enterprise," is given up: "Called 'indirect rule' there and 'apartheid' here, this experience was determined to prevent assimilation by keeping natives in their separate, 'customary,' ethnic places. It reified difference and was suspicious of native intellectuals" (130–31).[20] As a result, Mamdani writes, "South Africa, like equatorial Africa, had few institutions to nurture native intellectuals. At independence the institution-based intellectuals were mainly white. There was a native intelligentsia, but it was to be found mainly outside universities, in social movements or religious institutions. It functioned without institutional support" (131).[21]

Although Mamdani's is a highly schematic outline (its qualifications of "mainly" in the quote above indicate a need for substantial elaboration) and is not formulated as intellectual history per se, it does point the intellectual historian toward several important considerations touching on chronology and institutional location. An intellectual history of apartheid attuned to the divided political history presented by Mamdani would, in the first place, attend not only to the school and university system and to allied think tanks and cultural organizations but also to formations existing elsewhere, on which black intellectuals relied more than white, and from where an African intelligentsia can be said to have emerged: political organizations; cultural bodies; trade unions; religious groups; and, one would need to add, a diversity of venues for journalistic, political, devotional, and literary writing.[22] Mamdani's chronology and the racial division linked to it can be complicated and qualified. A fuller outline of apartheid's intellectual history would note that, for the African intelligentsia, institutions and practices dating back to the nineteenth century, though detached from the colonial "assimilationist enterprise," continued to provide support both within and outside the black universities Mamdani mentions ("No African Renaissance" 131–32). The legacy of "missionary" schooling, although eroded by apartheid education, remained a powerful one within the social movements to which Mamdani alludes, especially, but not only, those linked to the African National Congress.[23]

The intellectual historian of the apartheid era would supplement Mamdani's divide between black and white intellectuals with reference to at least two crucial areas. The first would be to distinguish between white Anglo–South African and Afrikaans intellectuals. Although it is accurate to say that both of these groups enjoyed privileged access to institutions during the apartheid era, the history of the Afrikaner-nationalist intelligentsia in certain respects parallels that of the black intelligentsia. A more complex chronology is essential. One has to distinguish a period of Anglo–South African political, cultural, and linguistic hegemony, when Afrikaner-nationalist thought emerged, not from the universities, but from within the Dutch Reformed Church and an array of cultural-political organizations (including the Afrikaner Broederbond and the Afrikaanse Taal- en Kultuurvereniging) from the time when, after the National Party came to power in 1948, the Afrikaans university system expanded and the bodies and think tanks they generated were tied more closely to the apartheid state and its policies.[24] The second area in which the intellectual historian would elaborate Mamdani's simple racial division is the alignment of radical white intellectuals (Afrikaner and Anglo–South African) with the liberation movements, the South African Communist Party, and the trade unions, and thus with the extra- or para-institutional formations on which they drew.[25] One can point to such white-led initiatives as the South African Institute of Race Relations as well as Alan Paton's Liberal Party, but the prime instance is the influence in the 1970s of Black Consciousness and the subsequent nonracial United Democratic Front and its affiliates on Whites in the universities, churches, and the legal profession.[26] It would also be essential to detail, in the context of the different outlets offered by the mainstream press and state-controlled electronic media, such singular cross-racial collaborations in publishing as *Staffrider* and the *Drum* magazine of the 1950s.[27]

The purpose of the amendments I have proposed to Mamdani's outline—one of the few that I am aware of to view the intellectual history of the apartheid era as an articulated whole rather than as a series of separate black and white, Afrikaans and English trajectories[28]—is not to criticize what is, after all, a programmatic statement addressing the specific post-apartheid challenges faced by the black intelligentsia. Rather, my purpose is, without ignoring the interests at work and the stakes involved after apartheid, to give the reader unfamiliar with the terrain and the campaigns waged there an overview of the racially and ethnically fissured intellectual history of the apartheid era and to suggest how, in its writing and rewriting, it could be more highly differentiated without having to remain rigidly compartmentalized.

My book is not an attempt at writing such a history. Although a chronology distinguishing the apartheid era from what came before and an awareness of complex differences in institutional location are elements critical to it, I see my study as distinct from an intellectual history of the apartheid era. The goal of my account of the intellectual and apartheid is, by identifying a structure of response across differences of time and location, to theorize the intellectual in terms of responsibility and complicity.

At the core of my book is how, both for N. P. van Wyk Louw, Geoffrey Cronjé, R. F. A. Hoernlé, and others, who imagined it and in different ways advocated its setting to work, and for those like Bloke Modisane, A. C. Jordan, Breyten Breytenbach, Nadine Gordimer, Rick Turner, N. Chabani Manganyi, and Steve Biko, who sought to overcome it, apartheid was the dominant venue of response and responsibility. It was around apartheid that each of these intellectuals articulated, not simply a position in support of, or in opposition to, a set of policies, but, more or less explicitly, the affirmation or denial of a basic human foldedness. In each case, whether complicity is located politically, socially, or in the intimacy of mental colonization and the psychosocial inscription of the body, an affirmation of a parochial filiation or affiliation is regarded as potentially at odds with a universalization or expansion of responsibility-in-complicity. At this basic level, the way in which each writer conceives of overcoming apartness, or of restoring joinedness or foldedness, is different. The solutions found are not always "political" in any simple sense. But in the work of each, the intellectual emerges as a figure of responsibility-in-complicity, one who points to the limits of universalization inherent in, and risked by, particular commitments.

Though as a theoretical project not confined to apartheid South Africa, mine is no less a "history of the present" (a scholarly counterpart perhaps to the Truth Commission's "concepts and principles" more than to its "institutional hearings"), it is possible that my rearticulation of complicity, along with the associated concepts of opposition and resistance, will yield new protocols for a writing of the intellectual history of apartheid, for its *continued* writing. One instance would be my casting of Black Consciousness not simply in terms of a history of political resistance but, when one reads Steve Biko, as a theorizing of the mental complicity that has to be negotiated in order for resistance to take place and for human freedom to be deepened. Another would be the abyssal complexity of the relationship between Afrikaner nationalism and apartheid that emerges from the essays of N. P. van Wyk Louw as I explain how, despite adopting much the same standard of responsibility for the intellectual as opponents of apartheid, he could nevertheless support apartheid.

In any case, I tacitly ask what the openings and limits of such an intellectual-historical project are as currently pursued, and to what extent the topic of the intellectual and apartheid, exemplary but not unique, is available for theoretical generalization in terms of responsibility-in-complicity. That is why my study is comparative, drawing parallels with Frantz Fanon and Ngũgĩ wa Thiong'o. And more importantly, it is why I begin with the colonial era in South Africa, treating Olive Schreiner and Sol T. Plaatje as precursors to the intellectual and apartheid to the extent that, although the concern of each is not solely with race apartheid in the narrow sense, each shows apartness and joinedness at work in ethically significant ways. It is also why my book begins, not with the typically privileged white intellectual or with the typically marginal black intellectual — the male figures commanding most of my attention — but with Schreiner, and it ends with the women who testify before the Truth Commission. The question is whether, when (as in the case of Schreiner and the women witnesses) the apartness in question is not racial in any narrow sense and the body is barred by virtue of its being sexed and gendered, there is still an articulation of complicity in general and narrow senses, and whether the account of responsibility-in-complicity I develop applies generally when it is a question of what it is to be an intellectual, a mind *in a body*. Broaching the history of sexuality and the place of the intellectual in it, this would imply another protocol not only for the writing of apartheid's intellectual history but also for that of the intellectual and apartheid. It is in the name of a necessary and impossible generalizing of responsibility that I am compelled to enter into such a questioning.

A related direction for questioning concerns literature. One might reasonably ask why, when it is a question of the intellectual and apartheid, when it is a question of complicity, I find myself concentrating, for the most part, on literary figures rather than, say, political theorists, lawyers, or even historians. The answer lies deeper than disciplinary location or the institutional conditions of emergence of the writer-intellectual at the end of the nineteenth century with an independent publishing market and press (Von Vegesack 13). The "actual literary structure" that Von Vegesack considers an "impediment" to his study of the intellectual (285) is not one to mine. To the extent that it relies on the possibility of one determinate figure taking the place of another (much as one word or phrase substitutes for another), a possibility that nevertheless allows it to retain for itself a minimal identity across repeated instantiations (what Derrida terms *iterability* in "Signature Event Context"), responsibility for the other is coextensive with what we imperfectly call the literary.[29] In several of the writers I examine, it is the literary that makes it possible for the particular other to operate as, and substitute for, a figure for the generalized responsibility demanded of the implied reader: Sol Plaatje's vernacular reader; Bloke Modisane's deceased father as the covert addressee of his autobiography; the stranger to whom hospitality is owed, drawn by A. C. Jordan from Tiyo Soga.

Although literature in the narrow sense can reveal an opening to responsibility, the literary is not confined to literature — as the Truth Commission's report with its "little perpetrator" acknowledges and as is audible at its public hearings. One thinks in particular of the special women's hearing the commission held in response to criticism from feminist observers that, in the first weeks of its hearings, the majority of witnesses were black women testifying to human rights violations to male relatives rather than violations to themselves. As striking as this intervention was, it ignored the widely noted fact that, from the first hearings, witnesses came forward to ask the commission for help in conferring the proper funeral rites on the deceased, thereby appearing on behalf of those who could not have testified on their own behalf: the dead. Advocacy is a version of the essential human foldedness whereby one can assume the place of another. As Derrida suggests in *Specters of Marx* (xix), justice may depend on responsibility assumed before the nonliving. In the same way as the commission assumes the responsibility of the perpetrator who does not come forward and disseminates that responsibility by making it generally available as a drama incorporating the "little perpetrator" in us all, the witness demanding proper funeral rites depends on the sense of an essential foldedness of human-being with the (nonliving and living) other.

The aporia, of course, is the fact that when one testifies on behalf of a father or a son or a daughter, one chooses a specific other over another and, as feminist critics of the Truth Commission observed, over oneself as an other. In the same way, the dead are never simply *the* dead; at the hearings, as in Modisane's autobiography, it is always a case of a *particular* dead one.[30] There is always, necessarily, a contamination of *the* other with *an* other.[31] Demanding decision, such contamination is basic to responsibility. As a mechanism of advocacy, the commission shares and renders apparent a contamination that, calling for careful negotiation, is also at the root of what it is to be an intellectual. Involving self-differing and substitution, advocacy shares as a condition of possibility the iterability that marks the literary. Literature — in a broad sense, including the acknowledgment of a "little perpetrator" and a receptivity to testimony — thus calls upon a reader to assume responsibility for an other in the name of a generalized foldedness in human-being (and perhaps beyond *human*-being).

To the extent that literature provokes such a questioning of the limits of filiation, it functions in the same way as the response set to work by Émile Zola and all of those who, whether disseminating his gesture or by independent invention, frame the intellectual as a figure of responsibility-in-complicity. This is the place of the literary in my writing of a history of the intellectual and apartheid, a task distinct, as I have indicated, from an intellectual history of apartheid. The history of the intellectual and apartheid yields a figure of responsibility-in-complicity who, opposing apartheid or differing from it, makes a radical affirmation of foldedness with the other, living and nonliving, but conducts a perhaps more radical vigilance for the particular complicities that, fostering apart-ness, would, sooner or later, eventuate his or her complicity as an intellectual in apartheid. This is why to write the history of the intellectual and apartheid is also to write the history of the intellectual — a history in which there is no responsibility without the troubling and enabling moment of complicity.

chapter 1
two colonial precursors

Apartheid forms and deforms the intellectual as a figure of responsibility-in-complicity. In order to overcome the apartness of apartheid, the intellectual opposing or differing from apartheid affirms a larger foldedness in human-being. He or she negotiates a complicity in whatever blocks the realization of that foldedness. In the name of this generalized complicity and responsibility, we witness a strategy of avoidance of certain determinate complicities in the narrow sense — or, as Derrida formulates it in *Of Spirit,* a choice between them.

Throughout its life span apartheid generated a common ensemble of complicities. These ranged from the support of specific policies and participation in certain institutions, to mental colonization. From each intellectual there emerges a version of generalized complicity related to the nature and extent of his or her involvement in that ensemble. Although encompassing a range of complicities, many of which it shared with other dispensations, apartheid attained a certain unity in the eyes of its opponents and dissidents. That is why it is accurate to treat it and its project of apartness, not as unique, but as exemplary. This allows one to begin with intellectual history but also to exceed it — to write a history of the intellectual as figure of responsibility-in-complicity, a figure *between* complicity and complicities.

When we leave the intellectual history of apartheid to trace its margins, its beginnings, and its legacies and no longer find the characteristic ensemble of complicities in place or find it shading into other formations, we witness a displacement of exemplarity. It is our chance to take up strands of other intellectual histories, other genealogies, and to ask to what extent they too yield dynamics of responsibility-in-complicity. When we read figures from before the apartheid era, we find a less-restricted set of complicities and means for their negotiation. These figures may be thought of as precursors, not simply in the sense of being earlier figures in a chronology, but as having a particular significance by virtue of what succeeds them. This is the picture presented by Jorge Luis Borges in his essay, "Kafka and His Precursors." According to Borges, Kafka's precursors exist because Kafka existed; we read other writers as Kafka's precursors because we have read Kafka. In the same way, once apartheid is identified as the predicament par excellence for the intellectual as a figure of responsibility-in-complicity, other earlier predicaments become precursors to that of the intellectual and apartheid. This is not to claim that the specific historical circumstances faced by these figures are themselves precursory to those of apartheid. My main concern is not with apartheid's precursors but with precursors to the intellectual-and-apartheid considered as an ethico-political predicament.

With Zola having been the major precursor in my introduction, I now turn to the specificities of South Africa. I argue that the responsibility engaged by earlier figures is structurally similar to that engaged by the later ones, and it becomes discernible as such by virtue of the latter. This does not mean that all of the earlier figures resemble each other or find themselves in identical historical situations. As Borges writes, although "the heterogeneous pieces I have enumerated resemble Kafka . . . not all of them resemble each other. This second fact is the more significant" (236).

Resembling in certain traits what comes later yet differing from one another, the precursors partake of a more capacious and more fluid agenda. Some of the complicities they negotiate strongly persist into the apartheid era. Some do not. Others emerge again to a significant degree only in its wake. That is what we find with Olive Schreiner and Solomon Tshekisho Plaatje. Although elements unite them — typically those anticipating opposition to apartheid — their concerns can also be heterogeneous. These distinct concerns render their work and careers exemplary, not just for the responsibility-in-complicity that apartheid provokes, but for that which comes afterward, when once-separate traits come to be joined: in Schreiner the figure of women, the embodiedness of intellect, and the social inscription of the body; in Plaatje advocacy, interpreting, and the problem of "ventriloquism."

Rather than pressing these two figures into the same frame — reducing one to the other, and their varied concerns to an occupation with the colonial makings of race apartheid — I maintain their heterogeneity, even as I note profound parallels, as a way of marking the limit of this work insofar as it is *determined* by apartheid. A consideration of other major figures of the period such as Smuts or Gandhi may have reinforced this limit. Plaatje and Schreiner each entertain a sense of a larger human foldedness as a way of avoiding complicity in the deepening social fissuring that would, once the colonial era drew to a close, coalesce into apartheid. It is Schreiner's position in an older genealogy, in what Foucault terms a "history of sexuality," that distinguishes her version of responsibility from Plaatje's. It is perhaps the passing of the apartheid era and its racializing of difference that enables us to read each writer for the conceptions of complicity in the general sense informing their respective positions. What is it in the name *of* that these writers strive to avoid complicity in the narrow sense? It is essential that we know this. It is not sufficient merely to make a checklist of their positions on a restricted set of political issues.[1] Although it is needful to know what sides they took and to expose any contradictory commitments, merely to do so is, in the final analysis, to pursue an anachronistic scholarly politics of strategic alliance insufficient for anything but a one-sided understanding of the intellectual as a figure of responsibility. They set responsibility-in-complicity to work in singular ways and they choose between determinate complicities. The choices they have, like those they make, are quite often different.

Despite their heterogeneity, each of the precursors imagines entry into, and participation in, intellectual life as an encounter in which distinctness and division are masked or suspended. Overcoming apartness, their respective literary strategies indicate generalizable ways of understanding the unstable articulation of complicities that goes to make a woman or a man an intellectual. When complicity emerges as a problem with entry into intellectual life and access itself becomes a question, it is necessary to adjust the trajectory (more or less a Marxist interpretation of Zola's stand in the Dreyfus case) from accredited "technician of practical knowledge" to "intellectual" as set out by Sartre ("Plea" 232, 244), and subsequently elaborated by Bourdieu in terms of the conversion of "cultural capital" into an ability to "criticize . . . the powers that be" ("Corporatism" 99–101).

In terms of this trajectory, the legitimating force of an intellectual's public stand derives from his or her accreditation or recognition as a mental worker. Thus, Émile Zola, as a celebrated novelist, could, on behalf of Dreyfus, enjoin a significant public toward his stance of responsibility-in-complicity. But how do we think of the intellectual who lacks accreditation, who does not have the standing of a Zola — or, moving to the South African context, of an N. P. van Wyk Louw or a Nadine Gordimer? Short of simply discarding the trajectory as a model, it is my sense that, although a certain legitimacy may implicitly be what is sought in the endeavor to participate in mainstream intellectual life, the issue of complicity as it emerges for marginal figures does not presuppose that such participation has already been achieved. Of course, to be an intellectual some minimal recognition will surely had to have been attained, but I doubt whether this condition of possibility can be reduced to a narrative element prescribing that the figure in question must, as Sartre and Bourdieu imply, already possess "cultural capital" in order for complicity to become a moral problem. Just as one could argue that with entry into intellectual life the figure entering is marked with at least some minimal recognition or legitimacy, one could say that the issue of complicity emerges in the attempt to gain access to it. Another way of saying this is that the issue of complicity arises with the accession to sociality, at the point of foldedness with the other. It is possible that the intellectual is nothing more than the figure who dramatizes the fact that this accession never realizes the generalized human foldedness that is sought but only generates more or less partisan versions of collaboration, loyalty, or affiliation, which must always be held responsible before (or through) a complicity that, though unrealizable, is conceived as generalizable.

With the history of the intellectual and apartheid and that history's precursors, opposition mounted in the name of a larger responsibility is variably distributed in ways that have to be taken into account. When, as in Schreiner's early writing and in Plaatje's late work and with Modisane during the apartheid era, it is a question of access, and the figures are more marginally positioned, it can appear that, in tracking their activities, it is simply a matter of showing their accommodations, compromises, and contradictory commitments. It will, I hope, be clear that this cannot be the end goal, for what is at stake is the very accession to intellectual sociality — and perhaps meaningful sociality itself. Bare sociality — human life, in a word — cannot be subject to critical judgment. In the same way, participation alone is no basis for judgment. Rather, it is the relationship between actual instances of participation and the possibility of generalizing or maximizing responsibility from such determinate complicities that calls for judgment. But judgments in this sphere can hardly ever be unequivocal, as we clearly observe with the precursors, before the ensemble known as apartheid is more or less firmly in place.

Although the precursors anticipate, in their shared concerns, an opposition to colonial forms of social apartness, they betray a division and singularity in the realm of complicities. In Schreiner's early work there is the question of the access of women to intellectual life. Her resolution, which suggests other genealogies for the intellectual — even another frame for a study of the intellectual and apartness — is later subject to her own tacit censure, and this, in turn, generates fresh complicities. Even in her later work, although actual entry of black African men and women into places of higher learning is registered, the evolutionary philosophy that would rule out participation by Bushmen (or San) remains unquestioned. It is in Plaatje's late work, where he builds on and alters his earlier reflections on the practices of the courtroom interpreter, that we find a more fundamental dispropriation of identity at work, a figuring of generalized complicity and responsibility. This division *within* Plaatje is an emblem for the division within opposition to apartheid between those with access and those gaining access. Responsibility-in-complicity must be universal. Since the type of complicity depends on one's specific situation, however, it follows that not all complicities from which responsibility arises are to be regarded as equivalent, although all are subject to judgment.

Olive Schreiner: The Intellectual in the History of Sexuality

This intel[l]ect is a good thing but it is not every thing.
—OLIVE SCHREINER, "Journal: Rattel's Hoek"

When Olive Schreiner's life and fiction are put together, we have a text that inscribes her as a writer in a genealogy of intellectual life older than apartheid and with its own peculiar margins. Although (as in Plaatje and those who follow) there is in Schreiner (1855–1920) a strong preoccupation with race and an attempt to mobilize race against racism in aid of an anticolonial cause (especially in her later works), the particularity of her life and written corpus, insofar as they touch on the intellectual, reside in an occupation with sexual difference. Her brief reference, in *Thoughts on South Africa* (written 1890–1901), to the entry of black women into mainstream colonial intellectual life, made in a footnote to a discussion of the relative capacity of Africans to assimilate white "civilization," is inseparable from that investment: "So considerable is the aptitude for abstract study displayed by the Bantu, that there are cases in which even Bantu females, preparing for the matriculation examination of the Cape University, are found not to be inferior to the average male Europeans sharing the same course of study" (127). Although what it identifies as a "considerable . . . aptitude for abstract study" in fact translates into no more than a few black women matriculating from the University of the Cape of Good Hope in the 1890s and early 1900s,[2] Schreiner's footnote conveys a sense of how she imagined a set of unspoken entrance requirements. The criterion is the "average male European"; to pass is "not to be inferior" to him. This standard resembles the one governing entry to intellectual life as Schreiner stages it in her earliest published novel, *The Story of an African Farm* (1883). Although the footnote to *Thoughts on South Africa* marks the figures racially ("Bantu female"; "male European"), suggesting the outline for a raced rewriting of the episode from her early work, the history of sexuality broached there is not displaced in the later work by a history of race or racial ethnicity.[3] The figures remain female and male, with the male the "average" against whom one measures oneself. The "Bantu female" assumes her place in a little modified version of the intellectual trajectory imagined for the white woman.[4]

It is in *The Story of an African Farm* that the complex relationship of sexual and intellectual life comes most strongly to the fore in a nexus of Schreiner's life and fiction. In her unfinished novel *From Man to Man* (1926), the sphere of mind is a chaotic and isolated zone separated from the work of mothering and almost entirely divorced from sociality; and *Woman and Labour* (1911) insists on the social function, within a clear division of labor, of women as mother-teachers. By contrast, *The Story of an African Farm,* when read along with Schreiner's letters and biography, stages the full-scale entry of the female intellectual into an intellectual sociality defined by men. The trouble is that in order to take part in it the female intellectual has, in effect, to cease to be a woman.

Like her female contemporaries in Victorian England, when Schreiner contemplated participation in intellectual life, she found it not only dominated by men in fact but also imagined as male sociality. At certain institutional nodes, this hegemonic imagining developed into a conception of the intellectual life modeled on love between men. At nineteenth-century Oxford, as is well known, liberal university reformers mobilized under the banner of a secular Hellenism. This Hellenism, with Benjamin Jowett its main proponent, was subsequently taken up by J. A. Symonds, Walter Pater, and Oscar Wilde, who, as Linda Dowling has shown, drew from Plato's dialogues to identify the life of the mind with male homosexual eroticism. Styled after ancient Greek *paiderastia,* as an affective model for the intellectual life it appeared to do little to facilitate participation by women.

Juxtaposing modern Europe and ancient Greece, Schreiner's later writing tacitly protests this foreclosure. Footnoting Jowett's translation of Plato's *Symposium* in *Woman and Labour,* Schreiner attributes the decline of Greek civilization to the marginalization of women from public life, their consequent intellectual etiolation, and its effects on the education of young children. Drawing on Jowett's commentary to the *Symposium,* Schreiner writes that "the abnormal institution of avowed inter-male sexual relations upon the highest plane was one, and the most serious result, of this severance" (*Woman and Labour* 85). Although Jowett alludes to "the greatest evil of Greek life" (Plato 534), he never reduces the erotic to the sexual, and he takes care to underline that among the Greeks homoeroticism was not an abnormal institution.[5] If Schreiner's feminist historicism in *Woman and Labour* reads as anti-homosexual and reflects the sexualization and pathologizing of the homosexual that took place late in the nineteenth century, in *The Story of an African Farm,* by contrast, a "Hellenist" ideology is strongly present. In that earlier work, however, its presence is not protested or questioned. That is because, in Schreiner's novel, the ideology is *enabling* for the woman—who is represented by a character who is not female but male and who enables a certain separation from sexuality in a narrowly biological sense of the eroticism Schreiner herself associates with the intellectual life.

As readers, we recover in fragments how, when Schreiner figures her own entry as a young woman into intellectual life, it is not through the female protagonist Lyndall but through the boy, Waldo Farber, the subject of "love glances" toward an unnamed male Stranger who leaves him with a book. Although in principle leaving no place for the woman, the masculine erotic model is used cryptically by Schreiner in order to figure female intellectual agency and erotic autonomy. Recovering and deciphering the fragments helps us pinpoint where Schreiner locates complicity and where responsibility emerges for her. As *Woman and Labour* suggests, when a woman successfully passes into intellectual life by becoming a "man," the continued marginalization of women in general from intellectual life is legitimated. Read in light of the later work, *The Story of an African Farm* stages a choice, in the name of a more capacious other-joinedness, between determinate complicities. In order to realize the foldedness in humanity promised by the intellectual life, the exclusion of women must be resisted, but as the novel does so, the continued marginalization of women from intellectual life is risked.

The genealogy of intellectual life into which Victorian Oxford inscribes itself is set out by Michel Foucault in *The Use of Pleasure,* the second volume of his *History of Sexuality.* Here Foucault explains how, in ancient Greece, philosophy as the disinterested pursuit of truth had its beginnings in rules regulating erotic concourse between men and boys. This Greek ethos prescribed that once the boy showed physical signs of maturity, the love relation between man and boy transform itself into friendship. It demanded "the ... conversion — an ethically necessary and socially useful one — of the bond of love ... into a relation of friendship, of *philia*" (201). Whereas the boy's body was the "right object" of the erotic relation, the signs of manhood it inevitably displayed dictated a shift away from it as an object of desire toward the development of "*philia,* i.e., an affinity of character and mode of life, a sharing of thoughts and existence, mutual benevolence" (201). Thus, in Plato's *Symposium,* though the body is not "excluded," the love of boys is taught to take truth as its ultimate and proper object: "Beyond the appearances of the object, love is a relation to truth" (*Use of Pleasure* 239). Born out of a problematization of desire in terms of an opposition of body and soul, and a subordination of body to soul, this displacement of the object of erotic love renders the genesis of "philosophy" complete. Read with an eye to more recent history, Foucault's account implies that, from

Greek antiquity onward, to engage in "philosophy"—and, in a wider sense, to participate in intellectual life—would have come to entail a sundering of mind and body. Men—and women, with the subsequent Christian elaboration of the topos—would henceforth come to intellectual life, not whole, but as "disembodied" intellects or spirits.

To judge from Schreiner's early work, intellectual women can be aided by the possibility of presenting the life of the mind as disembodied—of detaching, in a manner of speaking, mind from body, intellectual from sexual life. Although such a representation of the life of the mind may appear to resemble the topos received from ancient Greece, it is crucial to bear in mind that women take part in intellectual life against the social norm—in the face of the reproductive inscription of female sexuality. One might interpret Schreiner's assertions of intellectual disembodiment as anticipating an expected transformation between man and woman comparable to that between man and boy in ancient Greece. The transformation would in that case be from mistress or potential wife and mother to friend, from the sphere of the sexual—defined socially as the reproductive—to that of the intellectual. The young women of Schreiner's novel, prepared for motherhood, are not groomed as intellectuals. In contrast to the metamorphosis Foucault tracks in the Greek regulation of man-boy relations, a metamorphosis of this kind *subverts* rather than obeys the norm governing social relations between men and women.

The feminist bildungsroman typically regarded as the founding work of the South African novel in English, *The Story of an African Farm* mobilizes a narrative of intellectual "disembodiment" in the two stories of Lyndall and Waldo. Both stories present their protagonists with possibilities of connection, finally unrealized, with respective "Strangers" (see DuPlessis 21). The trajectory of the story of the colonial orphan Lyndall, whom Elaine Showalter describes as the English novel's "first wholly serious feminist heroine" (199), reveals how the entry of women into intellectual life can be at odds with the reproductive inscription of female sexuality. In order to resist this destiny, Lyndall thwarts desire. She will not marry her lover since, though moved by him sexually and pregnant by him, she sees no hope of intellectual companionship: "You call into activity one part of my nature; there is a higher part that you know nothing of, that you never touch" (*African Farm* 222).

The story of Waldo, introspective son of the farm's overseer, brings its protagonist near to the broaching of intellectual friendship, only to leave expectations of it unfulfilled. One day Waldo encounters a Stranger passing by the farm who interprets a wood carving he has fashioned for his father's grave by telling him an allegory of a "Hunter" who sacrifices his life on a long and lonely quest for truth. He departs, leaving Waldo a book, "a centre round which to hang [his] ideas" (*African Farm* 161). The exchange is Waldo's first moment of genuine intellectual reciprocity, and it marks his initiation into intellectual life. The Stranger finds the flashes of Waldo's eyes "more thirsty and desiring than the love-glances of a woman" (*African Farm* 153). The scene appears to hint at the roots of the norm for intellectual exchange uncovered by Foucault and set to work in Victorian Oxford. If so, the fact that the scene does not involve Lyndall, and that Waldo is a boy, plays out in the novel the difference between the paths into intellectual life taken by the young man and that by the young woman. Hinting at its displacement as "philosophy," a disinterested and self-sacrificing quest for truth, the story of the young man can entertain an eroticism. By contrast, since an expression of sexuality risks launching its protagonist into the social circuit of reproduction, the story of the young woman seeking her way in intellectual life strives to avoid it.

But in terms of the textuality of her own life, Waldo is Olive Schreiner, his initiation into intellectual life declaredly a fictionalization of hers. As Schreiner informs Havelock Ellis, the chapter "Waldo's Stranger" renders fictionally a pivotal event in her autobiography. One winter night in 1871, a young colonial official, Willie Bertram, stopped over at the rural mission station at Hermon in the Cape Colony where she was living with an aunt. When he departed, Bertram left the sixteen-year-old Schreiner a copy of Herbert Spencer's *First Principles* (1862), a magisterial reconciling of religion and science that alleviated her youthful unbelief: "He lent me Spencer's 'First Principles.' I always think that when Christianity burst on the dark Roman world it was what that book was to me" (Letter, 28 March 1884, in *"Other Self"* 39; see also 251, 435). As she explains, "The book that the Stranger gives to Waldo was intended to be Spencer's *First Principles*" (*"Other Self"* 39; see also Cronwright-Schreiner 80–84).

Bertram and his book mark the freethinking Olive Schreiner's entry into intellectual life away from her orthodox upbringing as a missionary's daughter.[6] It is thus fair to read "Waldo's Stranger" as Olive Schreiner's intellectual rite of passage, as, biographically speaking, an exchange between a young woman and an older man that has been rendered as the quasi-erotic encounter between an adolescent boy and a man. As such, the meeting of Waldo and his Stranger spells out the divergences between male and female intellectual trajectories. Interpreted in the light of Schreiner's autobiography and in juxtaposition with the story of Lyndall, the episode also reveals how a young woman might imagine and enact, even as she claims a certain disembodiedness, an eroticism she does not associate with reproductive life. *The Story of an African Farm* locates that displaced sphere of eroticism between man and boy. Like the cross-dressing in some of Shakespeare's comedies, the masquerade is subversive not only for imagining a way for a young woman to enter intellectual life but for staging, away from marriage, a place of active desire for her.

Still signing herself with the male pseudonym Ralph Iron in the preface to the second edition of *The Story of an African Farm* (1883), Olive Schreiner responds to reviewers of the first edition in a coded feminist statement on the intellectual life. Along with his resistance to writing "a history of wild adventure" demanded by the colonial adventure genre, Iron offers a feminist response to gendering in narrative formulae.[7] Iron affirms the art of the painter who paints from life, defending it from those who call for the predictable satisfactions of dramatic closure: "Human life may be painted according to two methods. There is the stage method. . . . But there is another method — the method of the life we all lead. . . . Life may be painted according to either method; but the methods are different. The canons of criticism that bear upon the one cut cruelly upon the other" (*African Farm* 23). Iron's critical exercise negotiates a crossing of sexual and intellectual exchange that Schreiner's ironic gender masquerade attempts to manage. As Ralph Iron, Schreiner addresses a readership's "feeling that a man should not appear upon the scene, and then disappear, leaving behind him no more substantial trace than a mere book; that he should return later on as husband or lover, to fill some more important part than that of the mere stimulator of thought" (23). In advocating a man's part as "the mere stimulator of thought," the bringer of the book, Iron also advocates the woman's part. *The Story of an African Farm*'s first Stranger, who appears to Waldo and leaves him a book, is not the man who appears at the farm later in the novel as Lyndall's lover. By not reappearing as Lyndall's Stranger, Waldo's Stranger fails to complete the romance or marriage plot. Failing also to complete the plot of intellectual companionship, he does not return at all; and when Waldo encounters him in town years later, the Stranger does not acknowledge him (*African Farm* 242–43). Iron's insistence on the Stranger's book, as he corrects metropolitan critical opinion, and his ironic emphasis on intellectual stimulation resist the canons of criticism to which he alludes. If that was all they were doing, there would be no obvious reason to leave unfinished the plot of intellectual companionship between Waldo and his Stranger. Fraternal homosociality would have been perfectly acceptable.[8] Iron not only mocks the critics but also diminishes the "mere book" and "mere" stimulation "of thought." This double irony suggests the force of further motives. These become apparent when Waldo is seen to play the woman's part, when this performance is related, if not, as Schreiner claims, to "the life we all lead," then to the life she as a woman writes for herself.

In the chapter entitled "Waldo's Stranger" it is still the woman (Schreiner) who passes as male (Waldo). Can we say that the early Schreiner's woman intellectual speculates and even capitalizes on a complicity that marginalizes women by admitting them to intellectual life only insofar as they are the same as men? This appears to be Schreiner's retrospective verdict. There may be room, though, for another hypothesis: that Schreiner supplements the masculinist version of intellectual life with a feminizing narrative of sexual danger. Schreiner's representation of the stimulator of thought as separate from the husband or lover, the mind as distinct from the body, can be interpreted as stemming, not from the normative conversion of an erotic man-boy relation, but from a position *marginal* to the institutionalized practices of intellectual life. In contrast to the position mapped out by Foucault in *The History of Sexuality,* the position I have in mind is historically specific to women.

Foucault shows that a historically specific problematization of erotic relations gives rise to a virtually universal model of intellectual exchange: "With the Greeks. . . . reflection on the reciprocal ties between access to truth and sexual austerity seems to have been developed primarily in connection with the love of boys" (*Use of Pleasure* 230). What does this genealogy of intellectual life help us to learn from Olive Schreiner? On the one hand, Schreiner lived and wrote at a time when it was common for intellectual life and intellectual friendship of a public kind to be coded as masculine.[9] It is thus possible to read "Lyndall's Stranger" in *The Story of an African Farm* and the subsequent exclusion, in Schreiner's story "The Buddhist Priest's Wife" (written in 1891–92) of the erotic from the intellectual friendship of women and men as adapting a topos handed down from the Greeks, one designed to regulate behavior between boys and men.[10] Since women enter intellectual life in violation of a social norm that inscribes female sexuality in reproduction, this adaptation and the admission of an eroticism not linked to reproduction would be transgressive in itself. The dynamics of the interchange between Waldo and his Stranger, at a time when the love of boys is no longer widely socially sanctioned, would be an exposure of the unacknowledged male homoeroticism actually fueling normative intellectual relations.

On the other hand, it is also quite possible that Schreiner's presentation in "The Buddhist Priest's Wife" of friendship as intellectual alikeness functions as a cover story for more familiar anxieties. The preface to *The Story of an African Farm* separates lover and teacher by setting the two Strangers apart. Without assimilating the two figures, the novel itself allows us to think that intellectual and physical exchange can be continuous. The concern here is not that the boy become a man and, according to Greek convention, render certain types of conduct unacceptable. Another life course faces Schreiner's young woman. When that course entails the social regulation of her sexual life in reproduction, the young woman's entry into intellectual life will necessarily be seen as transgressive. Since intellectual and physical exchange are in practice continuous, however, that transgressive entry implies contact with men and therefore risks a return to the prescribed life course of pregnancy and/or marriage. If that is why the life of the mind must be held separate from the life of the body, the "masculine" topos of the disembodied intellect or spirit can be given another genealogy. In entering intellectual life contrary to patriarchal norms, women can, in turn, be seen as consolidating another norm, which, although "feminine," combines old and new genealogies for topoi of disembodiment.

As the research of Helen Bradford shows, Schreiner's novels are acutely concerned about young women becoming pregnant. The social disgrace of unwedded pregnancy and the dangers of abortion are occasions for anxiety in novels about female participation in intellectual life.[11] Along with the threat of sexual violence, such sources of anxiety not only motivate narrative solutions in the form of separation of mind and body,[12] but they also give rise to the claim that a male intellectual companion is neither a lover nor a potential husband but a mere stimulator of thought. Emerging from Victorian commonplaces about female sexual conduct, this narrative solution comes to structure all intellectual exchange; it is, among other things, the way in which Schreiner figures an "anxiety of influence." To the extent that intellectual exchange is imagined to lead to risks and consequences of sexual congress specific to women, and to the degree that women undergo an imagined separation of mind and body, intellectual life itself undergoes feminization in this novel. It is in this context that Schreiner represents the pragmatic suspension of sexual difference customary in intellectual life as a provisional, albeit ambiguous strategy in "The Buddhist Priest's Wife." It is also in this context that during the previous decade Schreiner herself could script Waldo as boy-beloved and secure herself as proxy against the man as lover.

The preface to the second edition of *The Story of an African Farm* not only distinguishes between the characters of Waldo's Stranger and Lyndall's Stranger but draws a firm line between their roles. The stimulator of thought, Ralph Iron insists, is not the lover. Against the grain of the preface, the episode entitled "Lyndall's Stranger" stages a powerful link between intellectual friendship and sexual intimacy. Lyndall will not marry her Stranger on the grounds that her attraction to him is entirely physical:

"If you do love me," he asked her, "why will you not marry me?"

"Because, if I had been married to you for a year, I should have come to my senses, and seen that your hands and your voice are like the hands and the voice of any other man. . . . You call into activity one part of my nature; there is a higher part that you know nothing of, that you never touch. If I married you, afterwards it would arise and assert itself, and I should hate you always, as I do now sometimes." (222)

Lyndall does not say exactly what the "higher part" of her nature is. She keeps it in reserve. The novel, however, gives us the Stranger's construal of her words. His response is a curious mixture of paraphrase and desire. Taunting Lyndall, he associates the higher part of her nature with intellect and spirit, an association that only heightens his attraction to her:

"I like you when you grow metaphysical and analytical," he said, leaning his face upon his hand. "Go a little further in your analysis; say, 'I love you with the right ventricle of my heart, but not the left, and with the left auricle of my heart, but not the right; and, this being the case, my affection for you is not of a duly elevated, intellectual, and spiritual nature.' I like you when you get philosophical."

She looked quietly at him; he was trying to turn her own weapons against her. (222)

His taunts framed with desire—"I like you . . ."—the Stranger is, to Lyndall's mind, trying to subvert the very rule that she normally uses as a practical measure to keep male ardor at a distance. If the higher part of her nature is indeed her intellect, as the Stranger assumes, his "love" of her mind means that for her the intellectual life can no longer be a refuge from physical desire. That being the case, she prefers reticence.

Schreiner's novel narrates the difficulty of keeping sexual and intellectual life separate for purposes of sustaining the normative fiction of disembodied intellectuality. It is also a feminist commentary on that disembodied separation, an object lesson that there may be more to the idea of a separation of mind and body in friendship than a longing for spiritual or intellectual transcendence.[13] As previously noted, Foucault assigns the Platonic eclipse of the body a genealogy stemming from an anxiety associated with the maturation of the *eromenos*, the boy-beloved. For Schreiner's female characters, the attempt to remove the life of the body from the sphere of intellectual exchange appears to function as a way of imagining the avoidance of negative consequences, among them the bond of unwanted marriage associated with becoming pregnant. "I cannot be tied," Lyndall says (223). As their conversation suggests, the fact that Lyndall is carrying a child, or fears she might be, is the reason for the Stranger's offer of marriage: "I believe," Lyndall says to the Stranger, "that when you ask me to marry you, you are performing the most generous act you have ever performed in the course of your life, or ever will" (223). The novel proffers several other tacit signs that before Lyndall leaves the farm forever she is pregnant or at least believes that she is.[14] When intellectual and sexual life take place on a continuum, a pragmatic measure is required to hold them apart. Declaring mind and body separate is such a measure.

Staging the mind as disembodied, Schreiner's text not only acts to secure the woman from pregnancy and/or marriage when she interacts with male teachers and intellectual companions. The novel goes further.

By claiming, so to speak, that what was conceived mentally was the work of the woman alone, it effectively excludes the man, not only in his role as lover or husband but also as influence or "stimulator" of the intellect. Influence is minimized in *The Story of an African Farm* not only by eliminating or reducing the role of the man but by establishing the originality of Waldo's ideas through a manipulation of narrative time. Schreiner establishes the intellectual originality of her proxy male protagonist by placing "Waldo's Stranger," the episode of the coming of the book, just after "Times and Seasons," a lyrical episode comprising meditations on the "soul's life" attributed to Waldo. Curiously, the thoughts in "Times and Seasons," though in place before the Stranger arrives, resemble those that the Stranger and his book bring. By characterizing the Stranger as "mere stimulator of thought," the preface asks us to conclude that, whereas his coming is momentous — "'All my life I have longed to see you,' the boy said" (158) — the Stranger remains only a catalyst. Waldo's musings in "Times and Seasons," though indeed unripe, predate the Stranger's arrival. The temporal arrangement of the episodes allows readers to think that, whereas the Stranger (like Emerson,[15] whose influence is commemorated in the names of Ralph Iron and the characters Waldo and Em) is a vital stimulus to thought, the thoughts stimulated — in this case, those in "Times and Seasons" — would always have been the thinker's very own.

The "seasons" of "the soul's life" are "periods not found in any calendar" (*African Farm* 127). The chapter's seven divisions tell a story of infancy, religious doubting in childhood, and modified recovery of faith through pseudo-science (see Schoeman, *Olive Schreiner* 110). Schreiner can be read as giving form to the idea from Spencer's *First Principles* that "Religion and Science" are reconcilable, provided the adherents of each see them as only partially expressing a greater underlying truth (3–25), that there need be no conflict between religion and science writ large if each is viewed as "a constituent of the great whole" (21). Spencer helps Schreiner to imagine an intellectual departure from Christian orthodoxy that does not lead to mere atheism but instead to an affirmation of "truth." This is the philosophical gesture par excellence, one that brackets both the problem of influence and that posed by the physical presence of, and desire for, another human being. In other words, Spencer, like Waldo's Stranger, comes to stimulate thoughts, not to seduce and to subordinate the thinker to his authority.

The role of Spencerian evolutionary theory in Schreiner's *Weltanschauung* has been more widely discussed (by Lenta; Paxton; Barash) than how *First Principles* helps Schreiner and her characters deal with the question of influence. Spencer's book allows Schreiner to write a novel of ideas that, while strongly "Spencerian," is at the same time an intellectual autobiography that minimizes the role of influence, Spencer's included. In a nutshell, Spencer advocates transcendent truth against religious and even scientific authority: if the thinker apprehends truth, it is of secondary importance whether the truth apprehended is "his" or "hers," or indeed whether it happens also to be a truth revealed by religion or science. What is relevant for Spencer is whether or not authority usurps the place of truth. Schreiner both acknowledges and minimizes the contribution of the Stranger and his book. Registered through the character of Waldo, such ambivalence about influence constantly dogs Schreiner's self-presentation as a writer.

Spencer's place in Olive Schreiner's intellectual autobiography is unrivaled. As we noted, Schreiner borrowed a copy of his *First Principles* from Willie Bertram in 1871 and, as she informs Ellis, fictionalized that intellectual rite of passage in "Waldo's Stranger" (see Schoeman, *Olive Schreiner* 190–95). As far as anyone is aware, though, Schreiner never says (and Ellis never asks) why she stages the giving of the book in *The Story of an African Farm* as an encounter between men. Although Schreiner writes from a tradition that figures intellectual friendship as a relation between males, her insistence on the necessity of sexual difference for intellectual exchange alters the traditional topos. Though choreographed as an exchange between men, sexual difference, even the desire of the woman, enter into the transaction: Waldo, like Ralph Iron, takes the woman's part.

Revealing some of the social motivations for imposing a separation of mind and body, the facts of Olive Schreiner's biography enjoin us to interpret the gendered displacements in *The Story of an African Farm* as indications of a larger formation governing intellectual life. Hamilton Hope, Schreiner's cousin's husband, sent a letter to her with Willie Bertram that concludes with a piece of familial advice: "Don't get spooney on him. He's very intellectual they say" (Cronwright-Schreiner 81). The homoerotic exchange between Waldo and his Stranger may thus function as a cover story for patriarchal anxieties as well as for the way a young woman might negotiate their strictures. There are at least two anxieties. Hope's two sentences, extracted by S. C. Cronwright-Schreiner before he destroyed the original letter, could be read as hinting either that the "very intellectual" Willie Bertram is not interested in women or that he is a sexual threat to the young Schreiner, who would be seduced by his intellectuality. (Cronwright-Schreiner, Schreiner's husband and first biographer, who never knew Bertram, appears to favor the second reading, eliding the fact that Schreiner saw Bertram subsequent to the night at Hermon [Schoeman, *Olive Schreiner* 190]).[16] Given that Schreiner masquerades as Waldo, there are at least two possible motives for the incompletion of the plot of homosocial friendship between Waldo and his Stranger. These motives can be read as working at a tangent to those of Schreiner's family, as Schreiner/Waldo desires against its wishes. First, the boy (Waldo) is actually a young woman. Because she wants to be independent, this woman will not bind herself to a man (Waldo's Stranger). Second, the man (the Stranger), whether he is interested in women or not, has no desire for the boy (Waldo) who is a woman, even though she desires him. It is over against both the patriarchal injunction and its subversion that the character of Waldo, who receives the Stranger's book, plays out Schreiner's self-presentation as a writer and her ambivalent attitude to influence. Admitting eroticism without conjugal commitment, Waldo obviates a conventional resolution of the plot in marriage. As Waldo, Schreiner can also "get spooney" on the Stranger/Bertram, yet cast him, not as her major influence, but as "the mere stimulator of thought."

In *The Story of an African Farm,* the arrangement of narrative time in Waldo's story works both to acknowledge and to minimize influence, while a fiction of "disembodiedness" helps Lyndall imagine a zone of social and intellectual self-sufficiency linked with an eroticism not confined to reproduction. Read in the light of Schreiner's autobiography, these elements converge in "Waldo's Stranger" as Schreiner masquerades as a boy. It is in that episode that, in the context of drawing up a genealogy of intellectual life, the larger implications of Schreiner's intricate weave of fiction and autobiography become apparent. In *The Story of an African Farm,* Schreiner speaks through the male characters of Ralph Iron and Waldo Farber. Yet her men can also, as it were, become women.[17]

In "Waldo's Stranger," Waldo is feminized, and the Stranger is, reciprocally, the object of his gaze. While homoerotic, the process of intellectual stimulation in "Waldo's Stranger" depends, as it does in a number of Schreiner's texts, on sexual difference. Though the two protagonists are male, this difference is conceived as that between male and female, a duality with which Schreiner nearly always begins. The man excites the "woman": "At every word the stranger spoke the fellow's eyes flashed back on him—yes, and yes, and yes! The stranger smiled. It was almost worth the trouble of exerting oneself, even on a lazy afternoon, to win those passionate flashes, more thirsty and desiring than the love-glances of a woman" (*African Farm* 152–53). But the exchange is not figured simply as one between male and female. In the quasi-homoerotic space in which the episode takes place, Waldo's looks are "*more* thirsty and desiring *than* the love-glances of a woman" (my emphasis). This generates the possibility that the scene is neither one between men (Waldo is no longer a man), nor, to be sure, one between a man and a woman (Waldo is "more . . . than . . . [a] woman"), but instead puts into play another organization of sexual differences.

Opening such other possibilities may, however, encourage a powerful misogyny. To the Stranger, Waldo's being more than a woman implies that being a woman is unworthy. "Habits," he tells Waldo as he is about to ride off, "feed on the intellect like a woman sapping energy, hope, creative power, all that makes a man higher than a beast—leaving only the power to yearn, to regret, and to sink lower in the abyss" (160). Associated with male homosexuality and transposed into social terms, this is the abased womanhood that, in *Woman and Labour*, contributes to the end of Hellenic civilization.[18] Schreiner makes a choice between complicities in the name of a larger joinedness. This time it is not simply between exclusion or marginalization of women but also between misogyny and, to term it anachronistically but surely not inaccurately, an unacknowledged homophobia.

Women are marginal to the spectacle of intellectual exchange in "Waldo's Stranger." When interpreted as the fictional presentation of an exchange between a woman and man (Schreiner and Bertram), the episode can, however, be understood to address an anxiety about sexual intimacy and the baneful consequences it could hold for young, unmarried Victorian women. The narrative, as novel and autobiography, appears to admit an active female sexuality apart from the reproductive sphere. Figured as homoerotic and male, this erotic sexuality exposes a double genealogy for the forms of intellectual life. The episode of "Waldo's Stranger" suggests that the universal model for intellectual exchange—*inter alia,* the separation of mind and body, the privileging of mind over body, the "anxiety of influence"—can, in a way akin to Foucault's story of the beginnings of philosophy in Greek homoerotics, be assigned a genealogy in more modern norms pertaining to female sexual conduct. Both genealogies, one must not forget, depend ultimately on a depressed value being assigned to women, who are also invariably associated with the body rather than the mind (see Spelman). Nevertheless, what remains significant about *The Story of an African Farm* for the purposes of work toward a genealogy of intellectual life and the intellectual as figure of responsibility-in-complicity is that it does not call on us simply to replace a masculine with a feminine genealogy. In the cryptic act of making Waldo the intellectual woman's proxy, the novel textualizes what resonates with more familiarity in intellectual life today: the two sexual genealogies of disembodiment in all the intimacy of their articulation.

Such a separation of mind and body is challenged in South Africa after apartheid by feminist intellectuals acting in advocacy of women who appear before the Truth and Reconciliation Commission. By demanding that women be given the chance to testify to violations done to themselves, instead of merely to violations done to others, they implicitly respond to and oppose the "disembodiment" of intellect and its consequences for women fed by the two genealogies I have analyzed. Providing a protected yet still public space for testimony to violations involving sexual violence and abuse, and psychological torture manipulating the sociosexual inscription of the female body (Spivak's "internalized constraints seen as responsibility" [Translator's Preface xxvii]), these intellectuals imagine and set to work in the quasi-juridical forum of the Truth Commission's hearings, an entry into mainstream intellectual and political life that insists on the embodiedness of sexual difference and its social consequences. Like the strategies of post-apartheid gay and lesbian advocacy under the aegis of human rights and the Constitution,[19] the forms taken by this entry for both black and white women are ones unimagined, even unimaginable, for Olive Schreiner and her generation.

In terms of late-nineteenth-century intellectual history, the Hellenism on which Schreiner cryptically inscribes herself participated in an English imperialism that made its way from Oxford to the colonies. In Southern Africa its main representative was Cecil John Rhodes.[20] Initially an admirer of Rhodes and his intellect, Schreiner came to distance herself from his politics on meeting him: "As long as he and I talked of books and scenery we were very happy, but, when he began on politics and social questions, I found out to my astonishment that he had been misrepresented to me" (qtd. in Cronwright-Schreiner 279; see also First and Scott 198–205, 221–28). This was in reaction to Rhodes's vote for the Strop Bill in the Cape parliament in 1890 and subsequently for his covert support of the Jameson Raid of 1896. Schreiner's anti-imperialist allegorical novel *Trooper Peter Halket of Mashonaland* (1897) attacked Rhodes and the land-grabbing and murderous excesses of the British South Africa Company in Mashonaland and Matabeleland in present-day Zimbabwe.

As leading figures in the liberal anti-imperialist milieu of Kimberley in the late 1890s, Olive Schreiner and Samuel Cronwright-Schreiner were known and admired by Sol Plaatje, and he and Elizabeth Plaatje subsequently named their daughter Olive after Schreiner (First and Scott 219–21; Willan 47, 134). Although counted among the "friends of the natives," Schreiner and Cronwright-Schreiner were more critical of imperialism than Plaatje, who, as journalist and political leader after the failed deputation of 1919, declared loyalty to Britain in return for imperial protection for black South Africans and had even pledged African troops for the war against Germany and its allies. Schreiner, as a pacifist, condemned this stance (Willan 198; First and Scott 305). This filiation, and difference in affiliation, is one of the ironies of colonial South African intellectual history. It represents the heterogeneity of the colonial period, its continuities and discontinuities. We are squarely in the realm of taking sides, of complicities in the narrow sense, of divisions over specific issues of the day.

The heterogeneity of the period is also apparent when Plaatje devises an entry for the African, and cultural production in African languages, into mainstream intellectual sociality and circulation. Plaatje, to be sure, makes nothing like an appeal to Hellenism — which may have been disastrous, given that, at least in Schreiner, Hellenism is linked to evolutionary racism — but there is a deeper affinity between him and Schreiner, apparent when he stages, in his late work, a "secret" encounter between two implied readers speaking different languages. This affinity aside, the major difference is that in contrast to Schreiner, as an interpreter and an enfranchised black man, Plaatje speaks in his early work not, as one might expect after the end of a century of racialization and apartheid, from outside the colonial mainstream but, in some sense, as British imperialism's exemplary representative.

Sol T. Plaatje: "The Essential Interpreter"

The need to stage a covert encounter in order to enter an intellectual sociality from which one is marginalized or in which what one advocates does not easily circulate emerges in the work of Sol Plaatje (1876– 1932), albeit in quite a different way than in that of Schreiner. In Plaatje's case, in which through a system joining the circulation of money with linguistic translation, his writing in English facilitates reading in Setswana, the reader is drawn into an uncanny process whereby what he or she reads is not the sole object of his or her reading. In his preface to his historical novel, *Mhudi* (1930), Plaatje writes:

This book should have been published over ten years ago, but circumstances beyond the control of the writer delayed its appearance. If, however, the objects can be attained, it will have come not a moment too soon.

This book has been written with two objects in view, viz. (*a*) to interpret to the reading public one phase of 'the back of the Native mind'; and (*b*) with the readers' money, to collect and print (for Bantu Schools) Sechuana folk-tales, which, with the spread of European ideas, are fast being forgotten. It is thus hoped to arrest this process by cultivating a love for art and literature in the Vernacular. (21)

It would be wrong to see the split in address as racially symmetrical; as Plaatje implies, some of the historical events fictionalized in *Mhudi* — the murder of two Matabele tax collectors by the Barolong, the Matabele reprisals and the exile of the Barolong, the ill-fated alliance between the Barolong and the Boers to defeat the Matabele — may also have been unfamiliar to his contemporary readers of Setswana.[21] Yet, the "reading public" he projects and addresses, and whose curiosity for knowledge of "'the back of the Native mind'" is a demand inflecting his discourse, must be regarded as the place occupied by the white reader, or at least a reader able to split his or her awareness from "the Native mind." Called upon to make reparation for the forgetting that comes with "the spread of European ideas," this readership, one distinct from readers in "Bantu Schools," will provide the money necessary for the latter to be able to read "Sechuana folk-tales."[22]

There is, on the face of it, nothing mysterious about this appeal for cash, one of several Plaatje made for his folk-tale project (see *Selected Writings* 368–70, 375–81). Examined further, however, Plaatje's preface can be read as establishing a *technics* that will make possible a certain dispropriation. This dispropriation intimately links commerce and language, bringing together an appropriation of money from the book-buyer with the self-othering involved in translation between languages. If, by reading in English, reader (a) makes it possible for reader (b) to read in Setswana, a language reader (a) does not understand, a joined-ness is enabled in the midst of a radical split in address. The preface envisions a complicity in which one reader, by paying for the book, reads for another reader. In the sense that the complicity of reader (a) is enlisted without his or her needing to be aware of it, which parallels the way in which Waldo's Stranger does not know that he is effectively facilitating a young woman's initiation into intellectual life, we have a secret encounter. Irreducible to any voluntarism, since the ability of reader (a) to substitute for reader (b) depends entirely on the circulatory system activated by his or her book purchase, the process depends on technics.

The magic that technology could achieve in the realm of language fascinated Plaatje. A proponent of phonetic script as a way of preserving Setswana, Plaatje was impressed by the way it enabled speakers with absolutely no knowledge of the language to reproduce perfect sentences in it. Introduced to phonetics by the linguist Daniel Jones, Plaatje relates, "I saw some English ladies, who knew nothing of Sechuana, look at the blackboard and read phrases aloud without the trace of European accent" (*Selected Writings* 221). A more striking structural parallel is the simultaneous translation apparatus in use at the Truth Commission, where witnesses and commissioners can in effect speak and be heard in languages they do not understand.[23] In the phrase from the preface, "interpret to the reading public," we can hear the echo of Plaatje's own familiarity with an earlier version of this apparatus, which he embodied in human form.

Although not dominating it, secrecy of encounter and dispropriation are key elements in the account of the intellectual as advocate that can be drawn from a manuscript drafted by Plaatje twenty years before his preface to *Mhudi* and stemming directly from his activities as a court interpreter. Hardly a marginal figure, Plaatje's interpreter is the neutral switching point for an imperial and colonial rule whose promise of social justice and civic rights is then still taken seriously by black Africans. Before that promise is broken and the enforced social fissuring of segregation and apartheid brought an accompanying denial of substantive justice, it was not necessary to imagine interpreting in more radical terms.

Although the conditions of possibility for such a solution do lie in Plaatje's manuscript, his account of the interpreter can provisionally be linked to the more classical genealogy of the intellectual that comes down from Émile Zola, which I established in my introduction. To date nobody has remarked upon how, like W. E. B. Du Bois in the United States,[24] Sol Plaatje takes up, extends, and generalizes the project of advocacy and responsibility-in-complicity set to work for the intellectual in "J'accuse." Now that more than a century has passed, it is possible to think of Zola's intervention in the Dreyfus affair, not simply in European terms, but as an inaugural event in a global history of the intellectual. It is through such figures as Du Bois and Plaatje — and Frantz Fanon and Steve Biko, and even N. P. van Wyk Louw, who anticipates Jaspers's concept of "metaphysical guilt" — that a script for universal responsibility is globally disseminated.[25] In Plaatje's hands, Zola's project of advocacy is reoriented by its contact with local linguistic multiplicity and the attendant work of interpreting, which reveals a more basic structure and dynamics of responsibility-in-complicity. Before apartheid, but amid its colonial beginnings, Plaatje shows the makings of a minimal human foldedness that would counter complicity in what prevents its realization.

A tacit identification by Plaatje with Zola emerges in a petition Plaatje wrote on behalf of Sekgoma, a chief imprisoned without trial in 1906 by the British colonial authorities, who had sided with Mathiba, his rival to the Batawana chieftaincy in northwestern Bechuanaland. Characterizing Sekgoma as "the black Dreyfus," Plaatje joins his performance as an intellectual to a script adapted from Zola's advocacy. That Plaatje's Sekgoma-Dreyfus is "black" generalizes, and thereby reveals, the basic traits of the French case: a call for responsibility as advocacy on behalf of an other — an other who, being racially constituted, is in a classic sense not immediately kin to the one called to responsibility but can be projected as being kin through the mediating work of responsibility.

This positioning applies not only to the implied addressee of Plaatje's petition, who is imagined as British and white (*Selected Writings* 104–5), but also to Plaatje himself. As a loyal British subject and an enfranchised resident of the Cape Colony, he can split himself, in part, from the racial otherness he shares with Sekgoma. There is no inconsistency when Plaatje projects himself into the addressee's position by appealing to "British sense of justice" and "the sanctity of civilized rule" (*Selected Writings* 116, 118). From his advocacy of Sekgoma in "The Black Dreyfus," to his membership of the futile South African Native National Congress deputation to Britain to protest the Natives' Land Act of 1913, to his repeated declarations of imperial loyalty and his response to the rejection by Britain of black South African troops in the Great War (all documented in *Native Life in South Africa* [1916]), to the deputation he led to British Prime Minister David Lloyd George in 1919 to protest Union native policies (*Selected Writings* 257–64) — these were the basic principles Plaatje upheld in politics, even if, in some of his later writings, he began to question the wisdom of his advocated loyalty to the British Empire (*Selected Writings* 273). Through the imagining of a reading public in metropole and colony who embraced these principles with him, his strategy was to demonstrate and bring an acknowledgment of a widespread complicity in their abrogation. Like that of Zola, his call for responsibility is self-implicating and can be read as coming from a sense of his own part, simply by virtue of subscribing to those principles, in the arbitrary exclusion of others from their protection.

What is particular to Plaatje, however, is that his advocacy of Sekgoma is intimately related in conception to what he sets out as the responsibility of the courtroom interpreter in a multilingual colonial setting. Bringing together two senses of advocacy, Plaatje's conception of the intellectual supplements that of Zola by joining to the ethico-political responsibility of "J'accuse" a responsibility to language and the language of the other. Justice is situated at the point of convergence of these two senses of advocacy, with the court interpreter as the hinge between them.

The integrity of Plaatje's conception of the intellectual as interpreter has, however, been fractured by the very scholarly editing that helps to make it apparent. In the introduction to his edition of Plaatje's *Selected Writings* (1996), Brian Willan informs readers that "Plaatje's unpublished manuscript which combines 'The Essential Interpreter' and 'Sekgoma — The Black Dreyfus' has been separated in two" (4).[26] Sundered, its two parts distributed among texts and documents written at other times, the historicity of the manuscript, which was written in 1908 or 1909, is obscured. Plaatje himself had, according to Willan, begun to separate the manuscript into its two parts. For the links between his views on the duties of the court interpreter in South Africa, and his advocacy of Sekgoma to become visible, the two pieces of the manuscript have to be read over against each other.

Plaatje's account of "The Essential Interpreter" is framed in part as a memoir of his own employment as court interpreter in Mafeking from 1898 to 1902.[27] From out of that testimony another speaks, leading toward a claim for the "essential" place in "the administration of justice in South Africa" — and, I propose, in the administration of justice generally — of the office of interpreter. Before opening his memoir, Plaatje begins by drawing attention to a linguistic multiplicity that makes South Africa different from European countries, and to a system of colonial rule under which differences in language signify according to a hierarchy that codes them racially and ethnically:

> The administration of justice in South Africa is something entirely different from the same thing in Europe, where judge, plaintiff, defendant, counsel and witnesses all speak the same language. In South Africa, where the inhabitants are Englishmen, Dutchmen, and Kafirs of various races, there is hardly any court of law without its interpreter.
>
> I was at one time employed in the magistrate's court, Mafeking, under the Cape authorities, as an interpreter. (*Selected Writings* 51)

A shuttling of meaning takes place between the title "The Essential Interpreter" and the opening lines of the work it entitles. Routed through a play on the word *essential,* meaning shifts back and forth between contingency and essence; between a specific historical and biographical situation, and what is "essential" about the interpreter in the "administration of justice." Not allowing a reduction of either pole to the other, this movement suggests that Plaatje's text can be read, not merely as a self-implicating apologia for the employment of qualified interpreters,[28] but as a locally inflected iteration of what it means to stand for justice. It is in this sense that "The Essential Interpreter," along with its counter-part, Plaatje's petition on behalf of Sekgoma, is legible as a text on the intellectual and as a textual performance of what it is to be an intellectual.

At the turn of the twentieth century, court interpreters, along with teachers and ministers, were recognized members of the African petite bourgeoisie, the class that produced the bulk of the black South African intelligentsia.[29] A strong thread running through Plaatje's text is a plea for better remuneration of interpreters, a matter that touched him personally (*Selected Writings* 47–50), in order to guarantee accurate interpretation and thereby fulfill a necessary condition of possibility for justice. But "The Essential Interpreter" amounts to more than an expression of the professional claims and class aspirations of the black mental worker. It performs, in classic fashion, the transition from the figure referred to by Sartre in "A Plea for Intellectuals" as the "technician of practical knowledge," to the "intellectual," who begins to universalize responsibility by testifying to the wider ethico-political implications of his or her professional practice.

Tempted as we might be to assimilate the situation described by Plaatje to the collaboration envisaged by Macaulay's Minute on Indian Education (1835), which called for "a class who may be interpreters between us and the millions that we govern — a class of persons Indian in blood and colour, but English in tastes, in opinions, in morals and in intellect" (190), we should note that for Plaatje responsibility arises, not from a metaphor of mediated dominion presented to an imperial parliament, but from the sense of a standard of everyday forensic practice according to which the interpreter is bound to exist for each party equally. It is with this sense that there comes about the "certain idealism" that, as J. M. Coetzee reminds us, "is inherent in the way intellectuals conceive of themselves socially" ("Critic and Citizen" 109). Although rooted in the everyday practice of interpreting, Plaatje's conception of the intellectual is not exhausted by reference to professional ethos or social function, and, consequently, the sense of complicity from which responsibility emerges for him is not reducible to a simple discomfort with either.

When Plaatje relates how, while working in Mafeking for the Cape court, he refused to interpret without pay for the Resident Commissioner's office, at the time "also the court of appeal of the Bechuanaland Protectorate" (*Selected Writings* 52), it is not to demand a wage as much as it is to insist, at first through mildly mocking understatement, on the intimate link between "the services of an interpreter" and "the correct administration of justice." In this, the first of several formulations of the relationship between interpretation and justice, the interpreter features as an "adjunct," suggesting that the "essential" nature of the interpreter is to be an addition, but also that the essence of justice itself cannot be accomplished without this supplemental office: "I am told that this most important adjunct of the correct administration of justice went about begging for a hand until a street boy was obtained to interpret 'any-how'" (*Selected Writings* 52).

In Plaatje's subsequent formulations, what is "essential" about the interpreter lies in what joins this figure with the figure of the judge: "It is essential that every judge should clearly understand the evidence in any case upon which he sits in judgement, and the only means he has of attaining this in Southern Africa is by possession of a good interpreter" (*Selected Writings* 53). Although Plaatje writes of the court interpreter as a "means" to what the judge is to accomplish, the relationship between the two figures is a synecdoche. When a judge's duty to "understand the evidence" is inseparable, as it is in Southern Africa, from the ability to interpret from one language to another, the office of judge is inevitably, in part, the office of interpreter. It is not essential that judge and interpreter are embodied in one and the same person; what is essential is the relationship between judge and interpreter as interrelated functions of justice. As the fluidity of the genitive *of* in "by possession of a good interpreter" suggests, the relationship between the two functions is an intimate one in which the precedence of one over the other does not go without saying. That is why, in colonial Southern Africa, where judges are seldom multilingual, it is "importan[t]" to maintain the services of a "good interpreter."

After giving an example of how a court interpreter facilitates a "tri-alogue" between three parties, each of whom speaks a different language, Plaatje underlines the "essential" relationship between judge and interpreter — or, as a favorite phrase of Plaatje has it, "its true inwardness" — when he writes "that each . . . court should have not only a human tool who can reproduce a Kafir or Sechuana sentence in English but one whose conscience will never permit of any augmentation or garbling in his renditions" (*Selected Writings* 57). In other words, since he or she performs the judging function of "conscience," the interpreter cannot consistently be conceived simply as an "adjunct" to justice, a "human tool," or "a judge['s] . . . mouthpiece" (*Selected Writings* 59). The judge is possessed of the interpreter, the interpreter of the judge. It is in this mutual haunting that the interpreter is "essential" to the pursuit of justice; this is the deeper reason why "it is impossible for the South African courts to mete out substantial justice without the aid of good interpreters" (*Selected Writings* 59).

Once "The Essential Interpreter" is explicated in this way, "Sekgoma — The Black Dreyfus" is legible in its advocacy on behalf of the imprisoned chief, not merely as an act of political protest, but as a performance of the intellectual that, in insisting on the office of interpreter, joins ethico-political and linguistic responsibility. Such a joining, which I propose is integral to Plaatje's understanding of "substantial justice," can be analyzed at more than one level. It is, in one sense, easy to see how Plaatje takes up and extends Zola, making visible essential traits of "J'accuse" relating to advocacy and racial otherness. Contrasting South Africa with colonial India, where "they employ Native masters of arts and professors of literature — men of education and character — to act as interpreters," Plaatje writes: "The opposite policy almost universally pursued in this country is in the main responsible for Sekgoma's unfortunate position" (*Selected Writings* 60).

Alluding to a "series of faulty interpretations" in Sekgoma's case, Plaatje cites an instance when, in an interview of the disputing parties with the High Commissioner in 1906, "each time they spoke to His Excellency, Sekgoma's men had to speak through Mathiba's secretary who acted as interpreter between Lord Selborne and the Natives" (*Selected Writings* 60). "Where," Plaatje asks, "was His Excellency's interpreter? And if he had not one, why were not the services of a disinterested person procured for the occasion?" (60). Interpreting the role of essential interpreter, Plaatje steps in at the juncture at which justice has been miscarried through biased interpretation. Refusing to be an accomplice in injustice, Plaatje's intervention parallels that of Zola on behalf of Dreyfus. By being Sekgoma's advocate before a British public, Plaatje reinforces the centrality to justice of the everyday work of advocacy performed by the interpreter.

The implications of Plaatje's manuscript are, however, more radical. The local setting to work of Zola's text ultimately renders necessary an analysis of what is unthought in the Dreyfus case, where, although advocacy of the other is central, forensic interpretation in the narrow sense is not an issue. It is perhaps the fact that Plaatje writes before apartheid, and the consequent final divorce between race and political rights, that makes a fundamental structure of joinedness imaginable and makes the interpreter the representative figure for British imperialism as a force for global liberty and justice. With the Cape franchise still in place and imperial protection for Africans still conceivable, he is yet to undergo the alienation that Biko, Ndebele, and their generation do when their English-language education guarantees them nothing. With apartheid, and the colonialism that precedes it, as we see in Schreiner's *Thoughts on South Africa* and in Plaatje's *Native Life in South Africa,* there is an attention to complicities in the narrow sense; and it becomes a task to excavate from layers of apartness the visions of joinedness that drive anti-apartheid discourse or that make some, like Louw, question apartheid in some of its forms.

This is my reason for producing an account of Plaatje that attempts to go beyond—in the sense of an always-impossible *pas au-delà*—seeing him simply appeal to principles that, as a native intellectual, he has "internalized." I have sought to go beyond the failure of the imperial deputations he headed and his professions of loyalty to the empire, which, insofar as they promised African troops, alienate him from Olive Schreiner.[30] To attempt anything less is, in a sense, to capitulate to the depredations of apartheid and of the deformations of "unilateral" imperatives to oppose it on the intellectual history of South Africa. That is why I place the importance that I do on Plaatje's fragment on the "essential interpreter."

It is unusual to find much thought given to the deeper implications of the activity of courtroom interpretation. This is surprising—for is it by any means settled as to what is going on when interpretation takes place? The commonsense view is—to confine ourselves to the scene Plaatje narrates—that the judge, the accused, and the witness remain and leave as they entered. The task of the interpreter, in terms of this view, is to ensure that this personal integrity is maintained. He or she is bound by conscience to "reproduce a Kafir or Sechuana sentence," according to Plaatje, without "any augmentation or garbling in his renditions." But the interpreter is, in fact, the only party who does *not* undergo alteration in the process. That is because he or she is not a *party* at all, but is, as Plaatje puts it, a "human tool." Plaatje is strict in this regard: an interpreter who finds reason to add to the words of the accused or the witness ought better to testify instead (*Selected Writings* 57). Like the phonetic script that so captured Plaatje's imagination and the impersonal system of circulation implied in the preface to *Mhudi,* the function of the interpreter is, in terms of this conception, purely technical.

As with the apparatus for simultaneous translation used at the Truth and Reconciliation Commission, the technics embodied in the human form of the interpreter facilitate a process whereby the parties involved do not, so to speak, remain themselves. Undergoing a basic dispropriation, the judge who does not know the language of the accused or the witness must, in effect, be heard to speak a language he or she does not understand. This submission to the language of the other, which Derrida proposes as "the condition of all possible justice," but which appears "in all rigor . . . impossible,"[31] may be understood, in Levinasian terms, as a responsibility for the other and as responsibility for the responsibility of the other. In this instance, the responsibility of the other is a trueness to the grammar of a language, to its minimal truth. If, as Levinas writes in *Totality and Infinity,* justice is relation to the other — "the relation to others — that is to say, justice" (qtd. in Derrida, "Force of Law" 959) — then the technics of interpretation fulfill an essential condition of possibility for justice — in this instance, by making it possible, as a performance, for the judge to be responsible for the language of the accused. (This may be basic to all forensic procedure; where there is no translation involved, there is still the language of the other in the general sense.) In order for there to be justice, the law must cease, as it were, to be itself; it must allow itself to become other than itself, hearing and speaking a language it does not know.[32]

This account of justice, in terms of which it shares the same dispropriative structure as the technics of court interpretation, leads to an account of the intellectual that is at once true to Zola and yet entirely breaks with his problematic. By heading his petition "Sekgoma — The Black Dreyfus," Plaatje, like Zola, enacts responsibility as advocacy. But the "I" that, in Zola, does not wish to be complicit (and that is formed in the desire not to be) finds itself enabling a process whereby the parties concerned are, at least for the duration of the process and until a judgment is made, no longer themselves but folded together with one another (even if they do not know it). Although it stems from his specific location as court interpreter, surely the situation par excellence for imperial claims to justice, this dispropriation is a figure for complicity in the general sense.

This is not so different from what Plaatje makes more or less explicit in his preface to *Mhudi:* by reading this, you provide money so that others can read the folk tales. By reading this novel and responding to it as a reader, you are responsible, in more than one sense, for another reader. In this instance, money is mediated and alienated, not merely words, as in the courtroom. But in each case, the mediator *interprets.* In each case, the encounter between the parties is secret or quasi-secret. What passes is a secret. The position of the interpreter is not unlike that of Waldo in *The Story of an African Farm,* who functions as a proxy to figure Schreiner's entry into intellectual sociality by mediating and alienating her femininity for the Stranger in a secret encounter in which he does not know her true identity.

When justice is impossible in the juridico-political sphere, the secret or unwitting encounter, with more or less covert exchange, becomes a constant thread in anti-apartheid literature. In the 1950s in *Towards an African Literature* A. C. Jordan takes up and links the reciprocity of ubuntu to Tiyo Soga's messianic plea for hospitality among the ama-Xhosa a century before—which asks the reader to complete the verse from Hebrews: "Do not be forgetful to entertain strangers." When, a few years later, Bloke Modisane's *Blame Me on History* uses the "cover story" of protest literature to send a message to his deceased father via the "white liberal" reader, we are ready to identify, at the margins of apartheid intellectual life, a structure of responsibility-in-complicity that has to imagine a greater human foldedness in secret. The attempts of the Truth and Reconciliation Commission to "heal the nation" after apartheid, to repair broken social justice, depend on one's preparedness to be heard to speak in languages one does not know. The scene of larger or generalized joinedness counterposed to apartheid can thus be secret, phantasmatic, even impossible: one cannot speak a language one does not understand, and a woman cannot be a man. But we must all do the impossible. And, enabled by technics of various kinds, we often do.

Taking Sides: Late Works of Schreiner and Plaatje

In their attempts to imagine a joinedness against the apartness of late-colonial South African society, both Olive Schreiner and Sol Plaatje are overwhelmed, in major late works, by the increasing denial of and destruction of reciprocity and its conditions of possibility. These works take sides.

In Schreiner's *Thoughts on South Africa,* a volume composed of eight essays on the country, its peoples, and its political status written between 1890 and 1901 with several appended notes dating from roughly the same period, we find, on the one hand, a confession of complicity in race separation displaced into childhood, and, on the other hand, a vision of kinship implicated in the racism it would overcome. In the preface (1901) to *Thoughts on South Africa,* where she gives an account of her "early training," Schreiner confesses how, as a child, she "ma[de] believe that all the world belonged to me. That being the case, I ordered all the black people in South Africa to be collected and put into the desert of Sahara, and a wall built across Africa shutting it off" (17).[33] By contrast to the vision of Christian fellowship, complicity, and responsibility revealed to the protagonist of *Trooper Peter Halket of Mashonaland* (1897), in *Thoughts on South Africa* the colonial race separation informing the mind of the child Schreiner at play is imagined as surmountable in the very racial terms in which it is wrought. Contemplating the basis for political union in South Africa, Schreiner pointed to "a form of organic union which is possible to us" (*Thoughts* 56). According to Schreiner, "in our households, in our families, in our very persons we are mingled. . . . there is a sense in which all South Africans are one. . . . there is a subtle but a very real bond, which unites all South Africans, and differentiates us from all other peoples in the world. *This bond is our mixture of races itself*" (*Thoughts* 55–56).

Schreiner's anti-racist vision of mixture, in which the social shades into the sexual, but in which miscegenation is discouraged (*Thoughts* 95–130, 351–54), goes hand in hand with the political vision articulated in her pamphlet *Closer Union* (1908), in which a federation of South African states is preferred to the centralized government that the Union of 1910 would more closely approximate. The reason to reject "closer union" is that, from the point of view of her white reader, "we cannot hope ultimately to equal the men of our own race living in more wholly enlightened and humanised communities, if our existence is passed among millions of non-free subjected peoples" (31). Phrased as a passing of existence among others, the actual social and economic intimacy and interdependence of the races in South Africa, which Schreiner believes to be the foundation of any union, holds complicity in the general sense against the narrow race loyalty of Union. In the context of the contest over union, this opposition cannot be other than one-sided. Joinedness, although generalizable in terms of a passing of existence among others, is figured in terms of racial difference.

It is a troubling feature of South African intellectual history, of the history of the intellectual who opposes apartheid, that one of the most powerful moves, if not *the* most powerful move, against apartheid is a racist one. A version of anti-racist racism comparable to that of Schreiner is elaborated by Breyten Breytenbach in *A Season in Paradise* and *Dog Heart* (along with his ideas about linguistic hybridization) in order to resist the nationalist purism of Louw and others. Although not operating with a notion of hybridity, be it racial (like Schreiner, he eschewed miscegenation [*Selected Writings* 274–83]) or linguistic like Breytenbach's, Sol Plaatje imagines language as a condition of possibility for kinship. Plaatje's preface to *Mhudi*, in which we are able to read a radical dispropriation, comes before a novel in which possibilities for cross-racial kinship in a shared language are repeatedly undercut and in which a missed historical chance for it is dramatized as a predicament of linguistic incomprehension. Just as Schreiner's *Thoughts on South Africa* participates in racism by opposing mixture to separation, under the pressure of Union race politics, Plaatje's novel appears to stage a disastrous test to decide for or against a racial parting of ways: either one speaks the other's language or one does not. If one does, kinship may be possible; if one does not, kinship may be well-nigh impossible.

Mhudi is set in the 1830s, when the Barolong were dominated by the Matabele under Mzilikazi, who, having broken away from the Zulu kingdom to establish his own to the north, led the often bloody Mfecane to drive other groups from this territory. Allowing the Barolong to retain their land, Mzilikazi levied taxes on them. *Mhudi* relates the killing of Mzilikazi's two tax collectors by the Barolong around 1830, the subsequent Matabele reprisals, and the eventual military defeat of the Matabele by an alliance of Barolong and Boers, to whom the Barolong offer hospitality. These historical events are the setting for the romance of Mhudi and Ra-Thaga, who, uprooted separately during the Matabele raid, meet in the wilderness, have children, and finally make their way south back to the other exiled Barolong near Thaba Nchu (in present-day Free State Province) at about the time the Voortrekkers under Sarel Cilliers arrive in the region.[34]

As a historical novel, according to Tim Couzens, *Mhudi* displaces the colonial and Afrikaner-nationalist version of South African history in which the Great Trek is the central event of the early nineteenth century, making the coming of the Voortrekkers "merely another episode in the movement of South African tribes" (Introduction 7). Written around 1917, the year after *Native Life in South Africa* appeared, *Mhudi,* which is subtitled "An Epic of South African Native Life a Hundred Years Ago," seems to tie the events it narrates to what had taken place since Union in 1910. "It is my contention," Couzens writes, "that *Mhudi* is not only a defence of traditional custom as well as a corrective view of history, but it is also an implicit attack on the injustice of land distribution in South Africa in 1917" (Introduction 17). That would make Plaatje's novel, a prophecy and a warning to whites set in the 1830s (Introduction 18–19), a critical allegory of apartheid as it was developing after 1910.[35]

Mhudi's account of the military alliance against the Matabele between Chief Moroka of the Barolong and the Voortrekkers under Cilliers, described by Plaatje in 1932 as a "tragic friendship" (qtd. in Couzens, Introduction 11; see also *Selected Writings* 409), shares a textuality with *Native Life in South Africa* (126ff), foreshadowing a time when black South Africans, and not only the Barolong, would be dispossessed of their land. Reacting to the Trekker leader Potgieter's suggestion that "after killing off the Matabele and looting their property, they would make a just division of the spoil by keeping all the land for the Boers and handing over the captured cattle to the Barolong," Chief Tauana of the Ra-Tshidi clan exclaims: "'What an absurd bargain! . . . What could one do with a number of cattle if he possessed no land on which to feed them? Will his cattle run on the clouds! and their grass grow in the air? No, my lords; I would rather leave the Matabele where they are and remain a sojourner with my people in the land of the Selekas under my cousin, Moroka'" (*Mhudi* 141–42). As Plaatje points out in *Native Life in South Africa,* the Land Act of 1913 not only dispossessed Blacks of land, but it made it illegal for white landowners to lease land to black farmers, which, among other things, meant that their livestock would have nowhere to graze (*Native Life* 96). Making the South African native "a pariah in the land of his birth" (*Native Life* 21), the Land Act was the dubious reward for the Barolong alliance with the Boers; it was "the acme of ingratitude" (qtd. in Couzens, Introduction 16; see also *Selected Writings* 321–22).

Even as it makes its "prophetic" critique of the policies that would ground apartheid in the narrow sense, Plaatje's novel proposes a possible way of realizing a more durable alliance than the political one between Cilliers and Moroka. *Mhudi* suggests that this can take place through the learning of another's language. The chapters of the novel narrating Mhudi and Ra-Thaga's exile and the meeting that ends their mutual solitude firmly establish language as the basis of human existence.[36] Supplementing the historical narrative, the romance plot insists on language, insofar as it is the conduit for affect, as the essential dimension of human sociality:

With a drooping spirit [Ra-Thaga] mused over the gloom of existence and asked himself if he could speak still his own language; or if, supposing he met anyone and was addressed, he could still understand it. . . . "Until I met you [Ra-Thaga tells Mhudi], I did not believe that another of our tribe existed, and I had never expected to hear our language spoken again." . . . My only living friends [Mhudi tells Ra-Thaga] were the turtle doves whose language I thought I could almost understand. I think that if this solitude had been prolonged for another month, I should have been able to sing their songs and learn to converse with them; yet I longed for the company of a [well-spoken] man [uttering our language in a beautiful voice], like the one who appeared in my dream. (*Mhudi* 34–48)

The moments where shared language points to a lasting alliance between Black and White, to a stand against apartheid, are constantly undercut by the narrative, however, suggesting deeper fractures.[37] When Ra-Thaga and the young Boer de Villiers "made up their minds to learn each other's language . . . de Villiers taught Ra-Thaga how to speak the Taal and Ra-Thaga taught the Boer the Barolong speech," the narrator reminds us that "there was one special bond of fellow-feeling between them, namely, their mutual aversion to the Matabele" (*Mhudi* 114; see also 157). And when Hannetjie, de Villiers's wife-to-be, imagines a place for Mhudi in their household, it is as a servant: "Surely they would be proud to have for an ayah such a noble mosadi as Mhudi" (*Mhudi* 183). As Chrisman points out, the novel, which regularly provides parenthetical glosses, here "withdraws its translative function. . . . The discourse mimics the incomprehension between the two women" ("Fathering" 68); there is no meeting point, on an equal footing, between speakers of colonial Dutch and Setswana.[38] Among the novel's indications that there will be no genuine reciprocity between white and black (see also Plaatje, *Selected Writings* 410), language remains the exemplary meeting point of sociality and affect: "But, unlike the two men, they knew not each other's language, consequently she made a less favorable impression on Mhudi than de Villiers did on her husband" (*Mhudi* 183–84).

What happens, though, when Plaatje's text does not withdraw its "translative function?" As I have shown, in *Mhudi*'s 1930 preface this function can be understood as working in two ways. On the one hand, there is the interpreting of the "native mind" for the reader: history from a Barolong perspective, the incorporation of folk tales and proverbs in the novel itself, and the glossing of Setswana words and phrases.[39] But as I have proposed, the task of interpreter taken on by the preface is more radical and may be a response to a far deeper incomprehension than that figured between Mhudi and Hannetje. Inscribed in a different historicity, the 1930 preface, with its staging of a secret encounter, can be read both as a phantasmic overcoming of an absence of actual reciprocity and substantive justice, and as an active passage through that aporia. With the consolidation of Afrikaner nationalism and the rule of the National Party under Hertzog with its campaign in the 1920s for racial segregation and the disenfranchisement of Blacks (Plaatje, *Selected Writings* 370–74), the beginnings of apartheid are being read by Plaatje as a squandered chance of hospitality and friendship between black South Africans and Afrikaners. The only way that the white reader will aid the black vernacular reader is if he or she does not know, or fully know, what he or she is doing; like Bloke Modisane's white woman in "The Dignity of Begging," who will give money when she thinks she is being pandered to by a "beggar." This is a dark reading, to be sure. But is this not what has to take place, the very least that has to take place, when what is to be overcome is the profound and essential social division envisaged by apartheid?

One could ask whether Plaatje's placement of language at the center of his vision of social cohesion does not amount to just another linguistic nationalism. There is always the danger that language in a general sense may be yoked to one or other specific language, that a particular language may be used as an index of national identity. That is the inevitable complicity entered into by Plaatje when he appeals for the preservation of Setswana folktales, and it is the linguistic purism that is the obverse of his wonder at the dispropriative possibilities of phonetic writing. Plaatje is in some sense written by the history of "encounter" in which, as Jean Comaroff and John Comaroff show, a fluidity is lost and the novel ethnocultural entities of *sekgoa* (European ways) and *setswana* (Tswana ways) emerge and coalesce as rival identities (1:198–251).

There is a world of difference, however, between the dispropriative work of interpretation performed in "The Essential Interpreter," where it generalizes the responsibility of the intellectual — even in the preface to *Mhudi,* in which, although there is a colonial hierarchy of languages, it is not essential *which* languages are in dialogue — and the total appropriative identification of a particular language with a people. Afrikaans, the creole Dutch of black and white South Africans, has become the national language of the white Afrikaner *volk* by the time the first of Louw's nationalist writings appear in the early 1930s.

chapter 2

the intellectual and apartheid

> I don't know you. . . . perhaps,
> perhaps you are even honorable:
> but the Empire also uses honorable ones for its work
> to say the gentle words *after* the atrocity,
> *after* the striking down and the surprise attack.
> Even as you gently speak, blind power speaks.
> —Thusnelda, *Germanicus*, N. P. VAN WYK LOUW

"Problems of Europe"

One of the more intriguing turns in apartheid thinking was for N. P. van Wyk Louw (1906–70) to set out and to defend apartheid as a response, not merely to South African "race problems," but to "problems of Europe." This was the position Louw took as Extraordinary Professor in South African Language, Literature, Culture, and History at the University of Amsterdam as he lectured Dutch and Afrikaans students on the subject of South Africa's "Rassevraagstukke" (Racial Questions) in 1952. It was one of several contributions he made to the post–World War II debate on apartheid.

Prefiguring what was later implemented by the National Party state as "separate development," Louw argued that a form of multinational-ism would solve the problem, shared by South Africa and Europe, of racial domination. Pivotal to Louw's argument was the notion that a number of distinct national groups [nasies, volke], both white and black, comprised South African society in tenuous union. Imposing a separation of these groups from one another would, he claimed, foster the "full development" of each and prevent a single group from domi-nating the others. It followed for him that racial separation achieved by a separation of national groups was an "ethically just" response to the problem of racial domination. Louw not only phrased that problem as a "problem of Europe," but he framed a solution to it that he maintained was consistent with the European political tradition — even with liberal-ism, insofar as its goal of political liberty could be pursued consistently in terms of the principle of national self-determination.

Louw's position articulates the local with the international. In the wake of World War II and the Holocaust, state racism no longer com-manded the political, moral, and intellectual respectability it once had. White South Africans nevertheless brought D. F. Malan's National Party to power in May 1948, ceding it a mandate to make good its nebulous election promise of apartheid. Outside of the country, however, the new government and its supporters were rapidly forced onto the defensive. Afrikaner-Dutch relations reached a crisis. In August 1948, just after the National Party's victory, Queen Juliana of the Netherlands rejected the credentials of Otto du Plessis, the newly appointed South African am-bassador. Sending Du Plessis, who had been a leading member of the pro-Nazi Ossewabrandwag, to a country occupied by Germany during the war was a diplomatic faux pas (Kannemeyer, *Dokumente* 288). In Utrecht at the time to receive an honorary doctorate in literature from the Rijksuniversiteit, N. P. van Wyk Louw found his appointment to the editorial board of *Critisch Bulletin,* a Dutch journal, opposed "on the grounds of his 'nationalist' philosophy of life out of which 'racist' con-victions would flow" (Kannemeyer, *Dokumente* 287). The message to Afrikaners from the Netherlands seemed to be that the descendants of the early Dutch settlers were being untrue to their Western liberal-democratic heritage.

By the 1950s it had become necessary for Afrikaans intellectuals in Europe and in the United States to advocate and defend the perpetua-tion of racial domination, segregation, and separation on grounds other than those of inherent superiority and inferiority derived from biological and other racisms. The goal of intellectuals abroad was to show that, if the white electorate was out of step with Western history, Afrikaans thought was rigorously consistent with the Western tradition. The strategy of the intellectuals varied according to the audience they addressed.[1] Writing with an ear to American concerns and comparing race relations in the United States and Brazil, Dutch Reformed theologian Ben Marais defended apartheid on "practical" rather than scriptural grounds, but his comparison maintained racial categories of black and white.[2] Contrasting with that of Marais, Louw's vocabulary of *volke* and *nasies,* though ultimately not separable from racism, may, in terms of this diplomatic history, have reflected a terminological exchange of race for nationality made necessary in the aftermath of Europe's more direct experience of the war.[3]

But Louw's presentation of South Africa's race problems as European and his insistence that apartheid was a solution true to the traditions of Europe were also allied to a postwar tendency among Afrikaans publicists to claim and reinforce for Afrikaners, and for white South Africans more broadly, a European cultural identity. If not entirely unprecedented, their rhetoric and public spectacles placed an increased emphasis on links to Europe. This contrasted with the 1938 Ossewatrek [Ox-wagon Trek] — commemorating the centenary of the mass Boer migration into the African interior — which effectively established for the Afrikaner volk a local and even African unity and historical continuity distinct from white Anglo–South Africa.[4] The pageants and speeches of 1952 for the 300th anniversary of Dutch settlement were marked by showy affirmations of racial, ethnic, and cultural Europeanness. These festivities had a local and an international dimension. In South Africa, hoping to increase its electoral majority in the 1953 election, the National Party courted white English-speakers ideologically: "This meant promoting an accompanying wider settler nationalism, whose right to rule stemmed from its self-proclaimed role as bearer of 'civilization,' a role which started with colonial occupation in 1652" (Rassool and Witz 449). The dominance of an official rhetoric of white Europeanness can be gauged from counters to it by opponents of the Cape Town Riebeeck festival. Dr. Moroka, for instance, accused the organizers of ignoring the "role of Non-Europeans in South Africa."[5]

As these exchanges help to show, inside South Africa in the early

1950s, to be European was to be white. "European" and "non-European" were racial categories. Presenting South Africa's "race problems" as "problems of Europe," Louw joins South Africa and Europe in co-responsibility. These are not, I would argue, simply the calculating words of a diplomat: calling for a joining in co-responsibility is, as Zola and his inheritors affirm, the duty of the intellectual par excellence. In the case of Louw, however, the very instant this responsibility-in-complicity is broached, by evoking what it means locally to be "European" as it cannot avoid doing, the acknowledgment of complicity begins to undo itself by specifying its agent in racial terms. The invocation of Europe generalizes joinedness and responsibility internationally but bars it locally. Louw's appeal to Europe is, I propose, the moment at which his nationalism and the multinationalism deriving from it definitively become a racism. The deeper motivations for this terrifyingly equivocal moment and their implications for the topic of the intellectual and apartheid emerge once N. P. van Wyk Louw's texts in apartheid thinking are analyzed comparatively and in relation to what he wrote on the intellectual: from the 1930s, when his Afrikaner nationalism demanded of the volk that it make possible the attainment of "full humanity" for its members, to the 1950s, when that nationalism came to be what Louw considered a generally valid basis for his support and advocacy of apartheid as "separate development."

N. P. van Wyk Louw and Lojale Verset

Enjoying an iconic status in Afrikaans literary and cultural life — W. A. de Klerk (210) compares him to Milton — Nicolaas Petrus van Wyk Louw is still celebrated as a poet in Afrikaans. His long poem *Raka* (1941) used to be a standard prescribed work for South African school pupils. Yet today, as intellectuals reflect on their role after apartheid, it is Louw's thinking on the critical public role of the intellectual and his own career in South Africa and abroad that command a more urgent interest.[6]

Beginning in the early 1930s, Louw took upon himself the task of fostering, in a milieu intolerant of dissent, a culture of criticism in Afrikaans intellectual life. This he referred to as *volkskritiek:* criticism of, for, and from the volk. Spurred by the poet Uys Krige, who complained to his friend about provincialism and the "lack of self-criticism" in the world of Afrikaans letters (Letter to Louw, 30 July 1936), Louw, an educationalist by training, saw his early essays not only as didactic and informational but as encouraging a culture of criticism in nationalist circles. [7] A few years later Krige, who sided with the left in the Spanish Civil War, applauded Louw's essay "Die ewige trek" [The Eternal Trek] for "contain[ing], among other things, an excellent corrective to the kind of Afrikaners who are all too ready to decry as a 'traitor' another Afrikaner who does not agree with them politically" (Letter to Louw [1938/39?]). "Die ewige trek" was one of the essays collected in *Lojale verset: Kritiese gedagtes oor ons Afrikaanse kultuurstrewe en ons literêre beweging* (1939) (collected in *Versamelde prosa* 1:65–172), the book that emerged from these efforts. Its subtitle, "Critical thoughts on our Afrikaans Cultural Striving and our Literary Movement," gives an idea of the scope of what its main title announces. Depending on the extent to which one wishes to preserve its echoes of British parliamentarianism, *lojale verset* is translatable as "loyal resistance" or "loyal opposition."[8]

Despite its adversarial beginnings, lojale verset came to name the convention authorizing and regulating criticism by Afrikaans intellectuals of the apartheid era. For Afrikaans intellectuals such as André Brink and Breyten Breytenbach, who from the 1960s on publicly opposed apartheid, Louw's legacy possessed an ambiguous power: powerful for tapping the resources of the Afrikaans language; ambiguous because of the restriction, by censors, cultural bodies, and the Afrikaans university system, of what could be said in that language.[9] Although he invoked Louw during his trial in 1975, Breytenbach had two years earlier warned of the impotence of lojale verset: "We . . . have a small minority trying to grope their way to an alternative, probing, questioning view — and that, indeed, is where we should be careful, extremely careful, because even our questioning — our loyal resistance [lojale verset] — may again be swallowed up by and adapted to the prevailing culture; we become, in turn, fringes and frills, having contributed at best only to a renewal of the old" (*Season* 170). If thinkers such as Johan Degenaar and André du Toit found ways during the 1970s and 80s of turning Louw's writings against apartheid,[10] by the close of the latter decade, Etienne van Heerden could have a character in his novel *Casspirs and Camparis* speak of lojale verset as having "tamed generations of [Afrikaans] intellectuals" (405; trans. modified).

As some Afrikaans academics try to reclaim Louw from the critique of the late 1980s and early 1990s, principally the work of Gerrit Olivier,[11] the issue of lojale verset has moved out from debates within Afrikanerdom into a more inclusive public sphere. In the process, the term *lojale verset* has been retranslated back into English. In an exchange shortly after the April 1994 election, Njabulo Ndebele criticized Breytenbach, who had declared his "loyalty" to the African National Congress (ANC) to be one of "vigilant opposition," for having fallen back on "the old concept of 'loyal opposition.'" Given Breytenbach's advocacy of language and cultural rights, this was a potential source of "volkstaats of the mind."[12] Albie Sachs's widely circulated and discussed ANC in-house paper, "Preparing Ourselves for Freedom" (1989), which appealed for an end to "solidarity criticism" (20), had appeared to promise an openness to criticism not tied to party loyalty.[13] Ndebele's stated "ideal of criticism. . . . a genuine form of 'opposition' firmly grounded on a strong moral and ethical investment, completely home-grown and spawned by our revolution" ("Open Letter" 21), however, strikingly resembled Louw's notion of volkskritiek: "Great criticism emerges when the critic places himself . . . in the midst of the group he criticizes, when he knows that he is bound unbreakably . . . to the volk he dares rebuke" (*Versamelde prosa* 1:167).[14] Yet despite this resemblance, the words *lojale verset* and *loyal opposition* had become taboo.

What took place to make them so? Part of what happened to lojale verset can, as I have begun to suggest, be traced in Louw's own career as he became an apologist for apartheid in South Africa and in the Netherlands, setting, by his personal example, the limits of dissent. A recent biography has shed light on such previously obscure areas, relevant to an account of his apartheid thinking, as his Broederbond activities.[15] But documents relating to this and other areas remain either unavailable or restricted. In order to make sense of what Louw did or saw himself as doing as an intellectual, we still have to judge by what he wrote and said and by how, for whom, and where he wrote and said it.

Becoming a member of the Cape Town branch of the Broederbond in 1934, Louw presented a lecture at one of its meetings in November 1940 on R. F. A. Hoernlé's *South African Native Policy and the Liberal Spirit* (Steyn 1:126, 310–12). Having made this early contribution to the debate on race policy, he subsequently stayed close to what was agreed upon, if not in official circles, in such think tanks as the South African Bureau of Racial Affairs (SABRA), which were connected, through the Broederbond, to the National Party government. While his biography reveals no official mandate for his activities in the Netherlands (although he did once seek the ambassadorship), as an intellectual Louw assumed the task of promoting and defending Afrikaner-nationalist interests — what he refers to in a 1952 letter as "our cause" (Steyn 1:514–15; 2:647). This he did through an advocacy of apartheid in reaction to Dutch criticism of the newly elected National Party's race policies (see Jansen 322 n.6). During his European years (1950–58), Louw wrote much of his finest poetry.[16] On becoming professor in Amsterdam in 1950, he also began a diplomatic career of sorts: nearly all of his writings and utterances for Dutch and for South African audiences in defense of apartheid stem from the time he spent in Amsterdam. An account of apartheid apology abroad would be incomplete if it did not treat, along with Ben Marais's American reflections, N. P. van Wyk Louw's activities in the Netherlands. Whereas Louw appears not to have acted as a mouthpiece for official policy, as an academic he operated, as have many intellectuals, as an informal cultural-political ambassador.[17]

Whether or not Louw was a dissident, as some have argued (Brink, *Mapmakers* 25; Cope 64–67), he became a more controversial figure after his return to South Africa in 1958. Although disagreeing with their more liberal views, he stood up for the *Sestigers* [Sixties] on the grounds of their "renewal" of Afrikaans prose and poetry, and he intervened when Breytenbach's wife was denied a visa to South Africa, apparently on racial grounds.[18] In the context of a right-wing struggle for power in the late 1960s — referred to by Serfontein as *die verkrampte aanslag* — Louw was publicly attacked by Verwoerd over his play, *Die pluimsaad waai ver* (1966), and was subjected to a flurry of abusive letters in Afrikaans newspapers.[19] When he died in 1970, the government sent no representative to his funeral (Human).

Although Louw was an embattled figure and a guiding example of principledness to Breytenbach's and Brink's generation, his political thinking remained firmly within the cultural-nationalist vision of the volk on which he based his defense of apartheid — even when he called for white Afrikaners to embrace coloureds — or, as he put it, *Bruinmense* — as *óns mense* [our people] (*Versamelde prosa* 2:623–26). Apart from his remarks in defiance of Verwoerd on behalf of a muzzled F. R. Tomlinson on the Afrikaans service of Radio Nederland, he was hardly ever as openly critical abroad.

Besides Louw's own activities, there are, as Ndebele's response to Breytenbach reveals, more profound reasons to be wary of lojale verset.

They relate to the extent to which particular commitments make it possible to generalize responsibility-in-complicity, or, as Edward Said writes, to "universalize the crisis" (*Representations* 44). Although the ties entered into by each are different, the danger of restricting responsibility and critical agency to one's "own" is no less present in Ndebele than in Louw. The goal of the present analysis is not, however, to weigh the commitments of one intellectual against another. We perform such calculations every day; all of us carry with us a ready tabulation of our loyalties and those of others. But that does not mean that we fully grasp the algorithm we employ. If, as I propose, what we do is decide whether a particular filiation or affiliation generalizes responsibility-in-complicity, Louw's invocation of "Europe" presents an interesting difficulty. To point to "problems of Europe" is, in global terms, a way of drawing attention to race domination as a world crisis. There can surely be no quarrel with that in and of itself. Read in local terms, however, the universalizing appeal to Europe stands in the way of generalizing responsibility-in-complicity locally. Heard as the double speech of diplomacy, it draws attention away from South Africa's problems. Though deeply implicated in apartheid foreign relations, the difficulty in Louw's invocation is irreducible to it. As an analysis of his apartheid apology of the 1950s in the light of his nationalist writings of the 1930s will show, the problems of "Europe" begin well before Louw boards his boat for the Netherlands.

Louw had developed his position on apartheid in published essays dating back to 1947, engaging in dialogue with the works of the two other apartheid thinkers. His main interlocutor was the University of the Witwatersrand philosopher Hoernlé (1880–1943), a liberal and a leading figure in the Johannesburg Joint Council of Europeans and Natives and in the South African Institute of Race Relations. Though no record exists of any personal contact between the two men, the dialogue of ideas Louw staged with Hoernlé graphically illustrates Anglo-Afrikaans collaboration in the intellectual history of apartheid.[20] As Gerrit Olivier points out, Hoernlé's 1939 Phelps-Stokes lectures, delivered at the University of Cape Town and published as *South African Native Policy and the Liberal Spirit* (1939), provided the basis for the local adaptation of liberalism projected and publicized by Louw.[21] At the same time, Louw conducted a less openly declared, but nevertheless significant, minor dialogue with University of Pretoria sociologist Geoffrey

Cronjé (1907–1992). Although his uninhibited racism was not echoed by Louw, Cronjé's co-authored *Regverdige rasse-apartheid* [Just Race-Apartheid] (1947), a classic in apartheid writing, appears to have supplied Louw with the slogan under which he advocated and defended apartheid separate development and put forth an argument claiming the justness, for the volk, of that path: *voortbestaan in geregtigheid,* or "continued existence in justice."

A curious continuum of apartheid thinking — R. F. A. Hoernlé, N. P. van Wyk Louw, Geoffrey Cronjé — is revealed by Louw's advocacy of apartheid as a South African or African (Afrikaans) solution to problems of Europe.[22] Louw's professed adaptation, via Hoernlé, of the European liberal tradition as voortbestaan in geregtigheid effectively made it impossible for Europe and its intellectuals to absolve themselves of complicity in apartheid. As I have proposed, embracing Europe was a fatal gesture of filiation, since it went without saying for Louw that Afrikaners were the privileged inheritors of Europe's cultural and intellectual legacy and that black Africans were to be confined, in terms of the type of political representation allowed them, to the "traditions" distorted and frozen by invented ethnicities and "customary law" under colonialism.[23] Louw made almost no acknowledgment of more than a century of black appropriation of Christianity and the English language or of an even older appropriation of Dutch. Black politics was alleged to be stage-managed by "Communists" or white-liberal agitators. We not only witness the interpretive violence of Louw's reading of Hoernlé, a travesty in and of theory, but also the foreclosure, as Louw echoes Cronjé, of the African or "Native" as a partner in responsibility. If European tradition was indeed adapted, the racist coding of "Europe" meant that white, "European" political prerogative was, in all respects, left untouched; and black, "Non-European" opposition was unheard, or if heard, was unheeded.

Embracing Europe: Race and Nation

The years after World War II witness a proliferation of references in Louw's essays to what, in one formulation, he designated as "the great humanist tradition of *our* European West" (*Versamelde prosa* 1:503; my emphasis). Such filiative gestures reach a climax with the 1952 tercentenary of Dutch settlement in South Africa when Louw, teaching in

Amsterdam, had occasion to reflect as never before on the links between Afrikaners and Europe (*Versamelde prosa* 2:57–72). Louw's writings represented the Afrikaner volk, on a civilizing mission in Africa, more and more as a *European* volk. The volk would, Louw implied, at the same time bring about a renewal of European thought.

In *The Other Heading: Reflections on Today's Europe* (1991), Jacques Derrida characterizes the European intellectual as a figure of memory who, beset by assertions of European "cultural identity," guards against the "new"—which should be anticipated as the unanticipatable—becoming a repetition of what has been identified as "the worst": "the worst violences, those that we recognize all too well *without yet having thought them through,* the crimes of xenophobia, racism, anti-Semitism, religious or nationalist fanaticism" (10, 6; my emphasis).[24] The question is whether, as Nationalist propaganda claimed and proclaimed for Afrikaners and for Whites a "European" cultural identity, Louw's rethinking of liberalism adequately guarded what he saw as new from becoming a repetition of the worst.[25]

Louw's holding of the Afrikaner volk responsible, in political and intellectual life, before "the great humanist tradition of our European West" was a compromised assumption of responsibility. In "Vegparty of polemiek?" [Scrap or Polemic?] (1946), Louw qualifies responsibility before that "humanist tradition" with a rejection of "importe[d]" thinking as he attempts to reconcile liberalism with nationalism or, more precisely, with Afrikaner nationalism. There is some inconsistency in Louw's formulations; although "humanism and reason" are not "things . . . we came to South Africa to learn; it is part of our European heritage," the "abstract principles" of liberalism have to be thought through "with a view to our concrete situation" (*Versamelde prosa* 1:437, 504). Louw insists that liberalism's "demand for justice—economic and social—for the non-white group" be viewed differently in the context of "our multi-national state" (*Versamelde prosa* 1:503, 506). Unanticipated in the allegedly racially and ethnically homogenous European nation-states in which liberalism first emerged, a "multi-national South Africa" demands a new variant of "liberal" thinking.

The new thinking, Louw claimed, is prescribed not only by Afrikaner nationalists but by the "great liberalist," R. F. A. Hoernlé. For Louw, Hoernlé featured at once as opponent and ally, European and African. Louw writes: "Hoernlé—surely one of the few great South African liberalists — perceived and demonstrated this . . . with incomparable clarity in his *South African Native Policy and the Liberal Spirit:* 'classic' European liberalism had its origin in countries constituted as racially or nationally homogenous [lande met 'n homogene rasse- of volkesame-stelling]; it was almost mechanically imported into multinational [multi-nasionale] South Africa without *thinking through* the application of the principle *anew*" (*Versamelde prosa* 1:504; my emphasis). The crux of Louw's argument for renewal is the profusion of nations. Despite appearances, Louw is treating Hoernlé as an antagonist. "Liberalist" with its "-ist" bore a mocking, pejorative charge familiar to Hoernlé.[26] In order to examine the terms under which Louw received Hoernlé's text into his, we will need to return Louw's paraphrase to the procession of Hoernlé's text and resubmit it to the protocols of the latter. There are a number of places where Louw might have excised the fragment he quotes and from where he might be paraphrasing. In the preface to *South African Native Policy and the Liberal Spirit,* Hoernlé summarizes the content of his third lecture:[27]

The second line of thought, in Lecture III, is an analysis of the "liberal spirit" and of the meaning of "liberty." Its main purpose is to argue that "liberty" must always be understood as "liberties"; and that the two questions, viz. (a) what liberties to strive for; and (b) who is to enjoy them, have always been answered in concrete historical contexts, or settings, in such a way that an absolute claim, in other words, for unrestricted liberty for "all" men has, in practice, turned out to be a limited claim for specific "liberties" for a determinate class, or group, of human beings. Pursuing this line of thought, I argue, further, that the concrete historical setting in which the classical doctrine of liberalism was evolved, did not include the setting of a *multi-racial society,* such as we have here in South Africa, *in which, moreover, one racial group, and this one a minority group, is, and is determined to remain, the dominant group.* Of such a setting, the classical thinkers of liberalism had no first-hand experience. Hence, I hold that liberal ideals have to be re-examined and re-thought in their application to a society of this type. (vii–ix; final emphasis mine)

It is true that in *South African Native Policy and the Liberal Spirit* Hoernlé advocated "Total Separation" of black and white South Africa. What is debatable is whether he did so without reserve or merely, as Louw wanted to claim, because South Africa is "a multi-national" society.

First, Hoernlé refers throughout his lectures to a multi-*racial* society. He analyzes South Africa, not in nationalist terms, but in the racial language characteristic of prewar segregationism. Louw's alteration is an early example of how Afrikaans political thinking appended to the older discourse — on Black and White, "Native" and "European" — a notion of human associations as organically separate volkere.[28]

Second, Hoernlé's arguments keep steadily in view the eventuality that "Total Separation" — since it could in practice become the old "segregation as an instrument of domination" under a new name — will not bring about an end to white domination: "By 'Separation' . . . is meant literally a *sundering or dissociation so complete as to destroy the very possibility of effective domination.*"[29] For Hoernlé, it was not simply that, since South Africa is a multiracial or multinational society, as Louw claims, the "classic doctrine of liberalism" cannot be applied. The real reason is that "in South Africa . . . one racial group . . . is, and is determined to remain, the dominant group" and that "separate areas of liberty for separate racial groups seem the only alternative to domination in a racial caste-society" (*Native Policy* vii, 183). It is *force,* jealously guarding white monopoly on power and privilege, that actually precludes the doctrine of liberalism from being consistently applied in South Africa. For Hoernlé, the goal of any scheme of racial separation is the ending of white domination; a policy that fails to achieve this goal has no justification. Given that goal, "Total Separation" is "unrealizable in practice" (*Native Policy* 183). It is necessary but not sufficient to Hoernlé's argument that South Africa is made up many nations or races: what matters is whether one group, with no justification other than its self-affirmed racial or national identity, dominates another or all others. Louw, who maps the land as "multi-national," does not admit openly that what lies at the heart of his argument is domination by one racial group over another, and ultimately domination per se.

Third, and most crucial, Hoernlé himself makes a grave pragmatic concession to race domination by positioning it at the fulcrum of his argument.[30] Whether or not white domination is authorized by *South African Native Policy and the Liberal Spirit* may, finally, be unresolved. However, white supremacy is what stands *in the text* as the principal reason — indeed, the *only* compelling reason — that the South African situation demands a reexamination of "classical" liberalism. Having made such a concession, or left the question open, Hoernlé's syntax cannot guard itself against the aggressive reading Louw performs. The arguments of Louw and Hoernlé can be merged in order to gauge the support of each for racial separation. For the purposes of analysis, I emphasize portions of Hoernlé's argument that Louw, in "Vegparty of polemiek?" appears to suppress:

South Africa is a multi-racial/national society. Liberalism originated in European countries that were not multi-racial/national societies. *In South Africa one race dominates the other(s).* Liberalism has thus to be rethought in South Africa. *The goal of liberalism is to end all forms of domination. In South Africa Total Separation may put an end to racial domination. If it does so,* Total Separation can be seen as serving the goals of liberalism in South Africa.

In suppressing the motivating fact of racial domination, Louw suppresses what any reader of *Native Policy* knows to be the crux of Hoernlé's argument.[31] If Louw proceeds as if white domination were unimportant, yet all the while uncritically assuming it to be indispensable, Hoernlé accords it the utmost importance. Both men stipulate that European tradition has to be rethought in South Africa, but their reasons ostensibly differ. Louw presents his reasons as ontological — there *are* many races/nations — as if no further argument were needed. On the face of it, Hoernlé presents his reasons as pragmatic. By making white power the motivator of his pragmatism, however, Hoernlé effectively gives Louw and others an ontological argument for separate development. He does not advocate any other way of ending white domination; and to this extent, Hoernlé is correct to end his book with darkness.[32] There is no way out of the night into which he has led "the liberal spirit"; no way, in the final analysis, that he can find of freeing it from complicity in the domination — in this case, racial — that motivates his endeavor to rethink liberalism. In other words, as Hoernlé recognized, setting the liberal spirit against what in actuality *compels* it to be rethought may effectively divert the spirit toward the source of compulsion. Advocating "Total Separation" as a means to end white domination may in fact perpetuate it by other means (*Native Policy* 168–69). As Louw's reading shows, any concession to racism, whether substantive or syntactic, serves only to exacerbate the effect.

Louw's reading of Hoernlé is part of a major development in his nationalist thinking. Since the 1930s, as I will discuss in more detail shortly, N. P. van Wyk Louw had occupied himself with confirming the right of the Afrikaner volk to exist [bestaansreg]. His multinationalism of the 1950s, signaling a new departure in his thinking, implied a new task for the nationalist intellectual. In "Vegparty of polemiek?" Louw criticized Afrikaner nationalism for not having developed a "generally valid intellectual basis for its own struggle" (*Versamelde prosa* 1:500). The struggle to which Louw refers spanned a hundred years, from Boer opposition to British anglicization policies of the nineteenth century, to the Anglo-Boer War of 1899–1902 and the eventual attainment of official-language parity with English for Afrikaans in 1925. "I believe," Louw writes, "that if Afrikaans nationalism had possessed such a generally valid intellectual basis, it would also have found it far easier to make its struggle understood by everyone *inside and outside* South Africa" (*Versamelde prosa* 1:500; my emphasis).

Not yet in Amsterdam, Louw anticipates his role as cultural-political "ambassador." The intellectual basis he proposes at home and abroad is multinationalism, and it imitates the form of Afrikaner nationalism. In the past, Louw said, there were two things that Afrikaner nationalism had neglected to do: "1. It found no reasonable answer to the fundamental political question, 'What moral right has a small nation to want to continue to exist [voortbestaan] *as a nation?*'; and 2. In the heat of its own struggle for self-preservation, Afrikaans nationalism gave very little attention to the continued existence [voortbestaan] of *other* groups in South Africa as separate nations [aparte nasies]" (*Versamelde prosa* 1:500). To ask the "political question" in this way is to assume Afrikaner nationalism to be the privileged agent in and of South African history. If this assumption is unquestioned, Louw's point-by-point presentation lends his words an air of reasonableness (see Olivier, *N. P. van Wyk Louw* 256). The first point takes for granted that a "reasonable answer" is possible. The second, however, programs that answer by presupposing that "*other* groups" constitute "separate nations."

For Louw to present himself publicly as an intellectual is for him to present himself as rational. His rationality conceals, however, the violent cognitive remapping of the polity in postwar Afrikaner-nationalist thinking, which prescribed its sense of "cultural identity"—the *volkseie* [what is unique to the volk]—as the universal: Afrikaners constitute a volk—an entity bound by ties of race, ethnicity, language, culture, history, religion, and so forth—so all other groups must be volkere too.[33] Louw's jargon of rationality disguises a discursive formation of volkere, of "other" national groups, in the image of "the Afrikaner." Establishing a "generally valid intellectual basis" means, in effect, the "recognition" of African claims in the image of Afrikaner-nationalism:

Accordingly: the recognition of the national principle for the Afrikaner must *logically* include the recognition of it for other national groups in South Africa. We may then not speak of ourselves as "the volk of South Africa," but as "one of the volke of South Africa." We must think of the Union [of South Africa, which brought the former Boer republics and British possessions together as one white-dominated self-governing state in 1910] *consistently and radically* as a multi-national state and think through our problems within the boundaries created for us by the concrete political situation. (*Versamelde prosa* 1:502; my emphasis)

Louw argues that the Afrikaans nationalism that fought for Union "in many respects 'built better than it knew' [English in original] . . . promot[ing] in many respects the freedom of *everyone* in South Africa" (*Versamelde prosa* 1:502; see also 1:500). This is not a recognition of black political initiative — for Louw, at this time, black politics is conducted chiefly by white liberals (*Versamelde prosa* 1:503) — but rather a claim for "enlightenment" among the white guardians. The "national-thinking intellectuals" to whom Louw refers are white Afrikaner nationalists, who, though by no means recognizing an organized black *nationalism* (see Ashforth 153–55),[34] project distinct "black national groups" in need of "separate development":

The majority of national-thinking intellectuals have, at least in idle talk, paid tribute to the ideal of 'full development for all national groups in South Africa.' But one can also not submit any more in our defense. 'Full development' is never very 'full' for us when it concerns the development of the black nations [nasies]; and very often it is simply an ideological slogan, i.e. a little moral gravy over a rather unappetizing banquet of maize-porridge-and-nothing-besides. (*Versamelde prosa* 1: 502–3)

If subject to basic human needs (see *Versamelde prosa* 1: 505), Blacks cannot, Louw often seems to imply, be imagined as politically mature. Nevertheless, it would be unjustifiable for Afrikaner nationalism to "let itself [be] maneuvered into an . . . anti-liberal stance" because that would mean "having to be untrue to its own essence." It is the task of the intellectual, critical conscience of the volk, to object to such betrayals of essence and to redefine liberalism. Though "the Afrikaans intellectual cannot stand by with a clear conscience," he must *both* make the liberal "demand for justice" *and* oppose liberalism (as Louw does here) on the grounds that the application of its principles in South Africa "would mean that the small, relatively highly-developed Afrikaans volk and the English volk-part [volksdeel] would sink to [the status of] powerless minorities among a mass of blacks."[35] This would be tantamount to "national suicide." South Africa, where Blacks with their strength of "numbers" face up against Whites with their "cultural, economic and military supremacy," is in a " 'tragic' situation"; and the liberals refuse to recognize this (*Versamelde prosa* 1:505).

Hoernlé is introduced by Louw in order to argue that "separate development of the different groups" is the answer to "the checkmate of nationalities," a situation brought about, he claims, by the preparedness of the white minority to fight to maintain supremacy (*Versamelde prosa* 1:505). Added to Louw's silence on the justifiability of white supremacy in his reception of Hoernlé, such references to the "highly developed Afrikaans volk and the English volk-part," to "cultural supremacy," and to the cataclysmic prospect of "national suicide" suggest that in the final analysis what commanded Louw's far-reaching "thinking anew" of liberal principles was not so much a consistent ethnic or cultural nationalism as it was an undeclared and unquestioned *racism*.[36] The question that remains is the relationship between this commanding racism and Louw's nationalism as a whole. An exploration of this question demands an analysis, in the light of his debt to Geoffrey Cronjé, of his texts on the volk and its crises dating back to the 1930s, and the task of the intellectual contemplated in and assumed by them.

Criticism and Crises of the Volk: Bestaansreg and Voortbestaan in Geregtigheid

N. P. van Wyk Louw's early essays bear traces of the anticolonial origins of Afrikaner nationalism. These traces, which are integral to his vision of Afrikaner nationalism as a postcolonial formation, underlie his advocacy of a critical intellectual culture within the Afrikaner volk and indicate how, having fostered such a culture of criticism, Louw could later lend his voice to the advocacy of apartheid — not only as multinationalism but, in whatever form, as a basic apartness.

Addressing Afrikaans students at Stellenbosch University in March 1936, Louw characterized the becoming of the volk or nation as its passage from being a colony: "The most important change that a new community can undergo is the passage from colony to volk. The passage is only partly connected with political emancipation; it does not take place on a specific day, but has to work itself through in all areas of life over many years; it is a *spiritual* change" (*Versamelde prosa* 1:8). Louw, who had himself grown up in an Anglophile "Cape-Victorian culture" (Opperman, *Digters* 40; see also Schoeman, *Wêreld* 202), associates the "*spiritual* change" that takes place in the transition from colony to volk with the new community's move from having its direction determined by another, to being conscious of its individuality. This means not being content, in one's artistic vision — Louw is talking about literature — with being a picturesque local offshoot of Holland or England, but rather striving, while being bound into the volk, for full humanity [volledige menslikheid binne 'n volksverband] (*Versamelde prosa* 1:9). Louw envisions an attainment of the human and of humanity by way of the ties that bind him and others into the volk: an uninterrupted continuity between foldedness in the volk and foldedness in human-being. Ties to the volk do not, as Louw views it, stand in the way of generalizing responsibility-in-complicity.

In "Volkskritiek" (1939), Louw explicitly endeavors to unite this nationalist humanism with a notion of universal co-responsibility. Written after the banning of *The Turning Wheels* (1937), Stuart Cloete's unflattering novel about the Voortrekkers, Louw's short essay is a response to Afrikaners who reject and disqualify any criticism made by outsiders. He scoffs at such "hysteria"; after all, the British are able to laugh at a book such as *The English: Are They Human?* Even "destructive" criticism can be salubrious (*Versamelde prosa* 1:166–67). Louw's key move is to introduce, though uncertain as to whether it is from Dostoyevsky or Shestov, a statement of universal co-responsibility: "Every human being [mens] is co-responsible [mede-verantwoordelik] for all the evil that exists in the world . . . all sin is the sin of the whole of humankind [mensdom] . . . everyone is complicitous [medepligtig] in everything" (*Versamelde prosa* 1:168; see Dostoyevsky 190). Criticism, in terms of this formulation, is thought and writing that, in order to watch over more parochial commitments, presupposes not only a complicity in the act [medepligtigheid] but a more widely shared human foldedness in responsibility [mede-verantwoordelikheid]. The limits of its universalization are, however, in place with Louw from the beginning. Although writing of co-responsibility that "this ungraspable truth is the earth from which all great volkskritiek grows," he stipulates that "great criticism emerges when the critic places himself not outside, but in the midst of the group he criticizes" (*Versamelde prosa* 1:167–68).

Such qualifications are in clear breach of a rigorous notion of universal co-responsibility that renders one responsible and produces a corresponding critical imperative simply by virtue of one's being human. While Louw appears to set out a model valid for "every human being," he keeps returning to "us" [ons], to "the life of our volk" [ons volkslewe] (*Versamelde prosa* 1:168). Similar formulations of universal co-responsibility are taken up in arguably less-compromised ways by Jaspers, Fanon, Gordimer, and Biko.[37] But Louw's essay continually resists generalizing responsibility-in-complicity, ultimately denying others the right to criticize and bringing human-being back to the Afrikaner volk and its potential to bring forth the humanity [mensheid] of its members.

The ties imagined as enabling the attainment of full humanity for Afrikaners are the same ones that will subsequently mean withholding it from other Africans. As Louw's "Probleme van die intellektuele lewe in Suid-Afrika" [Problems of Intellectual Life in South Africa] (1940) attests, it was possible for an Afrikaans intellectual to treat black intellectual life as irrelevant, as if black Africans did not partake of "spiritual life." Foldedness with others of one's own volk — what Norval discusses in terms of the volkseie — becomes not simply a realization of "full humanity" for its members but complicity in the disavowal of shared humanity with others on the basis of race.[38] The volk claims and monopolizes the universal as uniquely its own [eie]. As Degenaar points out, the "nationalist" paradigm is "kept standing in its entirety" ("Politieke filosofie" 62).

When, in the 1950s, Louw's nationalist paradigm is tested in relation to an other or "outsider" defined not as English but as African, nationalism gives rise to multinationalism in dialogue with Hoernlé and Cronjé, and criticism of the volk is inextricably linked to crises of the volk. In "Kultuur en krisis" [Culture and Crisis], an essay deriving from five installments of *Die oop gesprek* (his column in *Die Huisgenoot*) dating from July to August 1952, Louw outlined what crisis means for the Afrikaner. After interpreting the history of the word *crisis* as indicating "the turning point, the point at which the decision between life and death falls" (*Versamelde prosa* 1:454), he identified "three kinds of situations that we, as Afrikaners, can call 'crises of the volk' [volks-krisisse], situations in which it really would concern the existence [bestaan] itself of our volk." Even as crisis shows the volk to be in danger, the assertion of crisis casts the volk into existence; as the volks-critic criticizes and reflects self-consciously, his rhetoric is an act of national—even multi-national—genesis. Following Paul Valéry's reflections on the crisis of the European "spirit" after World War I,[39] Louw enumerates three "crises":

1. When we are threatened with military attack (like Transvaal in 1899) or with being ploughed under (mass-immigration, etc.).
2. When a large part of our people themselves begin to doubt whether we must continue to exist as a volk [as volk moet voortbestaan]. . . .
3. When a large part of our volk comes to the dangerous belief that we do not have to live together [saam leef] *in justice* [in geregtigheid] with our fellow-volke [mede-volke] in South Africa—comes to suppose that *mere continued existence* [blote voortbestaan] is the main thing, not existence that is just [regverdige bestaan]. (*Versamelde prosa* 1:457)

Crisis three is a "danger of an ethical nature." It presents Afrikaners with an "ethical or even metaphysical" crisis (*Versamelde prosa* 1:460). Even when crises one and two no longer present themselves as crises, a volk "comes before the last temptation: to believe that mere continued existence [blote voortbestaan] is preferable to *continued existence in justice* [voortbestaan in geregtigheid]" (*Versamelde prosa* 1:462). This is a matter of life and death, for: "How can a small volk continue to exist for long when it is something hateful and something evil for the best inside—or outside—it?" (*Versamelde prosa* 1:463). It is by asking this question that the intellectual (or critic) articulates the "danger of an ethical nature" facing the volk as one that involves a relation between "inside" and "outside." In a momentary departure from the strictures of volkskritiek, it is a larger foldedness in human-being that is being sought. The volk is responsible to its "outside." The volk and its outside [mede-volke] are co-responsible [mede-verantwoordelik]: this is the weight and reach of "problems of Europe." At the crux of this version of co-responsibility, however, is not simply what the local means in a world context, but what a globalizing Eurocentrism means locally, in a space where "inside" and "outside" are differently constituted and where, although the structure of responsibility does not change, the response of the intellectual, as it is textualized in Louw, is not the same.

In order to make greater sense of how Louw's embrace of Europe allies nationalism and racism and how responsibility for the intellectual is compromised locally, it will help us to analyze the slogan of *voortbestaan in geregtigheid* in its intellectual-historical provenance, in its place in Louw's oeuvre as a whole, and in its semantics and etymology. Voortbestaan in geregtigheid links N. P. van Wyk Louw and Geoffrey Cronjé, figures commonly thought by Afrikaans intellectual historians to be quite different. Interpreted in the context of Louw's work, the slogan's semantics and etymology allow us to observe how voortbestaan in geregtigheid, implying existential continuity [voortbestaan], legitimates and makes transcendental a contingent historical abiding, and how it thereby contributes to the thinking of apartheid not merely as a liberal multinationalism (see Shaw) but as a doctrine prescribing a more profound apartness and foreclosure of joinedness with the other in human-being.

As Breytenbach's courtroom testimony suggests (Viviers 58), Louw is the one usually understood to have originated the phrase *voortbestaan in geregtigheid*. However, like *lojale verset,* with its overtones of Westminster, it is not his alone. In "Vegparty of polemiek?" Louw pondered the "moral right" of a small nation to exist and reproached "Afrikaans nationalism [for devoting] little attention to the continued existence [voortbestaan] of *other* groups in South Africa as separate nations [aparte nasies]" (*Versamelde prosa* 1:500). But *voortbestaan in geregtigheid* only appeared as a phrase in Louw's writing in 1952, in "Kultuur en krisis." The makings of "Louw's slogan" are to be found earlier, in *Regverdige rasse-apartheid* [Just Race-Apartheid] (1947), a classic work in apartheid thinking by Geoffrey Cronjé, written with the collaboration of W. Nicol and E. P. Groenewald. This is a book usually considered to articulate crude racist obsessions from which mainstream Afrikaner nationalist intellectuals preferred to distance themselves.[40]

Although it is tricky to separate racism and culturalism in Cronjé's text (see Norval 91–92), *Regverdige rasse-apartheid* can usefully be contrasted with Louw's postwar writings, which presented apartheid in expressly ethnic-nationalist rather than racial terms.[41] Cronjé presents a three-chapter argument in favor of a "total separation of the respective race groups" [algehele skeiding van die onderskeie rassegroepe]. In a section headed "The Bridging of the Distance between Reality and Ideal," he stipulates that "if there appears to be only one solution to [the racial] problems through which justice [geregtigheid] will come to pass, and through which the continued existence [voortbestaan] of the white race will be secured, the white race must set everything to work in order to make possible that solution" (147; see also 90–92).

Hoernlé consistently opposes white domination, but neither Cronjé nor Louw really questions it. Neither of them ever challenged the prerogative of Whites, specifically Afrikaners, to direct the schemes of racial/national separation they propose (see Cronjé, *Tuiste* 23, 226–31). While Louw often comes back to Hoernlé rather than to Cronjé (see Olivier, *N. P. van Wyk Louw* 229), his reception of *South African Native Policy and the Liberal Spirit* involved, as I have shown, a reduction of Hoernlé's syntax and thus a tacit assumption of Afrikaner prerogative and white supremacy.

Analyzing the semantics and etymology of *voortbestaan in geregtigheid* directs us to some of Louw's earlier works, where he was preoccupied with the right of the Afrikaner volk to exist, or its *bestaansreg*. This preoccupation runs through everything Louw wrote from the mid-1930s onward. Initially, Louw saw the bestaansreg of the volk being attained by writers. In terms of what Degenaar calls his "aesthetic nationalism" ("Politieke filosofie" 58–62; "Betekenis" 76–77), Afrikaans writers justify the existence of the volk—a spiritual rather than merely biological entity—as a separate language group by producing great works of literature. When Louw asks, "Is it not great literature that has to justify the existence [bestaan] of our volk as a separate language group [aparte taalgroep]?" (*Versamelde prosa* 1:164), the sought-after right to exist is the right to exist apart, as he later puts it, a "right to a separate existence" [reg op 'n aparte bestaan] (*Versamelde prosa* 1:465). The existing-apart of the Afrikaner volk would prescribe a generalized apartheid. The attainment of "full humanity bound up in a volk" and the "spiritual" transition from colony to volk are thus linked in conception to apartheid.

The seeds of Louw's advocacy of apartheid are sown at the same time as he works to open a space for criticism within Afrikaans intellectual life. The idea of producing great works of literature can thus be given a political emphasis. Rather than the work as final product, it is the rhetorical conduct of the work that justifies, and even renders just, the existence of the volk. Taking a political turn, the demand that writers justify the existence of the volk through works of literature is enacted by Louw's works on the occasion of the 1938 Ossewatrek: his essay, "Die ewige trek" [The Eternal Trek], and his choral play, *Die dieper reg: 'n Spel van die oordeel oor 'n volk* [The Deeper Right: A Play of the Judgment over a People]. When one reads against the grain of Louw's thinking, these works each figure a bestaansreg as having been achieved.

Both works establish the historical continuity of the volk rhetorically and dramatically and justify its permanence. The title of the essay "Die ewige trek" figures the century [eeu] being commemorated as an eternal [ewige, from *eeu* + *-ig*] journey. Like the German *Zug, trek* is also a "trait," even a "trace." The trek as "trace" broaches a path. And we might say, as did Derrida's *Of Grammatology,* that the trek "means that [the origin] was never constituted except reciprocally by a nonorigin, the [trek], which thus becomes the origin of the origin" (61). In the commemorative discourses on the occasion of the Ossewatrek, the Trek — with a capital *T* — works to institutionalize the trace. It makes history-as-past-present of the act of tracing and establishes the volk's unitary origin.[42] Although the 1938 Trek is staged as a repetition, the event it repeats only comes into existence through this enactment. Eschewing the popular historical interpretations and slogans one finds in the official Ossewa *Gedenkboek,* Louw's interventions in "Die ewige trek" and in *Die dieper reg* also help, as instances of the performative, to bring the volk into existence as an entity continuing through time. Just as the intellectual in "Die ewige trek" is a figure who, in contrast to the "intellectualist," chooses will over thought, deciding despite being able to foresee an "endless" series of outcomes (*Versamelde prosa* 1:99–100),[43] it is Louw as a writer who dedicates his work to securing, against all uncertainty, the volk's existence [bestaan, voortbestaan] and its right to exist [bestaansreg] as a separate language group [aparte taalgroep].

In *Die dieper reg,* a voice of Eternal Justice decides in favor of a band of Voortrekkers accused by a Prosecutor, or Accuser [Aanklaer] and spoken for by an Advocate [Voorspraak]. The Prosecutor is a caricature of a nineteenth-century English liberal philanthropist (the archetype being Dr. John Philip), and the words of the Advocate and Trekkers themselves recall Trekker apology of the same period, for instance a defense against charges of "land hunger," and the claim of a right to land on the basis of life sacrificed in its conquest and colonization (*Dieper reg* 21; see also Du Toit and Giliomee 216–18). In the end, a justification of another kind is staged, in terms of the will, against which Krige cautioned in his essay, "Cogito ergo sum." The Voice of Eternal Justice [Stem van Ewige Geregtigheid] intercedes in order to legitimate the deeds of the Trekkers:

> More than they know, did they do,
> and higher right before God preserve
> with one strong, hard deed
> than all wisdom that the word
> can catch in its brilliant nets
> after much searching for Good and Evil

> [Meer as hul weet, het hul gemaak,
> en hoër reg voor God behou
> met een sterk, harde daad
> as alle wysheid wat die woord
> in sy blink nette vas kan vang
> ná baie soek na Goed en Kwaad]. (*Dieper reg* 37–38)

In Louw's career after World War II, being an intellectual came to involve a choice between the roles of Accuser and Advocate. Although he was critical within Afrikaner circles, Louw chose to be an advocate or apologist, speaking on behalf of a volk faced by "foreign" foes at home and abroad. Against this background, voortbestaan in geregtigheid is another instance of how, as a writer, Louw guaranteed the bestaansreg of the volk. This was not so much by producing works of art as it was by producing works that, in terms of their formal and rhetorical conduct — at one extreme, figuring divine voice in quasi-transcendental "advocacy" — bring the volk into existence and represent it as having been granted a "right" to continued existence.

Etymology allows us to investigate further the nature of the existence guaranteed by Louw as a writer and to trace some of its less obvious European linkages. Etymologically, *voortbestaan in geregtigheid* conveys all the traits of Louw's activity as a nationalist intellectual justifying the existence of the volk through the production of works of literature. That is why translating it requires care. The historian Hermann Giliomee renders *voortbestaan in geregtigheid* as "survival in justice." Consonant with day-to-day exchanges between Afrikaans and English, his translation has the virtue of economy, but it deprives the phrase of some of its semantic and historical richness (as, no doubt, does my translation: "continued existence in justice"). The prefix *voort-* means "forth-." This connects it with the *voor-* in *Voortrekker.* Both *Voortrekker* and *voortbestaan* promise a future, presupposing an enduring entity with a past, a present, and a future. It is important to hear *bestaan* [existence] as a verb, "to exist," in Louw's evocation of *voortbestaan in geregtigheid,* as he occupies himself as a writer-intellectual with the right of the volk to exist [bestaansreg].

The word *bestaan* may be analyzed further etymologically. The prefix *be-* is a cognate of the Afrikaans preposition *by,* and of the German prefix *be-* and preposition *bei,* which are cognates of the English prefix *be-* and preposition *by.* The *OED* permits us to trace the *be-* in *bestaan* (like *bestehen*) to a spatial sense of *bí,* as in the Gothic *bistān. Staan* is a cognate of the German *stehen* and the English "stand" and "stay." Recalling what the "first man" is supposed to have said — in Dutch, but in what would have been a kind of crypto-Afrikaans: "'*Ik ben* een Afrikaner'" (*Versamelde prosa* 1:22; my emphasis)[44] — it becomes possible to reinterpret *existence* as *bestaan* along Heideggerian lines: as "*Sein bei,*" Heidegger's re-inscription of the Cartesian *cogito* — as *Ich bin* — in terms of Dasein's "being-in" [In-sein] and "being-in-the world" [In-der-Welt-sein] (*Being and Time* 54). The modern Afrikaans equivalent — *Ek is* — loses that echo of existence as *be-staan.* Rendering existence-as-bestaan in a colloquial South African English as "staying by" would convey the conceptual shift well.

Reinterpreting existence as located dwelling, as Heidegger does, has profound implications for an analysis of *voortbestaan in geregtigheid.* Interpreting existence as *bestaan* can end up converting what is local and idiomatic into the transcendental (as do Descartes's Latin and Heidegger's idiosyncratic German). *Voort-bestaan* could then be heard as legitimating, as historically unmarked existing, the persistence of a situated, local abiding — just as the affirmation "Ik ben een Afrikaner," divided between two languages, stands at the origin of Afrikaans, the basis of the existence of the volk as a separate language group. A Heideggerian analysis allows us to historicize claims about existence phrased as transhistorical. Allowing us to delve at their linguistic roots, such analysis is not only powerful in the context of European intellectual history, but it gives us a purchase on the most idiomatic of Afrikaans thinking. Encouraging us to think of claims about existence *as* historical, it enables us to think nationalist existential claims through historically.

This brings us to *geregtigheid*. Like the German *Gerechtigkeit,* it would, in scriptural translation, be rendered by the English "righteousness." Usually translated as "justice" in other contexts, *geregtigheid* functions, in a sense, as a supplement to *voortbestaan.*[45] But it is also its *location,* an abstract place *in* which the volk abides. In effect, like *Die dieper reg,* the catchphrase *voortbestaan in geregtigheid* can be read as setting the scene not only for a transcendentalization of bestaan, but for a legitimation of the local, historical act of tracing-forth [Voortrek], and of existing-forth [voort-bestaan]. Tracing [trek] is transformed from "land hunger" into a movement down the "right track" [orthós, rectus, rightwise, righteous, geregtig]. In so doing, a working correspondence is established between trekking forth [Voortrek, voortbestaan] and divine imprimatur [Reg, Ewige Geregtigheid]. Cast as an Advocate confronting a Prosecutor or Accuser, as in *Die dieper reg,* the intellectual acts, by staging justification, to secure the bestaansreg of the volk. The intellectual's words have the dual capacity to hold the volk responsible before Right, and to enact divine sanction. If voortbestaan in geregtigheid is what Louw's choral drama finally confirms for the Voortrekkers, the slogan also works to ratify "in advance" the subsequent existing-forth of the volk *as* right(eous) existence.

When the volk is faced with the third kind of crisis enumerated in "Kultuur en Krisis" — the ethical crisis — it is, however, the task of the intellectual, or culture-person [kultuurmens], "to remain at his own post," unmoved by overtures to be "an orator, an agitator, an organizer, a writer of pamphlets and folk songs" (*Versamelde prosa* 1:463–64). Culture-people, in their capacity as researchers and teachers and as artists and writers, have a duty not to make propaganda for "transitory issues." Among them, writers especially have to resist the temptation to "pay homage to the merely-transitory [alleen-verbygaande], or write for the demand of the market." As Louw says constantly, "they must make for the volk a durable culture [blywende kultuur] that will give it the right to an existence apart [reg op 'n aparte bestaan]" (*Versamelde prosa* 1:465).

As in earlier formulations of the necessity to claim and justify a right to existence [bestaansreg], Louw emphasizes separateness: "*aparte bestaan.*" The *apart-heid* of the Afrikaans volk programs an apartheid of, and for, all volkere. Not only is the volk transcendent — standing above human beings — but it stands apart, culturally distinct, from every other "volk." Being true [trou] to the volk, the writer imagines as abiding and enduring what is transitory, what passes [gaan verby], what is eternally trekking [ewig op trek]. This is what, in a slightly different sense, Isabel Hofmeyr calls "building a nation from words." It is as if, on the pattern of "personal identity," the writer "gives" the volk a cultural identity. The identity so fashioned abhors contact, which would, it is imagined, threaten its aparte bestaan. In an abyssal historical irony, given the origins of the tongue in which Afrikaner nationalists ground its existence (and to which Breyten Breytenbach constantly points), it shuns hybridity and measures purity.

This identity is — if indeed it is — no more than a step away from the phobia of "blood-mixing" [bloedvermenging] that so obsessed Geoffrey Cronjé, the "mind of apartheid."[46] If motivated in the final analysis by a racism that could not be argued away, Louw's version of apartheid flowed, if one examines the development of his ideas, from the establishment of the Afrikaans volk as separate from other volkere by him and other Afrikaans cultural workers. In these terms, the only way to justify the existence of the volk — as transcendental rather than contingent historical existence — was apartheid. Having come to grasp this, the question for Louw was how this voortbestaan of the volk could be in geregtigheid. He did not settle, as he had in the 1930s, for a theatrical representation of divine sanction alone — although traces remain — but began to consider justice in the conceptual language of politics.

The Lectures in Amsterdam

In a page in *Standpunte* from February 1964, Louw reminisced about his activities in the Netherlands, his work as forward-thinking Afrikaner-nationalist intellectual and unacknowledged ambassador of the newly elected National Party government:

(When I suggested in a course of public lectures in Holland about twelve years ago that a number of Bantu states would have to be established that would in time be independent and/or federated with the white state, I was often asked: "Does your government *want* to do it? *Will* it do it? Or is it just speculation?"; and I could only answer: "This is what Afrikaans-national intellectuals think . . . but whether a government will have the courage, that you must ask the government." From South Africa I received not the slightest echo in response to such talks; also no preparedness to publish such "unnational" thoughts.)

The thinking Afrikaner nationalist will have to learn no longer to wait with his thoughts until it suddenly (usually a little late) becomes "policy"; he will have to learn not to think as his newspaper leads him, but often a whole way ahead. ("Aantekening")

The course to which Louw alludes is "Rassevraagstukke in Suid-Afrika" [Racial Questions in South Africa], which took place at the Gemeente-lijke Universiteit of Amsterdam from 9 October 1952 to 27 January 1953. Louw set out for the participants a systematic account of South Africa's race question, based on an ethno-racial account of the situation and a reasoned defense of separate development. Though, as Louw claims, not yet the policy of the government, ethnic-national "separate development" was not a new idea, having been embraced officially by the Broederbond as early as 1933 (Dubow, *Scientific Racism* 250–51) and, as has been noted, discussed at meetings of Louw's own branch.

Before 1945 the major white political parties shared an ideology of segregationism as the guiding principle for dealing with the "native problem."[47] In the years after Union in 1910, a number of measures — for example, the Natives' Land Act (1913) and the Natives (Urban Areas) Act (1923) — implemented segregation on a large scale. Separate rural black "reserves" were established, and laws denied urban black workers the opportunity to compete equally with Whites. Despite such measures, there were calls for more drastic action. Even before World War II, black urbanization and economic competition were used by D. F. Malan's National Party to galvanize white voters — whether by appealing to economic self-interest or by exploiting racist fears. A good example is Malan's 1938 trek-festival speech.[48] The industrial boom of the war heightened demand for labor, and black urbanization increased. In its aftermath, however, demand leveled off, and competition among workers intensified. The National Party claimed to have stronger medi-cine than the old segregation, but in 1948 at least, no coherent scheme lay behind its electoral rallying cry of "apartheid." The slogan's vacuity did not, however, prevent the white electorate from ceding Malan and his party a mandate to represent its interests.

Though not always implemented as policy by the government,

"apartheid thinking" after 1945 was an endeavor by social scientists, theologians, and publicists such as Louw to give apartheid a meaning distinct from what had been known under segregation. Perhaps the most tangible body of Afrikaner thinking on the race question in the 1950s emanated from SABRA, which had been launched as an academic think tank by the Broederbond in September 1948 and which, during the 1950s, repeatedly found itself at loggerheads with the government over its proposed policy of "separate development" (Lazar, "Verwoerd" 363). A faction within SABRA believed that if the government put money into the reserves, territories could be established and developed with a view to eventually becoming politically independent black states within the existing borders of the Union. Sometimes presenting it as a solution to the *moral* problem of white domination, these SABRA intellectuals drafted several plans in the 1950s for realizing their vision. If SABRA's motives remained morally ambiguous, it is questionable what morality guided the government and its economic power base. For them, "development" would, in a word, have had to remain *under*development, so that the reserves would continue to produce a steady stream of proletarianized industrial labor. Although "separate development" became official policy in the mid-1960s before it was purged by Verwoerd in 1961, all of SABRA's schemes for it were more or less rejected by the government.[49]

This intellectual background gives us a way of making sense of Louw's claim that his Dutch lectures received no response from South Africa. The content of his lectures positioned Louw squarely with the then-disregarded SABRA intellectuals, "with whom," according to Hermann Giliomee, he "identified himself" (" 'Survival' " 533).

N. P. van Wyk Louw began his course in October 1952 with a few methodological remarks. One kind involves the relationship of the lectures to the European tradition. What Louw has to say marks out, in his view, a path for the regeneration of European thought: "We will have to think *through* [déúrdink] our whole traditional thought-world [denkwêreld]; reevaluate; create a new world of thought [wêreld van denk]" ("Rassevraagstukke" 1). In fact, Louw continues, the lectures are not so much about South Africa's problems, but "a course on: problems of Europe ['n kursus oor: probl[eme] van Europa]"; South Africa is a microcosm ("Rassevraagstukke" 3; "Bevolking" 1).

A second kind of methodological remark, connected to the first, concerns the process of thinking itself and establishes an intellectual analogy with the larger political goal: "We will have to *analyze* a great deal!!! Separate & then combine again" ("Rassevraagstukke" 2). The third type of remark pertains to ethics (in a colloquial rather than in any systematic sense). The study will busy itself with assembling and understanding the facts, but it is to be guided by ethical principles: "wetens[kaplike] studie onder leiding van etiese beginsels" ("Rassevraagstukke" 4). Accompanying these methodological remarks are four theses. The two most crucial are: first, that the Afrikaners are one of a number of volke in South Africa — they are not "*the* volk" [die volk]; and second, that "the Union of South Africa is an artificial unity. . . [for example,] 'Zululand' is not 'my land.' Cape Town is not the Bantu's land." These two theses guide Louw's entire analysis, dissecting the Union of South Africa in ethno-racial terms.

Let us examine these moves. As an intellectual, Louw makes South Africa's problems the problems of Europe. His renovative "thinking through" of traditional European thought is not, however, an abandonment of it. To interpret his gesture as an act of desertion would be to underestimate its ethico-political gravity. By appealing to European tradition and by demanding a renewal from within, Louw shows, in effect, how Europe can be held responsible for apartheid. The fact that Louw is able to appeal to the principle of ethnic-national self-determination, an artifact of the European Enlightenment, means that apology for apartheid comes easily enough from within a European "world of thought."

But that is not all. Louw was speaking in Amsterdam — and thus for a "we" that is also European — in 1952, the 300th year of European settlement at the Cape of Good Hope. By assuming the mission of rethinking what is in effect European "cultural identity," the poet-teacher also justifies and self-justifies — as essentially "European" — white, Afrikaner initiative in dominating and recharting the South African sociopolitical landscape. To reinvoke Derrida, this minority-directed "other heading," launched under the guise of a quest for a cultural identity sanctioned by "European" thinking, brings back the specter of racism, of white supremacy and the drive for (cultural, racial) apartness and purity.

In his introductory lectures, Louw considered briefly some "solutions." His ethical adjudication of these solutions is based on *economic* criteria: justice is done through a fair (though not necessarily *equal*) distribution of economic opportunities. He briefly dismisses the traditionally liberal solution—"complete and immediate equality (right to vote)"—as "ethically offensive" ("Rassevraagstukke" 10). The main debate among Afrikaners is between those who support "apartheid in *one* state: 'segregation,'" and those who envisage "apartheid in separate states: parallel development" ("Rassevraagstukke" 10). Louw proposes the latter. He rejects "apartheid in *one* state" because it "does not allow the full development of all" ("Rassevraagstukke" 12). Defenders of apartheid in one country, including Afrikaner business interests, were often accused of not being prepared to assist in creating economic opportunities in the reserves and of being only too willing to exploit black workers.[50]

Having accepted the correctness of parallel development and complete separation, Louw continues, there remains an alternative: immediate or eventual separation [afskeiding] ("Rassevraagstukke" 13). These choices also have to be assessed ethically; that is to say, for Louw, in terms of economic justice to those national groups presently denied it (which, for the sake of convenience, Louw refers to here, in standard culturalist parlance, as "the Bantu,"[51] although he routinely indicates the existence of five or six "national groups."[52] Louw's actual arguments against immediate separation do not appear in his notes,[53] but he gives reasons for eventual separation, a sundering he envisages taking place over fifty years, "a 50-year-plan" ("Rassevraagstukke" 13). One set of reasons is economic. The main thing is the *"development of the nat[ive] areas"* ("Rassevraagstukke" 13), which, given their current state, will take time. Without proper development in the reserves—for example, education—Blacks will object: "Bantu says: you want to give me something inferior" ("Rassevraagstukke" 13). The other reason for gradual separation is ideological, or "psychological" ("Rassevraagstukke" 14). White and Black alike need to be "educated"; the White, so that he "does not regard Bantu as permanent source of labor"; the Black, so that he "does not rely on his numbers (via *franchise;* or *violence*) to take over the whole country with all its resources" ("Rassevraagstukke" 14).

"And who," Louw asks, "will do the work of educating?" Neither White nor Bantu, but the "Intellectual—of 2 races. Outside of politics" ("Rassevraagstukke" 14). The Amsterdam lectures are Louw's contribution to the "work of educating"; he sees himself in conversation with the volk (see Van Rensburg, "'Hoe Praat'"). Not only is the intellectual a didact, but he is "of 2 races" [van 2 rasse]. Once again Louw projects black as mirror-image of white: although he assumes them to exist, there is no mention of what actual black intellectuals think of this apartheid vision and of what, if any, black intellectuals might be prepared to "educate" their respective "volkere" in it.

Geregtigheid

Deferring a solution — be it for fifty years or for some other notional period — means maintaining the status quo of domination and enforcing a nonnegotiable ethnic-national principle of analysis. We still, however, need to ask: What did *Louw* take to be the "ethical principles" guiding his analysis? Economic justice may be the principle he made most explicit. Do Louw's texts adumbrate any other sense of geregtigheid and voortbestaan in geregtigheid?

Louw's sense of economic justice is worth examining briefly. In 1950 the government appointed a commission of inquiry under the leadership of F. R. Tomlinson: "to conduct an exhaustive inquiry into and to report on a comprehensive scheme for the rehabilitation of the Native Areas with a view to developing within them the social structure in keeping with the culture of the Native and based on effective socioeconomic planning" (South Africa, Union of xviii). The Tomlinson Report found that the sum of £104,486,000 would be required of the government over ten years to begin developing the reserves as a viable "national home for the Bantu" (Union of South Africa, *Summary* 192–93, 101). The findings were rejected at the time by the government as too costly (SAIRR 1957 *Survey* 142–43; Ashforth, 149–94). Louw made a pointed response on Radio Nederland's Afrikaans service to the official reception of the Tomlinson Commission's findings in October 1956. Like other landmark official reports, such as the Carnegie Commission report on white poverty (1932), which Louw had reviewed in *Die Huisgenoot,* the Tomlinson report gave rise to a great deal of discussion in South Africa.[54] The government, however, forbade Tomlinson from speaking about the inquiry while on a visit to the Netherlands in 1956. Louw, who arranged an informal meeting of students with Tomlinson, all but calls the actions of the government censorship (see Human; Louw, *Versamelde prosa* 2:590ff). At the end of the second of his two radio talks, he outlined what he regarded as the most important implications of the report:

Eventual fair [billike] territorial separation with complete freedom for all
. . . that is something that even our most formidable opponents acknowledge as *ethically right* [eties juis]. But didn't they cheer when they could say:
"That is good, but impossible."

Our highest idealism would have been dashed against the hard economic
facts . . . to the joy of our enemies. Another, a great, sympathetic man,
Hoernlé, called this tragic discord our "Heartbreak House."[55]

And now with the Tomlinson Report a small ray of light has come: what
is ethically right, is *perhaps* . . . if the good will is there . . . not economically
impossible! (*Versamelde prosa* 2:593–594; Louw's ellipses).

Let us begin with Louw's invocation of Hoernlé, as one of "our most
formidable opponents." We have already observed that, although *enabling* a moral defense of apartheid, Hoernlé does not write in order to
mount one. In fact, Hoernlé shows how, given that it would be unlikely
to hasten an end to white domination, "Total Separation" might well
conflict with "liberal ideals" (*Native Policy* 183). While its complicity
with Louw's advocacy of apartheid must be acknowledged, *in its own
syntax* Hoernlé's "heartbreak house" scenario cannot be reduced to an
objection based on the economic impracticability of racial separation.
Toward the end of his final lecture, Hoernlé asks:

Why is [Total Separation] unrealizable? Because the *will* to realize it is not
there, nor is there any power on earth which can bring it into being. . . . The
White group as a whole cannot be conceived as agreeing of its own motion
to the sacrifices of power, prestige, and, not least, of economic advantage
and convenience, which would be involved in Total Separation. (*Native
Policy* 183)

Hoernlé does not allow that apartheid is ethically right [eties juis].[56]
On the contrary, his sense of impossibility is largely a moral one. For
Hoernlé, what makes Total Separation "unrealizable" or "impossible" *as
a means to ending white supremacy* is the will of certain protagonists of
race "separation" to use it as an instrument for perpetuating white domination (*Native Policy* 164).

By receiving Hoernlé as a foe, Louw makes his pragmatic advocacy of
apartheid into a guarantee of its rightness. Unlike Hoernlé, however,
Louw does not clarify his ethical criteria. He provides no explanation,
for instance, of how he imagines territorial separation guaranteeing

"complete freedom for all." If indeed "even [Louw's] most formidable opponents" do agree that separate development is "ethically right," it may be that economic criteria are indeed the remaining relevant criteria. However, numbers, even in a context of shared ethical assumptions, can never tell an ethical story if those on behalf of whom the scheme is projected are allowed no say. Ethics involves responsibility before the other. Economic forecasts tell us what schemes can be financed, but they cannot, in the absence of such responsibility, make them *right*.

Hoernlé was not the only one to argue that no scheme drawn up to perpetuate white domination could ever be right. That is what "opponents" — to whom Afrikaner-nationalist politicians never listened — repeatedly said. The Tomlinson Commission's findings were repudiated by delegates at the All-in African Conference, held in Bloemfontein in October 1956: "The concept of separate national homes for [the African people], coupled with the deprivation of basic opportunities and rights in the rest of the country, was totally unacceptable" (SAIRR 1956 *Survey* 153).

It is facile, in retrospect, to expose a disregard of black oppositional voices among white Afrikaans politicians and intellectuals. But to what extent was Louw himself ignorant about black South African political activity? From what is in his archive, it seems clear enough that he was abreast of developments within governmental structures. With his lecture notes can be found a clipping of a newspaper article reporting the final meeting of the official Natives Representative Council (NRC) in 1951, at which H. F. Verwoerd, then Minister of Native Affairs, "tells natives about apartheid." At this meeting, R. V. Selope Thema, a veteran moderate in the African National Congress, is reported to have objected: "It cannot be expected that whites and non-whites live separately, but that one section still makes the laws for the other" ("Minister vertel").

In *Die dieper reg,* the geregtigheid of the volk is contemplated, demanded, and ratified through dramatic performance. The Advocate defeats the Accuser, a caricature of a nineteenth-century liberal philanthropist. Black South Africans never appear on stage. Louw's postwar defense of apartheid as "separate development" elaborated this mise-en-scène politically. The volk's voortbestaan in geregtigheid was presented, through rational-seeming argument, as "possible." The scenario had changed slightly. The poet-didact no longer makes appeal to divine judgment, in order to defeat an Accuser. The Advocate instead attempts to assimilate the Accuser—the "liberalist" and "opponent" Hoernlé—by claiming that even he agrees that racial separation is "ethically right" [eties juis].

While Hoernlé and Louw both elaborated a racist text, it remains doubtful whether their agreement extended, as Louw maintained, to their respective opinions on the ethical correctness of apartheid.[57] The words of "liberalists" are manhandled, and black "opponents" are unheard in Louw's text of apartheid apology, except at its very margins. Basic journalistic convention, the duty to record two sides of a story, *audi alteram partem,* preserves a sentence or two of black protest; inassimilable for the critic of the volk, Selope Thema's words of protest are saved, but they are saved in silence.

The marginality of Thema's response to Verwoerd in Louw's archive redirects our attention to the mysterious quality of geregtigheid as "righteousness" and to how Louw as an intellectual put it to work. As a teacher in the Netherlands in the 1950s, Louw elaborated his apartheid vision. There, as writer-intellectual, he assumed the task of securing the Afrikaner volk a right to exist [bestaansreg] within a purportedly multinational country, demanding of and for the volk a righteous existing-forth [voortbestaan in geregtigheid]. We can surely have nothing against an intellectual demanding righteousness or justice; it may be that demanding justice is all a certain kind of intellectual, characterized by Foucault as "the man of justice" ("Truth and Power" 128), has ever done.

Justice, though, is not reducible to an application of the law—let alone to a system of laws that denies justice to the majority. The call for justice misfires when the larger structure of racism remains unquestioned. Van Wyk Louw staged an attainment of justice in an adversarial setting, from which the injured parties were absent, in which an Accuser and an Advocate vie for a verdict. Dramatically and historically, this presented him as an intellectual with a choice of one of two roles. Faced with the alternative, Louw elected to be Advocate, however much lojale verset appears to have prescribed that he be Accuser.

My goal has been more than a simple unmasking of diplomatic rhetoric in order to conclude that, in Afrikaans intellectual history, the promotion of nationalism abroad equals racism at home. It is too late; and in any case, the stakes are higher. Analyzed in terms of complicity, the Afrikaner nationalism of Louw's early work sought to generalize a foldedness in human-being blocked by British colonialism and cultural imperialism; this is the gravity of the notion that is full humanity bound up in a volk, in form no different from the campaign against mental self-colonization conducted by Black Consciousness forty years later. If in Louw's thinking of the 1930s, the entity referred to as the volk was, ideally, a bringer of humanity in the specific sphere that Afrikaner nationalism set itself to work, in the 1950s, as he developed a multi-nationalism on this pattern and proposed to set it to work more widely, the volk stood in the way of generalizing full humanity. If, in the 1930s, it was acceptable for the intellectual to defend the right of the volk to separate existence [aparte bestaan], in the 1950s, nationalist loyalty of this kind barred the way to a foldedness in human-being with those not accepted as members but for whom a mirror-image of separate national development was nevertheless prescribed. Although Louw would, in the 1960s, reach out to coloured people [Bruinmense] in the name of a shared language and history, this limited gesture, in which the human [mens] was qualified by color [bruin], only renewed the mortgaging to racism of his nationalism. The separate existence [aparte bestaan] cherished for the volk became the paradigm for the generalized apartness of apartheid.

It may be that we do not fault Louw so much for rendering Europe and its intellectuals complicit in apartheid or responsible for it (something that Europe could not avoid even if it wanted to), or even, if he was doing so, for shifting responsibility onto Europe alone (perhaps even thereby affirming *its* existing-forth in righteousness); but rather that we fault him for the deeper evil at work with the racism that this move entrenches. Enough intellectuals supported apartheid. Louw remains interesting because, although he never saw his support as beyond censure, as beyond responsibility, he nevertheless never ceased to defend it on what he regarded as purely nationalist terms. By internationalizing complicity and responsibility in the name of Europe, an apparently expansive and liberalizing move, and despite proposing national self-determination as a solution, when read in local terms, it is a case of narrow racial filiation standing in the way of what I am calling complicity in the general sense.

There are those who are simply excluded from responsible agency, whose portion is not "full humanity" but rather "full development." They are the same ones who are not consulted when decisions are to be made and whose protests are ignored. They are the ones in relation to whom a foldedness in human-being is foreclosed and, where it exists, is strenuously disavowed. Seen from another angle, this is also, as I hope to have demonstrated, the extent of what is to be undone by the intellectual who sets him- or herself against apartheid.

chapter 3
apartheid and the vernacular

In "What Price 'Négritude'?" the second chapter of *The African Image* (1962), Ezekiel Mphahlele gives two reasons why, for black South African writers and artists of his generation, "*négritude* is just so much intellectual talk, a cult" (40). Joining and disjoining complicity, the intellectual, and apartheid, both reasons imply the difficulty of entering into a relation with the other that does not imply the domination or marginalization that limit its realization as reciprocal foldedness in human-being.

The first reason is brutally political. Négritude thinking tacitly participates in apartheid ideology and policy and in its immediate British colonial precursor, "indirect rule," whereby Africans were denied access to colonial civil society and were ruled under "traditional chiefs" and "customary law" subject to the colonial government. This "bifurcated state," as Mamdani terms it in *Citizen and Subject* (16–23), was taken over by the National Party after 1948 as it elaborated apartheid as a system of ethnic-national "separate development." Such policies made many black intellectuals in South Africa wary of embracing African "tradition" and even of taking up Plaatje's address to the vernacular reader,[1] lest they fall into the arms of a system invented to deny black people access to basic political rights. There is thus a distancing by Mphahlele from vernacular intellectuals, and the work of A. C. Jordan (1906–68), the Xhosa novelist and scholar, is given short shrift. Jordan's portrayal, in his Xhosa novel, *Ingqumbo Yeminyanya* [The Wrath of the Ancestors] (1940), of the conflict between custom and Christian modernity is declared irrelevant when Mphahlele surveys "The Black Man's Literary Image of Himself."[2] "It is significant," Mphahlele writes, "that it is not the African in British-settled territories — a product of 'indirect rule' and one that has been left in his cultural habitat — who readily reaches out for his traditional past. It is rather the assimilated African, who has absorbed French culture, who is now passionately wanting to recapture his past" (25). One can, of course, question this conventionalized distinction between the French policy of assimilating a native elite and British "indirect rule," and the differences in cultural politics in Francophone and Anglophone Africa thought to emanate from it. Mphahlele's employment of the distinction nevertheless allows us to see how for South African intellectuals to embrace Négritude was to embrace apartheid. In Francophone Africa, in the Antilles, and in the French metropolis, Négritude meant an ambitious supplementing of the Western idea of humanity, as envisioned by Léopold Sédar Senghor, along with a recovery of an African or Black identity. Black Consciousness mobilized such thinking against apartheid in the 1970s. But in South Africa after 1948, Négritude appeared to mean submitting to an ethnic-national worldview that foreclosed, on racial grounds, any prospect of a larger humanity. That is why Mphahlele and other intellectuals kept their distance from it.

The second reason that black intellectuals eschewed Négritude, and the most important for Mphahlele, is that it appears to disavow the existence of "multi-racial communities like those in South Africa. . . . Our choral and jazz music, literature, dancing in South Africa have taken on a distinctive content and form which clearly indicate a merging of cultures" (*African Image* 28). This can be analyzed further. On the one hand, like other writers associated in one way or another during the 1950s with *Drum* magazine, where he was fiction editor, Mphahlele rejected the tribal identity imposed by the apartheid government. Breaking with the didacticism of earlier black writers such as R. R. R. Dhlomo, whose novel *An African Tragedy* (1928) dramatized the hazards of city life, they affirmed a hybrid urban culture. Writing of Nat Nakasa, fellow *Drum* writer Can Themba observed, "All those Africans who want to be loyal, hard-working, intelligent citizens of the country are crowded out. They don't want to bleach themselves, but they want to participate and contribute to the wonder that the country can become. They don't want to be fossilized into tribal inventions that are no more real to them than they would have been to their forefathers" (*World* 219). If only for a short time, and on a small scale, the urban culture, centered in Johannesburg, specifically in Sophiatown, brought black and white people together in ways that seemed to render tangible the idea of multiracial communities and a merging of cultures. Even novels of rural return such as Alan Paton's *Cry, the Beloved Country* (1948) and F. A. Venter's *Swart pelgrim* (1952) inadvertently registered black migration to the cities as inevitable. The state's policy of "retribalisation" in response to "African urbanisation" (Themba, *World* 235) ran directly counter to what Ezekiel Mphahlele, Lewis Nkosi, Can Themba, Nat Nakasa, and Bloke Modisane knew in their daily existence and celebrated in their writing. For them, apartheid "separate development" was a violent projection of the tribalism of Afrikaner nationalism. "I have to vote for my people's party," an Afrikaner nationalist tells Nat Nakasa, "How can I desert my people?" (*World* 13). When "my people" defines the Afrikaner-nationalist horizon for responsibility, as it did for N. P. van Wyk Louw, and this ethnically foreclosed responsibility is set to work as apartheid, drawing on the resources of the vernacular is a risk that few black intellectuals will take.

The juxtaposition of Mphahlele's two reasons for maintaining a distance from Négritude underlines the difficulty, for black South African intellectuals of this era, of setting to work ethico-political responsibility as a generalizing of foldedness with the other. As a positive response to Négritude, Mphahlele can, to be sure, point to cultural hybridity and small cross-racial communities. But even when separate development, which interferes with access to a "traditional past" and thus renders Négritude unacceptable, does not involve outright domination or repression, it can make cross-racial contact the site of an unwelcome and deforming intimacy. The taking up of colonial "indirect rule" into apartheid is only the external manifestation of a more deeply rooted evil.

Although the limited multiracialism unique to the 1950s is in part what turned Mphahlele and the other *Drum* writers away from Négritude and its project of African cultural retrieval, the foldedness with the white other — even the "liberal" — was not without an oppressive element. These intellectuals were dependent on Whites for access to mainstream intellectual life and a readership; *Drum,* a commercial magazine, was White-owned and managed. They were also generally the products, like their forebears, of English-language mission education and were thus the dubious beneficiaries of the broken liberal promise of citizenship.[3] Above all, they found themselves caught in more and less congenial everyday interactions with their more privileged white counterparts.[4] While cross-racial friendships certainly developed, the most striking images of self and other from the 1950s and early 1960s (and the ones Black Consciousness would take up) are of an oppressive existential intimacy.

A shared situation brought different responses. For example, Nat Nakasa resisted racial stereotyping—"To speak of the white man today means less than little to me"—and declared, echoing James Baldwin, that "Dr. Beyers [an Afrikaner nationalist] [is] inescapably part of me" (*World* 151, 160). Can Themba, however, wrote of a

crepuscular, shadow-life in which we wander as spectres seeking meaning for ourselves. . . . The whole atmosphere is charged with the whiteman's general disapproval, and where he does not have a law for it, he certainly has a grimace that cows you. This is the burden of the whiteman's crime against my personality that negatives all the brilliance of intellect and the genuine funds of goodwill so many individuals have. The whole bloody ethos asphyxiates me. (*Will to Die* 8–9)

For Themba, the "whiteman" has become a presence that, charging the whole atmosphere with his general disapproval, not only makes an ethical relation impossible by negating the reciprocal "goodwill" of the other but threatens the very existence of the other: "crepuscular, shadow-life in which we wander as spectres. . . . The whole bloody ethos asphyxiates me." The "whiteman" is of course not a particular person, but is a figure of generalized malevolence, one who enters the psyche to commit a "crime against my personality." This crime prevents the one possessed of "brilliance of intellect" and "funds of goodwill" from setting to work the responsibility folded into one's existence with the other. Compelled to take steps to resist apartheid, the intellectual is effectively prevented from doing so by its deformation of his or her relation with the other.

There is no more powerful account of this oppressive intimacy than Bloke Modisane's autobiography *Blame Me on History* (1963), where the black intellectual figures as a beggar dependent on the "charity" of a white reader. This subordinate dependence overdetermines the advocacy journalism of the *Drum* writers on behalf of black workers who are "illiterate and doomed to stay that way for the rest of their lives" (Nakasa, *World* 5) and others who do not have the relative privileges the writers enjoy. For Modisane (1923–86), however, responsibility emerges from yet another source. His book performs a work of mourning, manipulating the ambivalent intimacy of beggar and donor in order to address a message to his dead father. As is perhaps fitting for a group of writers several of whom died untimely deaths — Nat Nakasa (1937–65), Can Themba (1924–68), Henry Nxumalo (1917–56) — beneath the surface of Modisane's protest writing lies a relationship to the non-living. A condition of possibility for responsibility, this relation stands for the basic foldedness with the other motivating any opposition to apartheid in Modisane.

Responsibility before the dead animates the work of several African writers. In Amos Tutuola's *The Palm-Wine Drinkard* (1952), for instance, one can also trace an articulation of the author's mourning of his father, the encounter of the Drinkard with famine victims making their way to "Deads Town," and his efforts to end the famine (Tutuola 280, 295–96, 306–7). Their linking of filial and social responsibility through the work of mourning presents strong parallels between Modisane and writers like Tutuola, Ben Okri, Chenjerai Hove, and others, who variously elaborate the relationship between the living and the dead and the unborn. It is important to note, however, that, in each of these writers, doing so is irreducible to the practices of any specific cultural formation. At his father's funeral vigil, the fourteen-year-old Modisane finds himself ignorant of conceptions of death phrased in the vernacular: "'The poor man has gone to the ancestors.' They spoke in Sotho, Zulu and Xhosa, and most of the relationships of the symbols escaped me; I made polite gestures that the catering help was asking for me" (*Blame* 29). Imperfectly able to carry out funeral rites for his father as a young man, Modisane finds a substitute for them in the *literary,* in the possibilities of alterity offered by its structures of address.

There is a profound convergence between Bloke Modisane's literary work of mourning and A. C. Jordan's formulation of the ethics of reciprocity known as *ubuntu.* Ezekiel Mphahlele's appraisal of Jordan's novel cannot prevent us from witnessing how, in his essays of the late 1950s on Xhosa literature, Jordan brings the resources of vernacular language and culture to bear against apartheid. Gained through an invention of cultural memory, these are resources not of the past but of colonial and postcolonial *modernity*. The form they take is new. As with those of Bloke Modisane, Jordan's efforts form part of a literary project—the description of a "literary stabilization"—as he translates from a didactic essay by the Reverend Tiyo Soga written a century earlier in order to generalize responsibility-in-complicity. In each case, be it Modisane's address to the figure of his dead father (if not to *the dead* per se), or Jordan's insistence on the figure of the stranger in Soga, opposing apartheid is a matter of articulating narrow and general senses of complicity. This means, in each case, regulating the relation to a historically determinate other with reference to a figure of more or less transcendental alterity.

Responding to the "Situation"

Beggars . . . haunt all good liberals.
—J. M. COETZEE, *Doubling the Point*

HISTORY AND AUTOBIOGRAPHY

Readers of Bloke Modisane's *Blame Me on History* have recognized it as testimony to the human suffering brought about by apartheid.[5] It remains intractable, however, to critics who wish to explore it as a literary work. The book suggests various governing narrative structures but apparently always exceeds them. "Modisane in *Blame Me on History*," Jane Watts writes, "has no. . . . formal structural device to contain the disparate fragments of his life. Or rather the formal structure he attempts to impose fails to carry the book and disintegrates in the mind of the reader, as well as in the course of the narrative as the book progresses" (147). But "somehow . . . [it] maintains an encapsulating wholeness over its sixteen chapters and epilogue" (151).

Two factors, I suggest, generate this critical impasse. First, as I have indicated, critics tend to read *Blame Me on History* exclusively as a historical and political record. Second, Modisane's autobiography is usually read without reading the rest of his narrative prose.[6] As Modisane's expansive discussion in *Blame Me on History* of his early story "The Dignity of Begging" suggests, a consideration of these other writings illuminates the structure of the autobiography by revealing its motivations for deviating from a strict fidelity to history.

Summarizing "The Dignity of Begging," which appeared in *Drum* in September 1951, Modisane indicates how *Blame Me on History* figures him and other educated Blacks as beggars dependent on white charity. Having "bec[o]me cynical about my colour and my reaction to it" (*Blame* 88), Modisane imagines secretly avenging himself on Whites by manipulating their sympathetic responses; the eyes of Nathaniel Mokgamare, the beggar in "The Dignity of Begging," "plead for human kindness, but sneer behind every 'thank you, baas; God bless you, baas'" (*Blame* 89):

In my first published short story, "The Dignity of Begging," I created a satirical situation in which I sat back and laughed at the worlds which rejected. I projected myself into the character of Nathaniel Mokgamare, an educated African capable in any society of earning himself an independent living, but handicapped by being black in a society which has determined that black is the condition of being dependent on white charity, in the same sense that a cripple is dependent on public charity; but the beggar needs to be horribly deformed to arouse sympathetic patronage, and the African is disqualified by his colour from earning an independent living, hopelessly helpless in his incapacity to overcome the burden of his colour. (*Blame* 88)

An adherence to the conventions of anti-apartheid protest writing is strong in *Blame Me on History*. A figure of radical dependency, the beggar stands for the dependence of educated Blacks in a racist society. But—this is a "confession" of sorts—what had come to matter in the early 1950s for Modisane as a writer was the dynamics of begging and donation with its ruses and displacements of affect: a "transfer . . . [of] his demerits to where they finally belong, on the conscience of the overprivileged white public" (*Blame* 89). These dynamics take the place of a commitment to protest literature: "My writing showed a studied omission of commitment, the histrionics of tight-fisted protest" (*Blame* 88). Modisane's critics assume that a requirement of anti-apartheid protest writing (especially that aimed at uninformed international readers[7]) is an accurate chronicling of historical events. If that is so, *Blame Me on History*'s reevaluation of its author's earlier avoidance of protest may be read as a wish to supplement earlier writing in a genre to which criteria of verifiability applicable to history do not apply.

But autobiography, if capable of joining the writing of a life with a responsibility elaborated socially and historically, is not bound by the conventions governing the historian either; in *Blame Me on History*, the landmarks of apartheid history fulfill the generic demands of protest but at the same time operate as signs of another narrative. If *Blame Me on History* reframes "The Dignity of Begging" as an allegory of social protest, in the story itself Nathaniel Mokgamare begins another tale—of how he leaves his family out of irritation with their "excessive kindness" which "almost made me a neurotic" (12).

What *Blame Me on History* tells us about the black intellectual as a "beggar" can be applied to the textual performance of the book itself. Occupying the position of donor, the implied reader is subject to manipulation and, in the case of *Blame Me on History*, although called upon to respond out of conscience, is not a party to the full story. Reading with this dynamic in mind and attending to Nathaniel's asides about the ability of family life to produce neurosis allow us to read *Blame Me on History*'s account of the beginnings of Grand Apartheid, even as it is addressed to the reader of conscience, as a "cover story"[8] for a narrative of filiation. Never fully realized for the implied reader, this other narrative must be retrieved piece by piece from Modisane's autobiographical and fictional work.

Autobiography in *Blame Me on History* is, at first glance, the reflex of history. After describing the first of two terms of employment with Johannesburg's Vanguard Booksellers, Modisane tells us the reason he wanted to resume his studies and complete high school: "I wanted to rise above the messenger bicycle and the back door; what I did not realise was that I would never, in South Africa, be able to rise above the limitations imposed upon me by my colour, more eloquently articulated by Dr. Verwoerd: Natives should not be allowed to rise above certain levels of labour" (*Blame* 81). Refining the views of earlier educational planners who emphasized vocational training for the uplift of segregated communities (see Davis), Verwoerd had specified that "for [the Bantu] there is no place in the white community above the level of certain forms of labour." The place for educated Blacks, Verwoerd stipulated, was in their own communities: "Within his own community . . . all doors are open" (*Verwoerd aan die woord* 77–78). These "communities" were entities in the process of being defined in the invented "ethnic" vocabulary of "separate development" (see *Blame* 104). "Educated Africans" such as Modisane were effectively barred from performing intellectual labor within the "white community," although the community they shared with certain Whites was not white but, in a limited sense, as Mphahlele writes, a multiracial one. Whites were nevertheless typically the ones with the keys to what the Freedom Charter refers to as "the doors of learning and culture."

The fact that those who afforded them entry were by and large left-liberal Whites, often Jews (Kruger 580), influenced self-invention: if the ones accepting one did so out of conscience, what better way to present oneself than as a "beggar?" What better life story to tell than one protesting apartheid? Presenting oneself in such a way—the donor, addressed as "baas," is also the master—could, however, tacitly confirm the collective subordination of members of the group with which one was identified. An awareness of such implications, of which the intellectual, as portrayed by Modisane, is constantly reminded by less-privileged Blacks, is a significant source of a sense of complicity. As in the case of Olive Schreiner, whose *Woman and Labour* reads as a critique of the nature of her early imagining of entry into intellectual sociality, it is, ironically, the endeavor toward overcoming apartness that reinforces it.

The historical and social background to Modisane's autobiography helps to chart the terrain of complicities it negotiates in opposition to apartheid. A further articulation of these complicities with what I call complicity in the general sense takes place in the form of a filial drama of the kind to which Nathaniel Mokgamare alludes in "The Dignity of Begging." Disjoining autobiography from history, this articulation discloses itself with full force when we learn that Modisane's impulse to return to school makes itself felt four years after he joined Vanguard in 1947. This marks a departure of the autobiography from strict chronology, for Verwoerd's pronouncement on "levels of labour" comes from a speech on "Bantu Education Policy" delivered to Parliament in his capacity as Minister of Native Affairs in 1954, seven years later. I am not criticizing Modisane's account for being causally flawed or indicting his narrative for infidelity to history. Instead, I propose to read the sentence just quoted—"I wanted to rise above . . . certain levels of labour"—as a structure that, repeated in *Blame Me on History* in diverse narrative situations,[9] is basic to the textual performance and meaning of the work as a whole. In expressing the futility of Bloke Modisane's ambitions, the sentence generates a sense of synchrony. Recalling that, in "The Unconscious" (1915), Freud considered the processes of the unconscious to be "*timeless;* i.e., they are not ordered temporally, are not altered by the passage of time; they have no relation to time at all" (187; trans. modified),[10] it is possible to account for Modisane's distillation of chronology — which flaws the project of political protest without by any means undermining it — in terms of the filial motivations of the autobiography.

The significance of topoi of synchrony (or achrony) in Modisane's larger writing project is apparent from his short story, "The Situation" (1963). The relevant passage in the story does not make reference to verifiable events or chronology but represents, in the free indirect speech of its protagonist Caiaphas Sedumo, the figure of an intellectual — or, more precisely, the black intellectual:

> The darkness was creeping around him and when he got to his room he collapsed on to the bed and for hours stared at the ceiling. The darkness of the night blacked out the room, fusing him into it. He was obliterating himself, stopping the progress of time; annihilating it. The past, the present, the future, united into the frozen solidity of "now," the historic present. The incident with the farmers had demolished him, and there in the darkness the process of re-creation was shaping in clay the facsimile of man in the image of South Africa; it was a hollow man without reservoir of passion or human compassion. ("Situation" 12)

Black Consciousness invoked similar motifs — the "obliging. . . . empty shell," as Steve Biko writes in *I Write What I Like,* of the "black man . . . [who] has lost his manhood" (28–29) — in calling for a turning inward in order to address a collusion in psychic colonization and its social consequences. Modisane's texts insist that the psychic and the social both reside within a larger framework of reciprocity and responsibility. In order to remove from memory the recent past, his humiliation by a group of white farmers, Caiaphas Sedumo's erasure of identity is also an arrest of temporality: "He was obliterating himself, stopping the progress of time; annihilating it. The past, the present, the future, united into the frozen solidity of 'now,' the historic present." But the "self" is obliterated only for "the process of re-creation" to reinaugurate the destructive cycle by "shaping in clay the facsimile of man in the image of South Africa." When *Blame Me on History,* for its part, "stops the progress of time" by telescoping historical events, blame converges at a single point: Modisane's frustrated ambitions.

Although justifiably an object of blame, history is never held solely responsible. And if black sociality — "Go out among the people, lose yourself in the cacophony of noise" ("Situation" 12) — is a possible antidote to white racism, it brings for the "situation" its own alienation. The autobiography suggests a different venue for blame and rapprochement when it tells us that, at the funeral of Modisane's father, "commemorational rites to death [take place] over the body of the man who had passed on into — to nourish — cosmic life" (*Blame* 28). Echoing Caiaphas's self-obliteration, the passage of the father into cosmic life hints at a filiative allocation of blame and a corresponding attempt at reparation. A remedy for the corrosive effects of the disavowal of reciprocity that defines apartheid is sought, across the entire book, in the name of a reciprocity of living and dead. In terms of this analysis, the sentence "I wanted to rise above . . . certain levels of labour" acts as a "switch-word" (Freud, *Fragment* 65n) in a textual network that coordinates the narrative of historical witnessing and anti-apartheid protest addressed to the "liberal" reader with a message of filiation addressed by Modisane to his father. The latter functions, not as history or even as memory, but as a work of mourning. Structuring the autobiographical project as it emerges from the sources of "disaffection" elaborated by the book, this work of mourning is at the same time the engaging of a foldedness in human-being that stands as the minimal condition of possibility of any responsibility.

DISAFFECTION AND THE "SITUATION"

Nadine Gordimer observes in *The Black Interpreters* (1973) that "disaffected African intellectuals use the autobiographical form as a catharsis for the sufferings of second-class citizens with first-class brains" (7). The implications of Gordimer's observation can be explored in *Blame Me on History*. When Gordimer writes of "disaffected African intellectuals," from whom or what can the reader of Modisane's autobiography say that affect, or affection, has been withdrawn? On the one hand, *Blame Me on History* presents itself as a tale of a black intellectual disaffected not only from Whites but from black resistance organizations. "I burned my [African National Congress] Youth League membership card and retreated into a political wilderness," Modisane writes. "I was disillusioned beyond reconciliation, and decided to separate my life and interests from politics, until there shall rise from the slum of African politics a new and more professional liberation movement" (*Blame* 139). Like (or perhaps, unlike) Modisane, the African politicians cannot "rise from" their poverty. But the process that critics take to be Bloke Modisane's ascent to political consciousness, his growing allegiance to the Pan Africanist Congress (Watts 149; Mathabane x; see also Modisane, *Blame* 230–50), is also a movement, as it were, from "disaffection," through "catharsis," toward addressing Joseph Modisane, his late father — a passage steered between blame and rapprochement.

Sophiatown, Joseph Modisane, and Bloke are linked metaphorically in *Blame Me on History*. Joseph is brutally murdered: "The battered and grotesquely ballooned nightmare, hardly recognizable as a human being, was my father; the swollen mass of broken flesh and blood, which was his face, had no definition; there were no eyes nor mouth, nose, only a motionless ball" (*Blame* 26). "Sophiatown was like one of its own many victims; a man gored by the knives of Sophiatown, lying in the open gutters, a raisin in the smelling drains" (*Blame* 5). The first sentence of the book reads: "Something in me died, a piece of me died, with the dying of Sophiatown" (5). This sentence is a more cryptic statement in the context of Bloke's relation to his father. By accident, Bloke's given name (William) was written on his father's coffin: "The shock of seeing my name and not my father's on the coffin confused and frightened me, but it seemed symbolic somehow; I was officially dead, something I was later to exploit emotionally" (31). "William"'s death is confirmed as the bulldozers move in: "Something in me died, a piece of me died, with the dying of Sophiatown." This "piece" is, on one reading, the paternal part-object. His father has taken William/Bloke's name to the grave with him, but he remains encrypted, incorporated in Bloke in ciphered form. It is only years later, with the destruction of Sophiatown, that that part finally dies — or is killed.[11] The first time William dies; the second time, repeating the first, both Joseph and (a part of) William die.

The death of Joseph Modisane is a calamity for Bloke and his immediate family. "'We are cast-offs in the wilderness,' Ma-Willie said, in Sesutho. 'We are orphans, our *shield* is gone'" (*Blame* 27; my emphasis). Bloke leaves school, "a fourteen-year-old man responsible for a family of four" (*Blame* 28). His father's death leaves unresolved an ambivalence arising from his humiliation during a pass-raid by the police. "I was diminished. . . . My hero image disintegrated, crumbling into an inch high heap of ashes. . . . I hated the young [white police] constable for destroying my father" (*Blame* 24). Not only does Joseph Modisane make William/Bloke suffer through his suffering,[12] but in one of the starkest of *Blame Me on History*'s many ironies, by dying and leaving Bloke in charge of the family, he deprives his son of education and thus joins H. F. Verwoerd in consigning him to certain levels of labor. If the book tells the story of how Bloke Modisane was able to become a writer with an audience, it is addressed as much to readers of conscience as protest over what Verwoerd's policies did as to his dead father, who frustrated his son's ambitions by dying. It is for this reason that, read in conjunction with Modisane's short stories, *Blame Me on History* is not simply political protest but enlists its readers in order to reach his father. In so doing, it articulates the reader's complicity, in realizing an anti-apartheid narrative, in order to set to work a more basic responsibility.

In *Blame Me on History*, as in Peter Abrahams's *Tell Freedom* (13–14, 61–62), another of the autobiographies of the 1950s, injury to the face is a central motif. Bloke's vision of his father's face as unrecognizable, and as losing its "definition" and becoming a "motionless ball," recurs with the birth of a daughter:

Suddenly the features of her face began to blur, there was something un-differentiated about them, they were more red than black and the indefi-nition disturbed me; I was looking at a neutral face, possibly black, just a representative facsimile of millions of faceless masks; those who had seen her remarked that she looked like me, implying that our features were similar, but I have no face, I have no name, my whole existence slithers behind a mask called Bloke. I became desperate, here was a mask of millions of black faces, but I was determined that this was a face they shall not deface, I will define all its particularities. (*Blame* 74–75)

Modisane is a "nervous father" (*Blame* 74), contemplating succeeding at what his own father failed at. His daughter's face, mysteriously blur-ring into "indefinition," is a projection of the face of *his* father, whose dead face, a "swollen mass of broken flesh and blood . . . had no defini-tion." Like the figure of Caiaphas Sedumo, it is a "facsimile" ("Situation" 12). The "neutral face" is the face Bloke adopts after the death of his father. This de-faced Bloke-face substitutes for the face that died with his father.[13] Modisane's autobiographical project is to recreate the face of his father.

"Bloke" is a name adopted as a "*shield* against the thing I was" (*Blame* 167; my emphasis). Now a world of fantasy centered on Leslie Char-teris's character, "The Saint,"[14] the "shield" of the name replaces the paternal "shield" forcibly removed from him and the family. It becomes that shield, replacing the lost, "bad," part-object. A fictive appellation takes the place of his legal name: "People around us began to assume the label for my name, and gradually this label became a part of me I could not discourage; it began to overwhelm me, to become a piece of me, to impose a life of its own upon me. . . . It did not occur to me that in accepting this label I was to obliterate my legal name" (*Blame* 167).[15] In an inversionary turn of possession, the name "Bloke" becomes a part of him, then makes him a part of it.

Bloke progressively disintegrates, a process dramatized by a shift to the present tense. The collapse of distinctions he experiences demands sentences that will bring time to a standstill by harnessing metaphorically the interring of the father to the disappearance of the narrator's meaningful world. As in "The Situation," birth and death are linked through dust. The father dies, William dies, and Bloke is born: "The line between fantasy and reality is becoming less and less distinct; I cannot tell my friends from my enemies; everything is fading into dust. As the coffin of my father with my name on it had disappeared into the dust" (*Blame* 170).

Bloke escapes into a cinema, where he can "pretend the blackness from my hand." Like Caiaphas Sedumo, he can "lose [himself] into the darkness" (*Blame* 170). In Gordimer's terms, Modisane is "disaffected" from his father and his father's world but unable, as an African, to escape what Fanon calls "the fact of blackness" (*Black Skin* 109–40). In the cinema there is an association between neutralizing his "blackness" and compensating for a loss of a father, which is presented as the loss of a face. Providing the name "Bloke," the cinema might be a temporary alleviation; and being with Blacks in an environment where "blackness" is affirmed may, as Caiaphas thinks, resolve things socially. The ultimate recovery of a face and a self depends, however, on Modisane's recreation of the face of his father.

In losing himself and his self, Bloke becomes radically dependent on others, both "black" and "white" — whether less-privileged Blacks, racist Afrikaners, or patronizing liberal Anglo–South Africans. This dependence brings complicity. First there is the complicity of being a beggar, pandering to white authority and thereby reinforcing collective subordination. Then there is the complicity of the reader, the recognition needed for the autobiography to succeed, for it to be both political and filial protest. If not absolutely dependent on the taking up of a reading position given by racial authority and privilege, the cooperation of the listener or reader hinges, in Modisane's case, on being touched by the tale of a "beggar." Being disaffected, his sense of complicity comes not, as it does for N. P. van Wyk Louw and others who are better connected, from a desire to detach himself, but rather from a need to form attachments without which he cannot, in effect, be an intellectual. In the case of Caiaphas Sedumo, within what Fanon terms a "racist structure" (*Black Skin* 87), it is also a question of what it takes to be a human being. Opposition to apartheid, in this case in the form of protest literature, is not realized without broaching the complicity in a general sense in the name of which opposition is carried on, and in the name of which readers are summoned to join.

The second part of Gordimer's statement in *The Black Interpreters* refers to "second-class citizens with first-class brains." The educated — in Gordimer's terms, more intelligent — man is entitled to full civic rights but is denied them by the very people who profess to share this restrictive notion of democracy. Historically, "equal rights for civilized men" was the liberal promise. Colonial rule and apartheid, confirmed by Verwoerd's prohibitions, made it one that could not be kept. Without alternative ties to the black middle class, Modisane, as an "educated African," was doubly barred from intellectual life. That is another reason why, in the autobiography he writes, he assumes the persona of the "situation," presenting himself as a beggar, and why he writes, in the plural, of "the worlds which rejected" (*Blame* 88).

On one level, to speak of a disaffected African intellectual is to speak of someone who has withdrawn from the object determined by more "natural" filial ties, only to be denied the affection of the more desirable object put in its place. The disaffected African intellectual is, in the lore of the 1950s, usually a man. He is in love with the unattainable and denies "the community" for "individual" well-being.[16] Not only "rejected" by the African middle class but also mocked by other Africans, Modisane has no place, no citizenship, in either black or white society: "I am the eternal alien between two worlds; the Africans call me a 'Situation,' by Western standards I am uneducated" (*Blame* 218). An index of the "Situation" is language:

There is a resentment—almost as deep-rooted as the prejudice itself—against the educated African, not so much because he is allegedly cheeky, but that he fails to conform to the stereotype image of the black man sanctified and cherished with jealous intensity by the white man; such a native must—as a desperate necessity—be humiliated into submission. The educated African is resented equally by the blacks because he speaks English, which is one of the symbols of white supremacy, he is resentfully called a *Situation,* something not belonging to either but tactfully *situated* between white oppression and black rebellion. The English regard him as a curio, they listen to him with critical attention to detail as regard to accent, usage and syntax; when they have taken a decision they pronounce, and with almost divine tolerance and Christian charity, that the African speaks English beautifully; the more naïve listen with unmasked agony whilst the African is struggling with syntax to communicate his thoughts; they suffer patiently between interruptions to request the African to articulate with precision, but these self-same King's English enthusiasts will listen with enthrallment to a continental accent.

The Afrikaners are almost psychotic in their reaction to the English-speaking African, whom they accuse of talking back with insolence and aping the white man. (*Blame* 94; my emphasis)

In N. P. van Wyk Louw's poem, Raka is "the ape-man, he who cannot think." The assumption that Blacks are dark-skinned mimic men is not confined to those who indulge openly in racist violence and discrimination. Informed by "scientific racism" and galvanized by the "menace" of mimicry (see Bhabha 88), Louw's poem is a high-cultural version of the stereotype. Malan's National Party exploited the working-class Afrikaner electorate's fear of economic competition, and in the cities, where a knowledge of English gave one an edge, the "black Englishman" (*Blame* 90) was a rival. The *Drum* writers perceived that, as the language of commerce, English did bring material benefits. But even if, in the urban environment of Johannesburg, it seemed to promise some access to the privileges enjoyed by Whites, English was an ambiguous qualification in the eyes of ordinary black society.

"I walked about the streets of the bustling noisy city," Lewis Nkosi writes, "with new English words clicking like coins in the pockets of my mind"(7). There is hardly any comfort, however, in the pursuit of this kind of compensatory pleasure. Nkosi had "two sets of reality; one was the ugly world in which I lived my trapped life and the other, more powerful one, was the world of the books I read. . . . What was happening under my eye was filtered through the moral sieve provided by this foreign literature. It was clear that I was using literature as a form of escape; I was using it as a shield against a life of grime and social deprivation" (7–8). According to Nkosi, middle-class Blacks were occasionally reminded of their position of relative privilege by being forced by street toughs to recite Shakespeare (13).

Caiaphas Sedumo, the subject of "The Situation," is forced by the gangster Deadwood Dick to recite at gunpoint Mark Antony's funeral oration from *Julius Caesar* before a packed shebeen. He has to repeat it five times and is astonished by the shebeen-goers' familiarity with it; they interrupt him, and he realizes that their interjections derive from the screen version, which starred Marlon Brando.[17] Caiaphas, we recall, had been insulted and mocked by a group of Afrikaans-speaking white farmers; his English is their pretext. They had wanted to put him in his place: "'Be careful,' the farmer said. 'You city boys are spoilt—don't know your place; you're communists, the whole batch. We know how to deal with you—our boys on the farm are good boys. You be careful'" (11). The farmers not only represent a stereotype of firm paternal white supremacy on feudal lines. They also hint at another element of the rural-urban divide: the urban center, where migrants from all over the subcontinent meet, is potentially a place of working-class organization, whereas in the rural areas black resistance is thought to be contained more easily by manipulating localized "tribal" identities and fostering mother-tongue education. Blacks who speak English are a tangible threat to white rule newly articulated through manipulated black ethnicity.

Deadwood Dick, who has learned of the incident with the farmers, wants no less to put Caiaphas in his place. He tells Caiaphas, as he arrives at the Battleship shebeen, "'Heit, yourself, . . . bloody Situation. What's wrong with you situations actually? All you do is talk English—situation this, situation that; situating all the bloody time. You got no pluck'" ("Situation" 12). For the black intellectual, then, things seem no better with the gangsters than with the farmers. They also want him to be in one definite place and are impatient with his perpetual maneuvering, the "situating" that he does when threatened with violence. Battleship, the shebeen proprietress, advises him to "talk their language, talk to them in the dialect of the tsotsis; they're not fools, Caiaphas, talking in English is to situate yourself above them." But they have already responded with hostility to his use of "Heit," a colloquial greeting; they do not want him to situate for them as he does for the whites. "They say you are a coward," she adds, "you didn't raise a finger or open your mouth. These boys look up to you, you're a hero; *they look up to you to state their case*. When stupid farmers push you around *they* are humiliated" (13; my emphasis). As Battleship represents it, the motive behind the tsotsis' hostility is also the opening for the "situation" to advocate a cause and, by gaining a place from which to speak and an audience to address in protest, to become an intellectual. *Blame Me on History* grasps this opening with some ambivalence.

"THE DIGNITY OF BEGGING"

According to *Blame Me on History,* Modisane published his story, "The Dignity of Begging," just at the time when he would have been thinking of returning to high school, having left at the age of fourteen. As he tells us, he "created a satirical situation in which I sat back and laughed at the worlds which rejected." Nathaniel Mokgamare, the professional beggar, is "handicapped by being black in a society which has determined that black is the condition of being dependent on white charity, in the same sense that a cripple is dependent on public charity" (*Blame* 88). "The worlds which rejected" rapidly become a single white one, where "public charity" is "white charity" and a black skin is a horrible deformity. In terms of Gordimer's remark about citizenship, Nathaniel, by virtue of his dependence on charity, is excluded from the "public." Because he is black, he can never become part of that public and must therefore remain in a dependent position of charitable reception in relation to whites.

Time may have affected Modisane's memory of the story. Meant to illustrate the nastiness of both worlds, it only tells of the relation to one. Why does Modisane mention the story when it fails to say what he says it does? There are clearly tensions between the marks of identity Gordimer indicates — between being black, albeit educated, and being an *intellectual* — and the "masks" he adopts after the death of his father. As is revealed by the fabular texture of the story alluded to by Modisane's characterization of it as "a satirical situation," the citizenship of the intellectual, linked here to life itself, is more precarious than an exclusive consideration of racial factors would suggest.

Being a respectable petit bourgeois (he pretends to be a beggar),

"Nathaniel accepts the challenge, deciding that if he is condemned to be a beggar he would become a professional one, with the strict observance of the *ethics* of the profession" (*Blame* 88–89; my emphasis).[18] We are witnessing, perhaps, an example of "the appropriation of criminality in acceptable forms" (Foucault, *Discipline and Punish* 68) by the journalists of *Drum*. An exiled Nat Nakasa wrote, apparently in jest, that even if he did settle down and become a law-abiding citizen, he "would miss the experience of illegal living" that being black in South Africa demanded (Barnett 28). But "The Dignity of Begging" is not just a celebration of criminality. According to Modisane, it "is the reflection of the only possible life — with dignity and sanity — that the African could accept in order to accommodate South Africans" (*Blame* 89). The African must flatter whites and be "a master in the art of chicanery" (*Blame* 91).[19]

We can compare "The Dignity of Begging" with the more obvious duality of dependency and rejection of "The Situation," which first appeared in 1963, the same year as *Blame Me on History*.[20] Whereas "The Situation" brings both black and white society to book, as a fable of the intellectual, "The Dignity of Begging" is one-sided. Apart from telling us that Richard, Nathaniel's partner in begging, is "exploited" by his family, who send him out to beg, the story does not censure other Blacks. The summary of "The Dignity of Begging" in *Blame Me on History* speaks of accommodating "South Africans." Along with the book's looseness with regard to historical chronology, this apparent uncertainty surrounding the racial source of disaffection is another detail suggesting that, without ignoring its racial dimension, the story's significance can also be sought in the split in address that joins and disjoins a filial petition with the book's overt appeal to the reader.

If this search is a matter of reading, how are we to read "The Dignity of Begging"? It is possible, as David Maughan-Brown suggests, to reject the story for its inability to come to terms with material social conditions:

But the story is *not positing an alternative ethic* in the face of unbearable social and economic pressures. Both the narrator and his friend recognise themselves as being "parasites." . . . *Far from offering critical comment* on the criminalization of begging in a society characterized by gross inequalities in the distribution of income and wealth, the story implicitly endorses such criminalization. . . . This story is *less than revolutionary* towards the economic dispensation it takes for granted. (8; my emphasis)

There is a divergence of interpretation and of assumptions about the function of fiction between Maughan-Brown and Modisane. Modisane's goal is to illustrate the ambiguous position of the "Situation," not to provide a sociological analysis of crime and criminalization (Rabkin 131). The story functions as a fable. Ignoring specificity of literary genre, Maughan-Brown's prescriptive vigilance has difficulty locating the "alternative ethic" the story propounds.

Nathaniel and his friend, Richard Serurubele, are the self-declared parasites who feed from the social body as if it were a natural resource. "I think I will continue to drain the life-blood of the wonderful people of that big generous city, with the golden pavements," thinks Nat as they leave the magistrate's court. Richard is desperate:

"One of these days I'm going to kill myself," Serurubele says. "I can't go on like this, I'm tired of being a parasite. Why did this happen to me, tell me Nathan, why?"

How this man expects me to answer a question like that is beyond me. For one unguarded moment I almost told him to send his maker a telegram, and ask him all about it, but my gentler nature sees the harm such an answer can do.

"I don't know, Richard," I say. "But things like this happen; it is not in us to question why. Nature has a way of doing things and even then she gives something in return." ("Dignity" 11)

"Nature," Nathaniel says, has determined their fate but also "gives something in return." Although he knows better than to attribute agency to something as mystical as "Nature," Nathaniel thematizes a wish for distributive justice.

In a discussion of Marcel Mauss's *The Gift*, Derrida points to the ethical function that concepts of nature have, forming even "a Rousseauist schema," in theories of giving that attempt to distinguish giving from exchange: "It is nature that gives, and one must show oneself worthy of this gift. One must take and learn [prendre et apprendre] the gift of nature. From giving nature, one must learn to give, in a manner that is both generous and ordered; and by giving as nature says one must give, one will give it back its due, one will show oneself to be worthy, one will mark the right equivalence" (*Given Time* 66). The "parasite," as opposed to the virtuous purveyor of an "alternative ethic," is rejected by Maughan-Brown despite the fact that the semantic opposition between parasite and host can, as J. Hillis Miller shows in "The Critic as Host," be brought into question by etymology, and the interdependence of the terms asserted. Truly *ethical* conduct might thus well be to *enact* a narrative of justice and provision and responsibility within a context where it seems impossible, instead of fixing one's hopes dogmatically, as Maughan-Brown seems to, on some prescribed legal and institutional structure.[21] In this way, an "identity between the theoretical and the ethical" (Derrida, *Given Time* 66) could be entertained.

In his attention to "the ethics of the profession," Nathaniel implicitly puts into question the justice of Maughan-Brown's solution: "Why must I take a job when I can earn twice a normal wage begging? . . . I must uphold the dignity of begging. Whoever heard of a beggar working? It's *unethical,* that's all" ("Dignity" 11; my emphasis). The key word for Derrida in the longer of the passages I quoted from *Given Time* is "learn"; and "The Dignity of Begging" gives us a lesson in responsibility that we can take back to Modisane's autobiography. As with hospitality in Tiyo Soga, explicated by A. C. Jordan as ubuntu, the relation between guest and host is an ethical one. Rather than being a given, the identity of each party emerges in this relation.

The narrator of "The Dignity of Begging" is well aware of the dynamics of parasitism. A "well-dressed lady" is the latest subject of Nat's practiced skills: "She stops and looks at me as if she is responsible for my deformity" (12). The response of the apparently affluent woman to Nathaniel's self-staging constitutes an acknowledgment of responsibility for the state he projects. In this way, she gives him life as parasite. The effectiveness of the ploy, at least in this story, depends on the addresser being more aware than the addressee — conscious of the activity, if not the full implications of that staging: "I put on a gloomy face, bend lower than usual and let my deformed carcass shiver" ("Dignity" 12). Accordingly, we are presented initially with a Nathaniel who displays interiority and a Richard who only responds; the former decides not to disillusion him further with a cynical remark about dispatching a message ("send his maker a telegram") to which there can never be a response, let alone it reach its destination. In the world of "The Dignity of Begging," much depends on responses and on the respondent's relative obliviousness. A comparable complicity is enlisted on the part of the reader by Modisane's autobiography in order for its story and "cover story" to be told.

Finally, it is by being taken in by the machinations of a family "conspiracy," responding to a fictitious message sent via Richard, that Nathaniel is lured back to the countryside to his family (15–16). Parasitism requires the complicity of another. If "The Dignity of Begging" is, as Modisane says, a satirical representation of the "educated African," then the complicity in question is one that allows him to be an intellectual. Protest was one way black intellectuals could find a white audience and readership in the 1950s. Yet in simultaneously addressing a complaint to his dead father, Modisane subverts and supplements the narrow conventions of protest literature, demonstrating how they depend on a more basic structure of responsibility.

Blame Me on History's reasons for soliciting the attention of the reader are, considering the familial drama played out in "The Dignity of Begging," undeclaredly personal; and they give a structure to the book that the autobiographic historical chronicle does not. Implicit in the book's title are nagging questions. Who or what does one blame? Is it "me," or is it "history?" One's response to this question will determine where one's sympathies lie. The narrator, unlike Modisane's critics when they read the title univocally, is quite aware of this:

Rationalizations have their place and function. It is easy to blame the failure of my life on the colour-bar, in the same sense that it is easy for the white South African to be grateful to the colour-bar for his privileged positions. I could perhaps present eloquent argument that in a normal society I could have made this or that of my life. . . . And as a true South African I am tempted to blame the emptiness of my life on history, and pretend a reason for the loneliness, the need for love and companionship; but these are diversions. . . . But I cannot blame the hurt I have caused her [Fiki, his wife] to suffer on history; I had learned, but too thoroughly, to disregard the attentions of others; when I should have understood, I was callous and vindictive; I have never learned to accommodate her. . . . I was essentially concerned with the problems of living with my colour, and at the time I behaved as though I was the only black person in South Africa; I persecuted Fiki for her colour as viciously as white men did. (*Blame* 217–19)

Although authorship is progressively refused, and the blame moves from himself ("me") to "history," Modisane appears to be admitting that he cannot wholly blame, or be blamed on, history. He acknowledges some choice in the matter and appears to shoulder a degree of blame himself. How is the reader to respond? Some, as we have observed, repress the ambivalence found in *Blame Me on History* in favor of a reaction of mea culpa. They apologize in the name of history, giving Modisane his due as chronicler of the fifties without noticing the way in which their responses have been prefigured and predetermined by the beggar-text.

By reflecting on its title, Modisane's testimony becomes, for a moment, a confession. He not only recognizes that there are ones worse off than he is, but he admits that he has a hand in their subordination. His wife, Fiki, the granddaughter of Sol Plaatje, symbolizes his entry, as a "nobody's son," into the black middle class and intellectual elite. He is prepared to accommodate to Whites but not to her. He pursues white women, signs of an even greater prize: social acceptance among Whites, a share of white privilege, "being white" even: "I am able to admit that my marriage decomposed because Fiki is black; the women in the sex pilgrimage left me in a coma of screaming loneliness because they were black. . . . only the state of being white could satisfy me, and in a tedious succession I thought myself to be . . . lyrically in love with every white woman I met" (*Blame* 220). The rejection of black women may be a constitutive absence in the way responsibility is figured in Modisane's texts. At one level, in "The Dignity of Begging," the subject of the beggar's attentions is a "well-dressed lady," who, as the account of the story in *Blame Me on History* suggests, is imagined as white. At a more subterranean level, the drama of begging and donation is transacted between father and son.

Nathaniel Mokgamare ultimately finds the resolution he wants in respectable, idyllic rural retirement from the hazards of his profession: "I do not have to ask my father how the piano got here [from his Sophiatown room]. The conspiracy is all over his face. I find it difficult to hold back my tears when I read the message in his eyes. Welcome home, my son, his eyes said" ("Dignity" 16–17). Father and son are reunited, the father having made the son his own again by utilizing his chicanery. *Blame Me on History* makes "The Dignity of Begging" a part of the autobiography. Modisane's wish for a father whom he can not blame is fulfilled. The father's face is no longer undefined; his eyes are alive and transmit an indelible written message to which Nathaniel cannot but respond.[22] Modisane's larger autobiographical project succeeds by bringing the father back to life, by bringing back his face.

If this analysis sheds light on *Blame Me on History,* it is that the disaffection of the "Situation" is a result, not merely of racial or class inequality, but also, in this case, of the loss of a father. In the autobiography, the racial and class other is called upon to respond, but apparently not the father who takes his son with him to the grave. In the early story, though, the father sends a message of his own; there is a line to the "maker," although the message takes the reverse route. *Blame Me on History* (whose whole story is told in "The Dignity of Begging") can thus be read as a message to the departed. "I think that one writes also for the dead," Derrida says, speaking on the subject of autobiography. "One writes for a specific dead person, so that perhaps in every text there is a dead man or woman to be sought, the singular figure of death to which a text is destined and which signs" (*Ear* 53). Instead of reaching its deceased addressee, *Blame Me on History* errs and reaches living readers. Like the unnamed woman in "The Dignity of Begging," they can only respond as conscience dictates — or respond as history determines, if that is any different. In any case, what remains is the split in address and the articulation of more than one address in an inextricable codetermination.

To say that the autobiography errs in reaching living readers is not, of course, to say that there are not readers whom Modisane and other black autobiographers, like the black politicians of the day, do *not* reach. As far as I am aware, in his published work, N. P. van Wyk Louw makes no reference to black South African literature,[23] although in lectures in the Netherlands in 1951 on the literature of his country, he does discuss Peter Abrahams's early novels. Quoting from an article in the SAIRR's *Handbook on Race Relations* (1949) on "African Literature" by R. H. W. Shepherd, who writes that, in the sphere of written literature, "the African . . . has remained almost inarticulate" (609), Louw tells his students that very little has been written by "Bantu" writers and that the one example he gives, Thomas Mofolo's *Chaka* (1925), is a "historical novel — thus not socially of so much importance." (The same, despite its massive reference to the land question, would presumably have applied for Louw to Plaatje's *Mhudi,* which Shepherd mentions in the same paragraph along with Jordan's *Ingqumbo Yeminyanya,* J. J. R. Jolobe's essays, and S. E. K. Mqhayi's autobiography *U-Mqhayi Wase-Ntab'ozuko.*) "For this reason," Louw's lecture notes explain, "I will discuss with you the work of a *Coloured* writer who writes mainly about the Bantu."[24] Abrahams is "in any case extremely interesting: 'non-white' side of the 'wall'" ("By Abrahams" 1–2).

An extreme ambivalence pervades Louw's comments, in which literature and the social occupy shifting poles of intellectual investment. Although it is "difficult to impress upon you the *ineptitude,* [the] *superficiality.* . . . its inept[itude] as literature," the "main goal" is to "see whether there is something, a specific view [kyk], to be obtained at a *social* level" ("By Abrahams" 9). Having concluded that Abrahams's "*knowledge* [kennis] of the white man . . . [is] extremely deficient," Louw stages his response as a reader. Fracturing the progress of his lecture, the result is a complex passage of self-othering, in which the (white, Afrikaans, even Afrikaner-nationalist) reader is moved from exaggerated amusement to autocritical questioning:

100s of little details . . . made me *smile.* . . . Do *we,* Whites, see the Bantu just as erroneously [as Abrahams sees Whites]? I don't think so. (Never humble enough regarding our knowledge of 'other' people, volke . . .) *Serious side:* How difficult a 'meeting' of minds must be in a land where people do not know each other to such a degree! Were the *first* Afrikaans novels in which Bantus appeared not *equally inadequate?* For these reasons you must forgive me if I demand your attention for work which according to our standards is so weak. I regard it only as a *starting point* (in a not very talented writer) of what hopefully can become important for S.A. ("By Abrahams" 10)[25]

Once this interrogative parabasis is over, the "starting point" represented by Abrahams is shut off in a way that suggests an already existing foreclosure: "Not just *weak as lit.;* also without insight into the actual, tragic tensions in South Africa" ("By Abrahams" 12).[26] Although in the same breath appealing for "an openness, unconstrainedness for new thoughts" ['n oopheid, onbevangenheid vir nuwe gedagtes], as in his lectures on "Rassevraagstukke" the following year, "eventual separation [*skeiding*]" is the "'solution'" Louw proposes ("By Abrahams" 19). Responsibility can mean deciding in the night of nonknowledge, as Derrida argues in "Force of Law" (967), and openness can be a mode of responsibility. This being so, preoccupying oneself with the "knowledge" in the narrow sense possessed by and of the other can be a diversion — when the declared intellectual stance of "openness" is contradicted socially by a scheme of "eventual separation."

Kennis can, however, also be translated as "acquaintance, a relation, even a relation to the beloved," as André Brink reminds us, invoking in his novel *Kennis van die aand* [*Looking on Darkness*] (1973) a distinction made by Saint John of the Cross in his commentary to a line of his *Cántico espiritual: "To the mountain:* the full knowledge of the morning that, the revealed truth of God, face to face, too overwhelming for mortal man to endure; *to the hill;* the knowledge that comes in the darkness of the evening, of God in his creatures and works and wondrous ordinances — a form of knowledge grasped not with the intellect or the mind, but obscurely, intimately, intuitively, through a glass darkly, the way a lover knows his loved one in the night" (*Looking* 298/*Kennis* 305).[27] Knowledge need not be measured against divine knowing. There can, as Njabulo Ndebele's post-apartheid writings show us, be significant acquaintance, welcome or otherwise, without a high level of knowledge.

No matter the level of "knowledge," however, Louw's nonnegotiable solution remains apartheid. The opening to a relational "know[ing] each other" is choked by the allegation of empirical inadequacy. Relation is barred in advance. This is the fate of his single public opening to the other intellectual. For N. P. van Wyk Louw, black writing is processed like the letters from the African National Congress received by H. F. Verwoerd's secretary but never forwarded to the executive; or, if sent on, like the ones addressed to his predecessor, Advocate J. G. Strijdom, not acknowledged, and never acted upon.[28] As had the liberal R. F. A. Hoernlé in the days of "segregation," Louw tacitly assumed for himself and Afrikaners a type of ethico-political agency. This permitted them to address the "Natives," but not, in a way that truly became part of their sense of agency and responsibility, to listen to what black intellectuals were saying. It may be that, beyond the systematic restriction of black representation within "ethnic" channels outside of the civil society reserved for Whites and beyond the repression of political activity and the censorship of writers, "apartheid" will stand as a shorthand, among others, for this unheeding assumption of agency. At the same time as foreclosing reciprocal foldedness in human-being, apartheid withholds from the other the possibility of responsible agency.

The decades that followed saw political agency and initiative gradually shift out of white hands. In terms of intellectual history, one can mark this shift in the play of complicity in the narrow and general sense in

A. C. Jordan's text on Tiyo Soga, hospitality, and ubuntu. In Jordan, it is not, as it is in Modisane, the link to the dead person that stands as the transcendental horizon for responsibility, but rather it is the figure of the stranger. Something else is important in Jordan's reading and translation of Soga. In articulating empirical and transcendental figures of the stranger, what becomes visible is an assumption of responsibility. Although in some sense corresponding to an element in a vernacular cultural formation, as does Modisane's address to his father, this appears as something *new*. Having revealed his adolescent ignorance of conceptions of death and his hesitation about proper funeral rites (*Blame* 31–32), Modisane produces a literary substitute. In Jordan's text, which concerns itself with "literary stabilization," the cultural formation, fully an artifact of African modernity, is itself internally fractured. The responsibility assumed thus not only yields a version of complicity in the general sense—namely, ubuntu—but, in exemplary fashion, it avoids the trap of ethno-philosophical nostalgia by declaring itself complicitous with an "apartheid" in the narrow sense (in a fashion akin to Modisane, perhaps, when he indicts himself for employing the "colour-bar" as a screen for the persecution of his wife). In its historical actualization, ubuntu is perpetually lost.

"Loss of Ubuntu": A. C. Jordan, Tiyo Soga, and
the Invention of Cultural Memory

The epilogue to the interim Constitution of the Republic of South Africa (1993), a document drafted to act as a "historic bridge between the past of a deeply divided society . . . and a future founded on the recognition of human rights, democracy and peaceful co-existence and development opportunities for all South Africans," sets forth a series of needs. Rounding off the series is a need for ubuntu: "a need for understanding but not for vengeance, a need for reparation but not for retaliation, a need for ubuntu but not for victimisation." Warding off vengeance, retaliation, and victimization, each of these pairs is an attempt to frame what was absent, lacking, or lost in the apartheid era. The new dispensation, authorized by the constitution, is designed to rectify the situation.

In the case of ubuntu, a key word in post-apartheid politics and in Thabo Mbeki's "African Renaissance," the reparative syntax of the constitutional epilogue is particularly significant. Phrased in the Zulu formulation that has become dominant, *"umuntu ngumuntu ngabantu"* — a human being [umuntu] is a human being through human beings [abantu] — the concept of ubuntu is regularly embedded in sentences lamenting its loss. The report of the Truth and Reconciliation Commission (1998), for instance, cites Constitutional Court Judge Pius Langa: "During violent conflicts and times when violent crime is rife, distraught members of society decry the loss of *ubuntu*. Thus, heinous crimes are the antithesis of *ubuntu*. Treatment that is cruel, inhuman or degrading is bereft of *ubuntu*" (*Truth* 1:127). Read along with Langa's formulation, the epilogue to the interim constitution implies that reconciliation will come about not only when there *is* ubuntu, but when a state of ubuntu has been *restored*. A time is posited when there *will have been* ubuntu. If this were merely a time in the past, one could call this a process of remembering. But strictly speaking, the phrasing is in the future perfect: the time of ubuntu that is posited has never had an actual existence, but rather, it exists at the level of possibility. Without in any way detracting from ubuntu as a regulative ethico-political concept, this counterfactuality compels us, if we are to speak of memory, to call that bound up with ubuntu "invented memory." This invented memory is cultural to the extent that, in the emergence of ubuntu in contemporary public discourse, appeal is made to the explanatory resources of particular indigenous cultural formations.

To this immanent reading must be added a historical genealogy in which this temporality of the future perfect is itself repeatedly deployed as a way of managing the transition from one era to another and of effecting reconciliation between people and groups. Ubuntu has a history in black Christianity in South Africa, in the negotiations between missionaries and converts (see Friesen), and in dealing with the social effects of the simultaneous historical transition from existing formations to a more pervasive colonial modernity. The writings of Archbishop Desmond Tutu, where what Battle calls an "ubuntu theology" elaborates the Christian idea that "each person is not just to be respected but to be revered as one created in God's image" (Tutu 197; see also 31, 109), attest to this heritage, which provides resources for a fuller understanding, explication, and critique of the deployment of the concept in contemporary public discourse.[29] We find in that history a repeated emergence of ubuntu at times of historical crisis, when its loss is lamented. Somewhat like Louw's concept of voortbestaan in geregtig-heid, the strength of the concept of ubuntu is its ability, by inventing memory in the future perfect, to generate stability at a time of transition and to stage recovery at a time of loss.

The question remains: What will render the call for ubuntu, which is typically inextricable from the lamenting of its loss, concrete? Paradox-ically perhaps, it is the literary that does so. In the texts we are about to read, ubuntu is linked to hospitality and the injunction not to be forget-ful of the stranger, the figure of transcendental otherness. Just as with Modisane's address to his father, which also sets out to repair loss, ubuntu sets to work a general structure of responsibility beyond the living.

Although appearing as a character in a didactic essay, Jordan's and Soga's stranger remains a figure of some historical specificity. Linking the empirical and the transcendental, the works in question put forth a lesson in ubuntu. They link temporal alterity with the otherness of human-being. Uniting memory and responsibility, the stranger, as a mutable though constant presence, becomes the exemplary figure for ubuntu. As with Schreiner, where the encounter with the "Stranger" is the place of access to sociality and thus of accession to human-being per se (although that place is marked not as transcendental but as social),[30] for Jordan reading Soga, hospitality is at the crux of responsibility-in-complicity.

JORDAN AND "LITERARY STABILIZATION"

In the history of ubuntu, the efforts of Archibald Campbell Jordan (1906–68) are a major departure. Looking back to the 1860s and Soga's writings, A. C. Jordan extends the concept beyond a narrowly theologi-cal elaboration, suggesting how it can be an ethico-political counter to apartheid from within vernacular culture.[31] His writings of the late 1950s reveal how ubuntu, despite its own volatility as a concept and a linguistic entity, manages to bring stability; how, as figured in a work Jordan reads as part of a "literary stabilization," it can bring relative order at an unsettling historical conjuncture.

Among literary intellectuals of the left, A. C. Jordan is exceptional for his time. While Mphahlele and others associated ethnicity with the Ban-tustans, and the *Drum* writers celebrated the cultural hybridity of the city, Jordan, although, as his son Pallo Jordan informs us, not a stranger to Cape Town's District Six where he went to hear Xhosa storytelling (xxii–xxiii), insisted on the resources of vernacular structures of feeling. Like Ngũgĩ wa Thiong'o, Jordan wrote criticism in English and novels and stories in the vernacular (*Kwezo mpindo zeTsitsa* [Along the Bends of the Tsitsa], a book of tales and anecdotes, appeared in Xhosa in 1972). Jordan's work does not, however, display a strict bifurcation along linguistic lines; his versions of Xhosa tales of the supernatural [iintsomi], published after his death as *Tales from Southern Africa* (1973), were written in English, although they are said to evoke "oral tradition."[32] Between 1957 and 1960, as Lecturer in African languages at the University of Cape Town, Jordan wrote a series of twelve short articles under the rubric "Towards an African Literature" for *Africa South,* a quarterly edited in Cape Town and then in exile by Ronald Segal. More than a decade after he himself left South Africa for exile in the United States, Jordan's essays from *Africa South* were published posthumously as *Towards an African Literature: The Emergence of Literary Form in Xhosa* (1973).[33]

The sixth of the pieces, from the October–December 1957 issue of *Africa South* and chapter 6 of *Towards an African Literature,* is headed "Literary Stabilization" and discusses developments in Xhosa literature from the 1860s to the 1880s. As Jordan characterizes it, the period from around 1860 presents a paradoxical situation. Although he does not explicitly remark on it, from what he says, the history of literature runs counter to the main stream of history. On the one hand, "the period immediately succeeding that of the [Christian prophet] Ntsikana's disciples may be regarded as one of literary stabilization amongst the Xhosa-speaking Southern Africans." Later in the same paragraph, though, Jordan writes that "it must be remembered that this was a transitional period in every detail of the people's lives" (Jordan, *Towards* 53). What Jordan writes on literary stabilization is linked inextricably to his litany of the features of that transitional period — which one is tempted to read as an allegory for his own time of writing: an era of intensified racial *baasskap* [supremacy] under Strijdom, followed by the inception of Grand Apartheid, which, signally prefigured in Verwoerd's 1954 speech on Bantu education, made a mockery once and for all of the liberal missionary promise of equal rights for civilized men. It is within this larger frame — of allegory and of miming — that Jordan's analysis of Tiyo

Soga's writings of the 1860s transforms them into a response to the crisis of the 1950s:

While the missionary carried on his work as preacher and teacher, the soldier carried on with his own mission of conquest. While the missionary preached "peace on earth and goodwill towards men," the wars of dispossession were working towards a climax. The people had seen the disastrous effects of the Nongqawuse (Cattle-killing) Episode, which had impoverished them and driven thousands of their sons and daughters to seek work amongst their white conquerors; and the effects of the master-and-servant relationship between white and black were beginning to be keenly felt. Those who had accepted the teachings of the missionaries were no longer blindly optimistic about the motives of the white man. All this, and more, is reflected in the writings of the sixties to eighties of the last century. (Jordan, *Towards* 54)

The thread connecting Jordan and Soga is the impulse, on the part of one who has absorbed the culture of another, to harness the resources of his own cultural formation. In order to bring out the contradictions faced by Soga and other converts of his time, Jordan carefully balances a series of contrasting figures: the "preacher and teacher" versus the "soldier"; the "missionary" versus the "war of dispossession"; the "missionaries" versus the "white man." By the end of this series, a contrast between the entities in these pairs is no longer tenable, for "the effects of the master-and-servant relationship between black and white [are] beginning to be keenly felt." This relationship operates a synecdoche whereby the "missionary" is figured as part of a whole called "the white man." Under such circumstances, it is impossible simply to "accept the teachings of the missionaries" or to take at face value their preaching of "peace on earth and goodwill towards men." The words of the preacher and teacher are hopelessly contaminated and overdetermined by the racial political economy violently crystalizing around them (the catastrophic mass killing of cattle among the Xhosa in 1856–57, a step in fulfilling a millenarian prophecy predicting the resurrection of the ancestors and the dead cattle and a restoration of well-being in the country, was in part a response to the dislocations it had brought about).[34] Missionary Christianity, in short, is unmasked as colonial and capitalist ideology. Its ethics of peace and goodwill can no longer be credited as before. To remain silent and unthinking is to collude with the master in one's own enforced servitude. In 1950s, as in the 1860s, an alternative has to be found to overcome this troubling complicity.

JORDAN AND SOGA

Jordan finds an alternative in one of a series of essays written by Tiyo Soga (1829–71) between August 1862 and October 1864 for *Indaba,* a newspaper published at Lovedale, in which three-quarters of the articles were in Xhosa and the rest in English. The first black South African to be ordained as a Christian minister, Soga helped to render the Bible into Xhosa. He is best known for his Xhosa translation of part one of the *Pilgrim's Progress,* an influential event in the early history of vernacular written literature in Southern Africa (Jordan, *Towards* 53–54). Soga's essays, however, make a more immediate response to the social and political developments of the time and thus demand a careful consideration of the complex interrelationship between the history of literature, political history, and social history: "The essay of this period was . . . serious and didactic. Soga's essays reflect the social changes of the time very clearly" (Jordan, *Towards* 54).[35] Their mode of writing, situated between reportage and instruction, in the play of the empirical and transcendental, is integral to their ability to be read as lessons at Jordan's time of writing — or, for that matter, at any other time of writing.

It is in the course of this discussion that Jordan introduces the concept of ubuntu; or, more precisely, its *loss:* "[Soga's] essay on 'The Believers and the Pagans' . . . shows that the gulf is widening between the converted and the pagan. The converted has lost ubuntu [generosity, respect for man irrespective of position]. The pagan can no longer expect hospitality amongst the Christians. Soga gives an instance of a pagan traveller who spent a cold night in the open veld because none of the Christians in the village would admit him into their homes" (Jordan, *Towards* 55).

The first thing to note is that the word *ubuntu* does not occur in Soga's essay, "Amakholwa Namaqaba" (October 1864).[36] For Jordan to write of a loss of ubuntu is thus to translate and to generalize Soga's observations on the Christian converts' "lack of hospitality" [ukuvimba] toward those who remain outside the fold (the original title of Soga's essay was "Amakolwa na-MaXhosa angaphandle"). According to Mc-Laren, in Xhosa the transitive verb *-vimba* can mean to shut up, to store away, to be stingy toward, to refuse, to grudge. In Zulu, according to Doke et al., -*vimba,* which is a synonym of -*vala,* the word more commonly used in Xhosa, has a range of meanings: to close, to block up, to stop, to bar, to plug, to cork, to prevent. In Xhosa -*vimba* extends this closing and blocking up to relations between human beings. *Ukuvimba* might be translated as "closedness," even, in a psychoanalytic sense, as foreclosure: a rejection of an idea by the ego that is both intellectual and affective (see Spivak, *Critique* 4). This is the sense in which Soga's ukuvimba can be understood as a "lack of hospitality." The doors of the convert's house remain barred to the pagan, a state of "outsiderhood" made literal by his being forced to seek shelter outside [phandle]. The empirical and the transcendental mirror each other as the tale becomes an allegory of closedness, of a lack of hospitality, and of a loss of ubuntu. In the context of Soga's essay, ukuvimba is an attitude specifically toward the traveler or stranger [umhambi]. This makes of ubuntu a relation to the stranger, to the one not one's own, to the one not *of* one's own, to the one who has come to be treated as one not one's own. Hospitality is called for when the ties that make an other one's own do not exist or have fallen away. Hospitality is a way of owning—in a limited sense, through artifice of convention—the one who is not one's own, the one through whom one owns oneself and becomes who one is.

Although not out of the ordinary,[37] Jordan's "translation" is a far-reaching one. Ubuntu is no longer merely what is expected of people within a community toward members of that community but is what takes place between strangers. If ubuntu is commonly understood as *umuntu ngumuntu ngabantu* or as *umuntu ngumuntu ngabanye,* in the context of hospitality and the relation to the stranger, one must, in effect, speak of an attainment of human-being through an other not one's own. One's human-being is folded together with the other, the human-being of the other; and that other is the stranger. That is why ubuntu is, in a fundamental sense, hospitality. The quasi-apartheid that divides the amaXhosa, and denies the pagan a place to sleep among the believers, can be overcome by acknowledging a complicity, a folded-togetherness of human-being. In the most basic sense, ethics is a relation to the other. Ubuntu is an ethics of human reciprocity that shows that there is no ethics that is not also against apartheid. To identify a loss of ubuntu is thus to identify the evil, the untruth even, of apartheid in all its forms.

The power of Jordan's essay lies in locating, in the vernacular culture of the Xhosa converts, both a tendency toward apartheid and the antidote to it. Soga's fight is not reducible to what Attwell describes as his "intimate enmity" with his white missionary brethren.[38] Jordan's essay is more than a fable for the apartheid "host"; "Christians" is an unstable metonymy joining the "missionary," the synecdoche for the "white man," and the African convert, with Soga occupying both positions. Soga called on his readers to "examine yourselves" (176). Responsibility for apartheid, in a general sense, is assumed within the vernacular formation in order to propose, from within it, a more far-reaching countertendency. This acknowledgment is what has made ubuntu, in Tutu's theology and in the rulings of the Constitutional Court, a powerful counter to apartheid in the narrow sense as well as a compelling alternative to unmodified missionary Christianity.

Ubuntu operates a certain dispropriation. If set out in terms from Levinas (*Otherwise* 99–129; see also Keenan 19–23), as an ethics of responsibility, ubuntu captures how the relation to the other is prior to the selfhood of the self, how that relation is a condition of possibility for the selfhood of the self. One becomes who one is in responding to, and for, the other. A destabilization of identity, this dispropriation is also what makes possible any relative stability of identity. The syntax of ubuntu reveals such dispropriation at work. As I show in greater detail elsewhere ("Reading Lessons" 11), the phrase *umuntu ngumuntu ngabantu,* which, as the Truth Commission's report shows, is regularly taken as exemplary (*Truth* 1:127; also see Mbeki, "Culture" 259; Jabavu 69), operates according to a synecdoche. *Abantu,* the term on which the *umuntu*-ness of umuntu is supposed to depend, is, as the plural form of umuntu, itself dependent for its identity and propriety on umuntu. Abantu is not a given; it depends on an otherness of umuntu that divides it from inside. The communitarian interpretations of ubuntu abounding today thus presuppose what the formulation itself guards against taking as given: the community, the nation, et cetera.[39] Attending to the syntax as a whole of the formulation and its variants — instead of merely glossing ubuntu as "generosity, respect for man irrespective of position," humanity, respect for human dignity, the subordination of individual to collective — brings ubuntu to life as an ethics of responsibility standing watch over one-sided interpretation.

If such one-sided interpretation is unavoidable in practice, the question remains: What safeguards exist for the forming of alternative interpretations? Ubuntu has within it the ability to alter itself—as can be gauged from the fact that Jordan's essay juxtaposes "literary stabilization" with a comprehensive "transitional period." The stabilization offered by ubuntu is powerful but provisional; it cannot be appropriated with finality because it is responsibility, not rule. The other is prior to the self, and the self comes into being in a response to and for the other. Formalizing ubuntu as a communitarian alternative to human rights brings a provisional stability during a transitional phase. However, it is ubuntu's essential dispropriation—of *umuntu* and *abantu*—that works against any *single* formalization of human-being acquiring permanence as a basis for ethics and politics.

When articulations of ubuntu link ontology and temporality, as is apparent when a "loss of ubuntu" is lamented and when a recovery of ubuntu (rather than the pursuit of a program of "victimization") is thought to ensure national reconciliation and nation-building, dispropriation also affects the identity of the new nation as historical event. When the identity of the nation as an entity existing in time is no longer a given, what it means to remember or to forget is, in turn, altered. When the lament of a loss of ubuntu, with the tacit claim that it did once exist, is employed to bring provisional stability in the midst of transition, we can, as I have indicated, speak of invented memory and of invented cultural memory. It is precisely this element of invention, though, that, along with its active acknowledgment, has the potential to bring a dimension of responsibility to the management of transition. When memory of the past guides what is to be done now, ubuntu stands as an example of how, when that past is understood as invented, it can yield a structure of ongoing responsibility rather than a remedy meant to work once and for all.

The temporal dimension of ubuntu is apparent in Soga's formulation of the problem of hospitality, which is informed by the temporality of conversion. This conversion is a two-way process. On the one hand, Soga appeals to the New Testament to call for hospitality among the believers. He quotes, or rather translates, from Paul's epistle to the Hebrews: "Do not be forgetful to entertain strangers" [Imbuko yabasemzini ningayilibali] (Hebrews 13:2; qtd. in Soga 177). This reference to the earliest beginnings of Christian missionary work reinforces the association of the figure of the traveler [umhambi] with figures of strangeness or foreignness [abasemzini]. The reader is left to complete the rest of the verse, which reads: "for thereby some have entertained angels unawares" (Hebrews 13:2). On the other hand, Soga signs his essays in *Indaba* as "Unonjiba waseluHlangeni," which can be translated as "an enthusiastic enquirer into cultural origins" (Soga 150).[40] By linking the New Testament to a critique of ukuvimba, he also, so to speak, indigenizes Christian teaching. Jordan's "translation" of Soga may thus be read as a re-indigenization of Soga, even as a release of something that lies silent in Soga's text.

The figure of the "angel" in the rest of the verse from Hebrews marks the place of a transcendent alterity from which the figure of the stranger derives its power to provoke responsibility and thereby to condition the selfhood of the believer.[41] Ubuntu, notably in the interpretation given to it by Tutu, according to which human beings accrue dignity by virtue of being made in the image of God, also sets to work this play of the transcendent and the contingent. In Soga's essay, the stranger is also "prior" to the Christian self in the sense that he, being of the *amaqaba,* is the one closer to vernacular practice. This is the complex temporality of the responsibility taken up by the vernacular intellectual.

Whatever emphasis one lends to these reciprocal but uneven processes, it is important to note that what is being asserted — particularly in the case of Jordan, who is working out of Soga's missionary text — is something that emerges from the passage of conversion (Mphahlele's remarks about Négritude and assimilation apply). It is this irreversible and perhaps inevitable passage that produces the social division and alienation, the closedness or foreclosure [ukuvimba], that calls forth the necessity of hospitality toward the stranger, the nonforeclosure of his humanity, which Jordan, in turn, translates and generalizes as ubuntu. Each exists in the future perfect. There will have been, if division had not occurred, a state of hospitality, of ubuntu. This is, in a fundamental sense, invented memory, invented cultural memory, for there has always been division of some kind. If there had not been, there would be no calls for ubuntu, no lament for the loss of ubuntu — a lament effectively prior to ubuntu as a formulation of human-being, and one that generates that which it proclaims is lost but once prevailed. Human-being emerges in the articulation of the sense of its loss. Memory is also promise (Derrida, *Memoires* 138). All else—human dignity, community, and so forth—is an elaboration on what has been lost.

The invention of memory in the cause of reconciliation is, in the texts of Jordan and Soga that we are reading, inextricably bound up with the figure of the stranger who is denied hospitality and to whom hospitality is due. Here the ethical is bound up with remembering or, more precisely, un-forgetting. The fragment from Hebrews with which Soga ends his essay has as its last word an injunction not to forget: "*ningayili-bali*" [do not be forgetful]. "It must be remembered," Jordan writes (*Towards* 53). If the disasters of the past are to be avoided, the figure of the stranger must be continually reinvented. By linking ubuntu to hospitality, Jordan reminds us that there will always be an (and another) outsider who must be remembered, or not forgotten, who calls into question the existence of the collectivity. The stranger is at once possibility and risk.[42] Without forgetting the ethno-racial foreclosures that constrained its formulation and setting to work, this is also the admonition that N.P. van Wyk Louw attempted to make with volkskritiek and voortbestaan in geregtigheid.

What I have set out is not simply the philosophical play of ontology and its temporality. Ubuntu is rendered historical when it is connected to hospitality. The task of the intellectual is to be an advocate for the figure of the stranger—to insist on responsibility for the stranger as constitutive of collectivity itself. For the intellectual, the figure of the stranger is always specific or demands some specification: for Soga, the amaqaba or *amangaphandle;* for Jordan, the allegorical place left open for the reader to specify stranger and host. Soga's unreceived African, who a century later is also the figure at the limit of Louw's ethics, is today the *amakwerekwere,* the target of post-apartheid xenophobia and the subject of critical artistic work.[43]

In its setting to work, responsibility involves the play of the empirical and the quasi-transcendental, the constant oscillation of historical "transition" and "literary stabilization." Beyond the polemic over Négritude and vernacular culture, the occupation with the stranger and hospitality in A. C. Jordan's translation of Tiyo Soga complements, in the intellectual and literary history of the 1950s, the alterity of the figure of the dead one that, in Bloke Modisane's *Blame Me on History,* provides the basic structure of address for the anti-apartheid narrative. With Breyten Breytenbach and Steve Biko, however, the intimacy with the oppressive other that stands in the way of generalizing responsibility in foldedness with the other is largely unmitigated by an addressee figured as receptive to the intellectual's message — or, as Jordan's "allegory" suggests, a stranger / host willing to give / accept the hospitality that gives each party an identity.

chapter 4

prison writing

Suid-Afrikanerskap is 'n wordingsproses. Suid-Afrikanerskap loop deur die afbreek van apartheid en die help bou aan die groot Andersmaak. Ons máák mekaar.

[South-Africanhood is a process of becoming. South-Africanhood passes through a breaking down of apartheid and a helping to build the great Other-making. We *make* each other.]

—BREYTEN BREYTENBACH, "Fragmente van 'n groeiende gewaarwees"

As an Afrikaans poet and opponent of apartheid imprisoned on a charge of terrorism, Breyten Breytenbach occupies a liminal position: that of filiation, through language and ethnic origin, with ruling Afrikanerdom and white rule; and, as a consequence of embracing the anti-apartheid struggle and being jailed, that of a victim of apartheid's brutality. His autobiographical writings make their project the tracking of the divergent yet interrelated complicity in apartheid of "perpetrator" and "victim." In "A Note on the Relationship between Detainee and Interrogator," the second of six notes appended to his prison memoir, *The True Confessions of an Albino Terrorist* (1984), Breytenbach sets out the implications of this relationship for each of the parties. For the interrogator, there is, on the one hand, "the struggle for domination." This is "justified in terms of the exigencies of his job" (*True Confessions*

341/310).[1] On the other hand, "there is the effort to destroy," which Breytenbach separates from any simple justification in terms of professional exigencies. In an effort to explain that effort to destroy, he embarks on a series of speculations. These move, at least provisionally, from an indeterminate dynamics — "because the opposing forces are irreconcilable" — to inherent human pathology — "because there is the pathological human curiosity for killing, for altering permanently, or just 'to see'" — to a series of propositions that help to explain, from the perspective of the interrogator, how his intimacy with the prisoner can explode into violence:

because the dismantlement has revealed [a] *vis-à-vis,* a brother-I, a mirror-image or only a miserable human-conditioned pile of flesh and faeces which is unbearable and needs to be done away with; there is thus already the tendency to identify with the other (and the roles can be inverted) and the blind desire to force a solution to and a resolution of the irreconcilable contradictions — precisely because you cannot accept the (self)-image revealed to you, nor the knowledge that never the twain shall meet. (*True Confessions* 341)

Breytenbach's speculations progress from competing metaphysics of force and of human nature, to an account of human relationality. It is not simply that the interrogator destroys because opposing forces exist or because, like all human beings, he is curious to kill, alter, or "'see.'" Rather, it is because, in a situation of "opposing forces [that] are irreconcilable" and of "irreducible contradictions," the basic foldedness of human-being with the other is glimpsed but at once disavowed.

If, as Elaine Scarry proposes in *The Body in Pain,* torture brings about the "unmaking" of the victim's world, for Breytenbach the interrogation room consumes *all* of those involved. Identifying with the prisoner, the interrogator is faced with his own destruction. The "dismantlement" wrought by interrogation is, as Breytenbach sees it, mutual. His first step is to dramatize it from the side of the interrogator ("you"), for whom there can be no abstract, unvalenced reciprocity with the detainee. The terms in the reciprocal series — "[a] *vis-à-vis,* a brother-I, a mirror-image" — are tenuously united by hyphens that also disjoin them. These pragmatic signs establish a fragile fraternity and a tenuous specular correspondence. The image that comes to the interrogator is not, as far as he is concerned, his own. It is not an image of what he wishes to be. To identify with the prisoner is to identify oneself with, and as, "a miserable human-conditioned pile of flesh and faeces." For the interrogator, who is or is meant to be master of the situation, this dispropriating image, which unmakes *his* world, "is unbearable and needs to be done away with."

The other side of sensing a "brother-I" is a violent mimetic fraternity; as Breytenbach tells his interlocutor: "However strange it may sound, Mr Eye, I am convinced that some of the people they have killed in detention probably died when the interrogator was in a paroxysm of unresolved frustrations, even that the interrogator killed in an awkward expression of love and sympathy for a fellow human being" (*True Confessions* 50). Threatening to usurp one's place, the other becomes "a miserable human-conditioned pile of flesh and faeces," not in the sense of a shared and poignant humanity, but as what, presenting oneself with what one does not wish to be, "needs to be done away with." Like the instructions made public before the Truth and Reconciliation Commission that told the hit squads to eliminate or remove [elimineer, verwyder] anti-apartheid activists, "do away with" is open-ended in its incitement to violence (Tutu 240–41). The difference is that, according to Breytenbach, in the interrogation room, the interrogator is not executing an exceptional and secret instruction but playing out a scene that, in microcosm, represents apartheid in its essential traits.

Breytenbach's staging of interrogator and prisoner elaborates themes introduced in Afrikaans literature by N. P. van Wyk Louw in his poem "Die hond van God" [The Hound of God] (1941) and his dialogue "Heerser en Humanis" [Ruler and Humanist] (1947). In those works, personae of Inquisitor, and totalitarian ruler and prisoner, respectively, provoke questions into the meaning of human-being under theological and political strictures: "They call the instrument in my hands cruel, / inhuman; — because I cut through their human-being [mens-wees] / to seek the hidden godliness that I know to be inside" (*Versamelde gedigte* 146); "RULER: . . . I am man [die mens] in his emergence as ruler-animal, intelligent beast of prey. . . . I am MAN. . . . PRISONER: I am *man* [die mens], plain ordinary man . . . not man-as-animal and also not man-as-god. Composite, problematic man" (*Versamelde prosa* 1:512–15).

The questioning into human-being undertaken by Breytenbach, however, engages the specificities of apartheid. As J. M. Coetzee shows in his reading of Geoffrey Cronjé, apartheid may be understood as the legislation (as an economic and political system) of an aversion mediated by the black body apprehended metonymically as a sign of filth and contagion, and invested with intense but disavowed desire. Explained sociohistorically, as can be gauged from the Carnegie Report of 1932 and from the writings of Cronjé, a disavowal of a certain mirror-image led working-class Whites, competing with black workers with whom they lived side by side in urban slums, to enter the devil's pact of apartheid: economic privilege for the denial of the humanity of the other and hence of oneself.

The enforced separation of apartheid, which at least for Blacks could never achieve any essential apartness because of white domination and the oppressive intimacy of the white ruler,[2] is played out intensively in the place of interrogation. There the strict division of roles is undermined by the intimacy required by the interrogator, who then disavows the inevitable identification with the prisoner that results. Except in the case of Breytenbach, the body and the mind are not black, but those of an Afrikaans poet. By being a prisoner and by undergoing the specific treatment he describes, Breytenbach is able to *approximate,* in small part, the treatment undergone by Blacks under apartheid.[3] Under those conditions, he too finds himself a disavowed "brother-I."

Although interrogation is a "ritual" with "preordained roles," "the situation and the steps and the rules are always personalized and localized and in no way can the players be exonerated from their responsibilities" (*True Confessions* 341). This is especially important from the perspective of the prisoner, who, rather than simply being met with a denial of human foldedness, is faced with a perversion of that foldedness in the form of complicity in his own destruction. And this self-destructive collaboration takes place, not as an unwillingness to recognize one's "mirror-image" in the interrogator, but rather in a betrayal of solidarity—"the prisoner will end up confessing" (*True Confessions* 343)— with opponents of the system that prescribes this denial. It thus becomes, ultimately, a collaboration in this denial: "The self-disgust of the prisoner comes from the alienation he has been brought to. That in which he participated (because the mortification lies in that he is forced to participate in his own undoing) will play havoc with his conception of himself and it will forever modulate his contact with other people" (*True Confessions* 343).

This observation is borne out by the testimony of anti-apartheid activists before the Truth Commission. The specific pressures that force the prisoner to collaborate in his or her own "undoing," are, as I propose in chapter 5, one reason why the oppressive intimacy of the interrogation room is an imaginary site par excellence of the intellectual's negotiation of complicity — at once political and psychic — in apartheid. It is where one is brought to answer for one's convictions. The difference was that, in the case of Steve Biko, as it emerges from the inquiries into his death, the negotiation did not take place in the realm of the imagination alone, and his small "resistance" to participating in the denial of his "dignity" provoked a violent and murderous explosion by his interrogators.

Described in an appendix to *The True Confessions of an Albino Terrorist*, the relationship between detainee and interrogator functions as an allegory for the book as a whole, and for apartheid and the ways in which it perverts human relatedness. Behind Breytenbach's opposition to apartheid and his involvement in the clandestine resistance organization known as Okhela lies a philosophy, or a set of philosophical traits, which runs counter to the setting of human beings apart and the imposition of apartness on what is essentially joined. This philosophy is rigorous in its refusal simply to counter apartness with community. Breytenbach eschews "Liberalism" and speaks of what is "hazardous and dangerous." Given a humanist and teleological rendering, a fragment of the pre-Socratic thinker Anaximander provides Breytenbach with an expression of an original "separation" between human-being and a Being that is "boundless": "Man suffers because of his separation from the boundless, Anaximander said." Apartheid enforces separation, preventing a "liv[ing] towards . . . a greater, even metaphysical integration," and by denying the "sense of brotherhood" that, in the sphere of the social, gives meaning to it: "If there is a life force, Apartheid goes against it. Surely what we live towards is a greater, even metaphysical integration, however hazardous and dangerous. And just as surely we are inspired to do so by a profound sense of brotherhood" (*True Confessions* 74).[4]

Broaching the relationship between Being and beings, Breytenbach's philosophy of joinedness counters theological justifications of apartheid. The meaning of the note on the detainee and interrogator becomes clear as an allegory of apartheid: "Apartheid is a mutation of *power* and *greed*. No religion can justify it, except that warped doctrine the Afrikaners have fashioned from their desert faith. Their god is a cruel, White interrogator" (*True Confessions* 74). The Afrikaners worship a god who, like the interrogator, although possessed of a "profound sense of brotherhood," "goes against . . . a greater, even metaphysical integration." In the fragment from Anaximander, the words that "suffers" and "separation" appear to translate are *didonai diken* and *adikia*. Reading Heidegger's "The Anaximander Fragment" (1946) in *Specters of Marx* (23–29), Derrida emphasizes adikia as temporal anachrony: Hamlet's "time is out of joint." *Dikē,* of which adikia is an absence, is commonly translated as "justice." For Derrida, adikia is an expression of injustice as out-of-jointness and thus also of the possibility of justice: *didonai diken . . . tes adikias.*[5] Although not yielding a thinking of out-of-jointness as possibility of justice, some of the larger implications of Breytenbach's use of Anaximander emerge from this interpretive history. *The True Confessions of an Albino Terrorist* and Breytenbach's other writings on apartheid, particularly where hybridity is introduced as a counterconcept, make clear that justice can be realized only in the overcoming of "separation."

From time to time, Breytenbach's *True Confessions* are addressed to a "Mr Investigator," who changes here and there into Mr. I or Mr. Eye, as if to mime, in their self-investigation, the detainee's address to the interrogator, the one for whom one writes only to have one's "confession" torn up. Interrogator and investigator can fuse: "Mr Interrogator — sorry, Mr Investigator" (*True Confessions* 101). The work is a full-scale dramatization of the difficulty of separating other from persecutor, the basic foldedness of human-being from the oppressive presence of the other. Its wish is for an addressee who will affirm the sense of brotherhood that possesses him and, although the path is "dangerous and hazardous," will work with the one confessing toward an "integration" that is social and "even metaphysical."

For Breytenbach the path is blocked not only by the interrogator but by his brother-Afrikaner's stifling fraternity — which in *Giving Offense: Essays on Censorship* (1996) J. M. Coetzee associates with the mimetic rivalry in the writer's contest with the censor. In Breytenbach's own case, brother and "interrogator" literally merge. Not only would his exchanges with his interrogators have taken place in Afrikaans,[6] but his brother Jan, a commanding officer in the South African Army in its operations in Angola, was regarded as "an Afrikaner hero" (*True Confessions* 311). In the closed circuit in which he addresses himself, as he speaks the first version of *The True Confessions of an Albino Terrorist* into a tape recorder, he cannot be sure that he is not also addressing the interrogator or the censor, even though it is his wife who will read it first and correct it. Producing a text in an English that carries the echo of Afrikaans (see Coetzee, "Poet" 75) and is laced with transliterated French is a way of getting around these figures and of finding another reader.

It is within this fractured frame of address that *The True Confessions of an Albino Terrorist* marks out the basis of its understanding of apartheid and the responsibility-in-complicity and call for justice that emerge from it for the intellectual. In the years preceding Breytenbach's imprisonment, this involved negotiating a distance from the political legacy of N. P. van Wyk Louw: from lojale verset and voortbestaan in geregtigheid and from the task of attaining for the Afrikaner volk an aparte bestaan. We observe this at Breytenbach's 1975 trial and in the lecture he delivered at the University of Cape Town Summer School in 1973, which characterizes Afrikaners as a *bastervolk*. This hint or opening beyond a racial hybridity and Afrikaner-Coloured fraternity, which radicalizes Louw's overture to "Bruinmense" by detaching it from an ethnic essentialism in which the nature of *Afrikanerskap* is largely unquestioned, is elaborated in Breytenbach's more recent prose works. His self-declared *Suid-Afrikanerskap,* an alternative to the brittle "Afrikanerskap" of Louw and others, counters a separatist Afrikanerdom and its possessiveness over the Afrikaans language.

All of this comes to a head with Breytenbach's imprisonment, during which he turned away from Afrikaans and toward English, a move that, although without the permanence of Kenyan novelist Ngũgĩ wa Thiong'o's turn to Gĩkũyũ after being detained, is an act of refusing to be complicitous in the politics of a nationalist (and neo-colonialist) appropriation of national culture. In the case of both writers, we in turn observe a mimetic rivalry involving the ruler of the country. As J. M. Coetzee argues, in the case of Breytenbach, the rival is B. J. Vorster (*Giving* 215–18). For Ngũgĩ, the figure in question is Jomo Kenyatta. Here the shape of the exchange between the figure of writer/speaker and reader/interlocutor is formative of the act of resistance and in the negotiation of a complicity with the "interrogator" who cannot be wished away—for that complicity is no longer merely social and political but has become a game played and replayed in the psyche of the writer.

To me what matters is a quest for, an opening up toward a society in which *each and every one of us* may have his rightful share, within which we may accept responsibility for each other *on an equal footing.* . . . *That's* my loyalty. *That* is the substance of my South Africanhood.

— BREYTEN BREYTENBACH, *A Season in Paradise*

Hardly five years after the death of N. P. van Wyk Louw on 18 June 1970, the fight over his intellectual legacy began. Ostensibly a squabble over the dynamics and bounds of principled Afrikaner dissent, the perplexed discussion was, ultimately, about the meaning and fate of the human in apartheid South Africa. If, as I have been arguing, it is the task of the intellectual to affirm a basic human foldedness, and Louw's nationalism in essence embodied a restricted ethnic loyalty, Breytenbach's at times parodic reinscription of Louw's cultural-political vocabulary against apartheid was a deepening of intellectual responsibility in the name of openness to otherness and the other. The contestation of Louw's legacy, in which his was one intervention, culminated at Breytenbach's summary trial for terrorism of 21–27 November 1975.

With his publishing debut in 1964, Breytenbach was widely regarded as a bringer of renewal to Afrikaans poetry — and even as Louw's poetic heir (Galloway 34–37; see also Kannemeyer, *Geskiedenis* 2:471). His first collection of poems, *Die Ysterkoei moet sweet* [The Iron Cow Must Sweat], was awarded the APB-Prize. Louw, as chief adjudicator, observed that "it is not everyday — well, not every year or five years — that one encounters in Afrikaans good *and* new poetry." Louw heard in Breytenbach's poems "a sound almost completely its own" ("APB-Prys" 2).

Breytenbach had lived in Paris since 1961, where he had married a Vietnamese woman, Yolande Ngo Thi Hoang Lien.[7] Under the then-existing race laws, they would not have been allowed to live in South Africa. Yolande was denied a visa in 1964 when Breytenbach was awarded the APB-Prize, and the award ceremony had to be held at a restaurant in Paris the following year (Galloway 43). In 1973, however, the Afrikaner establishment attempted to rehabilitate the poet and allowed him and Yolande to come to South Africa for a ninety-day visit, during which he delivered his jaundiced "A View from Outside" (*Season in Paradise* 151–60) at the UCT Summer School. Breytenbach next came to South Africa in 1975. Bearing a false passport, he arrived on a clandestine mission to establish Okhela, whose aim was to build white support for the African National Congress and other liberation movements and to define the role of Whites in the black-led anti-apartheid struggle (*True Confessions* 389–90).[8] Agents of BOSS (Bureau of State Security), who had watched him from the outset, arrested him as he tried to leave the country. Breytenbach was charged with terrorism and, in exchange for a promise of leniency that was never kept, pleaded guilty.[9]

Before being sentenced, having been asked to do so by the security police, Breytenbach requested that he be permitted to make a statement to the court: "I do not want to make a political speech. It is about the circumstances of my life and will thus be an attempt at a confession of existence [bestaansbelydenis] and not a confession of faith [geloofs-belydenis]" (qtd. in Viviers 54).[10] In the light of the deal he thought he had made and the fact that the writing of his statement was stage-managed by the state, Breytenbach's "confession" provides a good example of the way in which Louw's name and thinking had come to operate in Afrikaans public discourse.[11] By the mid-seventies, the principle of lojale verset had, by and large, become a means for the Afrikaner establishment to contain and to regulate dissidence. There is no doubt that, as Giliomee says, Louw's thinking strongly influenced Afrikaner *verligtes*.[12] Nevertheless, not even verligtes were prepared to compromise the voortbestaan of the Afrikaner volk in its existing form, and they continued to put loyalty to their own before fidelity to an ideal of justice to the other.

The verligte newspaper editor Willem de Klerk (who claims to have invented the terms *verligte* and *verkrampte* ["Concepts" 520]) advocated the redemption of Breytenbach, "the prodigal son." He typifies attempts by the establishment at that time to contain the effects of a more radicalized lojale verset. Breytenbach's "confession [of existence]," according to De Klerk, "was something of a return to his place and his blood." The poet spoke, it is true, of the pain of exile and of the agony of disconnection from the language in which he wrote. Instead of "denationalizing" himself, De Klerk went on; the loyal Afrikaner retains his "connectedness with the volk" [volksverbondenheid], and takes his quarrel to his people: "As long as you cross swords with your people in love and respect, with pity almost, *like Van Wyk Louw,* you will remain standing and deliver service. But if you turn away and lash out behind on your way out as you yourself walk away from the fold you get lost in a wilderness" ("Breyten kan"; partially qtd. in Galloway 174–75; my emphasis). As I observed in chapter 2, by the 1980s, perhaps partly as a result of Breytenbach's trial and imprisonment, lojale verset — and the example of Louw — had lost most of its credibility among Afrikaners opposed to minority rule, despite attempts by some to reread Louw's works differently.

Breytenbach opens his "confession of existence" with paradox: "In my heart, Your Honour, the motivation for my actions was always love for my country. It is perhaps paradoxical, but for me it was about the continued existence of our volk [voortbestaan van ons volk], a continued existence with justice [voortbestaan met regverdigheid] *as Van Wyk Louw expressed it,* about the content and quality of our civilization" (qtd. in Viviers 58; my emphasis). In his "confession," Breytenbach departs from an attitude of simple fidelity to the volk and obedience to the laws of the country. His stand of civil disobedience recalls the court address of Nelson Mandela some thirteen years before, which invoked "civilization" in declaring respect for the law itself (*No Easy Walk* 125–61; see also Derrida, "Laws"). Breytenbach's departures from simple patriotism take place in the name of justice. In the process, he brings into dialogue Louw's two major dicta, insisting that lojale verset and voortbestaan in geregtigheid cannot be properly understood without each other and that neither can be attained unless the restricted project of securing an aparte bestaan for the Afrikaner volk is abandoned. The justice he advocates involves responsibility before the other. Breytenbach attempts to detach voortbestaan in geregtigheid from apartheid by formulating an account of human-being that counters its enforced separation with essential joinedness and hybridity — or, as he terms it in later writings, "other-making."

In declaring allegiance to the law itself and to justice as responsibility before the other, Breytenbach modified Louw's words in two ways. Although both *regverdigheid* and *geregtigheid* can be translated as *justice* or *righteousness,* a distinction can be made between *geregtigheid,* which is usually used in a transcendental sense, and *regverdigheid,* which is also practical and can be translated as *fairness.* Whereas Geoffrey Cronjé projected a *Regverdige rasse-apartheid* and made no bones about white prerogative, Louw used the word *geregtigheid* in his formulation in "Kultuur en krisis" (1952) in a way that rendered the located historical abiding of the volk transcendent and dissimulated its arrogation of historical prerogative. The use of the word *regverdigheid* is Breytenbach's first point of divergence. His second is in the preposition *met* [with], which replaces, and even displaces, Louw's *in* [in]. "A volk," Louw wrote, that "does everything it can in order to remain in existence [bly voortbestaan] . . . comes before the last temptation: to believe that mere continued existence [blote voortbestaan] is preferable to *continued existence in justice* [voortbestaan in geregtigheid]" (*Versamelde prosa* 1:462). With Breytenbach the notion that the continued existence [voortbestaan] of the Afrikaner could ever be one that is, in any transcendental sense, "in justice" [in geregtigheid] has been abandoned. All that is left is a justice or righteousness [regverdigheid] that can be brought to continued existence, added to it — something foreign and unassimilated. Yet, in this inaccurately rendered or badly recalled dictum (the address was written in prison while Breytenbach awaited sentencing) lie the seeds of future justice — because, in Breytenbach, the schism between Afrikaner survival and justice is made manifest.[13] The difference is that the new survival is no longer one in which the continued existence [voortbestaan] of the Afrikaner *as Afrikaner* is guaranteed. A "South Africa" emerges from the fissures left by the credo's disintegration, promising the "integration" he refers to when he invokes Anaximander in *The True Confessions of an Albino Terrorist*. "I believed that my actions were not directed against South Africa," Breytenbach continued, "but against what I regarded as injustices [onregverdighede]" (qtd. in Viviers 58).

Opposed to "injustices," this loyalty to the law itself forms part of a thinking of human-being. Its place in this "humanism" becomes evident when Breytenbach's courtroom invocation of "South Africa" against "injustices" is read alongside the address he gave two years before. Rapidly becoming a touchstone for a younger generation of Afrikaans intellectuals, "A View from the Outside" ['n Blik van buite] addressed participants, numbering several hundred, in an extramural seminar on the *Sestigers*.[14] Louw's cultural-political vocabulary was, as it would be at his trial, an uneasy point of departure,[15] as Breytenbach addressed directly the implication of Afrikaner ethnic identity in apartheid and, taking a cue from Black Consciousness, the role of white Afrikaners in the anti-apartheid struggle: "to work for the transformation of my own community" (*Season* 154). He begins by distinguishing his filiations from the restricted ones of lojale verset:

I am biased [Ek is partydig]. I take sides. Because to me what is at stake is the establishment of liveable conditions in our community. Because to me what matters is a quest for, an opening up toward a society [samelewing] in which *each and every one of us* may have his rightful share, within which we may accept responsibility for each other *on an equal footing*. Because, to me, it's a question of combating those institutions and edifices and myths and prejudices and untruths and idiocy and greed and self-destructive urges and common [English in original] stupidity which render such a society impossible. *That's* my loyalty. *That* is the substance of my South Africanhood [Suid-Afrikanerskap]. (*Season* 153, trans. modified)

Loyalty to one's "South Africanhood" amounts to opposing injustices, to an approximation of geregtigheid. This response before the other, a precondition for justice, is thus a responsibility engaged from within complicity in the deeds of a hegemonic group that acts in the name of an ethnic identity one shares, and in a set of terms that articulates and rationalizes its actions. In his summer school talk, Breytenbach translates Louw's precepts into new political terms and, to some extent, rids them of their transcendental aura. To be truly loyal, it is necessary to be partial, even to take sides. Even more: to be is to be partial, to be made up of parts that do not cohere into a unitary and immutable identity but that only cohere historically and with a provisionality that can ultimately only be preserved with violence. There is no existence without a departure; "South" [Suid] divides and supplements Afrikanerskap (*Afrikaner*hood becomes *African*hood). The Cape Town newspaper *Die Burger* slipped notably, reporting "Suid-Afrikanerskap" as "Afrikanerskap." The audience listened "in dead silence" ("Breyten kyk").[16]

Like Louw in the 1930s, Breytenbach declares allegiance to an ascendant national movement, except that this national movement stands, not for an aparte bestaan, but just for an existence free of the oppressive and exploitative intimacy of white domination. More significantly, unlike Louw, Breytenbach refuses to stop at simple fidelity to a particular volk. For Louw in the 1930s, humanity is fully realized in one's being bound up into a volk [volledige menslikheid binne 'n volksverband] (*Versamelde prosa* 1:9; see also 1:15), a boundness that presupposed, as a bare minimum, a shared language. As we have noted, in spite of reaching toward a more global responsibility in "Volkskritiek" (1939) and elsewhere, "a volk" continued to be only one volk; or, in "Vegparty of polemiek?" (1946), "Kultuur en krisis" (1952), and in the lectures on "Rassevraagstukke" (1952), a set of volkere propagated in its own form. Breytenbach, for his part, envisions a society (*samelewing* is literally a "living-together"),[17] a Suid-Afrikanerskap rather than an Afrikanerskap, from which he and other Afrikaners can draw life, "on an equal footing" with Blacks, as South Africans rather than as Afrikaners. He imagines a community more in accord with the "life force" to which he sees apartheid as opposed. His introduction of the English word *common,* a word heard in colloquial Afrikaans, demonstrates that, although disavowed by purists, an already enlarged community of "Afrikaners" exists. The Afrikaans language, he challenges, has no way of recognizing stupidity while it remains the sole property of a white Afrikaner community. "Afrikaans?" he asks, "Whose Afrikaans?" (*Season* 159).

Breytenbach's is a more expansive version of human-being, in which being an *Afrikaner* means what it says: being African. In his closing sentences, he generalizes the idea that language is the basis for group membership and shared and expanded humanity to include all those who can speak "Afrikaans," a language transformed, in the process, into a language of "humanness" unfettered by what his listeners know by Afrikaans:

Our first dimension is man [die mens] — in his sameness [eendersheid] and in his otherness [andersheid], in his humanness [mensheid]. Where there is something seeking expression, the language will expand where necessary to give expression to that something. . . .

I think that by taking cognizance of the nature of the struggle we are involved in and share, by making that struggle clearer — and even more: by taking a stand based on this knowledge — we expand our humanity [menslikheid] and our language.

Then only will we be freed from the traps of Apartaans [apartheid + Afrikaans = Apartaans], will we speak Afrikaans: one of the many languages of Africa. (*Season* 160)

Language produces (new) human beings as they engage in struggle. Breytenbach's humanism is a materialist one for which language is, as Raymond Williams puts it in *Marxism and Literature,* "practical consciousness" (35). It is not simply, as Lazarus argues, a nostalgia for "the humanism of pre-Nationalist Afrikaner culture" or for "traditional humanist values . . . surviving still in the heartland Afrikaner communities despite the burgeoning hegemony of Nationalism" (177, 176). Stating a precondition for community itself, although its roots are in anti-apartheid nationalist struggle, Breytenbach's formulation goes beyond any "traditional humanist values" in search of what constitutes the human as such. The struggle Breytenbach conceives is for "man" itself. That is why the struggle has to be made "clearer," with its participants "taking cognizance" and hence "expanding their humanity."

The version of human becoming outlined by Breytenbach in the peroration to "A View from the Outside" is a generalization, in positive terms, of his account of how apartheid is essentially tied to Afrikaner ethnic identity formation, and how a more or less generalized bastardy or hybridity [basterskap] can be an alternative:

We are a bastard people [bastervolk] with a bastard language [bastertaal]. Our nature is one of bastardy [basterskap]. It is good and beautiful thus. We should be compost, decomposing to be able to combine again in other forms. Only, we have walked into the trap of the bastard [baster] who has acquired power. In that part of our blood which comes from Europe was the curse of superiority. We wanted to justify [regverdig] our power. And to do that we had to consolidate our supposed tribal identity. We had to fence off, defend, offend. We had to entrench our otherness while retaining at the same time what we had won. We made our otherness the norm, the standard—and the ideal. And because our otherness is maintained *at the expense* of our fellow South Africans—and our South Africanhood [Suid-Afrikaansheid]—we felt threatened. We built walls. Not cities, but city walls. And like all bastards—uncertain of their identity—we began to adhere to the concept of *purity*. That is apartheid. *Apartheid is the law of the bastard.* (*Season* 156; final sentence English in the original)

Breytenbach had gone to the heart of Afrikaner-nationalist disavowal. The headline to the article reporting his lecture in *Die Burger* was "Breyten kyk van buite en sien bastervolk" [Breyten looks from outside and sees bastard volk]. When collective identity is defined in terms of racial purity, as it was for Afrikaners and for Whites under apartheid, bastardy is a threatening assertion. Breytenbach's first move is to set out a historical morphology that will function as an alternative to that embraced by Afrikaner nationalism. In terms of this morphology, the idea of a pure Afrikaner volk and a pure language is an invention, after the fact, by the hybrid [baster] who has attained and seeks to monopolize power (see also *End Papers* 55–56). N. P. van Wyk Louw's deployment of the eternal in "Die ewige trek," where the century [eeu] becomes an eternity [ewig] and the act of tracing [trek] becomes the Great Trek, are related turns of invention. Establishing the bestaansreg of the volk through the quasi-poetic generation of it and other volkere also functions in this way.

Breytenbach's strategy is to debunk these retrospective historical morphologies and to present what they conceal, not simply as a history of bastardy involving both Afrikaner and African (see *End Papers* 46), but as a generalization of bastardy as an alternative to the violence of purist identity formation and apartheid. Although here encompassing Afrikaners, the words "We are a bastard people with a bastard language" could apply to any human group, as could the remark "Our nature [aard] is one of bastardy." If an alternative Afrikaner history is fresh enough in the memory of the racist to be a sore point and to be disavowed — Breytenbach speaks of "the death of the memory" (*Season* 159) — it is also familiar enough to be able to function as exemplary for an essential human foldedness able to counter an apartheid ideology that, as it is allegorized in "A Note on the Relationship between Detainee and Interrogator" (*True Confessions*), maintains the propriety of its otherness at the expense of a shared but disavowed South-Africanness.

Everything turns on an otherness [andersheid] that, rather than being made the norm or ideal — as with Louw's aparte bestaan — names the transformative dimension of human-being, its ability to transform itself and to make itself other. This otherness is what Breytenbach, in more recent texts, such as his post-apartheid memoir *Dog Heart* (1998), calls, alluding to a novel by Jan Rabie, "the great transformation: the *groot andersmaak* [great other-making]" (69). The question that remains, as in the case of Louw and other ethnophilosophers, is whether, in the midst of this generalization of bastardy and of becoming-other, certain historically and locally determinate senses are not privileged. Breytenbach does not advocate, as Louw did, a paternalistic embracing of coloureds — or Bruinmense — as "our people" [ons mense], and in "A View from the Outside," he is not privileging Afrikaans as a language. His allusion to Rabie's *Die Groot Anders-Maak* (1964), a novel that "gives a picture," from a KhoiKhoi point of view, "of the disintegration of the Hottentot-nation around 1730," indicates a more radical self-othering. The living sign of this eighteenth-century making-other, described by a KhoiKhoi elder as "the greatest other-making in our nation's history," is a racially mixed "little Afrikaner" (Rabie, *Groot Anders-Maak* 124–25). As an authorial note to Rabie's novel explains, "the word 'Afrikaner' indicated for more than a century only bastard children with one Hottentot parent." A more fundamentally dispropriative version of Louw's gesture toward coloureds four years before, Rabie's novel asks the Afrikaner reader of the 1960s to put him- or herself in the place of the KhoiKhoi of the 1730s, who faced a choice between extinction as a nation and throwing in their lot with the encroaching Dutch farmers, as their military allies and servants.

In *Dog Heart,* however, there is the sense that, by drawing on the Western Cape interior as an exemplary region of racial and linguistic "bastardisation," Breytenbach limits the extent to which his intervention can be generalized. When it comes to Zulu, for instance — "Are there not other languages . . . which are even more the products of rooting and fruiting in this native soil?" — there is an unreasoned foreclosure of languages other than Afrikaans as merely instrumental: "Yes, I answer; but language is not just a tool, it is perhaps the closest we can come to a communal 'soul'" (*Dog Heart* 183). And more recently, Breytenbach has invoked Édouard Glissant's *The Poetics of Relation* in the name of language-based minority rights: "'The thought of errantry (*om te swerwe* [to wander]) is not apolitical nor is it inconsistent with the will to identity, which is, after all, nothing other than the search for a freedom within particular surroundings.' . . . The bastard has a right to full citizenship" ("Andersheid"; quotation from Glissant 20).

If his latest writings and statements — for example, in support of the neo-nationalist Group of 63 set up in May 2000, from which he subsequently distanced himself (see Rossouw; Breytenbach, "Reaksie") — dally with a cultural-nationalist politics of the kind Ndebele condemns, with *The True Confessions of an Albino Terrorist*, Breytenbach signaled "a definitive break with Afrikaans" according to André du Toit ("Breyten" 44). His first book in English, *The True Confessions of an Albino Terrorist* is a performance of responsibility-in-complicity as he perceived it at the time, a provisional refusal to write in a language flowing with the "poison of racism" (*Season* 159).[18] In each case, it would be a matter of *what* complicities are embraced along with a particular language at a particular time.

As a necessarily time-bound negotiation of complicity through the abrogation of a language, *The True Confessions of an Albino Terrorist* can usefully be compared with Ngũgĩ wa Thiong'o's turn, following the prison term chronicled in *Detained: A Writer's Prison Diary* (1981), away from English toward Gĩkũyũ as the language of his novels. Like Breytenbach's choice of language, Ngũgĩ's involves both a confrontation with postcolonial cultural politics and an intense psychic rivalry with the national leader.

Yes, No — to Language

Without ever being charged, Ngũgĩ wa Thiong'o was held in detention from 31 December 1977 until 12 December 1978. Like Breyten Breytenbach, Wole Soyinka, Jack Mapanje, Dennis Brutus, Jeremy Cronin, and other African writers imprisoned on political grounds by the governments of their countries, Ngũgĩ writes about the specific constraints of imprisonment on a writer.[19] And, like Breytenbach, Ngũgĩ also addresses the question of how responsibility for the intellectual emerges from an awareness of complicity:

Yes, No. Ndio, La. Two of the tiniest words in any language. But yes or no, one had to choose between them. To say "Yes" or "No" to unfairness, to injustice, to wrong-doing, to oppression, to treacherous betrayal, to the culture of fear, to the aesthetic of submissive acquiescence, one was choosing a particular world and a particular future.

It was not, of course, very cheering to know that most of those who had said "No" to the culture of fear and silence, had ended dying untimely deaths buried alive in desert places or left on hillsides for hyena's midnight feasts. Nor was it particularly cheering to contemplate that I was now in detention under a regime headed by an ex-detainee who had finally given in to years of imperialist blackmail and bribery. Would a political yes-man ever recognize the rights of a political no-man and the human and democratic necessity of that position? Would he, in other words, release a detainee who dared say "No" when he himself had said "Yes"? (*Detained* 97)

Detention is the hinge on which yes and no turn. The yes-man tries to convert the no into a yes by detaining the one who says No. Chapter 5 of

Detained gives examples of "two types of political prisoners: those who finally succumbed and said 'Yes' to an oppressive system; and those who defied and maintained 'Never!'" (81). To say No is to identify with trade unionist Makhan Singh and "'Mau Mau' detainee" J. M. Kariũki and to distance oneself from those who, after lengthy periods of detention, came around and said Yes: veteran East African nationalist Harry Thuku and independence leader and Kenyan president Jomo Kenyatta. Kenyatta is a *good* example because he is a *bad* example: one not to be emulated. By using Kenyatta, the prisoner turned jailer, as his example, Ngũgĩ is able to sustain and reinforce his No. If, in the case of the "yesmen," detention was a way of effecting an "about-turn" (*Detained* 90), in Ngũgĩ's case, the way to endure prison is to turn the conversionary logic of detention against itself by insisting on saying No. The example is the device *Detained* employs to perform the ruse of an absolute No.

A logic of repetition emerges, according to which the best way of surviving is to reiterate the original refusal. One way of reinforcing the No is to write a novel in Gĩkũyũ, since it is the writing of a play in Gĩkũyũ — together with a group of workers and peasants at Kamĩrĩĩthũ (*Detained* 72–80) — that appears to have been what led to the detention of the writer. This brings us to the question of culture and to another repetition, this time of a phrase, "a colonial affair," that "keeps on intruding into the literary flow of my mind and pen": "A colonial affair . . . a neo-colonial affair . . . what's the difference?" (*Detained* 29, 96).

Detained is not just a prison book, but a book that somehow makes it possible for Ngũgĩ to write, or *not* write, at least two books that were planned but never written: the one, entitled "A Colonial Affair"; the other, a biography of Jomo Kenyatta. At one level, *Detained* is both an anti-biography of Kenyatta — Kenyatta as (bad) example — and an indictment of postindependence Kenya as perpetuating colonial economic and political relations as a neocolonialism. Kenyatta uses detention in the same way as the colonialists did against him and others in the independence struggle of the 1950s, when a "pipeline" of detention camps was implemented to force "Mau Mau" fighters to confess their oaths and to offer them progressively more lenient treatment and eventual release in return for demonstrating a turning away from the aims of the movement.[20]

What is the difference? *Detained* works out a double response: historical and autobiographical, presenting the autobiographical as historical

(28). The goal of the book—to understand "the rituals of mystery and secrecy [that] are calculated exercises in psychological terror aimed [both] at the whole people . . . and at the individual detainee" (*Detained* 20)—suggests how a knowledge of history—Makhan Singh's resoluteness; Kenyatta's acquiescence—can provide examples, good and bad, that can help the detainee continue to say No—No to colonial education; No to a betrayal of Kamĩrĩĩthũ (98). *Detained* preserves the pattern of historical examples affirmed or refused. The most powerful example, the book suggests, is the one from which one disidentifies, yet with which one is, until the death of the other (162–63),[21] locked, in all its reversals, in a struggle of mimetic rivalry.

Part of the diagnosis of neocolonial Kenya is in terms of the politics of culture: Gĩkũyũ theater and literature is "national theater" and "national literature." This theater, created by peasants and workers, is aesthetically *superior* to the "unpalatable junk" staged at the Kenyan National Theatre (e.g., *The King and I; Jesus Christ Superstar*) favored by the comprador elite and underwritten by the Kenyan government (*Detained* 193; see also *Penpoints* 42–44, 48–50). Yet the Kamĩrĩĩthũ theater initiative is suppressed, and Ngũgĩ is detained. If, from the perspective of colonial and postcolonial Kenyan governments, detention is the hinge on which yes and no turn, culture helps the detainee to turn against saying the word the jailer wants to hear. It is by writing the novel translated as *Devil on the Cross* that the writer finally says No—a vocabulary of turning or "version" through writing that in *Detained* overcomes an "adversity" which might have made the petit-bourgeois Kenyatta and Thuku perform an "about-turn" (*Detained* 164, 90, 91), and succumb to pseudo-Christian "conversion" (see *Detained* 23, 86–87), to the ideology of the adversary. The colonial self is divided: one can succumb to an adversary within, reverting to type, to comprador petit-bourgeois identification or to English-educated colonial subjecthood (*Detained* 182; see also "Language" 20ff).

Because detention is the hinge on which yes and no turn, and the Gĩkũyũ novel a palpable but undeclared No to cultural domination, a great deal turns on the writing. Effectively yielding a Kenyan national literature in the form of works by Ngũgĩ, J. M. Kariũki, and others, prison is another place where the writer, within that confined space, contests the monopolization of the space of public discourse by the state: "Prison narratives by artist-prisoners are essentially a documentation of the battle of texts and of the continuing contest over the performance space of the state" (*Penpoints* 57). That literature is one born of a rivalry in which writers strive to free themselves from a range of complicities with their captors. For Ngũgĩ, to be committed to "national theatre" means not being allied with neocolonial rulers who allow a "National Theatre" to operate at the expense of the poor and marginalized. To say yes to the former and no to the latter is to elect a wider joinedness of nationality rather than to succumb to complicity in an official nationalism that operates in the interests of the rulers.

The implications of Breytenbach's choice to write his prison memoir in English rather than in Afrikaans differ from those of Ngũgĩ's decision to turn away from English in favor of Gĩkũyũ. The meaning of their respective acts of linguistic election depends on their relationship to the language in question and on the meaning of writing in it at a particular time. For Breytenbach, to write in English is to *not write in Afrikaans.* In South Africa in the mid-1970s, English is the language with the greater potential for political and cultural democratization. Whereas modern Afrikaans emerged in the late nineteenth century with the emergence of a united Afrikaner volk in the struggle against British imperialism, when the schoolchildren of Soweto rose up against the imposition of Afrikaans as medium of instruction in 1976, Afrikaans, not English, was regarded as the language of mental colonization. Although Afrikaans, having emerged in the mouths of slaves before being appropriated by Afrikaner nationalists (*True Confessions* 353), was spoken widely by coloureds and by black Africans in certain parts of the country, the official policy made it unavailable as a language of anti-apartheid struggle. The promotion of indigenous vernaculars at a time when the apartheid government was establishing ethnolinguistic Bantustans was viewed as divisive; and English, although the hegemony of its purist guardians was challenged by Njabulo Ndebele and others (including Jeremy Cronin, whose prison poems in *Inside* voice the many Englishes of South Africa),[22] represented unity in national struggle.

For Breytenbach, then, in contrast to Ngũgĩ's decision to write in Gĩkũyũ, it would have made little sense at the time to write in Afrikaans as a way of opposing a colonial or neocolonial hegemony associated with English. For him to write in Afrikaans would not have been to choose a different world—for not only was the Afrikaans language discredited among Blacks, but white Afrikaner dissidence, confined to an elite out of touch with working-class Afrikaners like those who guarded him (*True Confessions* 162–63), was efficiently contained. If, as he continued to insist in *The True Confessions of an Albino Terrorist*, "Afrikaans is a Creole language," and "to be African is to be a bastard" (353), the project advocated in "A View from the Outside" of democratizing Afrikaans in the name of creolization and bastardy was effectively stalled. For the Afrikaner to address the African other in Afrikaans was to speak as master.

Writing in Prison, J. M. Coetzee on Censorship and Apartheid

If the affirmation of "national literature" as a quasi-patriotic *defense* of Ngũgĩ's position failed to draw the sympathy of the authorities, the public, or his employer, the University of Kenya, an appeal to Breyten Breytenbach's status as a writer influenced the course of his imprisonment, the nature of the writings which emerged from it, and the sense of responsibility-in-complicity one finds in them. After representations on his behalf by members of the literary establishment, who pleaded the interests of Afrikaans literature, Breytenbach was permitted the privilege, under bizarre conditions, of continuing to write while in prison:

But I am the writer . . . I need to write . . . Soon after my sentencing I applied in writing, as always in prison, in duplicate, to the authorities for the permission to paint and write. Without my knowing about it, similar requests were being made from outside, emanating from the South African milieu of writers and academics. People who absolutely rejected me and my ideas and what my life stood for but who, perhaps from an obscure sense of uncomfortableness, if not guilt, and also, surely, because of a true concern for my work, applied to the minister to allow me to continue writing. "For the sake of Afrikaans literature." Was it a way for some of them to establish in their own minds their evenhandedness?

The request to paint was turned down. . . . Writing . . . I would be allowed to do, with the following conditions attached to the permission: that I would not show it to any other prisoner or warder (that went without saying since I had no contact with anyone); that I would not attempt to smuggle it out of prison; that I would hand it in directly upon completing anything or any part of any work; that I would not hoard or keep notes for the work and would destroy these immediately after finishing the work. In return I was assured that the work would be kept in safe-keeping for me. (*True Confessions* 159)

These conditions of writing reproduce and intensify, for the prisoner, the fraternal intimacy of Afrikaans cultural and political life. In his essay "Breyten Breytenbach and the Reader in the Mirror," in *Giving Offense,* J. M. Coetzee juxtaposes Breytenbach's prison and post-prison writings with the poetry he wrote before being incarcerated. Coetzee proposes that Breytenbach, at first in his poems and then through his clandestine actions, sought to provoke a confrontation with the policeman or censor on his own ground rather than in the elite language of poetry. According to Coetzee, many of Breytenbach's public statements on censorship are conventionally denunciatory and give little idea of the rivalrous projected intimacy of writer and censor, an intimacy continuous with that aggressively claimed with prime minister B. J. Vorster in his banned poem "Letter from Foreign Parts to Butcher" (1972) (*Giving* 215–18).

Like some of the prison poems, however, *The True Confessions of an Albino Terrorist* engages in the kind of "hidden contestatory dialogue" akin to that detected by Mikhail Bakhtin in Dostoyevsky, in which the self divides into an I and a you whose positions are interchangeable, with the phantasmatic figure of the policeman/censor: "For a time, at least, the policeman/censor of the imagination had been installed in Breytenbach as his mirror-self, and that writing had been, if not playing at the censor's game, at least playing a game with the censor" (*Giving* 223–24, 227, 232). In the context of Coetzee's wide-ranging work on censorship, in which he borrows from René Girard, this game is one of mimetic rivalry. According to Girard, human desire is triadic: the desirer takes another's desire as a model and imitates the other in his or her desire. What ensues is a dynamic of escalating rivalry over the desired object, which sees desirer and model become increasingly indistinguishable (*Giving* 90–93, 117–19). Girard makes it possible for Coetzee to read writer and censor as vying for the attentions of a reading public and helps him to "pass by two tired images of the writer under censorship: the moral giant under attack from hordes of moral pygmies and the helpless innocent persecuted by a mighty state apparatus" (*Giving* 118). Read in these terms, both Ngũgĩ and Breytenbach face, in their projects of writing, the difficulty of distinguishing themselves from intimate rivals whom they do not wish to resemble. Ngũgĩ does so by employing the ruse of the example to draw a clear line between Yes and No, between Kenyatta and Kariũki, between Kenyatta and himself. In his prison and immediate post-prison writings, Breytenbach does not, or cannot, draw as distinct a line.

The reasons for this, I propose, are related both to the peculiar circumstances under which he was permitted to write in prison (instead of being prohibited from doing so like Ngũgĩ and others) and to a sense of ethnic and linguistic implicatedness that predates and outlasts his imprisonment. In "A Note on the True Confessions of an Albino Terrorist," the first of those appended to the book, Breytenbach describes the process by which *The True Confessions of an Albino Terrorist* was composed. Speaking it onto a tape, the book "became the story of doing a book," the account of the exchange between writer and reader, speaker and interlocutor. After he had spoken it, Breytenbach relates, "my wife typed the tapes. . . . Therefore I was, in the first instance, in all intimacy, talking to her; telling her all which I'd had to hold back over the years" (*True Confessions* 338). Yolande Breytenbach is thus the one in relation to whom "telling" or writing can occur. She occupies the position of what Coetzee terms the "figure of the beloved," the one, in contrast to the "figure of the censor" (*Giving* 38), before whom one does not have to "hold back." But the address is irremediably split. The "you" addressed in the text mutates, and addressing it can mean interrupting the intimate address to the beloved. Sometimes the "you" is the implied reader, at other times the figure of Mr. Investigator, who is the internal interlocutor and counterpart to the narrator-I: "I have the earphones on my head and I speak to you and I listen to the voice coming back" (*True Confessions* 13).

Mr. Investigator can play a mediating role. *The True Confessions of an Albino Terrorist* contains a draft of a Christmas letter to Yolande, concerning which Mr. Investigator is asked: "Would you be so kind as to pass along the belated missive to her ladyship?" (*True Confessions* 306). The letter itself, a story in a punning idiom about a "bandit . . . who lived in Nosemansland" longing for "One Lady who lived far far away in another world called Pararis," is interrupted every so often by a number written between words, indicating the imminent approach and transgression of the 500-word limit enforced by the prison censor, and which the letter plays at circumventing by adding syllables to words. (*True Confessions* 306–8).[23] Access to the "figure of the beloved" is blocked by the "figure of the censor," who decides, in this case, how many words one can write and what one can write about. The letter, which "never arrived at its destination" (*True Confessions* 305), is thus addressed, "in the first instance," not to Yolande but to the censor.

This is another version of the fractured address of the writing Breytenbach was permitted to do in prison. "In these reports," Breytenbach writes in the "Apology" to *Mouroir*, a collection of his writings from prison, "there is an I and I's, a we, you's [jye], he's, she's, they's and you's [julles]. But *this* I is not *I*, and the you, dear reader, is not you; neither is the he the she the they or the you [julle] *you* [jý] or *you* [júlle]."[24] It is tempting to read this ontological indeterminacy of pronouns—there are a multiplicity of pronominal positions, but each is not coincident with a self with which it could be identified—simply as a gesture at the indeterminacy of all narrative address. With prison as their shared context of production, however, Breytenbach's poems and narrative prose are inflected by the same disruption as his letters. By collapsing the difference between the two activities and reducing each to its barest elements, imprisonment concentrates the link between two kinds of letters: literary and epistolary writing. Breytenbach's literary output, handed in to the authorities upon completion, is subject to the same surveillance as his correspondence. In both cases, the writer writes, uncertain of whether the reader he wishes to address will ever receive what he produces, and certain that those for whom he is forced to write will confiscate it:

A bizarre situation, Mr Investigator, when you write knowing that the enemy is reading over your shoulder; when you have to write as deeply down in yourself as you can because you need this to survive; writing in a desperate attempt at communication with the outside, with the world, with the people closest to you, knowing beforehand that it cannot reach them and knowing also that you are laying bare the most intimate and the most personal nerves and pulsebeats in yourself to the barbarians, to the cynical ones who will gloat over this. (*True Confessions* 159)

The process of writing, under these circumstances, is not so different from what happens when, like many security detainees,[25] Breytenbach is given a piece of paper and instructed to write. Here the mode of telling of *The True Confessions of an Albino Terrorist* slides into the form of the written confession demanded by the interrogator. The first appended note, which outlines an intimate process of composition and revision involving the beloved, cannot insulate itself from the second note, "A Note on the Relationship between Detainee and Interrogator." The relationship described in it is approximated in the address to Mr Investigator:

No, you won't catch me, Mr Investigator. I know how it is done. They let you sit down, they do not ask you any questions; they simply say, "Write"; and I've written volumes, volumes. . . . "Write," they say, and you write. Two sheets. "What must I write about, sir?" "*You* know: just write." And they come up and they read the two pages, and they smile and they tear it up. (*True Confessions* 28)

For the writer, these dynamics can contaminate the address to the figure of the beloved, which, as with the letter, is necessary in order to realize the literary work. Hence, for the book to be about the making of the book is also, to recall J. M. Coetzee, for it to be about the disruption of the writer-beloved dyad by the figure of the policeman/censor — or worse, about a potential lethal fusing of the two. The place of the beloved, in a radical reciprocity of I and you, is usurped, in various guises, by the master: "Mr Investigator . . . sir."

The most intriguing essay in Coetzee's *Giving Offense* is not on censorship per se, but deals with apartheid theorist Geoffrey Cronjé. A miniature masterpiece on the intellectual and apartheid, "Apartheid Thinking" relentlessly follows the obsessive metonymic association of Blacks with disease in Cronjé's academic writings.[26] Although identifying a degree of self-censorship in Cronjé, Coetzee does not directly relate Cronjé's "counterattack upon desire" to the activity of "the censor" — whose business is, as he puts it, "track[ing] 'the undesirable'" (*Giving* 169, 178, vii). A fact not mentioned in *Giving Offense* is that Geoffrey Cronjé chaired an official Commission of Enquiry in regard to Undesirable Publications which tabled its findings and recommendations in 1956. "The mind of apartheid" is therefore, in more than one sense, the mind of a censor.

What Breytenbach's *The True Confessions of an Albino Terrorist* suggests, by dramatizing the conditions of its writing, is that the disruption of the writer-beloved dyad by the figure of the censor emanates from the same basic impulse as brings about the violent denial of desire that underlies apartheid in thought and deed. In each case, the place of love is taken by violence. If "apartheid thinking" is bound up in this reflex, the intellectual who has thought apartheid is in a predicament. There is no simple avowal of desire to meet its disavowal. There is no dis-closure to correct foreclosure. Each approach, each opening to the other, is shadowed by a threat.

Breytenbach consistently acknowledges a complicity that, to his mind, makes him unable to say a simple No to Afrikanerdom. In "A Note on the True Confessions of an Albino Terrorist," he writes: "It was not my intention to take revenge on a system or on certain people — at least, I don't think it was. We are too closely linked for that" (*True Confessions* 339).[27] Once again, Breytenbach is not talking simply about his own linkages with Afrikanerdom, but he is setting out an account of apartheid in terms of a perversion of basic human foldedness, away from which one endeavors to turn, but of which one can never be confident of being free:

In the same way that the ideology of apartheid is only an aberration — a stillness — of what is potentially present in all of mankind, the butchers and the interrogators are not monsters but people like you and me. That is what makes them so horrible and so pitiful. And that is exactly why we must continue condemning and combating their acts. I believe that the torturer is as depraved by his acts as the one who is tortured. We will be fools and mere objects of history if we go looking for the causes of depravity in "human nature" only. We make society and society makes us. But there are certain fabrics once torn that cannot be mended again; certain transgressions that can never be condoned. (*True Confessions* 339)

Apartheid is represented, as it is in the "Note" which follows it, by the figure of the interrogator. It is the stilling of human potentiality by him, and by other police and prison authorities, a procession without end, that sets in motion the acts perpetrated in the interrogation chamber and in the censor's office, and that, on a systemic scale, constitute apartheid. The duty of the intellectual, for Breytenbach, is not to assume the existence of a position apart from it, but to condemn and combat from a position of acknowledged complicity — in the name of a basic human foldedness or "integration" that narrower modes of belonging deny.

Written on the pattern of its own writing, *The True Confessions of an Albino Terrorist* foregrounds the act of writing as an act of address involving an I and a you. The reciprocity of these two positions, a shorthand for the basic foldedness of the human self with an other, if never realized in a pure form, can be radically corrupted when one of the parties occupies, actually or phantasmatically, the position of master. When domination enters into basic foldedness, a range of complicities in the narrow sense develops. The responsibility taken up by the intellectual is to show how such complicities stand in the way of realizing, ethically and politically, a more equal reciprocity. Frantz Fanon, as we shall see, identifies an alienation whereby, for Blacks and Whites, racist fantasy stands in the way of love and the ethical relation. Insisting, by means of the figure of Mr. Investigator, that the I-you structure of address may at any time be contaminated by the figure of the interrogator, Breytenbach shows how apartheid, for which it can be read as an allegory, is not, as its name would seem to wish, a system of apart-ness at all, but an institutionalized intimacy of domination for its victims. Breytenbach adds to an oppositional understanding of apartheid the idea that, as an intellectual, it is not enough to resist the system in its more overt manifestations, but it is necessary to find the roots of the conversion of foldedness with the other into forms of complicity in its denial. This is what makes apartheid exemplary for the intellectual as a figure of responsibility-in-complicity. It is necessary to have not only an ideal of freedom or autonomy but an account of sufficient power to capture how that ideal is, at a fundamental level, susceptible to perversion as something like apartheid.

As Derrida argues, taking up the philological analyses of Benveniste and the thought of Levinas, the self, although, according to some of its original traits, a dispropriating openness of host to guest, becomes, under certain circumstances, "master of the house," a proper and proprietory self guarding itself against the other (Derrida, "On Cosmopolitanism" 16–17; Derrida and Dufourmantelle, *Of Hospitality* 39–41). These are the dynamics A. C. Jordan employs Tiyo Soga to reveal.

The relationship between detainee and interrogator, between prisoner and prison authorities, as set out by Breytenbach, dramatizes how a disavowal of shared humanity — "brother-I" — is embedded in social codes designed to preserve the structure of mastery. A visit to the censor illustrates that a prisoner cannot lay claim even to a token honorific of mastery: "Called me into the office. I sat down. 'Get up!' he screamed. Who the hell gave you permission to sit down like a . . . like a *mister!*'" (*True Confessions* 172). When these codes of domination-subordination are not observed by the prisoner and any hint of reciprocity is claimed, intense and destructive violence may ensue.

Although his generalization of bastardy against apartheid must be distinguished from the project of anti-racist self-recovery prescribed by Black Consciousness and its attendant tendency toward a purism of true and false consciousness (see Sole, "Reading" 22), Breytenbach does not hesitate to recognize the role of the latter in overcoming "spiritual domination" [geestelike baasskap] ("Fragmente" 13). In any case, the violence described by *The True Confessions of an Albino Terrorist* as a fact of prison life is no different from that faced by Steve Biko, whose Black Consciousness taught him and others not to collaborate, materially and psychically, in their own misuse.

chapter 5
black consciousness

The public marriage between the words *black* and *consciousness* has in some instances led to some panic and public consternation in certain sections of the South African public. There have been arguments, debates and naggings. It all happened so quickly that some observers have even suggested that the bogey of swartgevaar [black peril] was suddenly becoming real.
—N. C. MANGANYI, *Being-Black-in-the-World*

Almost all of what is known about the final days of the life of Black Consciousness leader Steve Biko (1946–77) comes from the lies and evasions, before bodies of legal inquiry, of those responsible for his death. It might be said, then, that we know nothing about those days—or nothing that can be separated from the untruths of its perpetrators, the only ones with him at the time. Steve Biko's death and its prelude remain obscured in a haze of prevarication. There is no one who can be trusted, as is usual in funerary remembrance of the dead, to "talk about how he died" (Biko, *Black Consciousness* 201). That blocks his being mourned and scars his legacy.

If, indeed, we can properly be said to know nothing of the circumstances of Biko's death, how do we talk about how he died? How do we narrate it? Is there a way of making it a part of an account of the intellectual and apartheid? Can Biko's death be reclaimed from the oblivion of the testimony of his killers and from the way that testimony consigns it to an entry in a litany of gross human rights violations of apartheid — or worse, a mention in the equivocal statements of those seeking amnesty for them? In order to do so, it will be helpful to talk about "traces" — for Derrida, marks of something that may never have been present but that nevertheless comes into being as those traces are deciphered. The result is something other than a knowing — more the writing of a life, a biography. The traces in question are those that are left on the body of Steve Biko and that surface in the speech of those exchanging words on the matter of his death. Circling around consciousness and its loss, they can be combed from documents emanating from two legal proceedings that took place twenty years apart.

After being transported, naked and comatose, 750 miles overland in the back of a police Land Rover from Port Elizabeth to Pretoria, Steve Biko died in a prison hospital on 12 September 1977.[1] An inquest into Biko's death was held in November 1977 in Pretoria's Old Synagogue, a deconsecrated place used as a court, to determine the cause of death and decide whether anyone would be prosecuted. Finding that "head injury with associated extensive brain injury" was the "cause or likely cause of death," the presiding magistrate concluded that "the head injury was probably sustained . . . when the deceased was involved in a scuffle with members of the Security Branch of the South African Police at Port Elizabeth." He ruled, however, that "the available evidence does not prove that the death was brought about by any act or omission involving or amounting to an offence on the part of any person" (Biko, *Black Consciousness* 293). There would be no prosecution of the policemen involved.

The second of the proceedings were the public hearings, between September 1997 and March 1998, concerning the applications by the policemen to the Truth and Reconciliation Commission for amnesty from prosecution in terms of the Promotion of National Unity and Reconciliation Act.[2] The respective proceedings occurred in different political worlds: the April 1994 election had brought nonracial democratic government, and apartheid security police no longer enjoy the state's protection. Yet in each, testimony and questioning return, as if compelled, to one motif and its variations — conscious, unconscious, consciousness — as if the truth, or one truth, of what took place resided there.

Whether Biko was conscious or unconscious is pivotal for testing the veracity of the police version of events. At the 1977 inquest, expert medical testimony was led to the effect that the five lesions found at the autopsy on Steve Biko's brain, which included "a contra-coup [*sic*] . . . an injury on one side of the brain, caused by a blow on the other side of the head . . . must have been followed by a period of unconsciousness of at least ten minutes, more likely fifteen to twenty minutes, and possibly up to one hour" (Woods 244–45; see also 248). When questioned by Sydney Kentridge, who appeared on behalf of the Biko family, as to "whether Mr. Biko lost consciousness at anytime [*sic*] during or after the alleged scuffle," Warrant Officer Beneke, one of the security policemen involved, replied that "he had not been unconscious" (Woods 252). In his closing summation, Kentridge argued that "when three of the leading pathologists of South Africa, and the leading neurophysician, said that in their opinions there must have been a period of unconsciousness, he had to submit that the court had to accept this as being so. The police account of the struggle completely excluded a period of unconsciousness, and it followed that in the case the injuries could not have been sustained during the struggle" (Woods 257).

When the signs of his body were read by those capable of interpreting them, it became clear that Biko could not have been conscious after the "scuffle" with the police. In the sphere of forensic questioning and argument, the fact that Biko was not conscious establishes the likely cause of his death and, though it is unable to draw the truth from the police, contradicts their account of how he was injured. Legal inquiry accords it no further significance. When read along with the more recent Truth Commission testimony, as the amnesty-seeking policemen are cross-examined by George Bizos, the question of consciousness in the record of the 1977 inquest accumulates an added weight.

The 1997–98 Truth Commission hearings for the five policemen, held in Port Elizabeth and Cape Town, revisited the medical evidence. In their written amnesty applications, the officers had altered their respective accounts of the "scuffle" to concur with the fact that Biko had lost consciousness. During this episode, they now testified, Biko was rammed, head first, into a wall of the interrogation room: "During this wrestling and fighting . . . the three of us grabbed Biko and moved with him in the direction of the corner of the room and ran against the wall into the wall with him" (Snyman 73). This happened after Biko's interrogators had taken exception to his sitting down on a chair:

MR BIZOS: Yes, but he was a proud man and . . . your self-respect would have been insulted if he continued sitting on the chair?

MR SNYMAN: Your Honour, we had to realise that he was a high profile person in the Black Consciousness Organisations. He was a president of one of these organisations and by sitting he maintained his own status.

MR BIZOS: I see. So that you were offended, personally offended that you, a White man, had a pretender of political power before him and that you were not going to tolerate [his sitting down] and you told him to get up? Is that correct?

MR SYNMAN: That is correct, your Honour. (Snyman 90)[3]

By sitting, Biko was perceived by the interrogators to be maintaining his status. He was seen as taking a stand. The result of being rammed into the wall was that Biko "appeared disorientated . . . completely confused . . . like someone who had been knocked out in a boxing match" (Snyman 20–21).[4] During cross-examination, Bizos challenged this revised account, recalling the witness to the 1977 inquest:

MR BIZOS: . . . Do you recall that it was the opinion of Prof Procter, of Prof Loubser — the Chief State Pathologist and Dr Jonathan Gluckman that your story could not possibly be true, because the contracoup [*sic*] injury on Mr Biko's [brain] would have lead to immediate unconsciousness as if it were a knock-out blow delivered by a heavy-weight boxer. Do you recall that?

MR SNYMAN: Your Honour, I cannot answer at this stage, but I can say that as we have stated, the way in which the head bumped against the wall, did in fact knock him out for a while, but he was not entirely unconscious.

MR BIZOS: In Pretoria, your evidence and your colleagues' evidence were shown to be false, because you said that Biko fell; that is where he must have got his injury above his left eye, but despite that, he continued to fight with strength and determination that not even four security policemen could bring him under control. Now, the convenient stage that you and your colleagues have changed the story to, was that he appeared to be confused, a sort of halfway stage to unconsciousness in order to make your story fit at least in part the medical evidence given by such eminent medical people. Isn't that the reason that you now changed your story, because you knew that unless you admitted at least in part, that portion, the medical evidence would again show that your evidence was false. Have you got anything to say about what I'm putting to you?

MR SNYMAN: Your Honour, what I have said in my application now, are the true facts. (Snyman 52)[5]

As the five adjust their story, Biko's loss of consciousness is the main narrative element they add. To the traces of consciousness and its loss deciphered from Biko's body by the pathologists at the Old Synagogue, the record of the recent hearings adds those sedimented in another medium: the speech of the policemen, and thus, fabricated or otherwise, the unreliable matter of their memories. As they trim their stories, even if only to accommodate the medical evidence, the effect of the repeated questioning and testimony concerning it is to establish Biko's loss of consciousness — not simply as remembered fact but as a pivotal and traumatic event. His consciousness and its loss obsesses them and their questioner, whose inquiries appear to go beyond what is necessary to falsify their testimony.

There is a certain sense to this — even a certain "truth." In the context of Black Consciousness, as a political and intellectual-historical formation, the codes governing the meaning of consciousness and its absence concatenate a series of traits. Crucial to the chain is the human being as intellectual, an embodiment of intellect and mind, who develops an awareness of the historical and psychical dimensions of his or her own oppression and active participation therein. This consciousness-raising leads to a resistance of such complicity. All these traits converge in the latest "memories" of the police, in the scenario that Bizos's questioning helps to construct: Biko, the leading figure in Black Consciousness, which teaches its followers to not participate in their own oppression, sits unbidden; he claims self-respect, refusing to be a collaborator with police in their racist denial of his human dignity; he is beaten, then his head is rammed into a wall; his consciousness is extinguished; the police, afraid of Biko's physical strength, his reputation for fighting back during interrogation, and of a movement they refer to as Black Power, have, at a symbolic level, accomplished their goal. Their panicked response to "the public marriage between the words 'black' and 'consciousness'" reveals a truth that can be heard screaming at the heart of their lies.

These lies not only allow us to reconstruct something of Biko's last days — as Bizos says, with the aid of forensic pathology, "even though none of us were there, we can work things out" (Nie[u]woudt 48) —

but also allow us, beyond forensic truth, to acknowledge the placement by Black Consciousness of complicity, and an awareness of it, at the root of what it is to be an intellectual. That is, if by an intellectual we mean someone who, through thought and its setting to work, assumes ethical and/or political responsibility. The actions of the police tacitly register that the complicity at stake is, specifically, complicity in the subordination of oneself and the group with which one is affiliated or identified. This is something that might have been uncannily familiar to them.[6] As Biko himself learned from Afrikaans students, there are striking resonances between Black Consciousness and Afrikaner nationalism. Language and culture were where it mobilized in the 1920s and 30s as it sought to help Afrikaners rid themselves of feelings of inferiority in relation to Britain and white Anglo–South Africans. As Biko noted in the SASO (South African Students' Organization) trial,[7] referring to the rejection by Soweto students in 1976 of Afrikaans as medium of instruction, "Language can help in the development of an inferiority complex" (*Black Consciousness* 24).[8]

The acknowledgment and negotiation of complicity, a basic impulse for Black Consciousness intellectuals, is not fully borne out in the intellectual history of the apartheid era. The politicized intellectual history of protest and resistance leads us to believe that oppositionality, along with solidarity, is essential to the intellectual.[9] Although lojale verset implies not only loyalty but resistance or opposition, Afrikaans intellectuals failed to "universalize" for others from the anticolonial origins of Afrikaner nationalism. When aparte bestaan was the prize, as for Louw, official-language status for Afrikaans went along with an unowned complicity in apartheid. Once it had become a name for mere Afrikaner-nationalist solidarity, Breytenbach and other Afrikaans intellectuals positioned in "complicity-willy-nilly" (Du Toit, *Sondes* 51) in apartheid were hard pressed to invoke lojale verset to extricate themselves from it. If Afrikaner nationalism ultimately made accommodation the norm, Black Consciousness reminds us that, for the intellectual, talk of resistance has no meaning when complicity is not negotiated.

Articulated in the writings of Steve Biko, the attention of Black Consciousness to complicity was widely taken up in South Africa in the 1970s. Influencing radical white intellectuals and setting the course of subsequent black cultural politics, Black Consciousness had developed an account of responsibility-in-complicity that went beyond the sphere of the political as traditionally understood. Borrowing from the writings of Frantz Fanon, it approached the psyche in ways fundamentally challenging any conception of the intellectual as "disembodied" and of his or her responsibility as purely intellectual. Addressing the psyche enlarged the field for political agency. It also altered what it meant to be an intellectual. When one is conscious of the corporeal dimension of one's complicity, responsibility entails bringing one's body into rebellion.

Black Consciousness, Apartheid, and Liberalism

Steve Biko set out the main lines of Black Consciousness in "I Write What I Like," a column he wrote for the *SASO Newsletter* between 1970 and 1972 under the pseudonym Frank Talk, and in other writings collected posthumously in a book by that title. The rubric and name unite thought ("I write") and desire ("I like"), intellectual practice and intentional autonomy, and are at the same time the performative instantiation of a subject ("I") in and through language, which exists in freedom (*francus* = free) ("Frank Talk").[10] Engaging in a project of writing of this kind renders its author exemplary in the way it permits the occupation of a writing subject-position of the thought of Black Consciousness it sets out. It was not until the SASO trial of 1976 that Biko, testifying for the defense, disclosed himself as the author (*Black Consciousness* 24). The structure of "I write" thus makes itself available to others, guarding against a cult of leadership in a vanguard movement (Biko, *I Write* 150) and providing for a generalizing diffusion of the project of intellectual liberation among those the "I" implicitly addresses as "you."[11]

Black Consciousness addressed several kinds of complicity in apartheid that, although separable for analysis, are interlinked. Two dealt with immediate questions of organizational strategy for SASO. As is well known, the organization took a stand against cooperating with white liberals, the traditional allies of Africans in anti-apartheid politics. It also condemned the growing participation of black leaders such as Gatsha Buthelezi in the ethnic "homelands" that the Verwoerd government began to set up in the mid-1960s as part of Grand Apartheid. The place of Black Consciousness in my account of the intellectual and apartheid lies, however, in its generalizing analysis of complicity in psychic terms, made available by "I Write What I Like" to an unnamed "you." The makings of a cultural-political lingua franca, its powerful analysis of racism as a mental phenomenon was taken up by both Blacks and Whites.

BLACK CONSCIOUSNESS AND WHITE LIBERALS

The beginnings of Black Consciousness are commonly traced to the break, in 1969, of SASO, a body representing black university students, with NUSAS (National Union of South African Students), the national umbrella body for student organizations. The ideological direction of NUSAS, SASO argued, was determined by white students, who embraced a liberal nonracialism that was out of touch with the realities of South African society, in which the interests of white students, as members of a group privileged by apartheid, diverged from those of black students, who were oppressed and exploited by apartheid: "It is rather like expecting the slave to work with the slave-master's son to remove all the conditions leading to the former's enslavement" (Biko, *I Write* 20–21).

Apartheid materially affected student unity; at conferences in the late 1960s, members of the respective bodies were housed in segregated university residences (Biko, *Black Consciousness* 6–8). At a more fundamental level, though, SASO argued that it was necessary for Blacks to attain political self-reliance and, rather than enjoying the hospitality of Whites, "we wanted to remove [the white man] from our table, strip the table of all trappings put on it by him, decorate it in true African style, settle down and then ask him to join us on our own terms if he liked" (Biko, *I Write* 69). This is eventually what happened. By the mid-1980s NUSAS was taking its direction from the black leadership, which had developed since 1976 (Budlender 235).

Although Bantustan leaders are said to have "sold their souls to the white man" (Biko, *I Write* 82), the "homelands" are not specifically identified, as they would be by Njabulo Ndebele (*South African Literature* 75–77), as places in need of mental decolonization. The links between intellectual and psychic alienation are, however, made insistently when it comes to debating political alliances with liberal Whites. One of the stated aims of SASO was "to boost up the morale of the nonwhite students, to heighten their own confidence in themselves" (Biko, *I Write* 5). As in Hegel and Hegelian thought, where the word *Selbstbewußtsein* bridges the two concepts, Black Consciousness links consciousness of the self and confidence in the self.

The relationship between breaking with white liberals and fostering black confidence is set out in companion columns in the August and September 1970 issues of *SASO Newsletter*: "Black Souls in White Skins?" and "We Blacks." Addressing the question from two sides, they address two parts of a black self divided against itself. "We Blacks," which I discuss later, addresses the question from the point of view of what it will take for Blacks to overcome dependence on Whites and white values, and what it will take for intellectuals to assist in negotiating this complicity. "Black Souls in White Skins?" the title of which parodies Fanon in order to challenge the basis of white identification with Blacks, moves from an accusation of Whites to an acknowledgment of black complicity and an assumption of responsibility. However fervid white identification with the black struggle is, continued black internalization of white values — black skin, white masks, in effect — stands in the way of effective interracial cooperation. Before "White Souls" can be addressed as equals, the part of the split black self that assumes a white mask has to be addressed. In these early writings, there is thus a constant turning-back, a performance of self-division-and-implication.

A refusal of the dynamics of advocacy and of activism by proxy is central to the analysis Biko presented. Historically, white liberals had, in a sense, spoken and acted for Blacks: "They have been doing things for blacks, on behalf of blacks, and because of blacks. When the blacks announce that the time has come for them to do things for themselves and all by themselves all white liberals shout blue murder!" (Biko, *I Write* 25). This relationship of tutelage had gone unquestioned, even, to a certain extent, among Blacks, who faced a void of political leadership after the imprisonment of Mandela and his fellow accused in 1964 and the crackdown on opposition that followed the State of Emergency in 1960. This was the context in which black students looked to NUSAS (Gerhart 257ff). Until Blacks gained self-confidence, Biko wrote, integration would remain "artificial . . . a one-way course, with the whites doing all the talking and the blacks the listening" (*I Write* 20).

It was thus necessary to put an end to the tendency to allow Whites to be self-appointed advocates, "verbalising all the complaints of the blacks beautifully" (*I Write* 21), and for Blacks merely to "echo" what the "Liberal" said (*Black Consciousness* 57–58). According to Biko, though, the point was not simply to blame white liberals for the results of centuries of racial oppression, but for Blacks to assume the task of overcoming it and its psychic consequences themselves: "As long as blacks are suffering from inferiority complex — a result of 300 years of deliberate oppression, denigration and derision — they will be useless as co-architects of a normal society where man is nothing else but man for his own sake. Hence what is necessary as a prelude to anything else that may come is a very strong grass-roots build-up of black consciousness such that blacks can learn to assert themselves and stake their rightful claim" (*I Write* 21).

Even though it is sometimes conceded by liberals that it was historically necessary, as Jean-Paul Sartre said of Négritude, as an "antiracist racism" ("Black Orpheus" 296), it nevertheless remains typical to see Black Consciousness as antithetical to liberalism and left nonracialism. The evidence, however, justifies the intellectual-historical hypothesis that, rather than confronting liberalism, Black Consciousness radicalized it as it took it out of the hands of its self-appointed white Anglo–South African custodians. Although relentlessly projecting the figure of the "white liberal" as the one whom one would want to avoid resembling (still a powerful projection for black intellectuals), and whom one needs to get out of the way so that one can communicate directly with one's authentic self, there is the strong sense in Biko's writings that Black Consciousness is proposed as the "true" inheritor of the liberal tradition. When Biko writes that "the very political vocabulary that the blacks have used has been inherited from the liberals" (*I Write* 63), he does not mean to reject liberalism as an ongoing emancipatory project. In fact, in terms of that project, Black Consciousness can instruct liberals: "If they are *true* liberals they must realise that they themselves are oppressed, and that they must fight for their own freedom and not that of the nebulous 'they' with whom they can hardly claim identification" (*I Write* 66; my emphasis).

When Biko gives a basic definition of freedom, it becomes clear how Black Consciousness can be proposed as a more "true" liberalism. It radicalizes the existing South African liberal tradition by defining freedom as freedom from submission, not only to white political leadership but also to white standards set in the psyche of Blacks as an internalized racism that enlists one's collusion in one's own subjection. Freedom, as the ability to act and speak for oneself instead of being spoken for by another, thus also depends on an overcoming of mental slavery: "Freedom is the ability to define oneself with one's possibilities held back not by the power of other people over one but only by one's relationship to God and to natural surroundings. . . . the most potent weapon in the hands of the oppressor is the mind of the oppressed" (*I Write* 92).

Black Consciousness is what Ngũgĩ, with less emphasis on the complicity of the victim, calls "decolonising the mind." It is thus necessary to distinguish between liberalism as an open-ended emancipatory project, and the political positions and strategies adopted by liberal Whites in South Africa; and between the project, and the projections by Black Consciousness—as by Afrikaner nationalists, who liked to speak of "liberalists"—of the figure of the "white liberal." This is why, even if there were some who might have embraced the label, my book has no separate division on white liberal intellectuals or on what Paul Rich terms "English-speaking intellectuals." The hypothesis could even be ventured that, well before the 1970s, the "liberal tradition" in South Africa, which is associated with mission-school education and the English language, was not white or necessarily "English-speaking," as is almost universally assumed, but was sustained in black intellectual and political life. Sol T. Plaatje would be a key figure in this history. Biko himself dates the end of white liberal political leadership to the late 1950s (*I Write* 20).

This is not to say that others could and did not lay claim to the "liberal tradition," as N. P. van Wyk Louw did in the name of an Afrikaner "liberal nationalism," turning Hoernlé's version of it to his own devices. But in actuality, those of its inheritors who deepened its principles and called for their more thoroughgoing application were black. We observe this in Nelson Mandela's speeches in court in the early 1960s, as Derrida so brilliantly shows in "The Laws of Reflection." We can discern it in the writings and courtroom testimony of Steve Biko too. The place taken, in the departure of each of its heirs, by the negotiation of complicity with what subjects oneself is, I would propose, an index of the strength of the claim of each party on the "liberal tradition."

WHITE LIBERALS AND BLACK CONSCIOUSNESS
By taking its lead from Black Consciousness, or at least allowing itself to be affected by it, subsequent left white politics tacitly acknowledged the validity of its implicit claim to "true" inheritance of the emancipatory project. The Study Project on Christianity in Apartheid Society (SPRO-CAS), which comprised six "study commissions" involving "academics

and researchers in . . . economics, education, law, the church, and the social and political sciences," is a case in point. Conceived in 1969 by dissident Dutch Reformed minister Beyers Naude's Christian Institute and the South African Council of Churches, it was initially perceived by Black Consciousness as being "a highly academic forum." But in 1971 or 1972 SPRO-CAS launched a Black Community Programme under Bennie Khoapa, "who helped gather together a group of black-consciousness radicals . . . including Steve Biko." At the same time, influenced by Rick Turner, a political scientist from the University of Durban who headed the political commission, the political direction of SPRO-CAS shifted from the "common-society liberalism" of Alan Paton's Liberal Party to a "pluralism" that attempted to take into account the racial barriers to political cooperation imposed by apartheid. "By the end of 1972," according to Rich, "black-consciousness ideology was beginning to exert a major impact on the work of white-run liberal organizations in South Africa. The SPRO-CAS Programme had led to strong demands by its black members for their own autonomous . . . space for the formulation of specifically black political demands."[12]

It was in this context that, in a debate in 1976 with Guy Butler, a writer and academic typically seen as standing for English-speaking liberal hegemony,[13] Mike Kirkwood (who set up the grassroots literary magazine *Staffrider* in 1978 at Ravan Press, an offshoot of SPRO-CAS) set out a three-stage "ontology of the colonizer." In terms of this "ontology," the "colonizer" first sheds ethnocentric assumptions, then yields political leadership: "In the third stage the initiative passes to the colonized" (qtd. in Attwell, "Problem" 125).[14] Whites had heeded Biko's message to them to stop speaking and acting on behalf of Blacks and to work to raise consciousness within their own — that is to say, "white" — communities (*I Write* 25). In addition to Breyten Breytenbach, who received this message in exile, and Rick Turner, to whom I return shortly, among those who took up this task, although none saw his or her activism as being *restricted* to Whites, was Nadine Gordimer.

In "Speak Out: The Necessity for Protest," a 1971 academic-freedom lecture for students at the University of Natal, Gordimer explicitly linked the emergence of Black Consciousness to the "failure of the liberal ideal in South Africa" (*Essential Gesture* 100). This failure she associates with a tradition of "radical-liberal" student protest that, historically, "has fallen . . . into the necessity to speak *for*, or demand on *behalf* of, people whose colour sets them aside." Responding to Black Consciousness's redirection of the liberal agenda away from white-black advocacy, Gordimer gave her audience a new task: "We shall need to see our efforts not so much as attempts to right wrongs on behalf of the blacks, as to set our society free of the lies on which it is built" (*Essential Gesture* 101–2). In this formulation, "our society" could refer either to South African society as a whole or to white society specifically. The context does not allow us to decide with certainty, and one retains the impression that a common society is figured as not yet realized.[15] Gordimer does not take the coincidence of part and whole for granted when, like Frank Talk, she links truth and freedom. In so doing, she articulates, in dialogue with Black Consciousness, a new version of the emancipatory project.[16]

From the beginning, Gordimer's acceptance of black leadership, which she has described, in quasi-religious terms, as an "offer[ing] [of] one's self" (*Essential Gesture* 264), was based on an acknowledgment, as a privileged middle-class White, of complicity, through acts of commission and omission, in apartheid. It is also based, perhaps, in an identification—at times cryptic, always reserved—of herself as a Jew with the struggle of blacks against apartheid. In her first novel, *The Lying Days* (1953), she writes of a Jewish character who eventually leaves South Africa to fight for the state of Israel: "In South Africa a quick sympathy from his own small struggle struck out and identified itself with the vast one" (159). Without adverting to the fact that it is a meditation on the Holocaust, Gordimer quotes in "Speak Out" from George Steiner's essay "A Kind of Survivor" (1965): "*Men are accomplices to that which leaves them indifferent*" (Steiner 150; qtd. in *Essential Gesture* 92). Hence the imperative to "speak out: the necessity for protest."

On the one hand, this citation links Gordimer and others with the European genealogy I outlined in the introduction, dating back at least as far as Zola's "J'accuse" (1898), of responsibility for the intellectual arising from a discomfiting awareness of complicity in social and political evil: "It is my duty to speak up; I will not be an accessory to the fact" (*Dreyfus* 43) ("La vérité, je la dirai. . . . Mon devoir est de parler, je ne veux pas être complice" ["Lettre" 97–98]). There are thus also echoes of Karl Jaspers's notion of "metaphysical guilt": "There exists a solidarity among men as human beings that makes each co-responsible for every wrong and every injustice in the world, especially for crimes committed in his presence or with his knowledge. If I fail to do whatever I can to prevent them, I too am guilty" (*Question* 32). Turned toward particular social and political responsibilities, Jaspers's formulation is taken up by Steve Biko (*I Write* 78) and Frantz Fanon (*Black Skin* 89n) and anticipated by N. P. van Wyk Louw in "Volkskritiek." At the level of generality articulated by Zola and those who follow him, a common stream feeds divergent positions. As I noted in chapter 2, Louw rapidly shifts from universal "co-responsibility" to responsibility within, and for, the Afrikaans volk. Each inscription of the minimal syntagma of universal responsibility-in-complicity runs the risk of delimiting responsibility as it attempts, within a specific situation of complicity, to universalize it.

When one takes into account her specific positionality, Gordimer's negotiation of complicity, always in the mode of Zola—assuming responsibility for the other, speaking the truth to one's own on behalf of the other—can be read as a down payment on the debt incurred by Dreyfus. Wary of the facile identification that Biko mocked in "Black Souls in White Skins?"[17] and never privileging Jewishness (let alone Zionism), Gordimer "universalizes" the plight of the Jew by identifying with, or at least putting her life at the disposal of, African liberation. This universalization is to be distinguished from the association by Sartre of intellectual and Jew (see Contat), which, as I show later, provides him with a privileged basis, powerfully challenged by Fanon in *Black Skin, White Masks*, for European solidarity with Third-World anticolonial struggles.

Gordimer consistently refuses to privilege an identity or identification: her Jew's struggle is a "small struggle"; the identification is imperfect. For her, assuming responsibility for the other takes on, historically, the form of responsibility for the self—in the narrow sense—by addressing the white community. This tacit acceptance of apartheid's boundaries is countered rhetorically by a resistance to speaking, not only as a Jew, but as a *white* South African, a speaking-position the privilege of which the Western media is, as Gordimer notes, complicitous in maintaining (*Essential Gesture* 263–64). Again, Gordimer's writing figures a common society, where she could speak simply as a South African, but never claims that it actually exists.

Before being shot dead at his home by an assassin in January 1978, Rick Turner prepared a second edition of his book *The Eye of the Needle: Towards Participatory Democracy in South Africa* (1972). Turner's approach to the question of complicity enables us to separate general and narrow senses in a way that the sociopolitical commitment of Gordimer and others who embraced Black Consciousness can obscure, although parallels do emerge in Biko when he talks about the "oneness of community" and "Man-centered society" of "African culture" (*I Write* 30, 40). Drawing on existentialism and on radical educators such as Paulo Freire, Turner emphasized the process of "socialization" (*Eye* 9ff). In a racist society, particularly for the "dominant group" (11), this is an obstacle to "laying [one]self open to the other" and "to the future" (23, 99; see also 104). In order to achieve social and individual freedom, it is necessary to "be free from hidden conditioning processes" (37; see also 52ff). Whereas Turner criticized Black Consciousness for not developing a critique of capitalism (98; see also Biko, *I Write* 63), his emphasis, from a Christian-socialist point of view, was also on the reflecting intellect: "continuous self-examination," "self-awareness, self-analysis, and self-criticism" (*Eye* 1–2, 23).

If, like Gordimer, Turner turned his attention to the ability of whites to change (*Eye* 122, 143), he attempted to shift the terms of analysis from race to systemic positionality: "The dominant group are also being socialized . . . and in one sense at least each group is as much a victim of the system as is any other. . . . In South Africa, whites as well as blacks are victims of the social structure. They are, of course, victims of a different kind: The bulk of the whites are responsible victims" (11). The responsibility of thinking Whites, then, is to acknowledge complicity in the social structure. For Whites, opposition to apartheid begins with the realization that they have been socialized as members of the dominant group. Without this moment, no effective opposition could take place. For Biko, who invoked Jaspers's notion of metaphysical guilt, the structure of responsibility Turner assigns to Whites can be generalized to Blacks, although differences in positionality mean that the specific content of the complicities and responsibilities differs. Assuming responsibility in this way, becoming an agent instead of a victim, is as crucial to Black Consciousness as it was to Karl Marx when, in *Capital*, he "attempted to make the factory workers rethink themselves as agents of production, not as victims of capitalism" (Spivak, *Critique* 357).

In contrast to Gordimer, who explicitly distinguishes white consciousness-raising from a tradition of liberal advocacy, Turner has nothing to say about the ethics and politics of "speaking for." Nevertheless, by pivoting around the difference between a foldedness of one's existence as a human being with an other and the socialized complicity in racism that blocks an opening to the other, Turner's work gives us a way of understanding complicity and responsibility as socially and systemically overdetermined (not just as racially distributed). It thus allows us to understand how Black Consciousness taught Blacks to see themselves as "responsible victims." It also helps us to make sense of why, when the issue of advocacy resurfaces with such force with the Truth Commission, it does so in unanticipated ways.

By setting out to "give a voice" to ordinary South Africans, the Truth Commission sought to be open to the other. It sought to extend hospitality. Yet the commission became the subject of criticism when it was found that women witnesses were testifying less to human rights violations done to them than to male relatives. A particular sense of openness to the other, although hinting at a fundamental relation of human foldedness—expressed as "community" by Biko (*I Write* 30, 41) and as ubuntu by the Truth Commission—was shown to have its own unquestioned limits. The impulse to speak truth on behalf of the other and to enable the other to speak—the impulse par excellence of the responsible mind negotiating complicity as an affirming of a larger foldedness and detaching itself from ties in its way—had not attended to the body and to the way in which sexual difference is inscribed socially. As I discuss in my final chapter, a special women's hearing was held by the Truth Commission. When the emancipatory project is taken from the hands of the stereotypical "white liberal" who speaks for the black African, the deepening of freedom can take less predictable turns.

Black Consciousness and Complicity

Biko's "We Blacks," the companion piece to "Black Souls," formulates matters more sharply in terms of one's own complicity in what one seeks to combat. Beginning in a confessional vein, the column firmly implicates its author in the dynamics it sets out to describe and analyze:

Born shortly before 1948, I have lived all my conscious life in the framework of institutionalised separate development. My friendships, my love, my education, my thinking and every other facet of my life have been carved and shaped within the context of separate development. In stages during my life I have managed to outgrow some of the things the system taught me. Hopefully what I propose to do now is to take a look at those who participate in opposition to the system—not from a detached point of view but from the point of view of a black man, conscious of the urgent need for an understanding of what is involved in the new approach—"black consciousness." (*I Write* 27)

The year the National Party under D. F. Malan came to power under the banner of apartheid, 1948 marks a rupture in time. Although he does not say so explicitly, beginning as Biko does with his "conscious life," we can read it as having been traumatic, an event he was not "conscious" of at the time but that would profoundly affect him. Like Bloke Modisane's *Blame Me on History,* which shifts Verwoerd's speech on education back into the late 1940s, Biko's autobiographical opening projects a later formation, "separate development"—apartheid was implemented under that name in the 1960s—back to the catastrophe of 1948. That is the name he gives the trauma. Nevertheless, what dominates Biko's capsule narrative of the self is the accession to consciousness: "my conscious life." That life "I have lived in the framework of institutionalised separate development." The institution of the subject ("I"), of conscious subjectivity, is coeval with the institutionalization of "separate development." Implicating the self, apartheid, no matter what name it is given, does not permit separate development. It locks one into an intimacy with it, invading the basic ties that constitute the self and infiltrating the ways in which the social self is formed: "My friendships, my love, my education."[18] It constitutes one as an intellectual: "[M]y thinking and every other facet of my life have been carved and shaped within the context of separate development." This is a growing awareness that comes with "consciousness," which makes one able to "outgrow some of the things the system taught me." Writing an exemplary life story, as the pseudonym helps him do, Biko dedicates his confession to others: "those who participate in opposition to the system." Its lesson is of professed self-implication, "not from a detached point of view but from the point of view of a black man"; in other words, by one whose consciousness, as he has become aware "in stages during [his] life," has been deformed by the system. What Biko presents as "the new approach—'black consciousness'" thus hovers between implication and departure. Before broaching "opposition to the system," Black Consciousness dedicates the life of the intellectual, as a "black man," to "an urgent need for an understanding of what is involved" in negotiating and overcoming this complicity.

The overwhelming tendency of both scholarly and popular accounts of Steve Biko and Black Consciousness is to explain them as a development in a history of political resistance to apartheid understood as a clash of clearly defined political forces. When this oversimplified narrative morphology is uncritically taken up in intellectual history, or in a history of the intellectual, the specificity of Black Consciousness is lost.[19] With it goes the chance to write the intellectual history of apartheid as one involving not only opposition but also complicity and its negotiation. The writings of the movement itself ought to lead us to revise the terms in which we write this history—indeed any history of the intellectual as a figure of responsibility who sets thought to work ethico-politically.

In "We Blacks," Biko writes:

One should not waste time here dealing with manifestations of material want of the black people. A vast literature has been written on this problem. Possibly a little should be said about spiritual poverty. What makes the black man fail to tick? Is he convinced of his own accord of his disabilities? Does he lack in his genetic make-up that rare quality that makes a man willing to die for the realisation of his aspirations? Or is he simply a defeated person? The answer to this is not a clearcut one. It is, however, nearer to the last suggestion than anything else. The logic behind white domination is to prepare the black man for the subservient role in this country. Not so long ago this used to be freely said in parliament even about the educational system of the black people. It is still said today, although in a much more sophisticated language. To a large extent the evil-doers have succeeded in producing at the output end of their machine a kind of black man who is man only in form. This is the extent to which the process of dehumanisation has advanced.

. . . . the type of black man we have today has lost his manhood. Reduced to an obliging shell, he looks with awe at the white power structure and accepts what he regards as the "inevitable position." . . . All in all the black man has become a shell, a shadow of a man, completely defeated, drowning in his own misery, a slave, an ox bearing the yoke of oppression with sheepish timidity.

This *is* the first truth, bitter as it may seem, that we have to acknowledge before we can start on any programme designed to change the status quo. It becomes more necessary to see the truth as it is if you realise that the only vehicle for change are these people who have lost their personality. The first step therefore is to make the black man come to himself; to pump back life into his empty shell; to infuse him with pride and dignity, to remind him of his complicity in the crime of allowing himself to be misused and therefore letting evil reign supreme in the country of his birth. This is what we mean by an inward-looking process. This is the definition of "Black Consciousness." (*I Write* 28–29)

In this passage we again observe a movement of emphasis from perpetrators ("evil-doers") to victims "complicit[ous] in" the evil they do ("letting evil reign supreme in the country of his birth"). The consequence of this is a barring of access to humanity, a "dehumanisation" phrased in terms of a loss of "manhood," even an emasculation ("ox"). In so doing, it echoes Modisane's *Blame Me on History,* which, although a banned work, was read by Biko and the other SASO activists (Lindy Wilson 29).

The masculinist terms of Black Consciousness rhetoric and practice are well known. "Black man, you are on your own," SASO leader Barney Pityana once declared (qtd. in Woods 35). Although women in the male-dominated movement evidently gained confidence by entering the arena of political debate and action and by embracing slogans such as "Black is beautiful," which helped black women and men reject white standards of beauty, the movement, while generating several women's organizations, did not produce a critique of existing gender relations out of its analysis of the psychic dimensions of racism (Ramphele, "Dynamics" 217, 220–21; *Across Boundaries* 66). While it does not *oppose* "manhood" to "womanhood" or "femininity," the terms of analysis put forward by Biko, concatenating an absence of manhood and emasculation with enslavement and subservience, concentrated on a human being and a human body figured as male. In foregrounding the blockage of access to humanity, Black Consciousness imagined that humanity as male; Mamphela Ramphele writes that as a woman in the movement one sought an "honorary male status" ("Dynamics" 219ff). The weight of this gendered foreclosure is apparent in the activism of women around the national constitution and the Truth Commission. Their interventions, I will propose, if not in direct continuity with the Black Consciousness project, indicate a direction Black Consciousness might have taken had it generalized its analysis of the body in terms of race in order to think gender and sexual difference.

Linked to the progression of "We Blacks" from perpetrator to complicitous victim is an analytic shift from abstract system to human subject. Biko moves from a diabolical "machine," the "educational system of the black people" devised by Verwoerd, to its dehumanized product: "a kind of black man who is man only in form." His account of "spiritual poverty" begins sociologically, providing a causal and structural explanation of the phenomenon. The crux of the analysis, however, is when Biko's diagnosis moves on from what is a rationalist explanation of intellectual formation, a sociology of "education" and socialization, to which his own autobiography can adhere, to an account that is psychic in emphasis.

Though interlinked, the kinds of truth produced by each account are different. Stressing systemic overdetermination, the first produces an analysis of "spiritual poverty" in much the same way as one would analyze material poverty and political oppression: ideology, decisions of the government, legislation, the nature of the resultant institutions, and so forth. The second of the accounts, or the second part of the account, guides us to the specificity of Black Consciousness and the responsibility it assigns to the intellectual. It explains how the "machine" has been so effective that, like Frankenstein, it has produced a new "man" — except that this is a man who does not turn against his creator. That is because his creator has installed himself in his mind as his master. In order to explain this, Biko turns to a psychoanalytic, or quasi-psychoanalytic, model: "people who have lost their personality." The truth provided by this model resides in complicity: "This *is* the first truth. . . . The first step therefore is . . . to remind [the black man] of his complicity in the crime of allowing himself to be misused." This truth — a psychic or moral truth — has to be acknowledged along with the epistemic truth of sociology if "spiritual poverty" is to be overcome. "Making the black man come to himself," engaging him in "an inward-looking process" — these are the essential traits of Black Consciousness: "This is the definition of 'Black Consciousness.'"

Although Biko does not employ the word, one could say that Black Consciousness, as an acknowledgment and negotiation by the oppressed of mental or intellectual complicity in his or her oppression, involves not only the conscious, analytical mind but also a coming to terms with the *unconscious*. The "evil," the "crime" in which he or she is complicitous, though framed in these moral and religious terms, is of the psyche and, it would follow, requires a psychic solution. To assume responsibility as an intellectual means not only applying one's mind to the analysis of social structures but also analyzing one's own psychic implication in them. This responsible self-consciousness is connected intimately to the body. Motifs of consciousness and its loss insistently recur in the hearings on Steve Biko's death when what is ostensibly at issue is the comportment and condition of his living and dead body. Why this should be so becomes more comprehensible once we turn to the taking up, by Black Consciousness, of the ideas of Frantz Fanon, whose adaptation of psychoanalysis transforms received notions of the intellectual and the extent of intellectual responsibility.

The Intellectual and Psychoanalysis, the Mind, and the Body:
Black Consciousness and Frantz Fanon

Steve Biko and the other university students whose debates attended the birth of Black Consciousness found resonance in the works of banned South African writers and in ideas from abroad (Gerhart 270ff.). The writings and recorded speeches of figures of the black diaspora — among them Malcolm X, Eldridge Cleaver, Stokely Carmichael, James Cone, and Martin Luther King — were particularly significant (Lindy Wilson 29). In elaborating his project, Biko borrowed and, I would propose, deepened, insights from Frantz Fanon, whose works first appeared in English in 1963, a few years before the debates began. In *Black Skin, White Masks* (1952), Fanon provided an account of how racism functions by enlisting the collaboration of its black victims through a psychic process of "internalization" or, as he adapted the concepts of psychoanalysis, "epidermalization." Through Fanon, Biko and his contemporaries were able to supplement the received sociopolitical account of racism as structurally overdetermined, with a theory of the psyche. The appropriation of Frantz Fanon by Frank Talk, whose name in part echoes Fanon's, also suggests how, as a theory of the mind and of the body, Fanon's *Black Skin, White Masks* can be read as an account of the intellectual and complicity.

Black Skin, White Masks confronts complicity at several levels as theoretical exposition blends with intellectual autobiography to produce, as it does in Biko, the productive tension of a self-implicating performance. Relying on existentialist and psychoanalytic morphologies of the self,

Fanon's text produces, from the beginning, an interweaving of general and narrow senses of complicity. In order to register the full force of Fanon's arguments, particularly at the level of ethics, it is essential to distinguish between these senses. If foldedness with the other is basic to human-being, it is a barring of access to this embrace by specific affiliations that stands in the way of full humanity.

The conduct of *Black Skin, White Masks* as a text makes the co-implication of complicity in general and narrow senses apparent from the start. Opening with an epigraph from Aimé Césaire that begins, "I am talking of millions of men who have been skillfully injected with fear, inferiority complexes," borrowing its own words from an other, the book draws its reader into an apocalyptic discourse already in full swing: "The explosion will not happen today. It is too soon . . . or too late" (9). Its negations reveal the makings of a dialogue, the existence of an other whose expectations are figured as differing and as forcing a differentiation: "I do not come with timeless truths. My consciousness is not illuminated with ultimate radiances." A few lines later the dialogue reaches or stages a crisis, with a question: "Why write this book? No one has asked me for it. Especially those to whom it addresses itself" (9; trans. modified). The crisis exposes, at once, a basic structure of address, involving self and other, and its fracture. If, as Fanon observes at the start of the first chapter, "The Negro and Language," "it is implicit that to speak is to exist absolutely for the other" (17), the irruptive question that arises foregrounds the difference and mixing of complicity in general and narrow senses.

When the operation of this basic structure of human-being is re-capitulated in chapter 2 of Fanon's book, "The Woman of Color and the White Man," the ethical implications are more overt: "Man is motion toward the world and toward his like. A movement of aggression, which leads to enslavement or conquest; a movement of love, a gift of self, the ultimate stage of what by common accord is called ethical orientation" (41). Standing in the way of "authentic love" for the black woman is "that feeling of inferiority or that Adlerian exaltation, that overcompensation, which seem to be the indices of the black *Weltanschauung*" (42). As critics have observed, the Martinican writer Mayotte Capécia, whose autobiography Fanon analyzes in this chapter, is the target of accusation more intense than that directed at the male authors he discusses.[20] The black woman, in love with "whiteness" (42), bears the larger part of burden of the imperative of self-criticism. Globally, the alienating implication in structures of racism, of one's social and affectual life, the giving of the self over to the other, catalyzes responsibility as ethical and sets the task of eliminating the desire for "whiteness" as complicity in the narrow sense, so that one can give oneself over to, and embrace, the other in ways that do not compromise a shared basic humanity. The main outline of Fanon's account has the "woman of color" as its blind spot; at a later stage, a relation with her is disavowed: "I know nothing about her" (181).

Yet a singular strength of *Black Skin, White Masks* remains the fact that it is written from a position of historical complicity—from the implication of the Antillean in a privileged relation to the French language and French culture: "The Negro of the Antilles will be proportionately whiter—that is, he will come closer to being a real human being—in direct ratio to his mastery of the French language" (18). As Fanon observes, the Antillean does not consider him- or herself to be black[21] and is taken by other Blacks in the French colonial system as a standard of a phantasmatic whiteness; Senegalese sometimes learn Creole in order to pass as Martinican (38). And Fanon himself, as a medical practitioner, finds himself talking down to Arab patients: "I myself have been aware, in talking to certain patients, of the exact instant at which I began to slip" (32). This awareness is dramatized rhetorically by passages in which Fanon would otherwise appear to participate in the racism he opposes: "When it comes to case of the Negro, nothing of the kind. He has no culture, no civilization, no 'long historical past'" (34).

To acknowledge such complicity is the responsibility assumed by Fanon, as he takes the situation of the Antillean as exemplary, not simply of being a victim of colonialism, but of being a racist perpetrator within it. Unlike Bloke Modisane and other masculinist writers on race, such as Malcolm X (68) and even Eldridge Cleaver (27–29, 187–89), however, he does not confess to a misogynist violence directed at one's own that we have registered at the level of his rhetoric. The project of his book is thus to separate narrow and general senses of the foldedness of human-being with the other and to free the black man from a complicity, in the narrow sense, with a captivating fantasy of being white. Because the minimal self-other structure of human-being as such is implicated, or instantiated, in a racist structure that produces black and white human beings, the opening to the black man of human-being in the general sense amounts to "the liberation of the man of color from himself" (10). Although Fanon does not want the black man to engage in self-accusation, if that means awaiting divine salvation (13), this acknowledgment of complicity is the fulcrum around which the book turns.

Black Skin, White Masks is, in one sense, the work *of* an intellectual *for* intellectuals — or, as Fanon puts it, those, as among the Antillean middle class (more or less diasporic), with access to the colonizing culture, affected by an "intellectual alienation." For that readership, which has not asked Fanon to write it, *Black Skin, White Masks* sets out complicity not only in terms of thought and intellectual life, but in terms of the implication of the psyche in a set of unconscious dynamics. The demand on the intellectual is thus for an ethical and a political response equipped to negotiate the pitfalls of consciousness and the ruses of the unconscious.

If, as a figure assuming responsibility out of a troubling sense of complicity, as I have proposed, the intellectual is an artifact of the last decade of the nineteenth century, his or her responsibility-in-complicity is radicalized in the twentieth century by psychoanalysis. That is, psychoanalysis becomes the site for a deepening of responsibility. This development, which is apparent in the practice in the 1930s of South African analyst Wulf Sachs, who foresaw an acceptance of political leadership as the outcome of successful therapy for his black analysand in *Black Hamlet*,[22] is clear in Fanon. "As a psychoanalyst," Fanon writes, "I should help my patient to become *conscious* of his unconscious and abandon his attempts at a hallucinatory whitening, but also to act in the direction of a change in the social structure" (100; see also Fanon, *Wretched of the Earth* 211).

Psychoanalysis as taken up by Fanon supplies yet another dimension to our emerging sense of the intellectual as a figure assuming ethical and political responsibility in a situation of acknowledged complicity. With the advent of psychoanalysis and even before, the intellectual can, as such early feminists as Olive Schreiner realized, no longer be thought of, historically or ethically, as a "disembodied mind" — even if that notion is a refuge for intellectuals frustrated by racial and sexual difference. As Jean-Paul Sartre wrote in *Anti-Semite and Jew,* analyzing the stereotype of the Jew as "abstract intellectual" by recalling the "disembodied philosopher" of Plato's *Phaedo:* "It is precisely this sort of disincarnation that certain Jews seek" (111). It is with this characterization that Fanon parts company with Sartre, whose *Anti-Semite and Jew* is otherwise a touchstone for *Black Skin, White Masks*'s arguments. Motivating the need for a "psychoanalytical interpretation of the black problem," Fanon notes, in a psycho-social bifurcation of analysis comparable to that put forward by Biko, that:

the effective disalienation of the black man entails an immediate recognition of social and economic realities. If there is an inferiority complex, it is the outcome of a double process:
— primarily, economic;
— subsequently, the internalization — or, better, the epidermalization — of this inferiority. (*Black Skin* 12, 13)

Although "the black man's alienation is not an individual question," Fanon stresses that, since "man is what brings society into being . . . any unilateral liberation is incomplete. . . . On the objective level as on the subjective level, a solution has to be supplied" (13).

In order to focus on the subjective dimension, Fanon adapts psychoanalytic terminology to account for how the black self is formed. In a basic sense, one's human-being depends on a relation to an other and thus involves an affectual and an ethical dimension, which, as Fanon notes, can be actualized or destroyed in a structure of linguistic address. This involves a process of phantasmatic identification, whereby one internalizes the other in ideal form. For the Antillean, who internalizes the other as "whiteness," it is more accurate to speak of "epidermalization," since the formation of his raced being takes place not only at the level of psychic structures but also socially, when he encounters Whites or a "white" gaze, and is, in so doing, deprived of access to whiteness — and thus to humanity, since his is a humanity that has been defined in relation to phantasmatic whiteness. To paraphrase Judith Butler on Althusser, he is complicitous in the power of "subjection" that, in forming him as a subject, subjects him to its regime (*Psychic Life* 2). Again, the middle-class Antillean is exemplary in being implicated in these dynamics, for until arrival in France, or until some other precipitating encounter with the white gaze, he or she has been unmolested in his or her access to whiteness. As a consequence of this psychoanalytic intervention, of this intervention *in* psychoanalysis, Fanon marks out his difference from Sartre.

In "The Fact of Blackness" [L'expérience vécue du Noir], perhaps the most intriguing chapter in *Black Skin, White Masks,* Fanon quotes from

Sartre's *Anti-Semite and Jew* as a counterpoint to his epigraph from Cé-saire: "They [the Jews] have allowed themselves to be poisoned by the stereotype that others have of them. . . . We may say that their conduct is perpetually overdetermined from the inside" (95; qtd. in Fanon 115). "All the same," Fanon responds, "the Jew can be unknown in his Jewish-ness. He is not wholly what he is. . . . I am given no chance. I am overdetermined from without. I am the slave not of the 'idea' that others have of me but of my own appearance" (115–16). Fanon develops an account of epidermalization in terms of a "corporeal schema" shared by all human beings, which, for black people in a racist social structure, is overlaid by a "historico-racial schema," an "epidermal schema" that shat-ters the corporeal schema of the black human being: "The other, the white man . . . had woven me out of a thousand details, anecdotes, stories" (111–12). This shattering is figured as having been precipitated by a child's fearful cry: "Look, a Negro! It was an external stimulus that flicked over me as I passed by. I made a tight smile" (111).

Fanon's analysis prompts him, in this meditative and quasi-autobiographical chapter, to challenge the relevance of Sartre's account of anti-Semitism, when it associates the Jew with reason (118–19), to an account of white-black racism. Even if, from Fanon's point of view, a fraternal identification with the Jew is possible — "The Jew and I. . . . I joined the Jew, my brother in misery" (122) — the specific nature of racism, as it is inscribed on the black body, sets its limit (see also 163), as it does in a different positionality for Gordimer. This limit is, to recall the French title of the chapter, "the lived experience of the black man." So Fanon turns to Léopold Sédar Senghor, who wrote in 1939 that the "rhythm" found in "Negro art. . . . affects what is least intellectual in us" ("Ce que"; qtd. in Fanon 122–23). "Since no agreement was possible on the level of reason," Fanon writes, "I threw myself back toward unrea-son. It was up to the white man to be more irrational than I" (123). This is what leads up to Fanon's famous rejection of Sartre's characterization of Négritude in "Black Orpheus," his introduction to Senghor's *An-thologie de la nouvelle poésie nègre et malgache* (1948), as "an antiracist racism," a dialectical negativity "intended to prepare the synthesis or realization of the human in a society without races" (qtd. by Fanon 133–34).[23] It is also what allows us to understand it as more than a simple rejection of white authority.

For Fanon, Sartre's account of Négritude is an "intellectualization of the experience of being black" (134). It points, in other words, to the limits of conceiving the intellectual to be "disembodied"—a concept that Sartre, although he points to how the Jew employs it in response to anti-Semitism, does not appear to question. Fanon's use of the word *intellectualization* is more than merely a pejorative, a retort to a Marxist philosopher's paternalism. It unites a critique of the foundations of intellectual practice, the concept of the intellectual as disembodied, with Fanon's theory of "epidermalization." The black intellectual has to affirm the body and make it part of his account, because racism will not allow him to be disembodied; and the unconscious psyche, if one is going to take that into account, operates at a social level and on the surface of the skin, not simply, as in the case of the Jew,[24] as an internalization by the ego of an ideal or poisonous idea. Philosophy is no escape since, as Olive Schreiner makes clear, intellectual life is always already social, and one's body is inscribed socially in different and unequal ways.

An appeal to the social inscription of the body is not, however, Fanon's main line of argument, as he summons Hegel, as a philosophical father-figure, to confront Sartre, the "born Hegelian":

A consciousness committed to experience is ignorant, has to be ignorant, of the essences and the determinations of its being. . . . In terms of conscious-ness, the black consciousness is held out as an absolute density, as filled with itself, a stage preceding any invasion, any abolition of the ego by desire.˙. . . Still in terms of consciousness, black consciousness is immanent in its own eyes. I am not a potentiality of something, I am wholly what I am. (*Black Skin* 134–35)

It is this gesture, analyzable in terms of a mimetic rivalry for the atten-tions of the figure of Hegel, that always makes me uncertain of whether Fanon's response to Sartre is a rejection or a disavowal—or whether he is playing at a disavowal, just as he tries on a racist's statements that he would not own but does. It seems to be made at a such high cost— namely, of Fanon's and Négritude's majority, both symbolically and intellectually, as Fanon affirms the "ignorance" of immanent experience. Aided by his psychoanalytic account of racism, Fanon produces an anal-ysis of Sartre's intervention; it is merely another way of imposing, at-tributing to the Négritude poets, a white ideal: "Not yet white, no longer wholly black, I was damned. Jean-Paul Sartre had forgotten that the Negro suffers in his body quite differently from the white man.

Between the white man and me the connection was irrevocably one of transcendence" (138; see also 225). Yet not only is it still Hegel who is summoned to bear witness, but Fanon's own analysis would tell us that it is impossible for him to avoid a dialectical relation with the figure of "the white man." Senghor's Négritude was itself the outcome of a passage through the French system of education and an attempt to supplement and deepen Western humanism; "Ce que l'homme noir apporte" is the title of his seminal 1939 essay.[25] It came after an encounter with the white gaze and could not have happened in ignorance of it. Perhaps this is why Fanon ends his chapter by writing, "Without responsibility, straddling Nothingness and Infinity, I began to weep" (140). Psychoanalysis radicalizes responsibility but renders old binaries and critiques defenseless. Sartre intellectualizes the experience of racism, but his position can only be criticized by a corresponding intellectualization — by not fully acknowledging one's complicity in the system one wants to move beyond, and by abrogating "responsibility" to Hegel, the dead white man who will authorize a "black consciousness" that disavows, impossibly, the presence of the "white man."

Biko and his contemporaries sometimes linked their Black Consciousness with Fanon's version. Barney Pityana works in and out of *Black Skin, White Masks,* using Fanon's phrases without quotation marks, and attributing other phrases to Fanon by enclosing them in quotation marks. Echoing what Biko writes in "We Blacks," he grafts Fanon's response to Sartre in "The Fact of Blackness" into a text where the emphasis falls heavily on complicity and where fragments of Fanon's philosophical language are taken up and capitalized but quickly translated into the terms of local political strategy:

Black Consciousness can therefore be seen as a stage preceding any invasion, any abolition of the ego by desire [Fanon, *Black Skin* 135]. The first step, therefore, is to make the black man see himself, to pump life into his empty shell; to infuse him with pride and dignity; to remind him of his complicity in the crime of allowing himself to be misused and therefore letting evil reign supreme in the country of his birth. This is what we mean by an inward-looking process. This makes consciousness, Black Consciousness, imminent [*sic*] in our own eyes. "I am not a potentiality of something," writes Fanon. "I am wholly what I am. I do not have to look for the universal. No probability has any place inside me. My [N]egro consciousness does not hold itself out as black [*sic,* Fanon's text reads "as a lack"]. It IS. It is its own follower [Fanon's text (*Black Skin* 135) ends here; Pityana substitutes block capitals for Fanon's italics]. This is all that we blacks are after. TO BE. We believe that we are quite efficient in handling our BEness and for this we are self-sufficient. We shall never find our goals and aspirations as a people centered anywhere else but in US. This, therefore, necessitates a self-examination and a rediscovery of ourselves. Blacks can no longer afford to be led and dominated by nonblacks." (qtd. in Woods 34)[26]

Where Biko wrote "This is the definition of 'Black Consciousness'" (*I Write* 29), Pityana has "This makes consciousness, Black Consciousness, imminent [*sic*] in our own eyes." Although Biko only sometimes wrote in such terms — "Black Consciousness makes the black man see himself as a being, entire in himself" (*I Write* 68) — there is, in both his and Pityana's formulations, an underlining of complicity. That complicity is usually in proximity to an insistence on a parting of ways with leadership by "white liberals." A rough analogy can be made between the disavowal by Black Consciousness of the authority of white liberals and the rejection by Fanon of Sartre's version of Négritude. In each case, what is disavowed is formative. Senghor, Césaire, and the other Négritude intellectuals came through the French education system and imbibed the Hegelian and Marxist teachings of the time, just as Biko and his contemporaries passed through mission schooling and experienced first-hand the liberal promise and its breach (see Comaroff and Comaroff 2:396). In the case of Black Consciousness, as I have argued, it is also a deepening, as liberalism is appropriated and radicalized (a basic dispropriability joins, disjoins, and rejoins "liberals" and liberalism) to the extent that such white intellectuals as Breyten Breytenbach, Nadine Gordimer and Rick Turner begin to formulate responsibility in the terms of Biko, Pityana, and others, and complicity becomes an essential part of their conceptual repertoire.

Calling on Hegel, Fanon's response to Sartre's "intellectualizing" of the experience of racism is a further intellectualization of racism and anti-racism. His passionate invocation of the Hegelian father and master, however, tends to make us forget his own provocative departure: the theorizing of race in terms of epidermalization, and a differing social inscription of the black body. This is where Fanon most directly challenges the notion of the intellectual as "disembodied intelligence" and thus also Alfred Weber's sociological notion of the intellectual class as a "free-floating intelligence" (Mannheim 137–38). Adapting psychoanalytic terms to supplement Sartre, Fanon compels us to think of the intellectual as a mind in a body. Historically, this has been a point of intervention for feminists, who point to the social inscription of the gendered body, a factor that, structuring intellectual life in its institutions, also functions at the level of the individual intellectual. Black Consciousness certainly took up Fanon's impassioned but, arguably, re-intellectualizing rejection of Sartre and his assertion of black being. What remains to be analyzed is the extent to which, when it set out responsibility-in-complicity for the reflective consciousness, it addressed the body.

BEING-BLACK-IN-THE-WORLD — APARTHEID AND THE INTELLECTUAL

In 1973 SPRO-CAS and Ravan Press published a small book of essays by clinical psychologist Noel Chabani Manganyi called *Being-Black-in-the-World* — the Heideggerian title of which alludes to Sartre's characterization of Négritude in "Black Orpheus" (314). Setting out Black Consciousness as "a new kind of responsibility" (21), Manganyi, more than any intellectual of the movement, makes the body part of an analysis of racism and of the complicity of its victims in it.

Like Fanon's *Black Skin, White Masks,* Manganyi's essay "Us and Them" begins with a basic account of human-being in its historicity, out of which he explicates the specificities of raced being in the South African context. Manganyi's Heideggerian terms allow him to move from a basic structure of human foldedness, of "being-in-the-world," to a set of alterable complicities of which it is the condition of possibility:

The basic structure of existence is historical. It is specifically man's historicity and his being a decisive being (man decides what to become) which have infused variations on this given existential structure. It is these two factors which have made it possible if not imperative for us to say that there is a mode of existence (of being-in-the-world) which may be characterised as being-white-in-the-world and being-black-in-the-world. There is sufficient documentation of the fact that the history of being-in-the-world (*In-der-welt-sein*) of the black and white races of the world is different. This history has been so different, in fact, that one is justified to talk in terms of a black and white existential experience. (*Being-Black* 27–28)

Manganyi moves rapidly from an invocation of the philosophical account of being-in-the-world as historical, to an explication of it in terms of race. His basic concept of being-in-the-world accumulates pieces of race thinking—"black and white races"—that inform the "documentation" he cites as evidence for "black and white existential experience." It is illuminating to compare this account with N. P. van Wyk Louw's voortbestaan in geregtigheid—which I explicated in terms of Heidegger's *"In-der-Welt-Sein"* and his translation of the Cartesian *cogito* as *"Sein-bei"*—as a making transcendental of the located, historical being of the Afrikaner volk, and an association of that existence with justice. Louw's declared project, to justify for the volk a separate existence [aparte bestaan], coincides with, and provides substance to, the larger project of elaborating apartheid thinking. Manganyi, who, like Biko, is always attuned to what Black Consciousness and Afrikaner nationalism share, is left with, and in turn elaborates, that legacy of ethno-racial nationalism and apartheid.[27]

It is here that is posed at its sharpest the question of apartheid and complicity, apartheid as a violent response to, a disavowal of, the other in whose proximity one exists [bestaan], and, in the case of Louw's "liberal nationalism," in relation to whom one wishes for a separate existence [aparte bestaan]. J. M. Coetzee has written about how the race thinking of Geoffrey Cronjé works as a disavowal of desire,[28] and how, for the white racist, the black body condenses an attractive and loathsome black "essence." Like Fanon, Manganyi begins from the premise that black people are ensnared in a similar ambivalence in relation to their own bodies. Apartheid, literally apartness, is commonly understood as a system of classification and separation. In a certain sense, we have deluded ourselves with the fantasy of Louw, Cronjé, and others. Just as Coetzee's reading of Cronjé allows us to see apartheid as a disavowal of inevitable intimacy—which Coetzee figures in terms of conscience and desire in his memoir, *Boyhood: Scenes from Provincial Life* (60, 64)—the lasting insight of Black Consciousness was that apartheid was not, in any essential sense, an achievement of separateness at all, but it was a system of enforced separation that, paradoxically, generated an unwanted intimacy with an oppressive other.

This is why apartheid is exemplary for making intellectual responsibility manifest as a negotiation of complicity: in the narrow sense, or in a range of narrow senses, the system decreed apartness; in a general sense, it disavowed relation, a foldedness in human-being with the other (one that, as Plaatje tries to show in *Mhudi,* had its own fractured historical manifestations as community). If such a disavowal of relation is what tends toward support for apartheid, it is an acknowledgment of this complicity and its disavowal at the heart of apartheid that is the essential starting point of any opposition to apartheid. Without it there would be no desire, no freeing of the desire, for things to be any different. If Louw's goal was to fashion a separate existence for the Afrikaner volk, Manganyi proceeds by acknowledging the illusory nature of such separateness, and to negotiate, in the context of the enforced separation of apartheid, the effects of a deeper intimacy.

Manganyi does not remain at the level of an existential ontology that, like apartheid thinking, disavows relation, but he insists on the dimension of the other in order to show how being-black-in-the-world unfolds historically. "Existence *(dasein),*" Manganyi writes, "is dialogue: relation" *(Being-Black* 28). Human existence bifurcates historically at "four different levels": "An individual has to relate himself first to his body as an existential fact. In addition to this dialogue with his body, relations have to be established with his fellowmen and sometimes God (god); with objects (material culture) and with time" (28). Although willing to attribute to "African ontology" a "primary focus on the existential situation in its totality; on dialogue as the most fundamental existential category" (39), Manganyi insists on its undermining by colonial and missionary efforts (40), and on "the destruction of traditional African approaches" in the area of social life (30). Each level of relation is set out in terms of the effect of colonial intervention, white domination, and capitalism. To be-black-in-the-world is to be alienated.

Manganyi's analysis is striking for treating intellectual alienation under the heading of the body. The intellectual thus operates, not in a "disembodied" realm of ideas, but at the level of corporeal images and impulses. This is what Coetzee's tracking of apartheid "thinking" and its phobia of blood-mixing reveals, as does Black Consciousness as it delves into the somatizing legacy of apartheid thinking. Colonialism inscribes the black body with oppressive intimacy. Apartheid has not separated black and white, for Blacks continue to measure their worth by white standards. The intellectual and the corporeal are joined in alienation.

Taking up the same phenomenology of the body as Fanon, Manganyi explicates corporeal being-in-the-world by again moving from a mini-

mal structure—the body's essential ambiguity—to the variegated production, in a zone of contact, of bodies as white and black, and the
mapping onto them of an epidermalized system of value, of "good" and
"bad." This system informs not only one's attitude toward one's body
but, more fundamentally, one's consciousness—one's awareness of who
one is and who one is able to "tell the world one is":

One of the legacies of colonialism in Africa has been the development of the
dichotomy relating to the body, namely the "bad" and "good" body. The
white man's body has been projected as the standard, the norm of beauty, of
accomplishment. . . .

The implications of this dichotomy are many and varied. An important
result of this state of affairs was the development of two different sociological schemas of the body. One of these schemas was black and bad and the
other was white and good. . . . Under ideal conditions of the "good body,"
the body becomes for the individual, a point of view (Mearlau-Ponty [*sic*]).
This means that the *individual schema* predominates over the *sociological
schema*. This last condition is one which has obtained in white societies for a
long time. In black communities on the other hand, through the artificial
and unnatural predominance of the sociological schema, the individual
schema has been traumatised and ceases to be a point of view; of telling the
world who one is. (*Being-Black* 28–29)

The social inscription of the body affects both social and intellectual
life.[29] Under apartheid, black and white exist in communities separated
by force. Yet "black communities" are haunted by whiteness as an ideal.
Where the "white man's body has been projected as the standard, the
norm of beauty, of accomplishment," the "the individual schema [of the
black body] . . . ceases to be a point of view; of telling the world who
one is." One's being-in-the-world is a condition of possibility for the
thoughts one has. Theory is informed by praxis in this basic sense. When
practical intervention can alter the sociological schema or one's relation
to it, bodies become a site of struggle. A corporealization of complicity
and resistance are implicit when Manganyi mentions, as one such initiative, the "Black is Beautiful" campaign: "A massive and creative campaign is essential to alter the negative sociological schema of the black
body. This is desirable from the point of view of its inherent aesthetic
potential, but also because of the unlimited social-psychological significance of the body as existential fact-situation" (29). Manganyi's agenda

advances that of *Black Skin, White Masks,* which, although it analyzes the corporeal dimension of racism and the complicity of its victims in it, does not propose more than an intellectual antidote: "I hope by analyzing it to destroy it" (*Black Skin* 14). The next step is taken in *The Wretched of the Earth;* in *Black Skin, White Masks,* Fanon's "black consciousness" remains at the level of the intellect and the intellectual.

One would never know, however, from Manganyi's account of "Black is Beautiful" that this campaign involved consciousness-raising among women. Although Manganyi draws support from an analogy between black being-in-the-world, and "a feminine mode of being-in-the-world" the existence of which he says has been "convincingly suggested" (*Being-Black* 37), he never allows sexual or gender difference to complicate the main, masculinist, lines of his analysis.[30] Generalized, the corporeal analyses of Fanon and Manganyi would also have situated the intellectual within the history of sexuality, within a history of apartness, although inextricably implicated in it, irreducible to race apartheid.

If the singularity of Manganyi's book lies in its insistence on the corporealization of intellectual alienation and the interpenetration of its "mental" and "corporeal" effects, we can, in the writers of Black Consciousness, nevertheless speak historically of a differential *distribution* of "mind" and "body." Remaining within Manganyi's terms, we could say that, if being-black-in-the-world is conditioned by the constant intervention of others, each representing the rupture of colonialism and the violence of apartheid, the corresponding being-*white*-in-the-world also varies. As we have noted, in the history of Black Consciousness and in the hearings concerning Steve Biko's death, the white "oppressor" is not imagined as unitary. The figure of the Afrikaner occupies a place different from the English-speaking white liberal and is linked to a different range of affect. One could say that, in the *dominant* imaginary of Black Consciousness, the Afrikaner represents dominion over the body; the Liberal, control over the mind. If liberation has been won from the former, the struggle for freedom from the latter continues.

BLACK CONSCIOUSNESS AFTER APARTHEID

This distribution of emphasis can be tracked, during and after apartheid, in the essays of Njabulo Ndebele, who, as a student, had begun to participate in Black Consciousness in the early 1970s ("Black Development").[31] As a writer and cultural critic, Ndebele carried forward and elaborated the intellectual project of Black Consciousness in the 1980s, when he observed that "we have given away too much of our real and imaginative lives to the oppressor and his deeds" and advocated, for writers, "working towards a radical displacement of the white oppressor as an active, dominant player in the imagination of the oppressed" (*South African Literature* 160, 73). This displacement is dramatized in his novella "Fools" (1985), when the teacher, Zamani, whose body resolutely absorbs a whipping from a "Boer" (Ndebele's stereotypical hairy-armed working-class Afrikaner male), realizes that "I had crushed him with the sheer force of my presence" (*Fools* 276). The echoes of Pityana, the later Fanon, and Négritude are unmistakable; it is the "presence" of the body, not the mind, that is set against, and overcomes, the "white oppressor." In the other stories in *Fools,* there are several different imaginings of an autonomous black intellectual and cultural life. Yet in this, the only appearance of a white character in the collection, the character is an Afrikaner — one does not find a "liberal" in any of Ndebele's stories[32] — and resistance assumes a corporeal dimension.

The "oppressor" returns in Ndebele's essays after 1990, but not in unitary form. The figure of the Afrikaner undergoes division. The "Boer" does reappear momentarily in "a brief encounter with the past," when a delegate at the 1990 Afrikaanse Skrywersgilde conference urges a questioner, uncertain about what language to use, to speak in Afrikaans: "I saw the compulsion to speak it in public at the risk of being denied access to public services. I saw the extent to which the little that I knew of the language when I was forced to use it in those situations became a confirmation that I was less than human" ("How" 12). In 1993 President F. W. de Klerk challenged Ndebele's appointment to the board of the South African Broadcasting Corporation on the grounds that he did not speak Afrikaans (Gevisser). More and more, however, the Afrikaner is the one with whom a tentative settlement is sought — and he or she is not confronted merely with the body. In "Guilt and Atonement: Unmasking History for the Future" (1991), Ndebele confesses that, having begun to write a novel "about a young Afrikaner boy": "I found I could not write the novel. . . . I simply did not know my main character. . . . All I had was a storehouse of stereotypes for which I had no use. . . . I know that I still cannot write it. At bottom is the fact that I do not know the people that my hero belongs to as a real, living community. . . . I am aware of a wall that is as formidable as ever. It is the wall of ignorance" (*South African Literature* 151).

Yet, despite this "wall," and despite not knowing much Afrikaans, Ndebele continues to be occupied by the figure of the Afrikaner—either as, in the case of Breytenbach, an antagonist who stubbornly clings to "volkstaats of the mind" ("Open Letter"), or as a potential partner in the invention of a national memory and consciousness. In "Memory, Metaphor, and the Triumph of Narrative" (1998), an essay in which he reflects on the Truth and Reconciliation Commission, Ndebele notes that, although a "psychology of maintenance . . . which made prejudice a standard mode of perception" predominated "among members of the white, mainly Afrikaner, working class" under apartheid, an acknowledgment of complicity—"an informal truth and reconciliation process"—is emerging from within the Afrikaner community (23–24). This Ndebele sees in Afrikaans literature, in the novels of Mark Behr, Karel Schoeman, and Jeanne Goosen (24). They are writing the novel—or the mirror-novel of the novel he cannot write. "Somewhere," Ndebele writes, "the story of the contemporary Afrikaans family will converge with the stories of millions of those recently emerged from oppression" (25).

In the same essay a personal anecdote reveals, quasi-allegorically, how the white liberal occupies a different and more troubling place than the Afrikaner. Ndebele and his wife are on a plane back to South Africa when the pilot announces that the national soccer team is ahead in a match against Cameroon. A white fellow-passenger turns around and asks Ndebele whether Cameroon is a good team, which Ndebele interprets as a pretense at a lack of prejudice (speaking to a black person), but also as implying that the national team, which is mainly black and supported by Blacks, is not good enough to beat a European team: "I am presenting, of course, the archetypal image of the bleeding-heart, English-speaking liberal South African, who has no idea why he is hated so much when he sacrificed so much for the oppressed. . . . Fellow South Africans of this kind are blissfully unaware that they should appear before the TRC" ("Memory" 26). When it does not assume the form of benefiting materially from apartheid (see Mamdani, "Reconciliation"), their complicity in apartheid takes the shape of a soul-murder, in their inability to relinquish control over the values that they tacitly pressure others to accept: "With their condescending platitudes, they have massacred hundreds and thousands of souls. . . . English-speaking South Africans have yet to acknowledge their willing compliance, by developing their own particular version of oppression, in the oppression of black people" ("Memory" 26). For a black intellectual elite that, if not mission-educated, often sent its sons and daughters to private schools in Lesotho and Swaziland — Ndebele, as his "Fools" would suggest, is a case in point — instead of the schools of Bantu education, the hegemony of Anglo–South African civility is powerful, and not easy to cast off. "Now we want to throw off the psychological burden of the past; now we want to hold onto it" (Ndebele, "Game Lodges" 122). If the Afrikaner is working among his or her own toward a slow and welcome convergence, the liberal on the national carrier — perhaps because a shared English language brings an intimacy that prevents the separation of identities possible in the case of the Afrikaner — is still the intrusive fellow passenger who sits nearby and wants to make conversation.

The Afrikaner or "Boer" and the Anglo–South African "liberal" are figures that represent psychocorporeal variants in the uncanny intimacy of apartheid: a wall of ignorance but centuries of projections,[33] and an unwelcome occupation of the black consciousness, or unconscious, by the figure of the un*known*, but by no means un*acquainted,* other. This is where the intellectual acknowledges the uncanny intimacy that is disavowed — the apartheid that is not and can never be an essential apartness, yet that destroys the basis for any meaningful community. Despite being "the primary agents" of apartheid ("Memory" 27), Afrikaners have made moves of acknowledgment. Intellectual responsibility has begun. The problem with the "liberal" is that he does not *think* but instead assumes a meaningful community where there has only been a hate-producing intimacy.

Ndebele, who does not say whether he responded to his white fellow-passenger, puts the onus on the "liberal" and puts only his own reaction down on paper. As in most of his essays and short fiction, Ndebele is more interested in emphasizing positive black achievement — in this case, sport — than in acknowledging black collusion in the operation of racist values. Yet despite taking on the guardians of English in "The English Language and Social Change in South Africa" (1986),[34] he remains persecuted in his mind, like William Makgoba (115–18) and others, by the "liberal," a figure who continues to rouse his anger. In openly questioning Afrikaner hegemony (which, not knowing Afrikaans, he cannot, in any case, embrace as intimately), he actively refuses to have a hand in perpetuating it ("Memory" 24; *South African Literature* vii–viii; "How" 12; "Open Letter"). For Ndebele the "liberal" is, ultimately, the nearer neighbor; in the context of furthering an emancipatory project based in his vocabulary, he may be the one whose influence is hardest to analyze and, though it must be, hardest to eradicate.[35]

The traces — a preliminary deciphering: When the intellectual registers an essential human foldedness, in opposition to apartheid, compromised by figures who represent an unwelcome and more or less unnegotiated intimacy, he or she can register it mentally, as Ndebele usually does, or, as others have done, add to that account the dimension of the body. Usually, though, "body" and "mind" are indissociable in complicity, responsibility, and resistance. That is what we hear in the inquiries into Steve Biko's death in police detention. The motifs of consciousness and unconsciousness, which recur in the hearings where it is a matter of the state and comportment of Steve Biko's body, uncannily trace the "truth" of Black Consciousness. In making a stand by sitting down, Biko acknowledges, is "conscious" of, his potential complicity in his own oppression. He refuses, in the comportment of his body, to be an accomplice "in the crime of allowing himself to be misused and therefore letting evil reign supreme in the country of his birth." The apartheid police deny a basic human foldedness; they harbor a phobia of him as a black person, which is exacerbated by tales of his retaliation during interrogation sessions. At a more banal level, as interrogators, they want to intimidate him, to "break" him by depriving him of his dignity. In the space of a few seconds, there is a "scuffle"; Biko's body is forcibly disciplined; he loses consciousness. The stage is set for his death and the inquests into it.

conclusion
"don't forget to tell us what happened to you yourself . . ."

Before it finished its work, the Truth and Reconciliation Commission held three special women's hearings and "attempted to amend its procedures in ways that would encourage women to speak." This took place in response to perceptions, voiced at a workshop held in March 1996 by the Centre for Applied Legal Studies (CALS) and articulated in a written submission, that "the Commission might be missing some of the truth through a lack of sensitivity to gender issues. . . . The CALS submission unashamedly focused on women in the belief that it is the voices of women that more often go unheard" (*Truth* 4:282).

It was not simply that women were not speaking. The problem was more complex. Women were speaking, but they were not speaking about their own experiences. They were instead bearing witness to what happened to others — and those others were, in many cases, men: "Women were by no means absent from other hearings of the Commission. . . . over half of those who spoke were women, but . . . the roles and capacities in which women and men spoke differed. . . . while the overwhelming majority of women spoke as relatives and dependants of those (mainly males) who had directly suffered human rights violations, most of the men spoke as direct victims" (*Truth* 4: 283; see also 289–90).

Reminded by CALS that nothing prevented it from asking victims questions about their own experiences (Goldblatt and Meintjes 19, 38), the Truth Commission changed course and asked women to provide other testimony. In addition to holding the special women's hearings, the commission enlisted the aid of witnesses in altering this tendency in April 1997 when it modified the form used to take initial statements from victims with a cautionary note: "IMPORTANT: Some women testify about violations that happened to family members or friends, but they have also suffered abuses. Don't forget to tell us what happened to you yourself if you were the victim of a gross human rights abuse" (*Truth* 4:283).

Like Black Consciousness, CALS shifted the activity of the intellectual from the mental to the corporeal and from theory to praxis by emphasizing embodiedness and its differential psychosocial inscription. By exposing a gendered foreclosure, however, this shift suggested a generalizing of the predicament of the intellectual and apartness on the terrain of the body, not in the history of race but of sexuality. It thereby tacitly challenged the privileged exemplarity of apartheid as historically determinate formation, for a history of the intellectual as a figure of responsibility-in-complicity. The chapter on the women's hearing in the Truth Commission's final report "underlines the fact that there were many women who suffered from the full range of abuses that fell within the Commission's ambit. It also, however, points out the particular ways in which these women might have experienced abuses. At the level of biology, it points to sexual abuses and threats. At a broader level, it looks at how gendered roles affected the experience and its aftermath" (*Truth* 4:284). By asking its questions differently and by addressing itself to the particular experiences of women, the commission had intensified its task of advocacy, of facilitating the testimony of victims of apartheid. As an intervention by feminist intellectuals, the CALS submission had amplified the scope of this advocacy and had brought about the involvement of women themselves in acknowledging and resisting their own part in the "silences" it had identified.

The intervention had, however, ignored another way in which the Truth Commission had adjusted its course in response to witnesses. As many observers have noted, early in the life of the commission, witnesses began to come forward at the hearings to petition it for bodies or remains of relatives who had been killed or "disappeared," for a gravestone, or simply for permission to visit a grave. Although not having budgeted for it, the Truth Commission undertook several exhumations and promised to obtain death certificates for those without them. In so doing, as I have argued elsewhere ("Ambiguities"), the commission fundamentally altered what it was doing. It could no longer be only a process of collecting evidence for a narrative of human rights violations. The epistemic project of making memory became, at once, an affective project of commemorating the dead. It is in this context that one would want to question the insistence of the CALS submission on how women witnesses do not speak of their own experiences, which is translated into the subsequent injunction to women by the commission: "Don't forget to tell us what happened to you yourself if you were the victim of a gross human rights abuse."

One of the examples of testimony cited by CALS and repeated in the commission's report is that of the widows of the Cradock Four, a group of Eastern Cape activists murdered in clandestine fashion by the state in June 1985:[1]

Many of the people who have already spoken in the TRC are wives and mothers of men who were killed. Many of these women were themselves detained and harassed by the police. Although these women are coming forward to speak about their husbands, fathers or sons, they should also be encouraged to speak about their own experiences. In the first week of the Truth Commission's hearings in the Eastern Cape, the widows of the "Cradock Four," came to speak about their murdered husbands. They themselves had been harassed and arrested, yet their stories were not probed and were treated as incidental. Our society constantly diminishes women's role and women themselves then see their experiences as unimportant. The TRC should empower these women so that they are able to locate themselves not just in the private realm as supporters of men but in the public realm as resisters to oppression. There is nothing in the Act which prevents these types of questions from being asked by Commissioners. (Goldblatt and Meintjes 19; see also *Truth* 4:293)

In terms of numbers, the witnesses of the first week's hearings were indeed predominantly women, testifying mainly to human rights abuses suffered by male relatives (*Truth* 4:289–90). Yet the significance accorded to this numerical figure, that women are simply not testifying to their own experiences, does not fully take into account the acknowledged fact that "the widows . . . came to speak about their murdered husbands." The construction of CALS, which is taken up in the final report, is one-sided; it is based on affirming the negative — women are *not* testifying to their own experiences — of a questionable description of what the witnesses *are* doing. If the witnesses are not simply bearing witness to the experiences of *men*, but to the experiences of those who have *died*, one cannot respond simply by concluding that such women ought to be encouraged to testify to abuses to themselves associated with their roles in the liberation movements. For feminists, to do so is necessary; but in the long run, other questions have to be asked. Appearing at public hearings, these women bear witness in ways that cannot simply be located in a "private realm." What they do resists being grasped in the opposition of public/private; it compels a reimagining of the political sphere.[2]

Apart from the fact that, in the process of mourning, the suffering of the victim shades into that of the bereaved, thus making it hard to separate victim and witness, I would propose that when the victim is dead, the testimony of the survivor is utterly different. In such instances, the witness speaks in the place of someone who cannot be present, cannot be summoned to appear, and cannot be asked to say more about their own experiences. With the death of the victim, there is only the advocate. This testimonial situation is, I would suggest, exemplary of the ethical relation and responsibility as a foldedness with an other who occupies oneself — in Levinas's terms, holds oneself hostage (*Otherwise than Being* 114, 124) — in advance. It is this responsibility before any living present that Derrida identifies as the condition of possibility of justice (*Specters* xix). As the third [terstis], the witness takes up the structural place of the one who is absent; this substitution is the condition of possibility of any number of instances of advocacy. To testify is to elaborate the foldedness with the other that I have been terming complicity in a general sense — and that, as a counter to apartheid, depends on the kind of dispropriation that Plaatje's advocacy of the vernacular reader in the preface to *Mhudi* secretly seeks to achieve.

The witness's collaboration with the statement-taker or questioner who, with the Truth Commission, helps her to tell her story, redoubles this basic foldedness. Despite the fact that, early in its life, the commission made itself willing to assist with funeral rites (see Krog, *Country* 204–5), neither the CALS submission nor the final report's chapter on women ever takes this basic structure and its relationship to the dead into account. In asking who speaks for whom and for whom not, it instead raises the question of complicity—to be sure, of women themselves, who do not speak on behalf of themselves—within a limited range of narrow senses: "Our society constantly diminishes women's role and women themselves then see their experiences as unimportant."[3] This is what it has to say on behalf of women who are absent.

In the light of such cases, where does responsibility-in-complicity lie? Advocacy is a site at which complicities are multiplied from a basic human foldedness that is also the condition of possibility for responsibility. Viewed in terms of advocacy (the word used by Said and others is *representation*), if he or she is not simply a more or less self-appointed advocate, the responsibility of the intellectual is typically a negotiation between various narrow senses of complicity: women who speak on behalf of men and not on behalf of themselves are complicit in their own silencing; Blacks who allow Whites to speak for them are collaborators in a racist status quo; and so on. Complicity cannot be avoided; one chooses, as Derrida writes in *Of Spirit,* in order to avoid the worst.

There is also the sense, as I have proposed in this book, that the intellectual also negotiates, at least tacitly, between quotidian complicities such as I have just mentioned, and a sense of a basic human foldedness that must be affirmed when choosing between affiliations can lead to its disavowal—between an acting-in-complicity and a responsibility-in-complicity. That is why, as I have argued, apartheid—which separates but could never achieve the essential separateness its name proclaimed— is exemplary for this kind of negotiation on the part of the intellectual.

As has been legible at least since Zola spoke out—*Mon devoir est de parler*—on behalf of Dreyfus (or, as Benda and Habermas write, on behalf of a principle), the link of advocacy to responsibility-in-complicity— *Je ne veux pas être complice*—is constantly made and remade in the daily work of the intellectual (as well as in the anti-intellectualism generated along with it). The intellectual represents the other, the principle that, being a part of oneself, the other ought justly to be represented, and that particular loyalties ought not to stand in the way. In Europe, the figure of the intellectual is, as Derrida suggests in *The Other Heading,* bound up historically with questions of hospitality and the stranger. When parochial loyalties are favored, the intellectual, aware of complicity, becomes a critic or opponent.

My book has moved repeatedly from the center of the political sphere—or "public sphere"—in which these notions emerged, toward its margins where, when one asks what it takes for the marginalized mind to be an intellectual, one has to attend to dynamics that are psychopolitical and even "literary" in nature and that involve not only the mind but the body, not only the living but the citizenry of the land of the dead. These peregrinations have, at the same time, sought to approach the limits of apartheid's exemplarity for a history of the intellectual.

Although bearing its seeds, the heterogeneity of colonial South Africa is irreducible to a prehistory of apartheid. This heterogeneity is plain when Olive Schreiner's writings are read as participating in an older history of sexuality. A more temporally circumscribed difference is apparent when Sol Plaatje, although later staging the fissuring of his implied reader, invokes Zola to appeal for justice within a British imperial system in which he could claim (if not consistently exercise) the rights of any other subject. In both cases, although its exemplarity remains intact, it is no longer privileged, and the uniqueness of apartheid as a site of complicity for the intellectual has been put into question.

When apartheid is the horizon for judgment, one seems bound to consider N. P. van Wyk Louw a "failed" intellectual, one who ultimately put loyalty to the volk ahead of a critique of racism. My judgment of Louw has been hard. Yet if we are to begin to write a history of the intellectual and apartheid and explain why it was possible for someone who in almost every other way stood for a culture of critical vigilance could have supported and actively promoted apartheid, it is with Louw that we have to begin. He, like other nationalists of his time, began as an advocate for the Afrikaner, particularly the proletarianized Afrikaans worker. Studying at the University of Cape Town, Louw wrote a B.Ed. thesis on *The Development of Agricultural, Industrial and Technical Education for Europeans in South Africa* (1928);[4] and one of his earliest published essays is a review in *Die Huisgenoot* of the Carnegie Commission's report on white poverty (1932). As a writer and educator, Louw conducted something like "social work." Many of his essays, early and late, appeared in mass-circulation newspapers and magazines.

The profession of social work, insofar as it grasps the social or the community as a totality, is one of the uncanny continuities, in intellectual work, between Afrikaner nationalism and African nationalism. In both formations, the work of women has been crucial, though underresearched. If the African nationalist intellectual conceived of a self-reliant African community, free of the influence of the white racist and of the tutelary "white liberal," the early Afrikaner nationalist imagined one free of Anglo–South African hegemony. This was the acceptable, anti-colonial face of Afrikaner nationalism. As my reading of Louw's prose has shown, the project of guaranteeing a separate existence [aparte bestaan] for the volk in relation to the expatriate part of the English volk also led Louw and other intellectuals to a definition of the identity of the volk in relation to the "mass" of black Africans. This is where, adapting the more overtly phobic racism of Cronjé and appropriating Hoernlé's liberal pessimism, the concept of a multitude of black volkere emerged.

The structure of responsibility-in-complicity of lojale verset, at best a safeguard against extreme political action in the name of the volk, in part an advocacy on behalf of a white Afrikaans proletariat not represented by an Anglo-identified urban Afrikaans middle class (to which Louw belonged) and competing with black workers, was always implicated in racism and anti-Semitism. Once the aparte bestaan of the volk became an obsession, to choose for the Afrikaner was to choose against anyone not perceived to be an Afrikaner. To be an Afrikaner, for Louw and others, meant to shut one's doors, in alliance with white Anglo–South Africans, against black Africans. It meant apartheid. A foldedness with that other was disavowed — the 1932 Carnegie Commission report dwells on intimacy of Afrikaner and African in mixed sections of the cities;[5] its fears of blood-mixing [bloedvermenging] are turned up a notch by Cronjé — in the name of a supposedly deeper foldedness with others of one's volk. Apartheid seldom allowed Africans to speak, and it ventriloquized ad lib: "Bantu says . . ."

Although lojale verset, with its parliamentary overtones, is a structure that could have been generalized or at least disseminated more democratically, the way in which Louw deployed it amounted to choosing one filiation over another, one subject of advocacy over another: the volk over British imperialism and Anglo–South African hegemony; then, and at the same time, the volk, in which Louw eventually hoped to include "brown" Afrikaners, over black Africans. With his involvement in the larger structure of racism unquestioned, his vision of a basic complicity-in-responsibility for the intellectual fell victim to apartheid. Having distinguished between the roles of Advocate and Accuser of the volk, N. P. van Wyk Louw chose in some circumstances to be the former and in others to be the latter, but when he was forced to choose between the two roles, as in the Netherlands, he usually chose to be an apologist rather than a critic.

The entrenchment of this position meant that, when Breyten Breytenbach took up lojale verset against apartheid by attempting to undo its connection with the Afrikaner volk and its aparte bestaan, he won relatively few Afrikaners over and went to prison for his attempts to set his vision to work. Going further than Louw — who had proclaimed in 1960 that "The brown people are *our* people" [Die bruinmense is óns mense] and had bitterly lamented it when his Afrikanerhood [Afrikanerskap] was cast in doubt ("Van Wyk Louw sê") — Breytenbach spoke of his being South African [Suid-Afrikanerskap] rather of than his Afrikanerskap, and of Afrikaners as a bastard-volk [bastervolk]. Breytenbach's attempted leftist rewriting of the nationalist project is, in obvious ways, far from the cooptative and appropriative rhetoric of Louw (and the tricameralism of the 1983 Constitution). Although Breytenbach's current thinking appears to center, in lyrical fashion, around the Afrikaans language and indissoluble racial and cultural bonds with coloureds and thus with the indigenous KhoiKhoi — but finds difficulty in imagining ties with Zulus, for instance — his statements of the early 1970s did suggest a generalization of human foldedness that, accompanied by a turn to English in prison, was less parochial and conservative and perhaps more promising of a generalization of bastardy or hybridity.[6]

It is highly unusual for a study of black resistance to apartheid to thematize complicity. As I have shown, however, the moment of assuming responsibility-in-complicity is integral to black intellectual life in South Africa and to the task that emerges for the black intellectual under apartheid. What is most striking about the writers I have examined is the fact that they view complicity, not simply in the political terms that dominate South African discourse — from Afrikaner nationalism and its dramas of loyalty and betrayal, to Black Consciousness and Bantustan leaders, to the investigations of the Truth Commission into the role of professional sectors during the apartheid era — but also in psychosocial terms that considerably complicate and enrich our understanding of why complicity and its negotiation should be an essential moment in intellectual responsibility.

Just as with Jordan and his brief text on ubuntu, in the works of both Modisane and Biko there is, within the immediate agenda of negotiating particular complicities, an opening for a basic structure of human fold-edness to emerge. The doubling of self and other, of living and dead, that saturates Breytenbach's *The True Confessions of an Albino Terrorist*, is anticipated by Bloke Modisane's *Blame Me on History*. The work of someone denied access to the mainstream of intellectual sociality, *Blame Me on History* and Modisane's stories figure a beggarly dependence, even parasitism, on the other — in this case, the guilty, patronizing white liberal. This social complicity, more or less representative for the *Drum* writers of the 1950s, also renders apparent the general structure of ad-dress and foldedness with the dead that underlies responsibility and justice. Modisane is one of the writers echoed by Black Consciousness when it proposed to pump life back into an empty shell of a "black man" and taught Blacks not to be complicitous in the crime of allowing them-selves to be abused in the country of their birth.

Although Steve Biko and Barney Pityana do not take up the brief mas-culinist self-critical moment of acknowledgment in Modisane of com-plicity in the subordination of women, Black Consciousness intensifies the link, constantly made before the Truth Commission, between com-plicity and advocacy, and between day-to-day complicities and modes of advocacy. The white liberal could no longer be permitted to represent, however "beautiful" his words, the concerns of Blacks. Guided by Biko, left-liberal Whites became advocates for the struggle within their own communities; for this Rick Turner was assassinated and Breyten Brey-tenbach jailed. It was up to Blacks, for their part, to examine their psyches and the conduct of their bodies for signs of collusion in their own oppression.

Exemplified in the death of Biko, Black Consciousness extended the intellectual's responsibility-in-complicity from the mind, via Frantz Fanon and the unconscious, to the body as a site of resistance. N. Cha-bani Manganyi's account of "being-black-in-the-world," uncannily reso-nating with Louw's ideas about Afrikaner abiding [voortbestaan], leads Black Consciousness back to a basic structure of shared human-being that, although imposed in colonial and apartheid South Africa as an unwelcome intimacy of race domination, is disavowed by apartheid ideology, which proclaims separateness as its goal but can only achieve imperfect separation. To the extent that it concentrates on the psychic as it plays out in the social inscription of the body, rather than on the merely political, and to the extent that it thereby acknowledges intimacy with the other as inevitable, Black Consciousness, at least in Manganyi's version, has the potential to reverse the psychic effects of apartheid without reproducing its political consequences.

With Schreiner it was the social inscription of the colonial female body that recast the history of the intellectual and apartheid within an older history of sexuality. Broached momentarily by Black Consciousness in its "Black is Beautiful" campaign of the early 1970s, gender, and its relation to advocacy, comes to the forefront after the end of apartheid as an alternative generalization, within the history of sexuality, of the predicament of the intellectual as a figure of responsibility-in-complicity. This has occurred not only in feminist interventions around the Truth Commission, where some of the women involved were once active in Black Consciousness, but also in polemics against white South African feminists. At a conference on Women in Africa and the African Diaspora (WAAD) held in 1992 in Nsukka, Nigeria, a group of African American delegates objected to the participation of white women and of men in the proceedings and demanded that they leave (Nnaemeka, "Women's Studies" 364).[7] Their position on white women was that, by virtue of being white, these scholars could not legitimately speak about the experience of black women; one statement was " 'I am sick and tired of white women telling me how I feel' " (qtd. in Nnaemeka 367). In response, members of the racially mixed South African delegation produced a statement during the conference suggesting "that all South Africans, irrespective of race, should be permitted to participate fully in this conference" (Statement 480). Objecting to what she saw as the imposition of ANC nonracialism in its drafting, Lumka Funani, one of the South African participants, later added her voice to the group objecting to the presence of white women: "African women have been dumb for years about their own experiences, leaving their white counterparts to talk for them, but I feel the time has come for us, as African women, to stand and talk for ourselves." Neither white nor coloured women, Funani claimed, "can . . . fully know the African experience" (414).[8]

Whereas the exchanges at and in the aftermath of WAAD are a particularly stark instance of resistance to advocacy and even a gainsaying of its *possibility* where experience is held to differ, the Truth Commission takes place in an atmosphere for some time highly sensitive to the ethics and politics of speaking on behalf of another. The women's hearing takes place as response to the sense that doing so is both impossible *and* necessary; that standing in for another is both a basic expression of human foldedness *and,* as it always is, a taking of the place of a particular other by a particular other, which is what necessitates the constant negotiation of who speaks for whom. As Jill Arnott observes, surveying the South African polemics in dialogue with Gayatri Chakravorty Spivak's "Can the Subaltern Speak?" portrayal can amount to a self-delegating "speaking for" (83). Folded into any act of representation or advocacy is an other-intendedness that makes it possible at once to portray and to betray.[9] The women's hearing attempts to negotiate this duplicity.

The critique of advocacy — speaking for and/or on behalf of — can be phrased as accusation of the advocate or as a self-critical awareness of complicity in allowing oneself to be represented in a way that does one harm. The latter stance is that of Black Consciousness, which situates responsibility-in-complicity at the foundation of what it is to be an oppositional intellectual. Whereas the women's hearing yielded some accusatory talk about the limits of black-white sisterhood — white women, both prison warders who mistreated political prisoners and those who sent parcels to soldiers "on the border," need to come forward as perpetrators (Masote 10) — the current interventions around the Truth Commission appear to be overwhelmingly in a spirit of autocritique. They seem, in this respect, to owe a great deal to the experience of women in Black Consciousness as well as to an older generation of women — some, such as Ellen Kuzwayo and Winnie Mandela, involved in social work — who were equally concerned, often but not always in political organizations, with fostering black community self-reliance and with maintaining, in more and less conservative ways, the social fabric of extended family and other networks. It is from this history, an *intellectual* history, that we hear not only the idea that women can collaborate mentally and corporeally in their own oppression, an element of consciousness-raising echoing Biko and his contemporaries, but the internal criticism that the anti-apartheid struggle is incomplete when women are still subject to discrimination and violence, and that the sexism and abuse of women in the liberation movements is largely unexamined.

During the struggle, and even after, women have to negotiate the sense that to examine this area is, as Thenjiwe Mtintso, head of the Commission for Gender Equality puts it, "in politics, to betray their solidarity . . . solidarity with male counterparts" (Masote 5). The immediate post-apartheid years saw the emergence of a Women's National Coalition, which, allying urban and rural women, successfully pressed for the explicit inclusion of gender in the constitution's equality clause but had less success in challenging the constitutional recognition of "traditional leaders" and "customary law" (see Albertyn). In the context of interventions around the Truth Commission, however, the form taken by criticism is typically not an accusation of men and a challenge to patriarchy but a self-criticism among women. Attending to the social inscription of the body, women negotiate a collusion in their own silencing.

Yet these critiques and autocritiques appear not to take into account what I set out above as the basic structure of advocacy — responsibility in foldedness with an other — which is a condition of possibility for complicities in the narrow sense. Again, as is so often the case, the actual hearings of the Truth Commission also produce elements that do not fit into the polemical positions that inform its report.[10] As Antjie Krog writes recently in a different context, "Oral stories make space for the exceptional, the unusual, and link it to the core values in all societies" ("Hundred").

There are signs, in the testimonies, of the dissemination of a general structure of responsibility. A first sign — it feels odd to be remarking an elision of male voices — is the fact that, at the women's hearing in Johannesburg, three men testified, two on behalf of wives and/or daughters who had been killed. The speech of support from Tokyo Sexwale is quoted from in the report, but the latter two witnesses — Simon Malakoane and Alli Maziya — are not mentioned. The report presents the women's hearing as an occasion for *women* to speak. To pursue what I proposed earlier, the significance of the testimony that provoked the CALS intervention is not that the witnesses are not testifying to abuses to men but that they are testifying in place of those who cannot testify. This instantiates responsibility before the dead, which is the condition of possibility for any and all responsibilities. The report proceeds as if this basic foldedness with the other were of no ethico-political significance, and that all that mattered were acknowledging and avoiding complicities in the narrow sense. At this level, the truth produced by the report is hopelessly (and necessarily) confused with a quotidian politics — albeit a profoundly "correct" politics.

A second sign can be identified in Thenjiwe Mtintso's moving opening remarks at the women's hearing. Mtintso, who had first been detained and tortured along with other Black Consciousness leaders in the 1970s and who later became a commander in Umkhonto we Sizwe, in effect testifies that she will not be testifying. Although saluting "the women that are coming forward to speak for themselves; to speak as actors, as active participants and direct survivors. . . . Not as relatives, not as spouses, not as wives, but as themselves; those that directly suffered," she confesses, "I must be honest with you that I am a coward. That is why I want to congratulate the women who are here. . . . they speak for many of us, like myself, who are still cowardly to talk about the experiences we went through. . . . As they try to free themselves today of the burden, they must know that they are freeing some of us who are not yet ready" (qtd. in Masote 5–6; see also Krog, *Country* 178–79). There can be no stronger affirmation of advocacy. In this case, the witnesses are not testifying on behalf of those who are dead, but of those who cannot, for a range of reasons, bring themselves to "come forward." In terms of what Mtintso says, it is not advocacy as such that is wrong, but the imposition on oneself of particular social roles and kinship positions through advocacy, as one testifies *as* a wife or female relative. If, in the context of funeral rites, there is the risk that women may be burdened with the social role of public mourners, which can cement such positions, the women's hearing suggests ways in which the basic structure of responsibility as foldedness with the other can be figured out of a female exemplarity that is, arguably, less compromised.

When the other does not or cannot come forward, and not only because he or she is dead, the opening toward a more basic responsibility is broached. Revealed before the Truth Commission in the exchanges between witness and questioner, are the makings of an imperative: one is always already occupied by another; and as an intellectual, one is called upon to act out of this being-occupied. In this sense the intellectual is an ethical figure — although not necessarily a figure of virtue. In its instantiation, occupation by the other may be more or less welcome or unwelcome: it may be embraced; it may be disavowed by instituting an "apartheid" that produces separation but cannot realize any essential apartness; or it may be acknowledged as "reality," with all the pragmatic day-to-day negotiations that this entails.

The anti-apartheid intellectual has historically pursued two strategies. The first has been to acknowledge, proclaim, and promote a basic human joinedness against apartheid. The idea that apartheid has achieved or could achieve some fundamental separation is not radically questioned. The second strategy has been to denounce apartheid's de facto disavowal of foldedness in human-being, and to resist the domination-in-separation that accompanies it. It thus rejects the idea of a realizable separateness that apartheid ideology asks us to accept. Advocating a refusal to collaborate physically and mentally in one's own subordination and that of others, it has also led to a critique of the politics of advocacy and a general skepticism concerning the efficacy of one's own version of opposition. If the first strategy mobilizes against the *evil* of apartheid, we could say the second strategy does so against its *untruth*.

The foregoing typology is deliberately schematic. But it allows us to see how the history of the intellectual and apartheid yields the possibility of another strategy, aspects of which are not wholly absent from the two that have typically been pursued. This strategy would involve insisting on an articulation in any given situation of general and narrow senses of complicity as foldedness in human-being. It would, in other words, call upon one to acknowledge one's occupation by the other, in its more and less aversive forms, but it would also maintain a *figure* of basic joinedness to stand watch over each intervention.

In the context of the Truth Commission, our present-day apparatus for measuring complicity and generalizing responsibility, such a strategy would foreground openings of the ethical understood in an extra-moral sense, especially at the hearings, and track ways in which such openings are one-sidedly reappropriated. It might, for instance, point to the cultural-essentialist interpretation of invocations of "custom" in the context of mourning, when such invocations can be read, in more basic terms, as naming a relation to the dead that makes possible each and every assumption of responsibility; or, as I have above, it might show how the interpretation of women testifying on behalf of men who have died as merely *not* testifying about themselves fails to explore the significance of what they *are* doing.

"I start with the late" (Masote 15). I have repeatedly used *the dead* to mark a limit to the privileging of one or other example, filiation, or affiliation. In the context of the women's hearing, "the late" can be deployed to mark such a limit. Yet it is important to remember that in referring to "the late" the witness refers to specific persons and calls upon others to join in specific commemoration. In terms of the strategy

I have been entertaining, although the relation to the nonliving cannot designate foldedness in human-being as such, it can be invoked to figure a limit to the usurping of human-being in the name of any single cause. This strategy is not content to privilege any one cause emerging at the margins of the history of sexuality, or the margins of the history of race, or the margins of any particular history — no matter how necessary the immediate demands of a given situation may be. It will thus always be more than merely oppositional. Foldedness in human-being is inevitably set against apartheid. Yet, insofar as every affiliation, oppositional or otherwise, is a restricted instantiation of that foldedness, and thus at risk of barring the way to its being generalized, it has no choice but at once to project itself beyond apartheid.

notes

Introduction

1 In "Racism's Last Word" (1986), Jacques Derrida explicates apartheid in terms of essential and quasi-ontological "being apart," and as making that apartness "the very law of the origin": "APARTHEID: by itself the word occupies the terrain like a concentration camp. System of partition, barbed wire, crowds of mapped out solitudes. Within the limits of this untranslatable idiom, a violent arrest of the mark, the glaring harshness of abstract essence [heid] seems to speculate in another regime of abstraction, that of confined separation. The word concentrates separation, raises it to another power, and sets separation itself *apart:* 'apartitionality,' something like that. By isolating being apart in some sort of essence of hypostasis, the word corrupts it into a quasi-ontological segregation. At every point, like all racisms, it tends to pass segregation off as natural — and as the very law of the origin" (331).

2 Hereafter, references to the *Truth and Reconciliation Report* will be cited in the text by volume and page number.

3 At the second of two conferences held in 1994 to discuss the idea of a truth commission, Albie Sachs observed: "In a sense our whole nation was complicit in what happened in the past and we must find appropriate ways of recognising that fact without diminishing the importance of focusing on the extreme violations which took place" ("Task" 107).

4 For an account of how the bad example operates, see Keenan 45–47.

5 An excellent overview of this history is provided by Von Vegesack, *De intellectuelen.*

6 Benda's writings on the Dreyfus case are collected in *Dialogues à Byzance* (1900). For details on this period in Benda's career, see Nichols 26–57.

7 All translations are mine unless otherwise indicated.

8 That is why I cannot endorse Judt's observation, in his reading of Benda's 1946 preface, that "whereas Benda's original use of the term in the edition of 1927 addressed the intellectual temptation to wander from the path of rigor and truth in the pursuit of political objectives, he and his postwar contemporaries now meant by *treason* something close to the opposite — an insistence upon following the dictates of one's own conscience even at the price of breaking ranks with one's political allies" (50–51). As I have suggested, whatever his political alliances, it is not a question of any change in Benda's usage of the word *treason;* in order to make any real sense of Benda, it is necessary to see that, as an analysis of his texts shows, his clerical purism was never tenable at a conceptual level and thus that his denunciation of treason, whether in theory or practice, will always have implied its supposed opposite.

9 Arendt was thinking of the Dreyfus affair when, on August 17, 1946, after reading *The Question of German Guilt,* she wrote to Jaspers: "It seems to me that what you call metaphysical guilt encompasses not only the 'absolute,' where indeed no earthly judge can be recognized any more, but also the solidarity which is the political basis of the republic (and which Clemenceau expressed in the words, 'L'affaire d'un seul est l'affaire de tous')" (*Correspondence* 54). Arendt's own account of the Dreyfus case is in *The Origins of Totalitarianism* (89–120).

10 "Every technician of knowledge is a *potential intellectual* since he is defined by a contradiction which is none other than the permanent tension within him between his universalist technique and the dominant ideology" (Sartre, "Plea" 244).

11 In his discussion of secular criticism at the beginning of *The World, the Text, and the Critic* (1983), Edward Said distinguishes between forms of responsibility-in-belonging that he refers to as "filiation" and "affiliation" (16–24). Useful for mapping complicities in the narrow sense, this distinction is based on another one, between nature and culture: *filiation* is family and nation; *affiliation* is professional guild and political party. A concept of complicity in a general sense does not have a place in Said's portrait of the critic, however, although for him criticism is "oppositional"; that is, it is opposed to the consolidation of authority, as systems of affiliation reproduce dynamics of filiation (29, 23). Without something like complicity in a general sense, a boundness irreducible to actual forms of responsibility-in-belonging but that instead implies their possibility, there is the risk that oppositionality might be simply a pragmatic choice between competing (af)filiations. Another objection to Said's distinction is that, whereas the passage from "filiation" to "affiliation" and the tensions between them provide a convenient narrative frame for the careers of particular intellectuals, the distinction between the two terms is weakened when, as is inevitable, the supposed naturalness of filiation is brought into question.

12 In *Secular Vocations: Intellectuals, Professionalism, Culture* (1993), Bruce Robbins

challenges the antithesis, shared by right- and left-wing commentators, of intellectual and professional, arguing that being an academic is not necessarily at odds with an oppositional or adversarial public stance. Analyzing contestatory discourse on the social position of intellectuals, Robbins privileges oppositionality (x–xi, 12, 79) without exploring its relation to complicity. He does, nevertheless, imply a relationship between oppositional advocacy and complicity in the general sense when he formulates an account of responsibility involving the projection of a "public": "The public is something like a professional unconscious. . . . There can be no clear border . . . between speaking to ourselves and speaking to others. Even at our most private, even in what we hope or fear may be professional soliloquy, we are to some extent looking over our shoulders, listening for other voices and adapting our own to what we think we hear. . . . We listen 'for' the public in two equivocal senses of the preposition: we listen so as to hear what the public may be saying, and we listen *to ourselves, on behalf of* the public, which is of course us too. Both senses invite us to surrender the illusion of a professional identity that is hermetically sealed and to recognize instead the social reality of an identity that is looser, less autonomous, more diversely populated" (89–90).

13 For an account of philosophical rhetoric employed by Heidegger and other university rectors to align the university with National Socialism, see Sluga.

14 With its more extensive meditations on the duty of European intellectuals, Derrida's *The Other Heading: Reflections on Today's Europe* (1991, 5–6 and *passim*), is a companion work to *Of Spirit.*

15 See "Derrida-Bourdieu"; Bourdieu, *Political Ontology;* as well as Adorno and Löwith.

16 See Spivak, "Responsibility" 24–25.

17 Derrida's protocols are thus different for Nietzsche, who prevented his ideas on the university, which were later taken up by the Nazis, from being published during his lifetime (*Ear of the Other* 24–26).

18 I allude to Nietzsche, "On Truth and Lying in an Extra-moral Sense." In "Critique of Violence" (1920), Walter Benjamin makes a useful distinction, in this connection, between an efficient cause and violence: "The task of a critique of violence may be circumscribed as the representation of its relation to right and justice. For an as-always efficient cause becomes violence in the precise sense of the word only once it intervenes in ethical relations. The sphere of these relations is designated by the concepts of right and justice" (*Reflections* 277; trans. modified).

19 This, as I take it, is the point made in a recent book by Christopher Kutz, *Complicity: Ethics and Law for a Collective Age,* in which accountability is framed in collective terms with reference to a set of relevant "respondents," and complicity is understood in a juridical or quasi-juridical sense as "acting together" (17–112). In the terms I am employing, complicity is not merely an acting together, but is (though the two cannot be regarded as coextensive) at the same time what establishes the horizon of judgment for that acting. The genealogy I

have set out makes it obvious that what most deeply occupies the intellectual is the orientation and scope of complicity in the latter sense.

20 For Mamdani's account of apartheid and the legacy of indirect rule, see his *Citizen and Subject*.

21 "Kept out of institutions of higher learning, [the native intelligentsia] mushrooms elsewhere: in the church and the mosque, as in the party and the union" (Mamdani, "Racism").

22 Willan's *Sol Plaatje: A Biography* is, among other things, an excellent study of early black South African journalism.

23 Nelson Mandela registers his debt to mission schooling in *Long Walk to Freedom* (144–45). The complexities of the missionary legacy for the African National Congress, as well as the Inkatha Freedom Party are explored by Comaroff and Comaroff (2:401–2). For a more literary account, see Chapman, "Red People."

24 Dubow provides a useful study of academic race thinking in South Africa before apartheid (*Scientific Racism* 20–245). On Afrikaans academics under apartheid, see Hugo. The role of literary and cultural organizations in Afrikaner nationalism is detailed by Hofmeyr; Kannemeyer (*Geskiedenis* 1:48–57, 86–88, 267–75); and Moodie (39–51, 96–115, 146–207), who also includes a discussion of the contribution of the Dutch Reformed Church to Afrikaner-nationalist ideology (52–72).

25 For a life of Bram Fischer, one of the most celebrated single examples, see Clingman.

26 Paton writes about the Liberal Party in *Journey Continued*. For an account of the influence of Black Consciousness on white radicals, see Rich (90–118). Abel details the part played, more generally, by lawyers in the struggle against apartheid.

27 On the press and broadcasting in South Africa, see the two collections edited by Tomaselli et al. For an intriguing account of Herbert Dhlomo's work for radio, see Couzens, *New African* 206ff. On *Drum,* see Chapman, *"Drum" Decade;* and, on *Staffrider,* Oliphant and Vladislavić.

28 Chapman's *Southern African Literatures* attempts a less "balkanis[ed]" study in literary history (xvi).

29 I am drawing on Roman Jakobson's account of the "poetic function" (356). For further accounts of reading, literature, alterity, and responsibility, see Attridge; Keenan; Spivak, *Critique*.

30 See Derrida, *Ear of the Other* 53.

31 See also Derrida, *Gift of Death* 82–115.

Chapter 1. Two Colonial Precursors

1 This approach is characteristic of recent scholarship on these writers. In the case of Olive Schreiner, the strategy of Anne McClintock is to show how, despite her advocacy of black women, Schreiner's feminism remained implicated in colonial racism. Laura Chrisman, although proposing an alternative view of "the

failure of . . . racism to ground itself in Schreiner's thought" ("Colonialism" 34), also confines herself to an assessment of the author's ideological commitments. To cite one example on Sol Plaatje, although not "offering the real Plaatje," David Johnson's presentation of "four Plaatjes" from different theoretical positions is conceived as a weighing of complicities in the narrow sense: "Fanon's obedient native reading European textbooks; Lenin's agent of British imperialism; Willan's reasonable black man shunned by white racists; and Spivak's fractured colonial subject [of collusion and resistance] produced by a discontinuous discursive network" (110).

2 The Cape of Good Hope University, an examining university founded in 1873, later became the University of South Africa (UNISA). The cumulative tabulation of matriculation results in the *University of the Cape of Good Hope Calendar* (1917–18) records the names of four black women between 1897 and 1913. Even in subsequent decades, female black matriculation candidates appear to have been the exception; in 1939 Lovedale entered only one (Shepherd, *Lovedale, South Africa* 421). T. D. Mweli Skota's *African Yearly Register* (1930) supplies statistics of black pupils up to Standard Eight, suggesting few at the matric level (392, 394). I thank Janine Dunlop for obtaining this information for me.

3 Schreiner's early works do not entertain the entry of black South Africans into colonial intellectual life. As Lenta points out, "The dependence of whites in all areas of their lives on black labour is faithfully recorded [in *The Story of an African Farm*], as faithfully recorded as the sense of the author and her characters that these suppliers of labour are inevitably excluded from the social and intellectual life of whites" (Lenta 25; see also McClintock). Nor does Schreiner credit black South Africans with a fully developed intellectual life of their own. In the nineteenth-century evolutionary race thinking informing all her writings, every modern European individual embodies all stages of human evolutionary development. In this thinking, Africans, supposed to embody fewer stages than Europeans, are typically not credited with the ability to elaborate science or philosophy, although they are attributed the capacity to produce art. Schreiner, perhaps alluding to the South African researches of philologist Wilhelm Bleek (1827–75) (see Dubow, *Scientific Racism* 78ff.), grants that "the language [the Bantu, who, according to Bleek, are more highly evolved than Hottentots or Bushmen] speak is of a perfect construction, lending itself largely to figurative and poetical forms, yet capable of giving great precision to exact thought" (Schreiner, *Thoughts* 98). The dichotomy between art, and philosophy and science might help to account for Waldo's childhood reverence for the Bushman (San) cave-painter (Schreiner, *African Farm* 42–43), who, though he once apprehended beauty, is not presumed to have pursued truth like Waldo's father, or truth *and* beauty as does Waldo himself. The early Schreiner would appear to have subscribed to the view that the disappearance of the San, almost total in the period and Karoo region in which she set *The Story of an African Farm,* is an outcome, not of the depredations of colonial whites, but of an inexorable evolutionary process (see Lenta 19).

4 A mimetic modeling of this kind comes to crisis in the letters, exchanged in the early years of apartheid, between Lily Moya and Mabel Palmer collected by Shula Marks in *Not Either an Experimental Doll.*

5 On this care, see Dowling 75. Schreiner's construal may be compared with the actual wording of the passage in Jowett to which she alludes: "There were many, doubtless, to whom the love of the fair mind was the noblest form of friendship . . . , and who deemed the friendship of man with man to be higher than the love of woman, because altogether separated from the bodily appetites. The existence of such attachments may be reasonably attributed to the inferiority and seclusion of woman, and the want of a real family or social life and parental influence in Hellenic cities; and they were encouraged by the practice of gymnastic exercises, by the meetings of political clubs, and by the tie of military companionship" (Plato 535). On the other hand, as Dowling observes, "Jowett's deep sense of Plato's undying philosophical power . . . would express in compelling terms the present significance of the Greek past to the Victorians, doing so even at the occasional cost of misrepresenting that past. Of this cost the salient example would always be Jowett's imperturbable transposition of Plato's remarks about the Greek love of boys to Victorian men's love of women: 'We may raise the same question in another form,' as Jowett said of the specifically homoerotic questions raised in the *Phaedrus,* 'Is marriage preferable with or without love?'" (Dowling 74; the embedded quotation can be found in Plato 406).

6 Her father, Gottlob Schreiner, worked for the London Missionary Society. As the novel makes clear, Olive Schreiner's analogy with Christianity and Rome indicates, not a restoration of Christian piety, but rather the pseudo-scientific overcoming of an agonizing period of rebellion and incapacity to affirm anything (*African Farm* 127–43).

7 Ralph Iron's assertions of autonomy from received literary and intellectual forms as a colonial writer is discussed by Gray and by Jacobson. Louise Green argues for the intimate links between the two projects.

8 I allude to Sedgwick's argument that, in contrast to the "lesbian continuum" identified by Adrienne Rich, the sphere of homosexual desire between men is discontinuous with other spheres of sanctioned homosocial desire such as "male bonding" and intellectual collaboration (1–3).

9 "Intellectual life, like so much else in Victorian culture and society, was divided into 'public' and 'private' spheres: the public sphere was male and signified intellectual leadership of the nation and the empire; the private sphere was female and signified intellectual cultivation of civilized discourse" (David 9).

10 First and Scott note that "as a writer, . . . or as a polemicist within South Africa, Olive Schreiner was almost inevitably a 'man,' given the distribution of roles within the culture." They go on to conclude, with a finality I cannot endorse, that "she found it impossible to ['live like a man, but like a woman as well'] successfully. Her sexual identity was split, and there was no way for her as a woman to integrate the powerful, aspiring part of herself (the 'masculine')" (335).

11 In Schreiner's posthumously published and unfinished novel *From Man to Man* (1926), rumors of the character Baby-Bertie's affair at the age of fifteen with her male tutor and subsequent pregnancy precipitate her ruin (81, 96–97, 167, 234, 326–27). Rebekah, the "sensual" Baby-Bertie's "intellectual" sister, marries a rich man she does not love in order to gain financial independence, but her writing is confined to a diary kept in a tiny room subdivided from the bedroom of her four children. For Schreiner marriage, at least without mutual "sympathy," is not a solution for the intellectual woman either (see *Olive Schreiner Letters* 91–94).

12 As a teenager, Schreiner went out to work, first as a shop assistant and then as governess to the children of various farmers. Some of her references to the first situation indicate sexual harassment (see First and Scott 72; Schoeman, *Olive Schreiner* 312–15). She later wrote: "I was the only girl I ever heard of as living five years as governess among the Boers without getting into some sort of sexual trouble" (qtd. in Schoeman, *Olive Schreiner* 315).

13 "When I am with you," Lyndall tells Waldo, "I never know that I am a woman and you are man; I only know that we are both things that think. Other men when I am with them, whether I love them or not, they are mere bodies to me; but you are a spirit; I like you" (*African Farm* 197).

14 In a prophetic dream, Lyndall's cousin Em sees a dead baby, and someone tells her, "It is Lyndall's baby." When Em tells Lyndall about her dream, she mutters to herself: "There are some wiser in their sleeping than in their waking" (219). In addition to Em's dream, there are times, as Bradford points out, when the text seems to tell us that Lyndall wants to abort her pregnancy. Riding wildly about in the farm buggy (193; see also 186) is "an action all too recognizable to Victorian women" as an attempt to induce miscarriage (Bradford 635; see also 639).

15 On Emerson and "stimulation," see Schreiner's letter to Havelock Ellis of 8 July 1885 in *"Other Self"* (369).

16 Cronwright-Schreiner destroyed many of the letters and journals that were the primary source material for his biography and, as more recent biographers and scholars have shown from what survived, often distorted facts and events by the way he quoted from the documents. Cronwright has also been criticized for not writing about key figures in Schreiner's life, like Karl Pearson. Considered by some to be vengeful and malicious, Cronwright's book has been the subject of systematic critical study by Liz Stanley (181–213).

17 The other instance is the new farm overseer, Gregory Nazianzen Rose, whom Lyndall mocks for his wifeliness and who dresses himself as a woman so as to attend Lyndall at her deathbed (*African Farm* 184, 251ff.). In contrast to that of Waldo, however, Gregory's metamorphosis is not associated with the intellect.

18 "Increasingly, division and dissimilarity arose between male and female, as the male advanced in culture and entered upon new fields of intellectual toil while the female sank passively backward and lower in the scale of life, and thus was made ultimately a chasm which even sexual love could not bridge. The abnor-

mal institution of avowed inter-male sexual relations upon the highest plane was one, and the most serious result, of this severance. . . . Man turned towards man; and parenthood, the divine gift of imparting human life, was severed from the loftiest and profoundest phases of human emotion: Xanthippe fretted out her ignorant and miserable life between the walls of her house, and Socrates lay in the Agora, discussing philosophy and morals with Alcibiades; and the race decayed at its core" (Schreiner, *Woman and Labour* 85–86).

19 For a critical account of these initiatives, see Botha and Cameron. For the judgments of the Constitutional Court of South Africa on, respectively, the constitutionality of the common law offence of sodomy and related statutory offenses, see National Coalition for Gay and Lesbian Equality and Another v. Minister of Justice and Others; and unfair discrimination on the grounds of sexual orientation and marital status, National Coalition for Gay and Lesbian Equality and Others v. Minister of Home Affairs and Others.

20 "It would be Jowett's distinction . . . to seek to bring the nation into the university — recruiting, reforming, and funneling ambitious plebeians and energetic peers alike into that civic elite of laity and statesmen whom he trusted . . . to take over the work of the English clergy. Nor did Jowett's ambition for an Oxford-trained elite pause at the nation's boundaries. 'I should like to govern the world through my pupils,' he once jested to Florence Nightingale . . . and by the end of the century Jowett's sally was scarcely an exaggeration. From Cecil Rhodes (Oriel) and Alfred Milner (Balliol) of Africa to George Curzon (Balliol) of India and C. H. Pearson (Oriel) of Australia, men from Jowett's college and university had come to preponderate in decisive posts throughout the empire. If the classic parallel which rose most frequently in the minds of such imperial proconsuls was that of Rome, the alternative imperial model supplied by the Greek colonial experience in Sicily . . . was never remote, and the pervasive ethos of Oxford Hellenism returns in force whenever we encounter, for example, Cecil Rhodes confiding that he traversed the South African veldt in the company of both Marcus Aurelius and *Marius the Epicurean*. . . . Constituting a quasi-platonic set of guardians at home and abroad, such men as Rhodes and Curzon were able to communicate through precisely the lingua franca of Literae humaniores which George Grote's brother John had earlier envisioned when he called classical study 'a point of intellectual sympathy among men over a considerable surface of the world' and a 'bond of intellectual communion among civilized men.' . . . Oxford graduates prospered from the civil service connection first established at Balliol by Jowett, not least of all because Jowett managed to arrange that classical studies would count for more points on the civil service exam than other subjects" (Dowling 72).

21 "By the merest accident, while collecting stray scraps of tribal history, later in life, the writer incidentally heard of 'the day Mzilikazi's tax collectors were killed.' Tracing this bit of information further back, he elicited from old people that the slaying of Bhoya and his companions, about the year 1830, constituted

the *casus belli* which unleashed the war dogs and precipitated the Barolong nation headlong into the horrors described in these pages" (*Mhudi* 21; see also Plaatje, *Selected Writings* 320–23, 348, 413).

22 David Schalkwyk writes, "There is no doubt that Plaatje would have set a far higher value on a book of such folktales — of which, Willan informs us, 'nothing at all has survived' — than on the novel itself, which he regarded as a mere means to a greater end" (24; citing Willan 336).

23 See Sanders, "Reading Lessons."

24 See Posnock 2. When Plaatje was unable to raise the money to attend, Du Bois read his address to the meeting of the 1921 Pan-African Congress in Paris on his behalf (*Selected Writings* 264–74).

25 I mean to invoke Derrida's concept of "dissemination," a "reading" irreducible to hermeneutic deciphering or decoding: "The semantic horizon which habitually governs the notion of communication is exceeded or punctured by the intervention of writing, that is of a *dissemination* which cannot be reduced to a *polysemia*. Writing is read, and 'in the last analysis' does not give rise to a hermeneutic deciphering, to the decoding of a meaning or truth" (Derrida, "Signature Event Context" 329).

26 For Willan's account of his rationale, see *Selected Writings* 3–4. For a critical appraisal of Willan's edition, see Schalkwyk.

27 Plaatje worked for the Mafeking magistrate's court, which was under the administration of the Cape Colony and, when the town was besieged by Boer forces (1899–1900), also interpreted for the courts martial (Plaatje, *Mafeking Diary* 37–38, 58).

28 His appeal for qualified "native interpreters" remains constant (see *Selected Writings* 252).

29 See Couzens, *New African* 5–6, 9–10.

30 Living in England at the time, Olive Schreiner, as a pacifist, was critical of Plaatje's advocacy of African support for the British War effort: "Olive knew of Plaatje and his book, but at the time the delegation visited England [*sic*] she was wary of him, for he 'advocates the natives coming here to help kill.' This was a reference to the decision of the Congress leadership to drop its agitation against the Land Act when the war broke out and to offer to enlist men for active service. Her pacifist convictions were paramount" (First and Scott 305; quoting Letter to Mrs. S. Solomon, 5 October 1916). It is one of the ironies of South African intellectual history that Sol Plaatje and Olive Schreiner effectively found themselves on different sides during the Anglo-Boer War, when Plaatje worked as an interpreter for the British at Mafeking, and Schreiner made speeches against the war (First and Scott 235–50; Schoeman, *Only an Anguish*).

31 "To address oneself to the other in the language of the other is, it seems, the condition of all possible justice, but apparently, in all rigor, it is not only impossible (since I cannot speak the language of the other except to the extent that I

appropriate and assimilate it according to the law of an implicit third) but even excluded by justice as law (*droit*), inasmuch as justice as right seems to imply an element of universality, the appeal to a third party who suspends the unilaterality or singularity of the idioms" (Derrida, "Force of Law" 949).

32 Despite the multilingualism common in South African court proceedings, the Minister of Justice has recently proposed that English be the sole language of record for the courts (Maseko and Kaschula).

33 This confession is repeated in *From Man to Man* as a story Rebekah tells her children (435).

34 For a accounts of the generic complexity of *Mhudi,* see Chennells, and Michael Green 50–62.

35 "*Mhudi,*" Tim Couzens writes, "is an attempt to create in mythical and historical terms the first South African national epic. . . . The novel becomes a kind of *extended* folk-tale which offers a moral. That moral is unequivocal: South Africa will only survive if all its citizens are afforded equality and if its unity is unswervingly kept in vision. Plaatje was implacably opposed to segregation and separatism" ("Sol T. Plaatje" 53).

36 For more on the significance of language, the "voice of nature," and its significance for "social co-operation" and the "social contract," see Couzens, "Sol T. Plaatje" 56–58.

37 Couzens writes, "By splitting the friendship of the individuals from the hostility of the peoples for one another, Plaatje has been able to give us both a glimpse of the possible ideal and a view of the real situation" ("Dark Side" 202).

38 Although, as Chrisman observes, "Plaatje uses women as figures through which to articulate a political vision, and critique, . . . at odds with the liberal non-racialist nationalism which the text endorses through the theme of the interracial alliance between baTswana and Boer," it would be inaccurate to imply that the intimacy between Ra-Thaga and de Villiers that corresponds to "the liberal humanistic idea that social and cultural difference can be transcended through interpersonal relationships" ("Fathering" 67–68) is unquestioned by the novel in other ways. For example, there is the repeated reminder that, although the men have affection for each other, in the final analysis, it is the alliance against the Matabele that keeps them together.

39 For a useful account of Plaatje's mediation of oral history, see Mpe.

Chapter 2. The Intellectual and Apartheid

1 Inside South Africa, intellectuals defending apartheid against foreign criticism did not always eschew racism. One of those to affirm it was G. B. A. Gerdener, Chairman of the South African Bureau of Racial Affairs (SABRA): "We have to lament that a great deal of the unfavorable foreign comment stands under the influence of the fear of the Germanic ideology of racial purity and racial superiority. Perhaps we can comfort ourselves with the assurance to the outside world that we have known the policy of racial purity and separate development for

more than a century and that it has appeared in our legislation for more than a generation" (5).

2   Marais, *Colour: Unsolved Problem of the West* (1952); also see Marais's *The Two Faces of Africa* (1964).

3   John Lazar suggests an interesting direction for further historical inquiry when he explores the global political motivations — a need for allies during the Cold War and rapid African decolonization to the north — for the paradoxical local affirmation of ties to the West by Afrikaner politicians who, in the 1950s and early 1960s, otherwise called for a republic free of any vestige, symbolic or otherwise, of colonial subordination (*Conformity and Conflict* 319–27).

4   On the 1938 trek, see Moodie.

5   Quoted in Rassool and Witz 464. The intensity of this rhetoric can also be gauged from B. M. Kies's attempt, in his lecture, *The Contribution of the Non European Peoples to World Civilization* (1953), to part "civilization" from its conjunction with "Europe" and the "West," and in so doing to wrest it from its racist appropriation by Afrikaner-nationalist ideologues.

6   Louw's "concept of the 'intellectual'" is treated exegetically by Pretorius. Confining itself to Louw's own writings, Pretorius's study does not explore any of the political and intellectual-historical questions that more recent scholarship, especially that of Olivier, has brought to the fore.

7   Early informational and didactic pieces include an extended two-part review in the mass-circulation magazine *Die Huisgenoot* [The House Companion, or Member of the Household] of the 1932 Carnegie Commission Report on White Poverty, a pivotal document in Afrikaner-nationalist mobilization, since it made visible the poverty of poor white Afrikaners and advocated specific measures of social uplift, including racial segregation and job reservation ("Armblanke-vraagstuk"); and a brief report on the historic national education conference of 1934 held in Cape Town and Johannesburg and marked (in Johannesburg) by intensive debate on "Native Education" (see E. G. Malherbe), which Louw, reporting on the initial Cape proceedings ("Konferensie"), does not, however, mention. Louw also wrote articles for the children's magazine *Die Jongspan* [The Youngsters] from 1937 to 1946, and he continued his South African journalism while in Amsterdam as a weekly column for *Die Huisgenoot* under the rubric *Die oop gesprek* [The open conversation]. See also Van Rensburg, "'Hoe Praat.'"

8   For a historical account of parliamentary "loyal opposition," see Lowell 437.

9   On academics at the Afrikaans universities, see Hugo.

10   Degenaar, "Politieke filosofie"; Du Toit, *Sondes.*

11   Olivier, *N. P. van Wyk Louw: Literatuur, filosofie, politiek.* Also see Olivier, "N. P. van Wyk Louw en Afrikaner-Nasionalisme: Die daad binne die geskiedenis"; "N.P. van Wyk Louw en die Afrikaner-Nasionalisme: Die Nasionaal-Sosialisme." For reactions to Olivier's book, see Du Plessis; Kannemeyer, "Deurtastende"; Van Rensburg, "Konfrontasie met Van Wyk Louw: Aflewering 1"; "Konfrontasie met Van Wyk Louw (Slot)."

12 Breytenbach, "Dear Mr. President"; Ndebele, "Open Letter" 21. For the right-wing appropriation of Louw of which Ndebele warns, see Jaap Marais, "Raka, deur NP van Wyk Louw: Die agtergrond en simboliek van die gedig in die eietydse samehang" and "Raka, deur NP van Wyk Louw: Die agtergrond en simboliek van die gedig in die eietydse samehang (2)."

13 Despite Sachs's intervention, as a party in government, the ANC has tended to attack its critics and to attempt to neutralize or co-opt them. The assault by Thabo Mbeki and his office on the scientists who signed the Durban Declaration on AIDS in July 2000 condemning Mbeki's questioning of HIV as the cause of AIDS is perhaps the most dramatic example ("Durban Declaration"; "Five Thou[s]and Scientists"; "Mbeki Consigns"). A discussion of the ANC's legal challenge to the release of the findings of the Truth and Reconciliation Commission on the organization in its report can be found in Tutu (208–13). On the post-apartheid role of left intellectuals in government think tanks, see Desai and Bohmke.

14 My translation of Louw's essay "Volkskritiek," part of a larger project of translating his writings on the intellectual into English, will appear shortly in *Metamorphoses: Journal of the Five-College Seminar on Literary Translation.*

15 Steyn, *Van Wyk Louw: 'n Lewensverhaal* (1998). While acknowledging the debt that Louw scholars will owe Steyn's monumental work, I note, however, my profound disturbance at two things: (1) Steyn, who writes as a nationalist, is never critical of Louw's advocacy of apartheid and in fact conveys the impression of being, for his own part, a post-apartheid apologist for apartheid; and (2) Steyn seeks to mitigate Louw's anti-Semitism and his advocacy, within the Broederbond in the 1930s, of discriminatory measures aimed at South African Jews (2:644–47, 784–88, 1111–14, 1135; 1:126–29).

16 About half of *Nuwe verse* (1954), and *Tristia* (1962). He also completed the verse drama *Germanicus* (1956), begun in the early 1940s.

17 "Because his academic duties encompassed more than literature, he was able to act in the Netherlands as a true ambassador for his country" (Grové, "Louw" 321). F. I. J. van Rensburg's account of Louw as tutor to the Afrikaans volk largely ignores his role as "ambassador" ("'Hoe Praat'").

18 On the *Sestigers,* see Louw, *Versamelde prosa* 2:87–185, 517–24; Louw "APB-Prys"; Cobden; "Prof. Louw." On Yolande Breytenbach's visa, see Louw, "Geagte Redaksie."

19 See Agtdrie; "Klein groepie"; Louw, "Groepie"; Verwoerd, *Verwoerd Speaks* 723; "Louw antwoord"; Louw, "Gesprek"; "Van Wyk Louw sê"; see also Olivier, *N. P. van Wyk Louw* 270.

20 See H. J. Simons: "The racist took over the concept of Separation from the liberal, translated it into Afrikaans as Apartheid, and turned it into a slogan of action" ("What Is Apartheid?" [March 1959] 17).

21 Olivier, *N. P. van Wyk Louw* 228–31; also see Olivier, "N. P. van Wyk Louw en R. F. A. Hoernlé."

22 On Hoernlé and apartheid, see H. J. Simons's two articles on "What Is Apartheid?"; and also Legassick.

23 On apartheid and the legacy of "indirect rule," see Mamdani, *Citizen and Subject.*

24 According to Derrida, "the irruption of the new . . . should be anticipated *as* the unforeseeable, the *unanticipatable* . . . in short, as that of which one does not yet have a memory. But our old memory tells us that it is also necessary to anticipate and to keep the heading [garder le cap], for under the motif — which can also become a slogan — of the unanticipatable or absolutely new, we can fear seeing return the phantom of the worst, the one we have already identified" (*Other Heading* 18; trans. modified).

25 In 1935 Louw supported measures against Jewish immigration as a member of the Broederbond (Steyn 1:126–29; Kannemeyer, *Dokumente* 83–85). In order to account for his sympathies with National Socialism, to Louw's anti-Semitism can be added an adherence to a principle of ethnic-national self-determination. The question of the right to national self-determination forced itself onto the European agenda with the Austrian *Anschluß* in March 1938 and the Nazi annexation of Sudetenland in October 1938 — less than two months before the main Ossewa celebrations. When Louw discusses the right of a volk to self-determination in "Die ewige trek," the essay he wrote for the 1938 Ossewatrek issue of *Die Brandwag,* his tone and choice of historical parallels convey some equivocation about the fate of Sudetenland: "Let me take an example from the latest European history: the 'rights' at stake in the recent break-up of the Versailles-Czech state. It would have profited no one to appeal to the 'right' in that struggle. Which right would be the highest? If we said: the right of the members of a volk to form a national state, then the Sudetenland should come to Germany, just as Transvaal and Free State should have had the right to unite in the 19th century; but if we say: the 'right' of treaties . . . and the 'right' of legally constituted states, then Czechoslovakia should have stayed undivided" (*Versamelde prosa* 1:100). Louw concludes: "Even the right of a volk to exist ['n volk se bestaansreg] is not something that remains safely written on unbreakable tablets, but something that must be created anew daily by its will and deed" (1:101). After the March 1939 Nazi invasion of Czechoslovakia, which lay outside of the German ethnic sphere, Louw's passion for National Socialism evidently abated (Olivier, *N. P. van Wyk Louw* 48).

26 "The spokesmen of the Nationalist section of the Afrikaner people are especially fond of hurling the word 'liberal,' or 'liberalist' [liberalis] as they like to say, at everyone and everything they regard as most *onafrikaans* [un-Afrikaans, even un-African]" (Hoernlé, *Native Policy* 103).

27 The first two lectures are "an analysis of present-day Native Policy in the Union, as a system of White 'domination,' or supremacy, tempered by what it has recently become fashionable to call 'trusteeship' or 'guardianship.'" Hoernlé's fourth and final lecture presents the results of "an attempt at re-thinking" liberal

ideals in the South African context: "They are that either *thoroughgoing parallel-ism*, or *total inter-racial assimilation*, or *total racial dissociation* (or *separation*), are compatible with the ideals of the liberal spirit, but that any half-measures in any one, or all, of these directions reduce in practice to our present system of domination-*cum*-trusteeship" (*Native Policy* viii, ix).

28 "Louw's summary of Hoernlé's views brings about a subtle paradigm shift: by referring to '[countries] constituted . . . racially or nationally [rasse-of volke-samestelling]' and a 'multi-national South Africa,' he adds the concepts of '*volk*' and 'nation' to Hoernlé's analysis, which in *South African Native Policy and the Liberal Spirit* and elsewhere, is concentrated on the question of *race*" (Olivier, "N. P. van Wyk Louw en R. F. A. Hoernlé" 247).

29 Hoernlé, *Native Policy* 168. "'Total Separation' envisages an organization of the warring sections into genuinely separate, self-contained, self-governing so-cieties, each in principle homogeneous within itself, which can then co-operate on a footing of mutual recognition of another's independence" (ibid. 169).

30 Sometimes his concessions are more than pragmatic and supply a moral basis, in terms of racial paternalism — "temporary . . . domination aiming at emanci-pation" — for the justification of white supremacy (*Native Policy* ix).

31 Louw's phobic negation of black domination might be read as a symptomatic admission of the repressed centrality of white domination: "the small, relatively highly-developed Afrikaans *volk* and the English *volk*-part [volksdeel] would sink to [the status of] powerless minorities among a mass of blacks. . . . [There would be] a 'plowing under' of the less numerous groups" (*Versamelde prosa* 1:505; see also 2:625).

32 Alluding to Isaiah 21:11–12, Hoernlé writes: "'Watchman, what of the night?' It is all too obvious that that watchman must report, not the breaking of the dawn, but an intensification of darkness" (*Native Policy* 185). In Isaiah 21:12, the watchman replies: "The morning cometh, and also the night: if ye will enquire, enquire ye: return, come."

33 According to Aletta Norval, apartheid displayed continuities and discontinu-ities with earlier segregationist discourse in that the racial division of segrega-tion was repeated in apartheid within the context of the *volkseie* — that is to say, in a context in which Afrikaner-nationalist intellectuals had begun to think of the volk as ethnically different and separate from the English section of the white population: "Although both discursive formations — segregation and apartheid — were structured with reference to racist exclusions, the context in which this exclusion took place makes it impossible to argue for an essential similarity between the two. Segregationist discourse was ordered around a pre-cise division between 'Europeans' and 'Natives,' and treated them both as ho-mogeneous categories. In response to this, the discourse of the volkseie sought to put into question the unity of the 'European' community, and extended this questioning to the homogeneity of the 'Native' community. Thus, even though the exclusionary black/white frontier was to continue to operate in the dis-course of apartheid, this frontier now functioned in a context where social

division was thought, in the first place, around the centrality of the volkseie. This is not to say that it was any less racist, but that these racist practices now operated in a context in which account had to be taken of the new organizing principle. Should one not recognize that, one would be unable to account for the effectiveness of this discourse in recasting social division and in prompting new images for identification not only for Afrikaners, but also for the wider black community. While a broad organizing principle, a new common sense, was in place by the mid-1940s, this did not mean that the detail of the project was worked out in fully fledged form. Quite the contrary: debates on the precise nature of apartheid within the Afrikaner community continued throughout the 1940s and well into the 1950s. It was only as a result of these debates, as well as of the resistance to the implementation of apartheid, that the nature of the project would begin to crystallize" (99–100). Curiously, Norval does not discuss N. P. van Wyk Louw. And, surprisingly, *Forty Lost Years,* Dan O' Meara's book on Afrikaner politics during the apartheid era makes no more than a passing reference to Louw's nationalist thinking (126).

34 Although there is no internal evidence, the multinationalism we find in Louw may also have been a reaction to Africanist demands for *national* self-determination supported by the Atlantic Charter, a compact made in 1941 between Franklin Roosevelt and Winston Churchill that "respect[ed] the right of all peoples to choose the form of government under which they live" (Brinkley and Facey-Crowther xvii).

35 A note on the word *volksdeel,* which I am translating as "volk-part": Afrikaner-nationalist intellectuals would argue that white Anglo–South Africans did not constitute a volk in their own right, but an expatriate local part [*deel*] of an international British volk—hence, a *volksdeel* (see D. F. Malherbe, *Afrikaner-volkseenheid* 25, 33–34).

36 "In constructing an intellectually coherent justification for apartheid, Christian-national ideologues frequently chose to infer or to suggest biological theories of racial superiority, rather than to assert these openly. For pragmatic as well as doctrinal reasons, the diffuse language of cultural essentialism was preferred to the crude scientific racism drawn from the vocabulary of Social Darwinism" (Dubow, *Scientific Racism* 246).

37 For a critique of Jaspers, see Lyotard, "German Guilt."

38 Ethnicity, race, and class were not the only fault lines. When Louw devised lojale verset, official Afrikaner-nationalist ideology still defined for women the role of *volksmoeders* [mothers of the volk] (see Elsabe Brink), which Afrikaans women intellectuals contemporary with Louw had to negotiate and overcome in order to enter intellectual sociality. In a short essay entitled "Gelykmaak en rangordening" [Equalizing and Rank-Ordering] (January 1939), Louw mocked, along with "'philanthropists'" and "communists," who advocate racial and economic equality respectively, "the champions of 'rights for women' who want to make the sexes equal, despite the difference in function" (*Versamelde prosa* 1:84).

39 In "The Crisis of the Mind" [La Crise de l'esprit], Valéry identifies three crises, the first of which is paralleled by Louw: "The military crisis may be over. The economic crisis is still visible in all its force. But the intellectual crisis, being more subtle and, by its nature, assuming the most deceptive appearances (since it takes place in the very realm of dissimulation) . . . this crisis will hardly allow us to grasp its true extent, its *phase*" (*Outlook* 25; trans. modified). Louw's writings on crisis also resonate with those of Edmund Husserl on the crisis of Europe: "The European nations are sick; Europe itself, it is said, is in crisis" (Husserl, "Philosophy" 270).

40 Olivier is thus not strictly correct to claim that Louw's "demand of justice" is new in nationalist discourse and is what differentiates him from Cronjé (Olivier, *N. P. van Wyk Louw* 216).

41 Rhoodie, writing in 1969 as a proponent of ethnic-national apartheid, then the official policy, underestimates the role of racism in Cronjé.

42 The names *Voortrekker* and *Groot Trek* both only gained currency in the 1870s in the time of the First Language Movement. Initially, *Groot Trek* was a translation of the English *Great Trek* (Van Jaarsveld 187f, 191f).

43 For more on the intellectual, the intellectualist, and figure of the seer [siener] in "Die ewige trek," see Sanders, "Complicities."

44 D. F. Malherbe dates the affirmation "Ik ben een *Afrikaaner*" back to 1706, attributing it to Hendrik Bibault, whose father was of French Huguenot extraction and whose mother was Dutch (*Afrikaner-volkseenheid* 41).

45 The phrase "in righteousness" [in geregtigheid] appears in the Old and New Testament many times. A troubling textual conjuncture, with its reference to a singular "his people," and to others as its "enemies," is in the song sung by Zacharias, father of John the Baptist, at his son's circumcision (I interpolate the Afrikaans): "And his father Zacharias was filled with the Holy Ghost, and prophesied, saying, Blessed *be* the Lord God of Israel; for he hath visited and redeemed his people [sy volk], . . . As he spake by the mouth of his holy prophets, which have been since the world began: That we should be saved from our enemies [vyande], and from the hand of all that hate us; To perform the mercy *promised* to our fathers, and to remember his holy covenant [heilige verbond]; the oath [eed] which he sware to our father Abraham, That he would grant unto us, that we being delivered out of the hand of our enemies might serve him without fear, In holiness and righteousness before him [in heiligheid en geregtigheid voor Hom], all the days of our life" (Luke 1:67–75; see also Genesis 17).

46 See Cronjé, *Tuiste* 66 and *passim;* Cronjé et al, *Regverdige* 71ff. and *passim;* Coetzee, "Mind of Apartheid" 17, 26, 32 n.17; W. A. de Klerk 203.

47 See Louw, "Rassevraagstukke" 10. According to Dubow, racial segregation functioned as a "consensus ideology" for Hertzog, Smuts, and their respective parties in the 1920s and 30s: "There was basic agreement between the SAP [South African Party] and the Nationalists on the need to preserve white supremacy. Racial segregation can indeed be seen as the counterpart to the cre-

ation of a unified white South African nation" (*Racial Segregation* 15; also see 133).

48 "I wish to speak to-day of the large-scale drift of our European population from the rural areas to the towns and of the struggle which the Afrikaans-speaking section particularly — many of them with Voortrekker blood in their veins — are waging in the towns to win their bread, to retain their Afrikaans tradition and background, and, not least of all, to keep South Africa a White Man's country" ("'Voortrekkers'").

49 "While the assumptions of the SABRA visionaries were informed by the same mix of racism and paternalism as their adversaries — and the same desire to maintain and rationalize white domination — their criticisms of Verwoerd and his supporters were not just differences about the most pragmatic way of securing white privilege. When the visionaries were finally purged in 1961, it was also because they had failed in the impossible task of infusing an inherently exploitative and oppressive programme with a consistent moral framework" (Lazar, "Verwoerd" 386).

50 See Giliomee, "'Survival'" 533. This was the position of Afrikaans business as represented by the Afrikaanse-Handelsinstituut (AHI, Afrikaans Commerce Institute). Arguing that development aimed at making the reserves economically self-sufficient would increase labor costs for white business and industry, it advocated separate urban residential areas (see Posel).

51 On the history of usage in racist discourse of the word "Bantu," see Dubow, *Scientific Racism* 104–7.

52 For example, Louw, "Die Afr[ikaan]se Beweging."

53 In a 1951 speech, Louw says that "immediate separation" would be "fatal for both [White and Bantu]" ("Geloftedag, 1951").

54 Louw, "Armblanke-vraagstuk"; see also W. E. G. Louw, Letter to N. P. van Wyk Louw, 8 January 1957.

55 In *Native Policy* 178–83.

56 Steyn reproduces Louw's claim uncritically, adding to it the absurdity that opponents of apartheid actually supported apartheid: "Louw supported 'the eventual fair territorial separation with complete freedom for everyone' at a time when even opponents of apartheid acknowledged something like it to be ethically right" (2:1135).

57 Cronjé, though, is unequivocal about where Hoernlé stands (*Regverdige* 92).

Chapter 3. Apartheid and the Vernacular

1 Mphahlele's discussion of Plaatje's *Mhudi* in *The African Image* (174–76) makes no mention of the "art and literature in the Vernacular" contemplated in the preface to the novel (Plaatje, *Mhudi* 21).

2 "[A]s hereditary chieftaincy is now a thing of the past, and the Government has for the last half-century been appointing chiefs who will obey it, in the place of

rebels, such a conflict is fast becoming irrelevant except as a symbol of the larger irony in black-white relations" (*African Image* 203).

3 According to John and Jean Comaroff, "colonialism . . . promised equality but sustained inequality; promised universal rights but kept the ruled in a state of relative rightlessness; promised individual advancement but produced ethnic subjection. In church and in state" (2:396).

4 "We were those sensitive might-have-beens who had knocked on the door of white civilisation (at the highest levels that South Africa could offer) and had heard a gruff 'No' or 'Yes' so shaky and insincere that we withdrew our snail horns at once" (Themba, *World* 229).

5 "No one with a conscience and a feeling heart can read Bloke's painful but ultimately uplifting story and long remain a neutral observer of the apartheid tragedy. One vividly grasps through his masterful delineations of South Africa's complex society that apartheid is a perverter of the human heart" (Mathabane viii); "Above all, the book is one about suffering, humiliation, the inability to change the circumstances of one's life, and the survival strategies of a black South African man of letters who does not possess anything at all, not even the most basic civil rights or his own name" (Obradović); "Of all the autobiographers who have written about the political ethos of this period, he is probably the only one to give a detailed, analytical critique" (Shava 35); "The book . . . provides, well within the framework of the individual development it sets out to trace, one of the most readable, informative and comprehensive guides to the history of apartheid, and of black opposition up to 1959, that is to be found" (Watts 149).

6 Or some readers separate their discussion of Modisane's stories from that of *Blame Me on History* (Barnett 184–85, 223–24). Other studies fail to mention his stories at all (Shava; Watts). Chapman ("More than" 201–2, 206) and Coste include discussions of the stories.

7 *Blame Me on History* was published in Great Britain and the United States in 1963. It was banned in South Africa, where it finally appeared in 1986. Traces of this history of publication can be found, to cite one example, in its gloss of "samp mealies" as "a sort of hominy dish" (*Blame* 31).

8 I borrow this term from Gilbert and Gubar who, writing about Jane Austen's novels, argue that, although "Austen's cover story of the necessity for silence and submission reinforces women's subordinate position in patriarchal culture," just as her heroines "manage to survive only by seeming to submit, she succeeds in maintaining her double consciousness in fiction that proclaims its docility and restraint even as it uncovers the delights of assertion and rebellion" (154, 168–69). Analogously, as a writer of an autobiographical work of political protest, aimed to some extent at "arous[ing] white consciousness to the plight of those racially dominated" (Sole, "Class" 160), Modisane not only portrays himself as a figure that laughs into its sleeve at its benefactors but, diegetically, makes use of the conventions of protest and its recognized literary forms to give a voice to a narrative neither easily declared nor fully realized.

9 Verwoerd's pronouncement itself is repeated twice (*Blame* 218, 306).

10 "The relation to time is bound up . . . with the work of the system *Cs*" (187; trans. modified). See also *Beyond the Pleasure Principle* (1920): "As a result of certain psychoanalytic discoveries, we are today in a position to subject to discussion the Kantian proposition that time and space are necessary forms of our thought. We have learnt that unconscious mental processes are in themselves 'timeless.' This means in the first place that they are not ordered temporally, that time does not change them in any way and that the idea of time cannot be applied to them. These are negative characteristics which can only be made clear by making a comparison with *conscious* mental processes" (28; trans. modified).

   According to Freud, in *Delusions and Dreams in Jensen's "Gradiva"* (1906), although the writer "directs his attention to the unconscious in his own mind, [and] listens to its possible developments and lends them expression instead of suppressing them by conscious criticism . . . he need not state [the laws which the unconscious must obey], nor even be clearly aware of them; as a result of the tolerance of his intelligence, they are incorporated within his creations" (92). In "Creative Writers and Day-Dreaming" (1908), Freud says that, for writers, "past, present and future are strung together, as it were, on the thread of the wish that runs through them" (148).

11 The dedication to the book runs as follows: "This book is for my mother MA-BLOKE and to the memory of my father JOSEPH who was killed by the Sophiatown which they bulldozed into the dust."

12 The humiliation of the father figure is also a critical scene in Peter Abrahams's *Tell Freedom* (1954), where Uncle Sam, cowed by a white man, beats the autobiographical Lee viciously for having raised his hand to a white boy. His Aunt Liza comforts him: "'It hurt him,' she said. 'You'll understand one day'" (32–34).

13 Paul de Man designates the address to the dead person and the positing of his or her response as the dominant figure of autobiography: "It is the figure of prosopopeia, the fiction of an apostrophe to an absent, deceased or voiceless entity, which posits the possibility of the latter's reply and confers upon it the power of speech. . . . The dominant figure of the epitaphic or autobiographical discourse is . . . the prosopopeia, the fiction of the voice-from-beyond the grave" ("Autobiography" 926–27).

14 "The Saint," a "reformed British gentleman crook who becomes a Robin Hood of crime," was the protagonist in a series of films made between 1938 and 1953 (Halliwell 987).

15 It also obliterates his mother's name, Ma-Willie, which changes with the name of her firstborn child, to become "Ma-Bloke" (*Blame* 167).

16 "He speaks for himself, thus cutting himself away from the community at the very moment when it is conducting a difficult fight" (Coste 45).

17 *Julius Caesar*, directed by Joseph L. Mankiewicz, MGM, 1953. *Deadwood Dick* is a Western film serial dating from 1940.

18 See also Modisane's desire for a "more professional liberation movement" (*Blame* 139).

19 "As long as he must submit to the White, the Black must 'play' the Negro. . . . As a result, the Black dwells in a certain ambiguity: Where does the game end? Where does it begin? Which of the two roles—the acted Black, the real Black— is authentic?" (Coste 47).

20 Modisane began writing *Blame Me on History* some years earlier. Sylvester Stein, chief editor of *Drum* in the 1950s, took the manuscript with him when he left the country in late 1957 (Stein 151).

21 I am in broad agreement with J. Hillis Miller's idea of "the ethical moment in the act of reading" as "a response to something, responsible to it, responsive to it, respectful of it," but I do not know whether it is always the case that the "ethical moment in reading leads to an act. . . . [in] the social, institutional, political realms" in the dissociated way that he seems to imagine (*Ethics* 4). Also see Sanders, "Reading Lessons" 8–9.

22 He has also given his father a packet of money, "his entire savings," that had been hidden in the back of the piano ("Dignity" 16).

23 His few references to "liberal" white writers such as Nadine Gordimer and Alan Paton are disparaging (*Versamelde prosa* 2:521–22). On Gordimer's response, see Steyn (2:1003). Despite his views on her fiction, in 1963 Louw's name appeared on a petition against censorship along with those of Gordimer and other writers and artists (Steyn 2:1156 n.81).

24 The fact that Abrahams represents Africans rather than coloureds may be why Louw does not discuss the work of S. V. Petersen, whose novel, *As die son ondergaan* (1945), is the story of a young coloured man who, frustrated in his ambitions to become a teacher, comes to the city, where he is tempted by sex and drink, before returning to the country (on Petersen, see Kannemeyer, *Geskiedenis* 2:169–71; see also Clinton 617). In June 1949, Louw and the other members of the *Standpunte* group tried, unsuccessfully, to solicit an article from Petersen on "the attitude of the coloured poet towards his community and the white community. He would also have to discuss critically what Whites were writing about coloureds and the possibility of a coloured having Whites appear in a story" (Steyn 1:523).

25 For a study of the representation of people of color in the Afrikaans novel, see Gerwel.

26 Steyn misrenders what Louw says about Abrahams as a "starting point": "Louw says he treats the work of a not very talented writer *not* as a starting point of what hopefully can be important for South Africa" (Steyn 2:645; my emphasis).

27 In the fragment that provides Brink with the title for his novel and that appears as one of its epigraphs, Saint John of the Cross subordinates evening knowledge to that of the morning: " . . . la noticia vespertina, que es sabiduría de Dios en sus creaturas y obras y ordenaciones admirables; la cual es . . . más baja sabiduría que la matutina." When the English version of Brink's novel appeared in 1974 as

Looking on Darkness, its title came from another of the epigraphs, a line from Shakespeare's Sonnet 27.

28 "The white power does not believe itself required to respond, does not hold itself responsible before the black people. The blacks cannot assure themselves, by return mail, by verbal exchange, by any look or sign, that any image of them has been formed on the other side, which may afterward return to it in some way. For the white power does not content itself with not answering. It does worse: it does not even acknowledge receipt" (Derrida, "Laws" 31; see also Mandela, *No Easy Walk* 131–38).

29 Critiques of the role of ubuntu in the ideology of post-apartheid nation-building have displayed little grasp of the linguistic intricacy, conceptual complexity, and historical genealogy of ubuntu; for an instance, see Richard Wilson (11ff.).

30 In Schreiner there is also a caution in relation to the stranger, an ironic inscription of Scripture (Matthew 25:35) as the chapter title "I was a stranger, and ye took me in" (*African Farm* 44ff.).

31 "Xhosa writers have long known: there is no retreat from modernisation, tradition has to revitalised and revalued in the present day. . . . In Xhosa literature this has resulted in strong intellectual writing by leaders such as the educationist Z. K. Matthews, the literary critic A. C. Jordan, and the statesman or politician Nelson Mandela. (There are numerous others.) What their writings and speeches have in common is that the two forces of the school people and the red people attach an enlightened universalism to a particular African concern. 'Red' traditionalism may be interpreted accordingly as both conservative (it is a bulwark against deracination) and progressive in a grassroots Africanism that holds the universalizing democratic language to local community account" (Chapman, "Red People" 40–41).

32 According to Pallo Jordan, A. C. Jordan "chose the Southern African tale — with its oral tradition, and hence not limited to a reading public — as the medium through which to express his protest against the existing order" (xxii).

33 For a biographical account of Jordan, see Kunene and Kuper.

34 On the cattle-killing, see Peires.

35 Lindi Nelani Jordan writes, incorrectly, that A. C. Jordan "merely mentions Soga" (ix). A. C. Jordan's framing of Soga is complex, and its brevity cannot be read as indicating that Jordan saw Soga as unimportant, let alone as justifying the notion that "this is because Tiyo Soga's writings do not reflect the cries and anguish of the African people, but rather, are an exhortation to the people to join the new society, where Soga believed there was 'abundance of life' for all" (ix). It is clear from A. C. Jordan's discussion that Soga had no illusions about the "new society."

36 When citing the Xhosa text of "Amakholwa Namaqaba," I refer to the version in Bennie (51–53).

37 When, for instance, Archbishop Tutu addresses the hearing of the Truth and Reconciliation Commission at East London on 18 April 1996, the simultaneous

translator renders his acknowledgment of the ubuntu of the witnesses as follows: "The people who've come forward here are people of quite extraordinary character. [Thank you] very much for your hospitality [ubuntu]. The world is amazed as it hears the harrowing stories that you have been telling. That there can be this willingness to forgive, this humaneness" (SABC, disc 1, track 6; production script on-line: http://www.sabctruth.co.za/bones.htm [11 April 2001]; last interpolation mine). The relationship of ubuntu to the thematics of forgiveness alluded to here demands a separate treatment lying beyond the scope of the present study.

38 For an alternative account of Soga's position, see De Kock 179–84, 206–7 n.12.

39 Arguing that ubuntu is one name for an ethics of cooperation arising among the poor across the globe, Deacon makes a critique of the post-apartheid appropriation of ubuntu in corporate management. Lacking in Deacon's account, however, is a thorough linguistic analysis of formulations of ubuntu current today.

40 Soga's journal reveals his curiosity about, and need for instruction on, "the ceremonies [for] a heathen burial" (Soga 31–32).

41 Soga's essay was written before the Xhosa translation of the Scriptures was completed. In the Xhosa Bible published by the British and Foreign Bible Society in London in 1927, the word for "angels" is *izithunywa,* or "messengers," a rendering consonant with the original Greek (*angeloi*).

42 Soga appears to register the dimension of risk in the earliest of his essays in *Indaba,* "A National Newspaper" [Ipepa le-Ndaba Zasekaya]: "We are fed up with half-truths by travellers who pass near our areas [ngamahamba-nandabǝ]" (Soga 152).

43 For accounts of the 2000 exhibition, Kwere Kwere: Journeys into Strangeness, see Dodd; Edmunds; "Documenting."

Chapter 4. Prison Writing

1 The second page reference is to the Taurus edition, as a typesetting error in the Faber edition results in this phrase being absent from it. I have used the Taurus edition whenever I have corrected the Faber edition.

2 As Breytenbach observes in a pre-prison text, "Vulture Culture: The Alienation of White South Africa" (1971), "Apartheid is the state of being apart. . . . It is the space of the White man's being. It is the distance needed to convince himself of his denial of the other's humanity. It ends up denying all humanity of any kind both to the other and himself. . . . But that which may be a psychic purge for the White . . . is a physical straining for the Black; the confines and the confinement of his condition, the maiming of his possibilities" (*End Papers* 53).

3 I am claiming a little more than Breytenbach himself does: "Still, if what I had to describe is of any documentary value it can only be because I tried, as a White African who has had the privilege to enter into a world known only too well by the majority of South Africans, to paint as *fully* as *possible* my view of *that* society as it exists *now*" (*True Confessions* 340).

4 The saying of Anaximander, in a slightly different form, also appears as an epigraph to *Mouroir: Mirrornotes of a Novel,* a collection of Breytenbach's prison writings: "Every individual does penance for [his] separation from the boundless."

5 "Beyond right, and still more beyond juridicism, beyond morality, and still more beyond moralism, does not justice as relation to the other suppose . . . the irreducible excess of a disjointure or an anachrony, some *Un-Fuge,* some 'out of joint' dislocation of Being and in time itself, a disjointure that, in always risking the evil, expropriation, and injustice (*adikia*) against which there is no calculable insurance, would alone be able to *do justice* or to *render justice* to the other as other?" (Derrida, *Specters* 27).

6 It appears to be an exception when the prison censor, a staunch Afrikaner nationalist whom Breytenbach calls Major Schnorff, will not speak to him in Afrikaans: "He refused my Afrikaans. Spoke his quaint English to me" (*True Confessions* 173).

7 For biographical treatments of Breytenbach, see Weschler; also Walzer 210–24.

8 "I was recruited in the early 1970s [by the ANC] for the specific purpose of creating forms of aid to militant White opposition to the Apartheid regime in the country, of establishing these points of aid abroad, of helping the White militants in obtaining a basic training when abroad, permitting them to carry on the struggle clandestinely upon their return to the country" (*True Confessions* 77).

9 Minister of Justice Jimmy Kruger had, apparently without Cabinet approval, promised him a lighter sentence of five years in exchange for his counsel's not politicizing the trial. Kruger failed to keep his word, denying that he had made any such agreement, and Breytenbach served seven of the nine years of his sentence (see Galloway 196–98, 208; *True Confessions* 61). Breytenbach was put on trial again in 1977 on similar charges but, with the help of skilled defense lawyers, was found innocent (*True Confessions* 242–52).

10 The journalist Jack Viviers, who gained Breytenbach's confidence, turned out to be working for the security police (*True Confessions* 70–71). Although I cite his book as the most accessible source for Breytenbach's speech, I have tried to draw on it only when the text corresponds with what was reported in newspapers at the time (see ". . . Ek was dom").

11 "Read it — you will also hear the insidious voice of the controller in it. This was in the hands of [security police colonel] Huntingdon a week before the trial commenced, and Vorster had it on his desk before it was read in court" (*True Confessions* 63).

12 The term *verlig* is usefully defined in relation to *verkramp,* its antonym: "It is difficult to translate the term 'verkramp.' The nearest word in English would be 'cramped' or 'ultra-conservative.' The German word 'verkrampfen' also conveys something of the meaning of the Afrikaans word, i.e. 'to become rigid or motionless as the result of a cramp.' The word is used in a metaphorical sense to indicate a specific outlook on life. Expressing an attribute, the word becomes

'verkrampte.' 'Verlig' may be translated by 'enlightened' (either a person or a point of view. However, in the context of South African politics, the word was originally used in a negative sense. Used attributively the word becomes 'verligte'" (W. J. de Klerk, "Concepts" 519).

13 Breytenbach's contestatory dialogue with Louw has not ceased. Alluding to voortbestaan in geregtigheid, Breytenbach writes, "Survival knows no justice. Even though a simulacrum of justice is often considered the vehicle of survival," in a recent contribution to a book on the Truth Commission ("Appendix" 163).

14 "Breytenbach," writes André Brink, "was very reluctant to take part, but I managed to persuade him" (Introduction to Breytenbach, *Season* 14). See Polley for a compendium, without Breytenbach's address, of the summer school proceedings. On the impact of the address on younger Afrikaans intellectuals, see Du Preez (3).

15 There are at least two other parodic allusions to Louw in "A View From the Outside," when Breytenbach speaks of "lending [Afrikaans literary] work a right to existence [bestaansreg] by assigning it [to students]"; and when he declares that "I want to come as close as I can in my work to the temporal [die verbygaande] — not the infinite [nie die ewige nie]; that has always been around" (*Season* 157, 160; see Louw, *Versamelde prosa* 1:164, 465).

16 Another notable "slip of the pen" occurred when "A View from the Outside" was reproduced as part of *Rapport*'s 1975 trial coverage. The word *bevegting* ("combating," in the phrase "combating . . . institutions" [*Season* 153] in the passage quoted earlier in this paragraph) is printed as *bevestiging* [confirmation] ("Ek skaam my vir my volk . . ?").

17 A great deal of weight is put on "life" in "A View from the Outside," which constantly contrasts what it proposes with the deathliness of the status quo: "André Brink intimated the other evening that there might be a resurrection [heropstand] of us Lazaruses, not that there was ever any insurrection [opstand]. . . . As a matter of fact, one of the things I specifically want to ask this evening is whether there is still some life left in us, or are we totally mummified [uitgevrek] as a result of our petit-bourgeois mentality?" (*Season* 152; trans. modified). The first, Afrikaans, edition of *Season in Paradise* was published in 1976 under the pseudonym B. B. Lasarus.

18 Since then, however, Breytenbach, although continuing to write in English, has published several books in Afrikaans.

19 Soyinka, *The Man Died*; Mapanje, *Chattering Wagtails* as well as "Of Orality and Memory" and "Containing Cockroaches"; Brutus, *Letters to Martha*; Cronin, *Inside* as well as "No Unnecessary Noises".

20 On the "pipeline," see Kariũki 79–82, 126ff.

21 Kenyatta died in August 1978, while Ngũgĩ was in prison.

22 See Ndebele, "The English Language and Social Change in South Africa" (*South African Literature and Culture* 98–116). Also see Mothobi Mutloatse's introduction to *Forced Landing*. On language policy more generally, see Alexander.

23 "Bandit" is a rendering of the Afrikaans *bandiet* [convict]. "Nosemansland" is a

variant of "No Man's Land," Breytenbach's code-word for South Africa. Another of Breytenbach's specular alter egos, Don Espejuelo (Master Mirror), is the author of a book entitled *On the Noble Art of Walking in No Man's Land* (*Mouroir* 256). "One Lady" is an anagram of "Yolande."

24 *Mouroir* 1. I cite the Taurus edition. The "Apology" is omitted in the English-language edition, as is the dedication: "These texts are dedicated to my old cell-mate and my master: Don Espejuelo."

25 See, for example, the Truth Commission testimony of Deborah Matshoba (3).

26 "Apartheid Thinking" is a condensed version of "The Mind of Apartheid."

27 See "A View from the Outside": "I cannot and will not dissociate myself from this mess" (*Season* 154).

Chapter 5. Black Consciousness

1 Material in this paragraph on Steve Biko's death and the subsequent inquest is drawn from Woods 176–261; and Biko, *Black Consciousness* 279–98.

2 Amnesty is conditional on the act or acts for which amnesty is sought being: (a) committed with a political objective; (b) commensurate with the achievement of that objective; (c) disclosed in a full account of the act or acts in question (for further details, see South Africa, Promotion 4 [20]). The applications of four of the five policemen failed (Snyman et al., Application). The application of the fifth, Gideon Nieuwoudt, was separated from those of the others, and is still pending.

3 See also Siebert 2: 48; Nie[u]woudt 65–66, 80.

4 See also Snyman, Testimony 2–3, 4, 20, 21, 52f, 61, 80, 98, 108; Siebert 1: 27ff; 2: 12–13,15,21; Marx 60, 65; Nie[u]woudt 21f, 29, 34, 35, 40, 43, 48, 87, 95, 145.

5 See also Nie[u]woudt 34, 43.

6 According to N. Chabani Manganyi, "the victory of black consciousness cannot be revoked because it was and still remains a psychological and spiritual one. . . . It challenged the white power structure since it dared to expose the pariah status of black South Africans and in so doing threatened to repeat, in the perceptions of Afrikanerdom, what Afrikanerdom had gone through not so long ago in its fight against anglicisation" (*Looking* 175).

7 The trial of nine leaders of SASO and the BPC (Black People's Convention) took place in Pretoria from August 1975 to December 1976. According to Gerhart, the trial, although ending in imprisonment for the accused, "instead of contributing to the suppression of Black Consciousness ideology . . . by giving the accused a continuous public platform through the press, merely disseminated that ideology more widely" (298). The testimony of Steve Biko as an expert witness for the defense is reprinted in Biko, *Black Consciousness.*

8 "When I addressed a group in Cape Town . . . I spoke about our viewpoint, and incidentally this was found most acceptable by the Afrikaner students. They said to me in no uncertain terms: This is the way Afrikaner nationalism developed,

right; we wish you guys well. . . . [Johan Fick, president of the Afrikaner Studentebond] recognized what I was saying as what had been said in his history" (*Black Consciousness* 144).

9   The dominant narrative for the direction of political resistance is well captured in the title of Karis and Carter's monumental five-volume *From Protest to Challenge: A Documentary History of African Politics in South Africa, 1882–1964* (1972–).

10 In Biko's letters to Aelred Stubbs, frankness of utterance is a condition of possibility of relation but can also disrupt it: "I have in some parts of this letter spoken very frankly — not to kill my friendship with you but rather to preserve it"; "A lot of friends of mine believe I am arrogant and they are partly right. Often what I call a critical frankness sounds much sharper than was intended and tends to assume holier-than-thou proportions. The problem with me is that I often take friends for granted and do not cater for the protective subjectivism that we all suffer from" (Stubbs 174, 176).

11 As Aelred Stubbs observed, "perhaps the political genius of Steve lay in concentrating on the creation and diffusion of a new consciousness rather than in the formation of a rigid organisation" (182). In a similar vein, Ellen Kuzwayo writes: "Steve was model of black consciousness . . . for young and old alike. . . . Steve Biko is dead; but his spirit will live forever" (47).

12 Rich 110. The preceding quotations in this paragraph are also from Rich (101–9).

13 A useful selection of Butler's essays and lectures is edited by Stephen Watson. For a critical response to Butler's claims for English, English-speaking South Africans (ESSAS), and mission-school education, see Ndebele's "The English Language and Social Change in South Africa" (*South African Literature* 98–116).

14 Attwell characterizes Kirkwood's three-part "ontology" as a "brilliant piece of rhetorical inversion . . . [of] the three phases identified by Fanon in the development of the national culture of indigenous peoples" ("Problem" 125). To Attwell's elegant formulation one would need to add that it also represents, in a more direct way, an acceptance of the agenda laid down for Whites by Black Consciousness.

15 See Gordimer, "My New South African Identity."

16 In "Relevance and Commitment" (1979), Gordimer readily admits to "using the schema of a Black Consciousness philosophy" (*Essential Gesture* 139). See also "The Essential Gesture" (1984): "the white writer's task as 'cultural worker' is to raise the consciousness of white people, who, unlike himself, have not woken up" (*Essential Gesture* 293).

17 In her second novel, *A World of Strangers* (1958), Gordimer uses the narrator, an Englishman come to work in South Africa, to pose questions about attempts by left-liberal whites to identify with distant causes: "'It's so ridiculous when you're trying to identify yourself with the other person.' . . . 'Of course,' she said, smiling reminiscently. "But it's a risk you have to take sometimes'" (70).

18 It is interesting to note, in the context of this figuring of exemplarity, that Biko's

education was not conducted by "Verwoerd" but by the "missionaries." Biko attended St. Francis College at Marianhill, Natal, "a liberal Catholic boarding school and one of the few remaining private high schools for Africans in South Africa" (Gerhart 259–160). This biographical fact appears to participate in the displacement whereby anger is transferred from Bantu education to the white liberal.

19 The exception is Gail Gerhart, whose study situates Black Consciousness in a political and intellectual tradition of African nationalism dating back to the early years of the twentieth century. Particularly provocative is her linking of elements of Black Consciousness to the idea of self-reliance put forward by Anton Lembede, who became the first president of the African National Congress Youth League in 1944 (45–84).

20 For a critical summary of the debate on Fanon's reading of Capécia, see Sharpley-Whiting. Although Fanon does indeed conclude his discussion of René Maran in the chapter on "The Man of Color and the White Woman" with the concession that "'there was a touch of fraud in trying to deduce from the behavior of . . . Mayotte Capécia a general law of behavior of the black woman with the white man,'" this seems insufficient to justify the conclusion that "Fanon's diagnosis of Capécia's affective erethism is unique to this woman of color" (Sharpley-Whiting 66; embedded quotation from Fanon, *Black Skin* 81). Elsewhere Fanon uses Capécia in an even more generalizing way: "I am thinking impartially of men like Gobineau or women like Mayotte Capécia" (*Black Skin* 13).

21 "In the Antilles perception always occurs on the level of the imaginary. It is in white terms that one perceives one's fellows" (*Black Skin* 163n; see also 25ff, 29, 31, 153, 172–73, 191ff., 193, 197).

22 As Jacqueline Rose points out, this development is more overt when Sachs revises his book as *Black Anger* (1947).

23 On the impact of Fanon's response on Sartre's subsequent work, see Bernasconi.

24 It is important to note that, although he does not make the distinction in *Anti-Semite and Jew,* in "Black Orpheus" Sartre writes: "A Jew—a white man among white men—can deny that he is a Jew, can declare himself a man among men. The Negro cannot deny that he is Negro, nor can he claim that he is part of some abstract colorless humanity: he is black" (296). Fanon's response to "Black Orpheus" suggests, however, that Sartre's conclusions do not fully take this distinction into account.

25 Wole Soyinka analyzes Senghor's project in terms of forgiveness (*Burden of Memory* 93–144).

26 Woods does not date this text. It probably comes from after July 1970, when Pityana succeeded Biko as second president of saso. Biko's "We Blacks," which it echoes, appeared in September 1970.

27 saso was founded in 1969 amid a debate that "arose because of the tendency not to want to do what appears to conform with government policy—i.e., to segregate against another group" (*I Write* 11). This tendency became known in

subsequent writings as the "'morality' argument" (*I Write* 17; see also 50, 68). Despite setting out clearly its arguments for a separate organization, and coming out against apartheid separate development, SASO was, in its early years, permitted to operate on black campuses by the apartheid state, which saw its strategic separatism as according with separate development (Stubbs 157–58; Gerhart 268–69).

28 Coetzee appears to echo Fanon: "the Negrophobic woman is in fact nothing but a putative sexual partner—just as the Negrophobic man is a repressed homosexual" (*Black Skin* 156).

29 This idea informs Manganyi's reading of the myth of Sisyphus: "I the black Sisyphus am social—not metaphysical" (*Mashangu's Reverie* 16).

30 Here it is worth turning to Spivak's account of the ethico-political implications of a transcoding of value (*Critique* 103ff, see also *Outside* 281–82). See also my "Postcolonial Reading." When beauty is turned into goodness, we have an assumption of agency in complicity, rather than a lamenting of victimhood.

31 As O'Brien notes, "Ndebele's theory, though it has evolved along with South African politics for nearly twenty years, had its origins in the Black Consciousness movement" (72).

32 This is in contrast to earlier writers such as Modisane and Mphahlele, whose "Mrs. Plum" satirizes the Black Sash human rights organization. In an exchange between the narrator, Mrs. Plum's domestic worker, and her employer's daughter, the organization is mocked for speaking on behalf of Blacks: "For your people. I ask her I say, What for? My people are in Phokeng far away. They have got mouths, I say. Why does she want to say something for them? . . . Kate raises her shoulders and drops them and says. How can I tell you Karabo? I don't say your people—your family only. I mean all the black people in this country" (*In Corner B* 168–69).

33 In "Liberation and the Crisis of Culture" (1990/1994), Ndebele writes of "a chasm of engineered ignorance, misunderstanding, division, illusion, and hostility . . . that highlights the national tragedy of a people who have long lived together, but could do no better than acknowledge their differences. They have done so with such passion as would suggest that perhaps they sensed something in common between them which neither of them was prepared to acknowledge; the awesome responsibility entailed by such an acknowledgement may have been too daunting" (3–4).

34 This was arguably a "loyal" critique. In "The University: Redefining Commitments" (1987), Ndebele notes that "South African English-speaking liberal universities have long proclaimed themselves the custodians of the liberal tradition" (1). I would argue that here, once again, it is not liberalism as a basic emancipatory project that is being challenged—Ndebele contrasts "the liberal posture" and "the mass struggle for liberation" (6–7)—but the control that white institutions have over defining the shape of that project.

35 In many of his post-apartheid writings, Ndebele is haunted by "confusion," which he sees it as his duty as an intellectual to lessen. In his 1991 preface to

South African Literature and Culture, he accuses the National Party of "appropriating many of the ideals of the liberation movement. One effect of such appropriation is to reduce the capacity of those ideals to inspire a visionary optimism among the oppressed" (viii). To make this case seems less difficult than distinguishing the vocabulary of the mass anti-apartheid struggle from that developed historically by liberalism in South Africa. One might thus interpret the "hatred" of the figure of the liberal to a mimetic rivalry and violence born of the difficulty, for Ndebele and others, of making such a distinction.

Conclusion

1 The Cradock Four were Matthew Goniwe, Fort Calata, Sparrow Mkonto, and Sicelo Mhlauli.
2 Judith Butler questions the Hegelian opposition of kinship and politics in *Antigone's Claim*. For a slightly different interpretation of *Antigone* in an African context, see Sanders, "Ambiguities."
3 The CALS submission notes that "many feminist theorists have attempted to explain why women sometimes collude in their own oppression and are even complicit in the oppression of other women" (Goldblatt and Meintjes 25).
4 Without going into detail, Louw's thesis also considered the education of Africans and the duty of white educators to make provision for it: "The native is not only *in* South Africa, but *of* South Africa. The native question cuts across the whole of our life, social and economical. The white man's task in South Africa is to adjust his environment to the individual, and any scheme of education for the European, which leaves out the black man, must be futile" (qtd. in Steyn 1:69).
5 In his review of the Carnegie Commission's report, Louw reproduces, without comment, its views on racially mixed urban areas: "'Long-term economic equality between poor whites and the great majority of colored people, and proximity of their residences to one another, [must] have the tendency to bring about social equality among them'— and 'the weakening of the social color separation line is now in some parts visibly underway'" ("Armblanke-vraagstuk" 63).
6 On the geographical limits of Breytenbach's vision, also see Coetzee, "Against."
7 A range of accounts and responses are reprinted in Nnaemeka, ed., *Sisterhood* 389–468.
8 A self-described white feminist from South Africa made this a point of self-criticism: "However supportive a white feminist might be of her black 'sister,' she is not an historical inhabitant of a black woman's subject position and needs to maintain a rigorous interrogation of her *own* subject position while listening to black women articulate *their* situation" (Ryan 199).
9 On other-intendedness, see Spivak, *Imperative/Imperatives*.
10 See Sanders, "Reading Lessons."

bibliography

Abel, Richard L. *Politics by Other Means: Law in the Struggle against Apartheid, 1980–1994.* New York: Routledge, 1995.

Abrahams, Peter. *Tell Freedom: Memories of Africa.* 1954. New York: Macmillan, 1970.

Adorno, Theodor W. *The Jargon of Authenticity.* Translated by Knut Tarnowski and Frederic Will. Evanston, Ill.: Northwestern University Press, 1973.

Agtdrie [pseud.]. "Dan hoop ek dat die staatsgreep slaag." *Die Burger,* 5 January 1967, 8.

Albertyn, Catherine. "Women and the Transition to Democracy in South Africa." In *Gender and the New South African Legal Order,* edited by Christina Murray, 39–63. Cape Town: Juta, 1994.

Alexander, Neville. *Language Policy and National Unity in South Africa/Azania.* Cape Town: Buchu Books, 1989.

Anyidoho, Kofi, ed. *The Word behind Bars and the Paradox of Exile.* Evanston, Ill.: Northwestern University Press, 1997.

Arendt, Hannah. *The Origins of Totalitarianism.* 1951. San Diego: Harcourt, 1973.

Arendt, Hannah, and Karl Jaspers. *Correspondence, 1926–1969.* Translated by Robert and Rita Kimber. Edited by Lotte Kohler and Hans Saner. New York: Harcourt, 1992.

Arnott, Jill. "French Feminism in a South African Frame? Gayatri Spivak and the Problem of Representation in South African Feminism." In *South African Feminisms: Writing, Theory, and Criticism, 1990–1994,* edited by M. J. Daymond, 77–89. New York: Garland, 1996.

Ashforth, Adam. *The Politics of Official Discourse in Twentieth-Century South Africa.* Oxford: Clarendon Press, 1990.

Attridge, Derek. "Innovation, Literature, Ethics: Relating to the Other." *PMLA* 114, no. 1 (1999): 20–31.

Attwell, David. "Intimate Enmity in the Journal of Tiyo Soga." *Critical Inquiry* 23, no. 3 (1997): 557–77.

———. "The Problem of History in the Fiction of J. M. Coetzee." In *Rendering Things Visible: Essays on South African Literary Culture,* edited by Martin Trump, 94–133. Johannesburg: Ravan, 1990.

Barash, Carol L. "Virile Womanhood: Olive Schreiner's Narratives of a Master Race." In *Speaking of Gender,* edited by Elaine Showalter, 269–81. New York: Routledge, 1989.

Barnett, Ursula A. *A Vision of Order: A Study of Black South African Literature in English (1914–1980).* Cape Town: Maskew Miller Longman, 1983.

Battle, Michael. *Reconciliation: The Ubuntu Theology of Desmond Tutu.* Cleveland: Pilgrim Press, 1997.

Benda, Julien. *Dialogues à Byzance.* Paris: Revue Blanche, 1900.

———. *La Trahison des clercs.* Ed. René Étiemble. Paris: Bernard Grasset, 1958.

———. *The Treason of the Intellectuals (La trahison des clercs).* 1928. Trans. Richard Aldington. New York: Norton, 1969.

Benjamin, Walter. *Reflections: Essays, Aphorisms, Autobiographical Writings.* Translated by Edmund Jephcott. New York: Harcourt, 1978.

Bennie, W. G., ed. *Imibengo.* Lovedale: Lovedale Press, 1935.

Bering, Dietz. *Die Intellektuellen: Geschichte eines Schimpfwortes.* Stuttgart: Klett-Cotta, 1978.

Bernasconi, Robert. "Sartre's Gaze Returned: The Transformation of the Phenomenology of Racism." *Graduate Faculty Philosophy Journal* 18, no. 2 (1995): 201–21.

Bhabha, Homi K. "Of Mimicry and Man: The Ambivalence of Colonial Discourse." In *The Location of Culture,* 85–92. New York: Routledge, 1994.

Biko, Steve. *Black Consciousness in South Africa.* Edited by Millard W. Arnold. New York: Random House, 1978.

———. *I Write What I Like.* Edited by Aelred Stubbs. San Francisco: Harper, 1986.

Borges, Jorge Luis. "Kafka and His Precursors." In *Labyrinths: Selected Stories and Other Writings,* edited by Donald A. Yates and James E. Irby, 234–36. Harmondsworth, U.K.: Penguin, 1970.

Botha, Kevan, and Edwin Cameron. "South Africa." In *Sociolegal Control of Homosexuality,* edited by Donald J. West and Richard Green, 5–42. New York: Plenum, 1997.

Bourdieu, Pierre. "The Corporatism of the Universal: The Role of Intellectuals in the Modern World." Translated by Carolyn Betensky. *Telos* 81 (1989): 99–110.

———. *The Political Ontology of Martin Heidegger.* Translated by Peter Collier. Stanford: Stanford University Press, 1991.

Bradford, Helen. "Olive Schreiner's Hidden Agony: Fact, Fiction, and Teenage Abortion." *Journal of Southern African Studies* 21, no. 4 (1995): 623–41.

Bredin, Jean-Denis. *The Affair: The Case of Alfred Dreyfus.* Translated by Jeffrey Mehlman. New York: George Braziller, 1986.

Breytenbach, Breyten. "Andersheid en andersmaak, oftewel die Afrikaner as Afrikaan (Brief gerig aan Frederick van Zyl Slabbert)." [2000]. On-line: ⟨http://www.mweb.co.za/litnet/seminaar/afrikaan.asp⟩.

——. "Appendix 1." In *Dealing with the Past: Truth and Reconciliation in South Africa,* edited by Alex Boraine, Janet Levy, and Ronel Scheffer, 160–65. Cape Town: IDASA, 1994.

——. "Dear Mr President." *Die Suid-Afrikaan* 50 (1994): 20.

——. *Dog Heart (A Travel Memoir).* Cape Town: Human and Rousseau, 1998.

——. *End Papers: Essays, Letters, Articles of Faith, Workbook Notes.* New York: Farrar, 1986.

——. "Fragmente van 'n groeiende gewaarwees." *Vrye Weekblad,* 17 August 1990, 12–13.

——. *Mouroir (bespieëlende notas van 'n roman).* Emmarentia: Taurus, 1983.

——. *Mouroir: Mirrornotes of a Novel.* New York: Farrar, 1984.

——. "Reaksie." Open letter to Johann Rossouw. *Wilde-Als,* 18 April 2001. On-line: ⟨http://www.rebellie.org/wildeals_v1.htm⟩.

——. *A Season in Paradise.* Translated by Rike Vaughan. New York: Persea Books, 1982.

——. *The True Confessions of an Albino Terrorist.* Emmarentia: Taurus, 1984.

——. *The True Confessions of an Albino Terrorist.* London: Faber, 1984.

"Breyten kyk van buite en sien bastervolk." *Die Burger,* 15 February 1973, 5.

Brink, André P. Introduction. *A Season in Paradise* by Breyten Breytenbach. Translated by Rike Vaughan, 9–17. New York: Persea Books, 1982.

——. *Kennis van die aand.* 2d ed. Cape Town: Human and Rousseau, 1982.

——. *Looking on Darkness.* New York: William Morrow, 1975.

——. *Mapmakers: Writing in a State of Siege.* London: Faber, 1983.

Brink, Elsabe. "Man-made Women: Gender, Class, and the Ideology of the *Volksmoeder.*" In *Women and Gender in Southern Africa to 1945,* edited by Cherryl Walker, 273–92. Cape Town: David Philip, 1990.

Brinkley, Douglas, and David R. Facey-Crowther. *The Atlantic Charter.* New York: St. Martin's Press, 1994.

Brutus, Dennis. *Letters to Martha, and Other Poems from a South African Prison.* London: Heinemann, 1968.

Budlender, Geoff. "Black Consciousness and the Liberal Tradition: Then and Now." In *Bounds of Possibility: The Legacy of Steve Biko and Black Consciousness,* edited by Pityana et al., 228–37. Atlantic Highlands, N.J.: Zed Books, 1992.

Butler, Guy. *Essays and Lectures, 1949–1991.* Edited by Stephen Watson. Cape Town: David Philip, 1994.

Butler, Judith. *Antigone's Claim.* New York: Columbia University Press, 2000.

———. *The Psychic Life of Power: Theories in Subjection.* Stanford: Stanford University Press, 1997.

Carnegie Commission of Investigation on the Poor White Question in South Africa. *The Poor White Problem in South Africa: Report of the Carnegie Commission.* 5 vols. Stellenbosch: Pro-Ecclesia, 1932.

Chapman, Michael, ed. *The "Drum" Decade: Stories from the 1950s.* Pietermaritzburg: University of Natal Press, 1989.

———. "More than Telling a Story: *Drum* and Its Significance in Black South African Writing." In *The "Drum" Decade,* edited by M. Chapman, 183–232.

———. "Red People and School People from Ntsikana to Mandela: The Significance of 'Xhosa literature' in a General History of South African Literature." *English Academy Review* 10 (1993): 36–44.

———. *Southern African Literatures.* London: Longman, 1996.

Chennells, Anthony. "Plotting South African History: Narrative in Sol Plaatje's *Mhudi.*" *English in Africa* 24, no. 1 (1997): 37–58.

Chrisman, Laura. "Fathering the Black Nation of South Africa: Gender and Generation in Sol Plaatje's *Native Life in South Africa* and *Mhudi.*" *Social Dynamics* 23, no. 2 (1997): 57–73.

———. "Colonialism and Feminism in Olive Schreiner's 1890s Fiction." *English in Africa* 20, no. 1 (1993): 25–38.

Cleaver, Eldridge. *Soul on Ice.* 1968. New York: Delta, 1992.

Clingman, Stephen. *Bram Fischer: Afrikaner Revolutionary.* Cape Town: David Philip, 1998.

Clinton, Iris A. "Literature of the Cape Coloured." *Handbook on Race Relations in South Africa,* edited by Ellen W. Hellmann and Leah Abrahams, 615–18. Cape Town: Oxford University Press, 1949.

Cobden, Michael. "Professor Louw Tells of His War of Words with . . . 'the Minister-Kissers.'" *Rand Daily Mail,* 2 February 1967, 2.

Coetzee, J. M. "Against the South African Grain." *New York Review of Books,* 23 September 1999.

———. *Boyhood: Scenes from Provincial Life.* New York: Viking, 1997.

———. "Critic and Citizen: A Response." *Pretexts* 9, no. 1 (2000): 105–7.

———. *Doubling the Point: Essays and Interviews.* Edited by David Attwell. Cambridge: Harvard University Press, 1992.

———. *Giving Offense: Essays on Censorship.* Chicago: University of Chicago Press, 1996.

———. "The Mind of Apartheid: Geoffrey Cronjé (1907–)." *Social Dynamics* 17, no. 1 (1991): 1–35.

———. "A Poet in Prison." *Social Dynamics* 11, no. 2 (1985): 72–75.

Comaroff, Jean, and John Comaroff. *Of Revelation and Revolution.* Vol. 1. *Christianity, Colonialism, and Consciousness in South Africa.* Chicago: University of Chicago Press, 1991.

———. *Of Revelation and Revolution.* Vol. 2. *The Dialectics of Modernity on a South African Frontier.* Chicago: University of Chicago Press, 1997.

Contat, Michel. "The Intellectual as Jew. Sartre Against McCarthyism: An Unfinished Play." *October* 87 (1999): 47–62.

Cope, Jack. *The Adversary Within: Dissident Writers in Afrikaans.* Cape Town: David Philip, 1982.

Coste, Jean. "The Masks of Modisane." *World Literature Written in English Newsletter* 19 (1971): 45–54.

Couzens, Tim. "The Dark Side of the World: Sol Plaatje's 'Mhudi.'" *English Studies in Africa* 14, no. 2 (1971): 187–203.

———. Introduction. *Mhudi* by Sol T. Plaatje, edited by Stephen Gray, 1–20. Oxford: Heinemann, 1978.

———. *The New African: A Study of the Life and Work of H. I. E. Dhlomo.* Johannesburg: Ravan, 1985.

———. "Sol T. Plaatje and the First South African Epic." *English in Africa* 14, no. 1 (1987): 41–65.

Cronin, Jeremy. *Inside.* Johannesburg: Ravan, 1983.

———. "No Unnecessary Noises Allowed, OK?" *Ingolvane* 1, no. 2 [1990]: 8–12.

Cronjé, Geoffrey. *'n Tuiste vir die nageslag: Die blywende oplossing van Suid-Afrika se Rassevraagstukke.* Johannesburg: Publicité, 1945.

Cronjé, Geoffrey, Wm. Nicol, and E. P. Groenewald. *Regverdige rasse-apartheid.* Stellenbosch: CSV Boekhandel, 1947.

Cronwright-Schreiner, S. C. *The Life of Olive Schreiner.* London: T. Fisher Unwin, 1924.

David, Deirdre. *Intellectual Women and Victorian Patriarchy: Harriet Martineau, Elizabeth Barrett Browning, George Eliot.* Ithaca, N.Y.: Cornell University Press, 1987.

Davis Jr., R. Hunt. "Charles T. Loram and the American Model for African Education in South Africa." In *Apartheid and Education: The Education of Black South Africans,* edited by Peter Kallaway, 108–26. Johannesburg: Ravan, 1984.

Deacon, Moya. "The Ethic(s) of (U)ubuntu." *Ubuntu in a Christian Perspective.* Institute for Reformational Studies Study Pamphlet no. 374, edited by M. Deacon, J. H. Smit, and A. Shutte, 29–43. Potchefstroom: Potchefstroomse Universiteit vir Christelike Hoër Onderwys, 1999.

Degenaar, J. J. "Die betekenis van N.P. van Wyk Louw voor mijn eigen denken." In *Voortbestaan in gerechtigheid,* edited by Jan Biezen, 68–80. Leiden: Dimensie, 1985.

De Klerk, W. A. *The Puritans in Africa: A Story of Afrikanerdom.* London: Rex Collings, 1975.

De Klerk, W. J. "Breyten kan ook gewete word." *Rapport,* 30 November 1975, 16.

———. "The Concepts 'Verkramp' and 'Verlig.'" In *South African Dialogue: Contrasts in South African Thinking on Basic Race Issues,* edited by N. J. Rhoodie, 519–31. Johannesburg: McGraw-Hill, 1972.

De Kock, Leon. *Civilizing Barbarians: Missionary Narrative and African Textual Response in Nineteenth-Century South Africa.* Johannesburg: Witwatersrand University Press, 1996.

de Man, Paul. "Autobiography as De-facement." *Modern Language Notes* 94 (1979): 919–30.

———. "Die politieke filosofie van N. P. van Wyk Louw." In *Moraliteit en politiek*, 55–91. Cape Town: Tafelberg, 1976.

Derrida, Jacques. "Derrida-Bourdieu: Débat." *Libération*, 19–20 March 1988.

———. *The Ear of the Other: Otobiography, Transference, Translation.* Translated by Peggy Kamuf and Avital Ronell. Edited by Christie McDonald. 2d ed. Lincoln: University of Nebraska Press, 1988.

———. "Force of Law: The 'Mystical Foundation of Authority.'" Translated by Mary Quaintance. *Cardozo Law Review* 11, nos. 5/6 (1990): 921–1045.

———. *The Gift of Death.* Translated by David Wills. Chicago: University of Chicago Press, 1995.

———. *Given Time: I. Counterfeit Money.* Translated by Peggy Kamuf. Chicago: University of Chicago Press, 1992.

———. "The Laws of Reflection: Nelson Mandela, in Admiration." Translated by Mary Ann Caws and Isabelle Lorenz. In *For Nelson Mandela,* edited by Jacques Derrida and Mustapha Tlili, 13–41. New York: Seaver Books, 1987.

———. *Memoires for Paul de Man.* Translated by Cecile Lindsay, Jonathan Culler, Eduardo Cadava, and Peggy Kamuf. Rev. ed. New York: Columbia University Press, 1989.

———. *Of Grammatology.* Translated by Gayatri Chakravorty Spivak. Baltimore: Johns Hopkins University Press, 1976.

———. *Of Spirit: Heidegger and the Question.* Translated by Geoffrey Bennington and Rachel Bowlby. Chicago: University of Chicago Press, 1989.

———. "On Cosmopolitanism." Translated by Mark Dooley. In *On Cosmopolitanism and Forgiveness*, 3–24. London: Routledge, 2001.

———. *The Other Heading: Reflections on Today's Europe.* Translated by Pascale-Anne Brault and Michael B. Naas. Bloomington: Indiana University Press, 1992.

———. *Points . . . Interviews, 1974–1994.* Translated by Peggy Kamuf et al. Edited by Elizabeth Weber. Stanford: Stanford University Press, 1995.

———. *Le problème de la genèse dans la philosophie de Husserl.* Paris: Presses Universitaires de France, 1990.

———. "Racism's Last Word." Translated by Peggy Kamuf. In *"Race," Writing, and Difference,* edited by Henry Louis Gates Jr., 329–38. Chicago: University of Chicago Press, 1986.

———. "Signature Event Context." In *Margins of Philosophy.* Translated by Alan Bass. Brighton: Harvester Press, 1982. 307–30.

———. *Specters of Marx: The State of the Debt, the Work of Mourning, and the New International.* Translated by Peggy Kamuf. New York: Routledge, 1994.

Derrida, Jacques, and Anne Dufourmantelle. *Of Hospitality.* Translated by Rachel Bowlby. Stanford: Stanford University Press, 2000.

Desai, Ashwin, and Heinrich E. Bohmke. "The Death of the Intellectual, the Birth of the Salesman." *Debate* 2 (1997): 10–34.

Dhlomo, R. R. R. *An African Tragedy: A Novel in English by a Zulu Writer.* Lovedale: Lovedale Press, 1928.

"Documenting the Experience of Being an Alien in the Land of Apartness." *Sunday Independent,* 9 April 2000, 12.

Dodd, Alex. "Once It Was Called Apartheid, Now It's Xenophobia. Same Difference." *Sunday Independent,* 4 June 2000, 11.

Doke, C. M. et al. *English-Zulu Zulu-English Dictionary.* Johannesburg: Witwatersrand University Press, 1990.

Dostoyevsky, Fyodor. *The Brothers Karamazov.* Translated by David Magarshack. Harmondsworth, U.K.: Penguin, 1982.

Dowling, Linda. *Hellenism and Homosexuality in Victorian Oxford.* Ithaca, N.Y.: Cornell University Press, 1994.

Dubow, Saul. *Racial Segregation and the Origins of Apartheid in South Africa, 1919–36.* New York: St. Martin's Press, 1989.

——. *Scientific Racism in Modern South Africa.* Cambridge: Cambridge University Press, 1995.

Du Plessis, Bertie. "'n Laaste baken verkrummel." *Die Beeld,* 3 May 1993, 8.

DuPlessis, Rachel Blau. *Writing Beyond the Ending: Narrative Strategies of Twentieth-Cenury Women Writers.* Bloomington: Indiana University Press, 1985.

Du Preez, Max. "Vrydagoggend." *Vrye Weekblad,* 7–13 June 1991, 2–3.

"The Durban Declaration." *Nature* 406, no. 6 (July 2000): 15–16.

Du Toit, André. "Breyten se Confessions." *Die Suid-Afrikaan* 1 (1984): 44–46.

——. *Die sondes van die vaders: 'n Poging tot die verkenning van die posisie van die Afrikaner-intellektueel in die komende legitimiteitskrisis van die Afrikaner-nasionalisme en die apartheidsorde.* Cape Town: Rubicon, 1983.

Du Toit, André, and Hermann Giliomee. *Afrikaner Political Thought: Analysis and Documents. Volume One: 1780–1850.* Berkeley: University of California Press, 1983.

Edmunds, Paul. "Strange Journeys." *Mail and Guardian,* 7–13 April 2000, 20.

"Ek skaam my vir my volk . . ." *Rapport,* 30 November 1975, 5.

". . . Ek was dom en onbesonne — jammer." *Rapport,* 30 November 1975, 5.

Fanon, Frantz. *Black Skin, White Masks.* 1952. Translated by Charles Lam Markmann. London: Pluto Press, 1986.

——. *The Wretched of the Earth.* 1963. Translated by Constance Farrington. New York: Grove Weidenfeld, 1968.

First, Ruth, and Ann Scott. *Olive Schreiner.* New York: Schocken, 1980.

"Five Thou[s]and Scientists Sign Aids Declaration." *Mail and Guardian,* 1 July 2000. On-line: ⟨http://www.mg.co.za/mg/za/archive/2000jul/01julpm-news.html#aids⟩.

Foucault, Michel. *Discipline and Punish: The Birth of the Prison.* Translated by Alan Sheridan. Harmondsworth, U.K.: Penguin, 1979.

——. "Truth and Power." In *Power/Knowledge: Selected Interviews and Other Writings, 1972–1977,* translated by Colin Gordon et al., edited by Colin Gordon, 109–33. New York: Pantheon, 1980.

———. *The Use of Pleasure.* Volume 2 of *The History of Sexuality.* Translated by Robert Hurley. New York: Random House, 1985.

Freud, Sigmund. *The Standard Edition of the Complete Psychological Works of Sigmund Freud.* Translated by James Strachey et al. London: Hogarth Press and the Institute of Psycho-Analysis, 1953–.

———. *Beyond the Pleasure Principle.* 1920. *Standard Edition,* 18:1–64.

———. "Creative Writers and Day-Dreaming." 1908. *Standard Edition,* 9:143–53.

———. *Delusions and Dreams in Jensen's "Gradiva."* 1907. *Standard Edition,* 9:7–93.

———. *Fragment of an Analysis of a Case of Hysteria.* 1905. *Standard Edition,* 7:7–122.

———. "The Unconscious." 1915. *Standard Edition,* 14:159–215.

Friesen, J. Stanley. *Missionary Responses to Tribal Religions at Edinburgh, 1910.* New York: Peter Lang, 1996.

Funani, Lumka. "The Nigeria Conference Revisited." In *Sisterhood, Feminisms, and Power: From Africa to the Diaspora,* edited by Obioma Nnaemeka, 411–17. Trenton, N.J.: Africa World Press, 1998.

Galloway, Francis. *Breyten Breytenbach as openbare figuur.* Pretoria: HAUM, 1990.

Gedenkboek van die ossewaens op die pad deur Suid-Afrika: Eeufees, 1838–1938. Compiled by Dirk Mostert. Cape Town: Nasionale Pers, 1940.

Gerdener, G. B. A. "Die buiteland en die naturellevraagstuk in Suid-Afrika." *Journal of Racial Affairs* 3, no. 2 (1952): 4–10.

Gerhart, Gail M. *Black Power in South Africa: The Evolution of an Ideology.* Berkeley: University of California Press, 1978.

Gerwel, Jakes. *Literatuur en apartheid: Konsepsies van 'gekleurdes' in die Afrikaanse roman tot 1948.* Bellville: University of the Western Cape, 1988.

Gevisser, Mark. "Behind the Tussles for the SABC Board." *Weekly Mail,* 4–10 June 1993, 2, 6.

Gilbert, Sandra, and Susan Gubar. *The Madwoman in the Attic: The Woman Writer and the Nineteenth-Century Literary Imagination.* New Haven: Yale University Press, 1979.

Giliomee, Hermann. "'Survival in Justice': An Afrikaner Debate over Apartheid." *Comparative Studies in Society and History* 36, no. 3 (1994): 527–48.

Glissant, Édouard. *Poetics of Relation.* Translated by Betsy Wing. Ann Arbor: University of Michigan Press, 1997.

Goldblatt, Beth, and Shiela Meintjes. "Gender and the Truth and Reconciliation Commission: A Submission to the Truth and Reconciliation Commission." Report. Johannesburg: Centre for Applied Legal Studies, University of the Witwatersrand, 1996.

Gordimer, Nadine. *The Black Interpreters: Notes on African Writing.* Johannesburg: SPRO-CAS/Ravan, 1973.

———. *The Essential Gesture: Writing, Politics and Places.* Edited by Stephen Clingman. New York: Knopf, 1988.

———. *The Lying Days: A Novel.* London: V. Gollancz, 1953.

———. "My New South African Identity." *New York Times Magazine,* 30 May 1999, 40–43.

———. *A World of Strangers.* 1958. London: Jonathan Cape, 1976.

Gramsci, Antonio. *Selections from the Prison Notebooks.* Translated by Quintin Hoare and Geoffrey Nowell Smith. London: Lawrence and Wishart, 1971.

Gray, Stephen. "Schreiner and the Novel Tradition." In *Southern African Literature: An Introduction,* 133–59. New York: Barnes and Noble, 1979.

Green, Louise. "The Unhealed Wound: Olive Schreiner's Expressive Art." *Pretexts* 6, no. 1 (1997): 21–34.

Green, Michael. *Novel Histories: Past, Present, and Future in South African Fiction.* Johannesburg: Witwatersrand University Press, 1997.

Grové, A. P. "Louw, Nicolaas Petrus van Wyk." In *Dictionary of South African Biography,* edited by W. J. de Kock et al., 4:318–24. Pretoria: Nasionale Boekhandel, 1968–.

Habermas, Jürgen. "Heinrich Heine and the Role of the Intellectual in Germany." In *The New Conservatism: Cultural Criticism and the Historians' Debate,* translated by Shierry Weber-Nicholsen, 71–99. Cambridge: MIT Press, 1989.

Halliwell, Leslie. *Halliwell's Film Guide.* Edited by John Walker. New York: Harper, 1995.

Heidegger, Martin. *Being and Time.* Translated by John Macquarrie and Edward Robinson. San Francisco: Harper, 1962.

———. "Heidegger's Letter to the Rector of Freiburg University (4 November 1945)." In Karl August Moehling, "Martin Heidegger and the Nazi Party: An Examination," 264–68. Ph.D. diss. Northern Illinois University, 1972.

———. "The Self-Assertion of the German University." Translated by Karsten Harries. *Review of Metaphysics* 38, no. 3 (1985): 470–80.

Hoernlé, R. F. Alfred. *South African Native Policy and the Liberal Spirit.* Cape Town: University of Cape Town, 1939.

Hofmeyr, Isabel. "Building a Nation from Words: Afrikaans Language, Literature and Ethnic Identity." In *The Politics of Race, Class, and Nationalism in Twentieth-Century South Africa,* edited by Shula Marks and Stanley Trapido, 95–113. London: Longman, 1987.

Hugo, Pierre. "The Politics of Untruth: Afrikaner Academics and Apartheid." *Politikon* 25, no. 1 (1998): 31–55.

Human, J. J. "N. P. van Wyk Louw en die Verkrampte Aanslag." 1975. Typescript 2.z.25. J. S. Gericke Library, Stellenbosch University, South Africa.

Husserl, Edmund. "Philosophy and the Crisis of European Humanity." In *The Crisis of the European Sciences and Transcendental Phenomenology: An Introduction to Phenomenological Philosophy,* translated by David Carr, 269–99. Evanston, Ill.: Northwestern University Press, 1970.

Jabavu, Noni. *The Ochre People.* 1963. Johannesburg: Ravan, 1982.

Jacobson, Dan. Introduction. *The Story of an African Farm* by Olive Schreiner, 7–24. Harmondsworth, U.K.: Penguin, 1993.

Jakobson, Roman. "Closing Statement: Linguistics and Poetics." In *Style in Language,* edited by Thomas A. Sebeok, 350–77. Cambridge: MIT Press, 1960.

Jansen, Ena. *Afstand en verbintenis: Elisabeth Eybers in Amsterdam.* Pretoria: Van Schaik, 1996.

Jaspers, Karl. *The Question of German Guilt.* 1946. Translated by E. B. Ashton. Westport, Conn.: Greenwood Press, 1978.

Johnson, David. *Shakespeare and South Africa.* Oxford: Clarendon Press, 1996.

Jordan, A. C. *Kwezo mpindo zeTsitsa.* 1972. Lovedale: Lovedale Press, 1974.

———. *Tales from Southern Africa.* Berkeley: University of California Press, 1973.

———. *Towards an African Literature: The Emergence of Literary Form in Xhosa.* Berkeley: University of California Press, 1973.

———. *The Wrath of the Ancestors.* 1940. Translated by A. C. Jordan and Priscilla Jordan. Alice: Lovedale Press, 1980.

Jordan, Lindi Nelani. Introduction to *Towards an African Literature: The Emergence of Literary Form in Xhosa* by A. C. Jordan. Berkeley: University of California Press, 1973.

Jordan, Z. Pallo. Foreword to *Tales from Southern Africa* by A. C. Jordan. Berkeley: University of California Press, 1973.

Judt, Tony. *Past Imperfect: French Intellectuals, 1944–1956.* Berkeley: University of California Press, 1992.

Kannemeyer, J. C. "'n Deurtastende kritiese ondersoek?: Gerrit Olivier oor N. P. van Wyk Louw." *Tydskrif vir Letterkunde* 32, no. 2 (1994): 54–69.

———. *Die Dokumente van Dertig.* Cape Town: Juta, 1990.

———. *Geskiedenis van die Afrikaanse literatuur,* vol. 1. Rev. ed. Cape Town: Human and Rousseau, 1984.

———. *Geskiedenis van die Afrikaanse literatuur,* vol. 2. Cape Town: Human and Rousseau, 1983.

Karis, Thomas, and Gwendolen Carter et al. *From Protest to Challenge: A Documentary History of African Politics in South Africa, 1822–1964.* 5 Vols. Stanford: Hoover Institution Press / Bloomington: Indiana University Press, 1972–.

Kariũki, Josiah Mwangi. *"Mau Mau" Detainee: The Account by a Kenya African of His Experiences in Detention Camps, 1953–1960.* Nairobi: Oxford University Press, 1963.

Keenan, Thomas. *Fables of Responsibility: Aberrations and Predicaments in Ethics and Politics.* Stanford: Stanford University Press, 1997.

Kies, B. M. *The Contribution of the Non-European Peoples to World Civilization.* Cape Town: Teachers' League of South Africa, 1953.

"Klein groepie wil beheer verkry." *Die Burger* 7 November 1966: 7.

Krige, Uys. Letter to N. P. van Wyk Louw. [1938/39?]. 2.K.1.41.14. J. S. Gericke Library, Stellenbosch University, South Africa.

———. Letter to N.P. van Wyk Louw. 30 July 1936. 2.K.1.41.2. J. S. Gericke Library, Stellenbosch University, South Africa.

———. "Cogito, ergo sum." *Die Brandwag,* 17 February 1939, 7, 48.

Krog, Antjie. *Country of My Skull.* Johannesburg: Random House, 1998.

———. "A Hundred Years of Attitude." *Mail and Guardian,* 11 October 1999. On-line: ⟨http://www.mg.co.za/mg/news/99oct1/11oct-boer.html⟩.

Kruger, Loren. "The Drama of Country and City: Tribalization, Urbanization, and Theatre under Apartheid." *Journal of Southern African Studies* 23, no. 4 (1997): 565–84.

Kunene, Daniel P., and Hilda Kuper. "A. C. Jordan 1907–1968." *African Arts* 2, no. 2 (1969): 24–27.

Kutz, Christopher. *Complicity: Ethics and Law for a Collective Age.* Cambridge: Cambridge University Press, 2000.

Kuzwayo, Ellen. *Call Me Woman.* Johannesburg: Ravan, 1985.

Lazar, John. "Conformity and Conflict: Afrikaner Nationalist Politics in South Africa, 1948–1961." D.Phil. thesis. Oxford University, 1987.

——. "Verwoerd versus the 'Visionaries': The South African Bureau of Racial Affairs (SABRA) and Apartheid, 1948–1961." In *Apartheid's Genesis, 1935–1962,* edited by Philip Bonner, Peter Delius, and Deborah Posel, 362–92. Johannesburg: Ravan and Witwatersrand University Press, 1993.

Lazarus, Neil. "Longing, Radicalism, Sentimentality: Reflections on Breyten Breytenbach's *A Season in Paradise.*" *Journal of Southern African Studies* 12, no. 2 (1986): 158–82.

Legassick, Martin. "Race, Industrialization, and Social Change in South Africa: The Case of R. F. A. Hoernlé." *African Affairs* 75 (1976): 224–39.

Lenin, Vladimir Ilích. *What Is to Be Done?* Translated by Joe Fineberg, George Hanna, and Robert Service. Edited by Robert Service. Harmondsworth, U.K.: Penguin, 1988.

Lenta, Margaret. "Racism, Sexism, and Olive Schreiner's Fiction." *Theoria* 70 (1987): 15–30.

Levinas, Emmanuel. *Otherwise than Being or Beyond Essence.* 1974. Translated by Alphonso Lingis. Pittsburgh: Duquesne University Press, 1998.

Louw, N. P. van Wyk. "Aantekening by tydsgebeurtenisse." *Standpunte* 17, no. 3 (1964): 67.

——. "Die Afr[ikaan]se Beweging die Toekoms in." Holograph Notes. [1948?]. Notebook. 2.X.18. J. S. Gericke Library, Stellenbosch University, South Africa.

——. "Die APB-Prys vir 1964." *Kriterium* 3, no. 1 (1965): 1–3.

——. "Die Armblanke-vraagstuk." *Die Huisgenoot,* 19 May 1933.

——. "Bevolking." Holograph Lecture Notes. 1952. 2.L.A.27(5). J. S. Gericke Library, Stellenbosch University, South Africa.

——. "By Abrahams." Holograph Lecture Notes. 17 April 1951. 2.L.A.13(4). J. S. Gericke Library, Stellenbosch University, South Africa.

——. *Die dieper reg: 'n Spel van die oordeel oor 'n volk.* Cape Town: Nasionale Pers, 1942.

——. "Geagte Redaksie." Typed Letter. 26 May 1965. 2.Br.11. J. S. Gericke Library, Stellenbosch University, South Africa.

——. "Geloftedag, 1951." 1951. Manuscript 2.To.2(3). J. S. Gericke Library, Stellenbosch University, South Africa.

——. *Germanicus.* 1956. Cape Town: Tafelberg, 1975.

——. "Gesprek." *Wurm* 4 (1966): 4–14.

———. "'n Groepie wil die literatuur probeer oorheers." *Die Burger,* 31 January 1967, 12.

———. "Konferensie van die nuwe onderwysbond." *Die Huisgenoot,* 27 July 1934.

———. *Die pluimsaad waai ver; of bitter begin.* 1966. 2d ed. Cape Town: Human and Rousseau, 1987.

———. "Probleme van die intellektuele lewe in Suid-Afrika." *Groot Nederland* 38, no. 1 (1940): 466–78.

———. *Raka.* Translated by Antony Dawes. Cape Town: Nasionale Boekhandel, 1968.

———. "Rassevraagstukke in S[uid]-A[frika]." 1952. Holograph Lecture Notes 2.L.A.27(1). J. S. Gericke Library, Stellenbosch University, South Africa.

———. *Versamelde gedigte.* Cape Town: Tafelberg/Human and Rousseau, 1981.

———. *Versamelde prosa.* 2 vols. Cape Town: Tafelberg/Human and Rousseau, 1986.

———. "Volkskritiek/People's Criticism." Translated by Mark Sanders. *Metamorphoses: Journal of the Five-College Seminar on Literary Translation* 10, no. 1 (2002).

Louw, W. E. G. Letter to N. P. van Wyk Louw. 8 January 1957. 158.K.Lo.29(83). J. S. Gericke Library, Stellenbosch University, South Africa.

"Louw antwoord die 'groepie.'" *Die Transvaler,* 2 February 1967, n.p.

Lowell, A. Lawrence. *The Government of England.* Vol. 1. New York: Macmillan, 1908.

Löwith, Karl. "Les implications politiques de la philosophie de l'existence chez Heidegger." *Les temps modernes* 2, no. 14 (1946): 343–60.

Lyotard, Jean François. "German Guilt." In *Political Writings,* translated by Bill Readings and Kevin Paul Geiman, 127–34. Minneapolis: University of Minnesota Press, 1993.

McLaren, James. *A New Concise Xhosa-English Dictionary.* Cape Town: Maskew Miller Longman, 1963.

Macaulay, Thomas Babington. "Thomas Babington Macaulay on Education for India." 1835. In *Imperialism,* edited by Philip D. Curtin, 178–91. New York: Walker and Company, 1971.

McClintock, Anne. "Olive Schreiner: The Limits of Colonial Feminism." In *Imperial Leather: Race, Gender, and Sexuality in the Colonial Contest,* 259–95. New York: Routledge, 1995.

Makgoba, M. W. *Mokoko: The Makgoba Affair: A Reflection on Transformation.* Florida Hills, South Africa: Vivlia, 1997.

Malcolm X and Alex Haley. *The Autobiography of Malcolm X.* 1964. New York: Ballantine, 1973.

Malherbe, D. F. *Afrikaner-volkseenheid.* Bloemfontein: Nasionale Pers, 1942.

Malherbe, E. G., ed. *Educational Adaptations in a Changing Society: Report of the South African Education Conference Held in Capetown and Johannesburg in July 1934, under the Auspices of the New Education Fellowship.* Cape Town: Juta, 1937.

Mamdani, Mahmood. *Citizen and Subject: Contemporary Africa and the Legacy of Late Colonialism.* Princeton: Princeton University Press, 1996.

———. "The Racism at the Heart of the Ivory Tower." *Mail and Guardian,* 1 September 1997. On-line: ⟨http://www.mg.co.za/mg/news/97sep1/9sep-racialism_makgoba.html⟩.

———. "Reconciliation Without Justice." *Southern African Review of Books,* November/December 1996, 3–5.

———. "There Can Be No African Renaissance Without an Africa-focused Intelligentsia." In *African Renaissance: The New Struggle,* edited by Malegapuru William Makgoba, 125–34. Cape Town: Mafube/Tafelberg, 1999.

Mandela, Nelson. *Long Walk to Freedom.* Boston: Little, Brown, 1994.

———. *No Easy Walk to Freedom.* London: Heinemann, 1965.

Manganyi, N. C. *Being-Black-in-the-World.* Johannesburg: Ravan, 1973.

———. *Looking Through the Keyhole: Dissenting Essays on the Black Experience.* Johannesburg: Ravan, 1981.

———. *Mashangu's Reverie and Other Essays.* Johannesburg: Ravan, 1977.

Mannhein, Karl. *Ideology and Utopia: An Introduction to the Sociology of Knowledge.* Translated by Louis Wirth and Edward Shils. New York: Harcourt, 1954.

Mapanje, Jack. *The Chattering Wagtails of Mikuyu Prison.* Portsmouth, N.H.: Heinemann, 1993.

———. "Containing Cockroaches (Memories of Encarceration Reconstructed in Exile)." In *The Word behind Bars and the Paradox of Exile,* edited by Kofi Anyidoho, 46–79. Evanston, Ill.: Northwestern University Press, 1997.

———. "Of Orality and Memory in Prison and Exile (A Personal Note on How to Survive the Chaos of Incarceration)." In *The Word behind Bars and the Paradox of Exile,* edited by Kofi Anyidoho, 19–45. Evanston, Ill.: Northwestern University Press, 1997.

Marais, B. J. *Colour: Unsolved Problem of the West.* Cape Town: Howard Timmins, 1952.

———. *The Two Faces of Africa.* Pietermaritzburg: Shuter and Shooter, 1964.

Marais, Jaap. "Raka, deur NP van Wyk Louw: Die agtergrond en simboliek van die gedig in die eietydse samehang." *Die Afrikaner,* 26 November 1993, 4, 10.

———. "Raka, deur NP van Wyk Louw: Die agtergrond en simboliek van die gedig in die eietydse samehang (2)." *Die Afrikaner,* 3 December 1993, 4, 10.

Marks, Shula, ed. *Not Either an Experimental Doll: The Separate Worlds of Three South African Women.* Bloomington: Indiana University Press, 1988.

Marx, Ruben. Testimony before the Truth and Reconciliation Commission of South Africa. Port Elizabeth. 8 December 1997. Transcript. *Truth and Reconciliation Commission Website.* On-line: ⟨http://www.doj.gov.za/trc/amntrans/pe7/2bik01.htm⟩.

Maseko, Pamella, and Russell H. Kaschula. "Beating the Paralyses." Review of *Discourse in a Multilingual Courtroom: A Court Interpreter's Guide* by R. Moeketsi (1999). *LitNet—Seminar Room.* n.d. On-line: ⟨http://www.mweb.co.za/litnet/seminarroom/courtinterpret.asp⟩. 1 December 2000.

Masote, Sheila. Testimony before the Truth and Reconciliation Commission of South Africa. Johannesburg. 28 July 1997. Transcript. *Truth and Reconciliation Commission Website.* On-line: ⟨http://www.doj.gov.za/trc/special/women/masote.htm⟩.

Mathabane, Mark. Foreword to *Blame Me on History* by Bloke Modisane. New York: Simon and Schuster, 1990.

Matshoba, Deborah. Testimony before the Truth and Reconciliation Commission. Johannesburg. 29 July 1997. Transcript. *Truth and Reconciliation Commission Website.* On-line: ⟨http://www.doj.gov.za/trc/special/women/matshoba.htm⟩.

Maughan-Brown, David. "The Anthology as Reliquary? *Ten Years of Staffrider* and *The Drum Decade.*" *Current Writing* 1 (1989): 3–21.

Mbeki, Thabo. "Culture: The Barrier Which Blocks Regress to Beastly Ways." In *Africa: The Time Has Come: Selected Speeches,* 257–60. Cape Town/Johannesburg: Tafelberg/Mafube, 1998.

"Mbeki Consigns Aids Declaration to Bin." *Mail and Guardian,* 4 July 2000. On-line: ⟨http://www.mg.co.za/mg/za/archive/2000jul/04julpm-news.html#mbeki⟩.

Miller, J. Hillis. "The Critic as Host." In *Deconstruction and Criticism,* edited by Harold Bloom et al., 217–53. London: Routledge, 1979.

——. *The Ethics of Reading: Kant, de Man, Eliot, Trollope, James, and Benjamin.* New York: Columbia University Press, 1987.

"Minister vertel naturelle van apartheid." Unknown source. 1951.

Modisane, Bloke. *Blame Me on History.* 1963. Johannesburg: Ad Donker, 1986.

——. "The Dignity of Begging." In *The "Drum" Decade: Stories from the 1950s,* edited by Michael Chapman, 10–17. Pietermaritzburg: University of Natal Press, 1989.

——. "The Situation." *Black Orpheus* 12 (1963): 10–16.

Moodie, T. Dunbar. *The Rise of Afrikanerdom: Power, Apartheid, and the Afrikaner Civil Religion.* Berkeley: University of California Press, 1975.

Mpe, Phaswane. "'Naturally These Stories Lost Nothing by Repetition': Plaatje's Mediation of Oral History in *Mhudi.*" *Current Writing* 8, no. 1 (1996): 75–89.

Mphahlele, Ezekiel. *The African Image.* New York: Praeger, 1962.

——. *In Corner B.* Nairobi: East African Publishing House, 1967.

Mutloatse, Mothobi, ed. *Forced Landing: Africa South, Contemporary Writings.* Johannesburg: Ravan, 1980.

Nakasa, Nat. *The World of Nat Nakasa.* Edited by Essop Patel. 2d ed. Johannesburg: Ravan, 1985.

National Coalition for Gay and Lesbian Equality and Another v. Minister of Justice and Others CCT11/98 (9 October 1998). On-line: ⟨http://www.concourt.gov.za/judgments/1998/gayles.pdf⟩.

National Coalition for Gay and Lesbian Equality and Others v. Minister of Home Affairs and Others CCT10/99 (2 December 1999). On-line: ⟨http://www.concourt.gov.za/judgments/1999/natcoal.pdf⟩.

Ndebele, Njabulo. "Black Development." In *Black Viewpoint,* edited by B. S. Biko. 13–28. Durban: SPRO-CAS Black Community Programmes, 1972.

———. *Fools and Other Stories.* Harlow, Essex: Longman, 1986.

———. "Game Lodges and Leisure Colonialists." In *blank —— Architecture, Apartheid and After,* edited by Hilton Judin and Ivan Vladislavić, 119–23. Cape Town: David Philip, 1998.

———. "How Representative Is South African Literature?" In *The Ghostly Dance: Writing in a New South Africa,* 1:12–15. Cape Town: IDASA, 1990.

———. "Liberation and the Crisis of Culture." In *Altered State? Writing and South Africa,* edited by Laura Chrisman, Kenneth Parker, and Elleke Boehmer, 1–9. Sydney: Dangaroo, 1994.

———. "Memory, Metaphor, and the Triumph of Narrative." In *Negotiating the Past: The Making of Memory in South Africa,* edited by Sarah Nuttall and Carli Coetzee, 19–28. Cape Town: Oxford University Press, 1998.

———. "An Open Letter to Breyten Breytenbach." *Die Suid-Afrikaan* 50 (1994): 20–21.

———. *South African Literature and Culture: Rediscovery of the Ordinary.* Manchester: Manchester University Press, 1994.

———. "The University: Redefining Commitments." Lecture typescript. Senate Lecture Series, University of the Witwatersrand, 2 September 1987.

Ngũgĩ wa Thiong'o. *Detained: A Writer's Prison Diary.* London: Heinemann, 1981.

———. "The Language of African Literature." In *Decolonising the Mind: The Politics of Language in African Literature,* 4–33. London: James Currey, 1986.

———. *Penpoints, Gunpoints, and Dreams: Towards a Critical Theory of the Arts and the State in Africa.* Oxford: Clarendon Press, 1998.

Nichols, Ray L. *Treason, Tradition, and the Intellectual: Julien Benda and Political Discourse.* Lawrence: Regents Press of Kansas, 1978.

Nietzsche, Friedrich. "On Truth and Lying in an Extra-Moral Sense." In *Friedrich Nietzsche on Rhetoric and Language*, edited and translated by Sander Gilman, Carole Blair, and David Parent, 246–57. New York: Oxford University Press, 1989.

Nie[u]woudt, Gideon. Testimony before the Truth and Reconciliation Commission of South Africa. Cape Town. 30 March 1998. Transcript. *Truth and Reconciliation Commission Website.* On-line: ⟨http://www.doj.gov.za/trc/amntrans/ct10/niewoudt.htm⟩.

Nkosi, Lewis. "The Fabulous Decade: The Fifties." In *Home and Exile, and Other Selections,* 3–24. Rev. ed. London: Longman, 1983.

Nnaemeka, Obioma, ed. *Sisterhood, Feminisms, and Power: From Africa to the Diaspora.* Trenton, N.J.: Africa World Press, 1998.

———. "This Women's Studies Business: Beyond Politics and History (Thoughts on the First WAAD Conference)." In Nnaemeka, ed., *Sisterhood,* 351–86.

Norval, Aletta J. *Deconstructing Apartheid Discourse.* London: Verso, 1996.

Obradović, Nadežda. Review of *Blame Me on History* by Bloke Modisane. *World Literature Today* 65 (1991): 353.

O'Brien, Anthony. "Literature in Another South Africa: Njabulo Ndebele's Theory of Emergent Culture." *Diacritics* 22, no. 1 (1992): 67–85.

Oliphant, Andries Walter, and Ivan Vladislavić, eds. *Ten Years of Staffrider, 1978–1988*. Johannesburg: Ravan, 1988.

Olivier, Gerrit. "N. P. van Wyk Louw en Afrikaner-Nasionalisme: Die daad binne die geskiedenis." *Die Suid-Afrikaan* (December 1989): 38–39, 42.

———. "N. P. van Wyk Louw en die Afrikaner-Nasionalisme: Die Nasionaal-Sosialisme." *Die Suid-Afrikaan* (February 1990): 28–29, 32.

———. "N. P. van Wyk Louw en R. F. A. Hoernlé: Aantekeninge by N. P. van Wyk Louw se gedagtes oor die Suid-Afrikaanse rassepolitiek." *Tydskrif vir geesteswetenskappe* 35, no. 4 (1995): 243–53.

———. *N. P. van Wyk Louw: Literatuur, filosofie, politiek*. Cape Town: Human and Rousseau, 1992.

O'Meara, Dan. *Forty Lost Years: The Apartheid State and the Politics of the National Party, 1948–1994*. Johannesburg: Ravan, 1996.

Opperman, D. J. *Digters van Dertig*. Cape Town: Nasionale Boekhandel, 1953.

Paton, Alan. *Cry, the Beloved Country: A Story of Comfort in Desolation*. 1948. Harmondsworth, U.K.: Penguin, 1987.

———. *Journey Continued: An Autobiography*. New York: Collier, 1988.

Paxton, Nancy L. "*The Story of an African Farm* and the Dynamics of Woman-to-Woman Influence." *Texas Studies in Literature and Language* 30, no. 4 (1988): 562–82.

Peires, J. B. *The Dead Will Arise: Nongqawuse and the Great Xhosa Cattle-Killing Movement of 1856–57*. Johannesburg: Ravan, 1989.

Pityana, N. Barney, Mamphela Ramphele, Malusi Mpumlwana, and Lindy Wilson, eds. *Bounds of Possibility: The Legacy of Steve Biko and Black Consciousness*. Atlantic Highlands, N.J.: Zed Books, 1992.

Plaatje, Sol T. *Mafeking Diary: A Black Man's View of a White Man's War*. Edited by Brian Willan, John Comaroff, and Andrew Reed. Athens: Ohio University Press, 1990.

———. *Mhudi*. 1930. Edited by Stephen Gray. Oxford: Heinemann, 1978.

———. *Native Life in South Africa*. 1916. Johannesburg: Ravan, 1982.

———. *Selected Writings*. Edited by Brian Willan. Johannesburg: Witwatersrand University Press, 1996.

Plato. *The Dialogues of Plato*, vol. 1. Translated by B. Jowett. 3rd ed. Oxford: Clarendon Press, 1892.

Polley, James, ed. *Verslag van die Simposium oor die Sestigers, gehou deur die Departement Buitemuurse Studies van die Universiteit van Kaapstad, 12–16 February 1973*. Cape Town: Human and Rousseau, 1973.

Posel, Deborah. *The Making of Apartheid, 1948–1961: Conflict and Compromise*. Oxford: Clarendon Press, 1991.

Posnock, Ross. *Color and Culture: Black Writers and the Making of the Modern Intellectual*. Cambridge: Harvard University Press, 1998.

Pretorius, Rena. *Die begrip 'Intellektueel' by N .P. van Wyk Louw*. Pretoria: Van Schaik, 1972.

"Prof. Louw: 'Laat ons nou swyg!'" *Die Vaderland*, 2 February 1967: n.p.

Rabie, Jan. *Die Groot Anders-Maak.* Cape Town: Human and Rousseau, 1964.

Rabkin, David. "Drum Magazine (1951–1961) and the Works of Black South African Writers Associated with It." Ph.D. Diss. University of Leeds, 1975.

Ramphele, Mamphela. *Across Boundaries: The Journey of a South African Woman Leader.* New York: Feminist Press, 1997.

———. "The Dynamics of Gender within Black Consciousness Organisations: A Personal View." In *Bounds of Possibility: The Legacy of Steve Biko and Black Consciousness,* edited by Pityana et al., 214–27. Atlantic Highlands, N.J.: Zed Books, 1992.

Rassool, Ciraj, and Leslie Witz. "The 1952 Jan van Riebeeck Tercentenary Festival: Constructing and Contesting Public National History in South Africa." *Journal of African History* 34 (1993): 447–68.

Rhoodie, N. J. "G. Cronjé se beskouing van die Suid-Afrikaanse Blank-Bantoe-problematiek, soos weerspieël in sy onmiddelik na-oorlogse geskrifte." *Mens en gemeenskap: Huldigingsbundel vir prof. dr. G. Cronjé,* edited by J. E. Pieterse et al., 41–81. Pretoria: Academica, 1969.

Rich, Paul B. *Hope and Despair: English-speaking Intellectuals and South African Politics 1896–1976.* London: British Academic Press, 1993.

Robbins, Bruce. *Secular Vocations: Intellectuals, Professionalism, Culture.* London: Verso, 1993.

Rose, Jacqueline. "Wulf Sachs's *Black Hamlet.*" In *The Psychoanalysis of Race,* edited by Christopher Lane, 333–52. New York: Columbia University Press, 1998.

Rossouw, Johann. "Groep van 63 byeen oor minderheidsbelange." [2000]. On-line: ⟨http://www.mweb.co.za/litnet/seminaar/63.asp⟩.

Ryan, Pamela. "Singing in Prison: Women Writers and the Discourse of Resistance." In *Sisterhood, Feminisms, and Power,* edited by Obioma Nnaemeka, 197–212. Trenton, N.J.: Africa World Press, 1998.

SABC (South African Broadcasting Corporation). *South Africa's Human Spirit.* Sound Recording. Johannesburg: South African Broadcasting Corporation, 2000. 6 Compact Discs.

Sachs, Albie. "Preparing Ourselves for Freedom." In *Spring Is Rebellious: Arguments about Cultural Freedom by Albie Sachs and Respondents,* edited by Ingrid de Kok and Karen Press, 19–29. Cape Town: Buchu Books, 1990. 19–29. Reprinted in *Writing South Africa: Literature, Apartheid, and Democracy, 1970–1995,* edited by Derek Attridge and Rosemary Jolly, 239–48. Cambridge: Cambridge University Press, 1998.

———. "The Task of Civil Society." In *The Healing of a Nation?* edited by Alex Boraine and Janet Levy, 103–9. Cape Town: Justice in Transition, 1995.

Sachs, Wulf. *Black Hamlet: The Mind of an African Negro Revealed by Psychoanalysis.* London: Geoffrey Bles, 1937.

Said, Edward W. *Representations of the Intellectual: The 1993 Reith Lectures.* New York: Vintage, 1994.

———. *The World, the Text, and the Critic.* Cambridge: Harvard University Press, 1983.

South African Institute of Race Relations (SAIRR). *A Survey of Race Relations in South Africa, 1956–1957*. Compiled by Muriel Horrell. Johannesburg: SAIRR, [1957].

——. *A Survey of Race Relations in South Africa, 1955–1956*. Compiled by Muriel Horrell. Johannesburg: SAIRR, [1956].

Sanders, Mark. "Ambiguities of Mourning: Law, Custom, Literature, and Women before South Africa's Truth and Reconciliation Commission." *Law Text Culture* 4, no. 2 (1998): 105–51.

——. "Complicities: *Of Spirit* and Van Wyk Louw's *'lojale verset.'*" *Imprimatur* 1, no. 2/3 (1996): 162–72.

——. "Postcolonial Reading." *Postmodern Culture* 10, no. 1 (1999). On-line: ⟨http://muse.jhu.edu/journals/pmc/v010/10.1.r_sanders.html⟩.

——. "Reading Lessons." *Diacritics* 29, no. 3 (1999): 3–20.

Sartre, Jean-Paul. "A Plea for Intellectuals." In *Between Existentialism and Marxism: Sartre on Philosophy, Politics, Psychology, and the Arts,* edited by John Mathews, 228–85. New York: Pantheon, 1974.

——. *Anti-Semite and Jew.* 1948. Translated by George Joseph Becker. New York: Schocken, 1995.

——. "Black Orpheus." In *"What Is Literature?" and Other Essays,* 291–330. Cambridge: Harvard University Press, 1988.

Scarry, Elaine. *The Body in Pain: The Making and Unmaking of the World.* New York: Oxford University Press, 1985.

Schalk, David L. *The Spectrum of Political Engagement: Mounier, Benda, Nizan, Brasillach, Sartre.* Princeton: Princeton University Press, 1979.

Schalkwyk, David. "Portrait and Proxy: Representing Plaatje and Plaatje Represented." *Scrutiny2* 4, no. 2 (1999): 14–29.

Schoeman, Karel. *Olive Schreiner: A Woman in South Africa, 1855–1881.* Translated by Henri Snijders. Johannesburg: Jonathan Ball, 1989.

——. *Only an Anguish to Live Here: Olive Schreiner and the Anglo-Boer War, 1899–1902.* Cape Town: Human and Rousseau, 1992.

——. *Die wêreld van die digter: 'n Boek oor Sutherland en die Roggeveld ter ere van N. P. van Wyk Louw.* Cape Town: Human and Rousseau, 1986.

Schreiner, Olive. "The Buddhist Priest's Wife." In *Stories, Dreams and Allegories,* 61–80. London: T. Fisher Unwin, 1923.

——. *Closer Union.* 1908. Cape Town: Constitutional Reform Association, 1924.

——. *From Man to Man; Or Perhaps Only. . .* 1926. Reprint: London: Virago, 1982.

——. "Journal: Rattel's Hoek, 24 July–23 September 1876." Holograph manuscript. Harry Ransom Humanities Research Center, University of Texas at Austin.

——. *"My Other Self": The Letters of Olive Schreiner and Havelock Ellis, 1884–1920.* Edited by Yaffa Claire Draznin. New York: Peter Lang, 1992.

——. *Olive Schreiner Letters. Volume 1, 1871–1899.* Edited by Richard Rive. Oxford: Oxford University Press, 1988.

——. *The Story of an African Farm.* 1883. Johannesburg: Ad Donker, 1986.

——. *Thoughts on South Africa.* 1923. Edited by Margaret Lenta. Johannesburg: Ad Donker, 1992.

——. *Trooper Peter Halket of Mashonaland.* Boston: Roberts Brothers, 1897.

——. *Woman and Labour.* 1911. London: Virago, 1978.

Sedgwick, Eve Kosofsky. *Between Men: English Literature and Male Homosocial Desire.* New York: Columbia University Press, 1985.

Senghor, Léopold Sédar, ed. *Anthologie de la nouvelle poésie nègre et malgache de langue française.* Paris: Presses Universitaires de France, 1948.

——. "Ce que l'homme noir apporte." 1939. In *Liberté I: Négritude et humanisme,* 22–38. Paris: Seuil, 1964.

Serfontein, J. H. P. *Die verkrampte aanslag.* Cape Town: Human and Rousseau, 1970.

Sharpley-Whiting, T. Denean. "Fanon and Capécia." In *Frantz Fanon: Critical Perspectives,* edited by Anthony C. Alessandrini, 57–74. New York: Routledge, 1999.

Shava, Piniel Viriri. *A People's Voice: Black South African Writing in the Twentieth Century.* London: Zed Books, 1989.

Shaw, Gerald. "Seeking to Merge SA Identities." *Cape Times,* 13 January 1995, Top of the Times Supplement.

Shepherd, R. H. W. "African Literature." In *Handbook on Race Relations in South Africa,* edited by Ellen Hellmann and Leah Abrahams, 599–611. Cape Town: Oxford University Press, 1949.

——. *Lovedale, South Africa: The Story of a Century, 1841–1941.* Lovedale: Lovedale Press, n.d.

Showalter, Elaine. *A Literature of Their Own: British Women Novelists from Brontë to Lessing.* Princeton: Princeton University Press, 1977.

Siebert, Daniel Petrus. Testimony before the Truth and Reconciliation Commission of South Africa (1). New Brighton, Port Elizabeth. 11 Sept. 1997. Transcript. *Truth and Reconciliation Commission Website.* On-line: ⟨http://www.doj.gov.za/trc/amntrans/pe1/siebert.htm⟩.

——. Testimony before the Truth and Reconciliation Commission of South Africa (2). Port Elizabeth. 8 December 1997. Transcript. *Truth and Reconciliation Commission Website.* On-line: ⟨http://www.doj.gov.za/trc/amntrans/pe7/2biko1.htm⟩.

Simons, H. J. "What Is Apartheid?" *Liberation* 35 (March 1959): 12–17.

——. "What Is Apartheid?" *Liberation* 36 (May 1959): 16–25.

Skota, T. D. Mweli, ed. *The African Yearly Register: Being an Illustrated National Biographical Dictionary (Who's Who) of Black Folks in Africa.* Johannesburg: R. L. Esson, 1930.

Sluga, Hans. "Metadiscourse: German Philosophy and National Socialism." *Social Research* 56, no. 4 (1989): 795–818.

Snyman, Harold. Testimony before the Truth and Reconciliation Commission of South Africa. New Brighton, Port Elizabeth, South Africa. 10 September 1997.

Transcript. *Truth and Reconciliation Commission Website.* On-line: ⟨http://www
.doj.gov.za/trc/amntrans/pe1/snyman.htm⟩.

Snyman, Harold et al. Application in Terms of Section 18 of the Promotion of National Unity and Reconciliation Act No. 34 of 1995. Decision by Amnesty Com-
mittee of the Truth and Reconciliation Commission of South Africa. 1999. On-
line: ⟨http://www.doj.gov.za/trc/decisions/1999/99Snyman.html⟩.

Soga, Tiyo. *The Journal and Selected Writings of the Reverend Tiyo Soga.* Edited by
Donovan Williams. Cape Town: A. A. Balkema, 1983.

Sole, Kelwyn. "Class, Continuity and Change in Black South African Literature
1948–1960." In *Labour, Townships, and Protest: Studies in the Social History of
the Witwatersrand,* edited by Belinda Bozzoli, 143–92. Johannesburg: Ravan,
1979.

———. "Reading the Nation." *Southern African Review of Books,* Sept./Oct. and
Nov./Dec. 1995: 20–22.

South Africa, Republic of. Constitution of the Republic of South Africa. Act 200 of
1993. On-line: ⟨http://www.doj.gov.za/trc/legal/sacon93.htm⟩.

———. Promotion of National Unity and Reconciliation Act. Act 34 of 1995. On-
line: ⟨http://www.doj.gov.za/trc/legal/act9534.htm⟩.

South Africa, Union of. *Summary of the Report of the Commission for the Socio-
Economic Development of the Bantu Areas within the Union of South Africa.* Pretoria: Government Printer, 1955.

Soyinka, Wole. *The Burden of Memory, the Muse of Forgiveness.* New York: Oxford
University Press, 1998.

———. *The Man Died: Prison Notes of Wole Soyinka.* London: Rex Collings, 1972.

Spelman, Elizabeth. "Woman as Body: Ancient and Contemporary Views." *Feminist Studies* 8, no. 1 (1982): 109–31.

Spencer, Herbert. *First Principles.* 4th ed. New York: D. Appleton and Company,
1888.

Spivak, Gayatri Chakravorty. "Can the Subaltern Speak?" In *Marxism and the Interpretation of Culture,* edited by Cary Nelson and Lawrence Grossberg, 271–313.
Urbana: University of Illinois Press, 1988.

———. *A Critique of Postcolonial Reason: Toward a History of the Vanishing Present.*
Cambridge: Harvard University Press, 1999.

———. *Imperative zur Neuerfindung des Planeten/Imperatives to Re-Imagine the
Planet.* Edited by Willi Goetschel. Vienna: Passagen, 1999.

———. *Outside in the Teaching Machine.* New York: Routledge, 1993.

———. "Responsibility." *Boundary 2* 21, no. 3 (1994): 19–64.

———. Translator's Preface. In *Imaginary Maps* by Mahasweta Devi. New York:
Routledge, 1995.

Stanley, Liz. *The Auto/biographical I: The Theory and Practice of Feminist Auto/biogra-
phy.* Manchester: Manchester University Press, 1992.

Statement from the South African Delegation Regarding the Request by Some
Participants that Whites Be Excluded from Presenting Papers at the WAAD

Conference. In *Sisterhood, Feminisms, and Power,* edited by Obioma Nnaemeka, 479–80. Trenton, N.J.: Africa World Press, 1998.

Stein, Sylvester. *Who Killed Mr. Drum! A Historical Caprice.* Bellville: Mayibuye Books, 1999.

Steiner, George. "A Kind of Survivor." 1965. In *Language and Silence: Essays on Language, Literature, and the Inhuman,* 140–54. New Haven: Yale University Press, 1998.

Steyn, J. C. *Van Wyk Louw: 'n Lewensverhaal.* 2 vols. Cape Town: Tafelberg, 1998.

Stubbs, Aelred. "Martyr of Hope: A Personal Memoir." In Biko, *I Write What I Like.* 154–216.

Themba, Can. *The Will to Die.* Edited by Donald Stuart and Roy Holland. London: Heinemann, 1972.

———. *The World of Can Themba: Selected Writings of the Late Can Themba.* Edited by Essop Patel. Johannesburg: Ravan, 1985.

Tomaselli, Keyan, Ruth Tomaselli, and Johan Muller, eds. *Currents of Power: State Broadcasting in South Africa.* Bellville: Anthropos, 1989.

———, eds. *Narrating the Crisis: Hegemony and the South African Press.* Johannesburg: Richard Lyon, 1987.

Truth and Reconciliation Commission of South Africa Report. 5 vols. Cape Town: Truth and Reconciliation Commission, 1998.

Turner, Richard. *The Eye of the Needle: Toward Participatory Democracy in South Africa.* 2d. ed. Maryknoll, N.Y.: Orbis, 1978.

Tutu, Desmond Mpilo. *No Future Without Forgiveness.* New York: Doubleday, 1999.

Tutuola, Amos. *The Palm-Wine Drinkard and My Life in the Bush of Ghosts.* New York: Grove, 1984.

Valéry, Paul. *The Outlook for Intelligence.* Translated by Denise Folliot and Jackson Matthews. Princeton: Princeton University Press, 1962.

Van Heerden, Etienne. *Casspirs and Camparis: A Historical Entertainment.* Translated by Catherine Knox. Johannesburg: Viking, 1993.

Van Jaarsveld, F. A. "Die ontstaansgeskiedenis van die begrippe 'Voortrekkers' en 'Groot Trek.'" In *Lewende verlede,* 173–200. Johannesburg: Afrikaanse Pers-Boekhandel, 1962.

Van Rensburg, F. I. J. "'Hoe praat jy met 'n hele volk?' (N. P. van Wyk Louw)." *Literator* 17, no. 1 (1996): 57–75.

———. "Konfrontasie met Van Wyk Louw (Slot)." *Tydskrif vir geesteswetenskappe* 35, no. 3 (1995): 184–96.

———. "Konfrontasie met Van Wyk Louw: Aflewering 1." *Tydskrif vir geesteswetenskappe* 32, no. 2 (1995): 84–94.

"Van Wyk Louw sê dit maak bitter seer." *Die Burger,* 13 June 1966, 11.

Venter, F. A. *Swart pelgrim.* Johannesburg: Boek-van-die-Maand-Klub, 1952.

Verwoerd, Hendrik Frensch. *Verwoerd aan die Woord: Toesprake 1948–1962.* Edited by A. N. Pelzer. Johannesburg: Afrikaanse Pers-Boekhandel, 1964.

———. *Verwoerd Speaks: Speeches, 1948–1966.* Edited by A. N. Pelzer. Johannesburg: Afrikaanse Pers Boekhandel, 1966.

Viviers, Jack. *Breyten: 'n Verslag oor Breyten Breytenbach.* Cape Town: Tafelberg, 1978.

Von Vegesack, Thomas. *De intellectuelen: Een geschiedenis van het literaire engagement 1898–1968.* Translated by Petra Broomans and Wiveca Jongeneel. Amsterdam: Meulenhoff, 1989.

"'Voortrekkers Still Fighting' — Dr. Malan." *Rand Daily Mail,* 17 December 1938, 19.

Walzer, Michael. *The Company of Critics: Social Criticism and Political Commitment in the Twentieth Century.* New York: Basic Books, 1988.

Watts, Jane. *Black Writers from South Africa: Towards a Discourse of Liberation.* London: Macmillan, 1989.

Weschler, Lawrence. "An Afrikaner Dante." *New Yorker,* 8 November 1993, 78–100.

Willan, Brian. *Sol Plaatje: A Biography.* Johannesburg: Ravan, 1984.

———. Introduction to *Sol Plaatje: Selected Writings,* edited by Brian Willan. Johannesburg: Witwatersrand University Press, 1996.

Williams, Raymond. *Marxism and Literature.* Oxford: Oxford University Press, 1977.

Wilson, Lindy. "Bantu Steve Biko: A Life." In *Bounds of Possibility: The Legacy of Steve Biko and Black Consciousness,* edited by Pityana et al., 15–77. Atlantic Highlands, N.J.: Zed Books, 1992.

Wilson, Richard A. "The Sizwe Will Not Go Away: The Truth and Reconciliation Commission, Human Rights and Nation-Building in South Africa." *African Studies* 55, no. 2 (1996): 1–20.

Woods, Donald. *Biko.* New York: Paddington Press, 1978.

Zola, Émile. *The Dreyfus Affair: J'accuse and Other Writings.* Edited by Alain Pagès. Translated by Eleanor Levieux. New Haven: Yale University Press, 1996.

———. "Lettre à M. Félix Faure, Président de la République." In *J'Accuse. . . : La Vérité en marche,* edited by Henri Guillemin, 97–113. Brussels: Complexe, 1988.

index

Arendt, Hannah: "banality of evil" in, 3; Dreyfus case in, 6, 214 n.9

Atlantic Charter, 227 n.34

Autobiography, x, 23–25, 28–29, 35, 44, 98–103, 115–16, 174, 231 n.13

Bakhtin, Mikhail, 152

Baldwin, James, 96

Bantu Education, 100–101, 122, 195, 239 n.18

Barolong, 40, 52

Barrès, Maurice, 4

Bastardy and *basterskap. See* Hybridity

Benda, Julien, 5–6, 201, 214 n.8

Benjamin, Walter, 215 n.18

Benveniste, Émile, 157

Bering, Dietz, 4

Bertram, Willie, 28, 35–36, 37

Bestaansreg (right to exist): of Afrikaans volk, 70, 77, 81, 145, 225 n.25

Bibault, Hendrik, 228 n.44

Biko, Steve, 7, 14, 15, 48, 74, 102, 129, 135, 158, 159–96, 204–5; "Black Souls in White Skins?" 167; "I Write What I Like," 165–66; "We Blacks," 167, 174–79, 186–87

Bizos, George, 161–63

Black Community Programme, 170

Black Consciousness, 14, 15, 91, 93, 96, 141, 158, 159–96, 198; complicity in, 164–66, 167, 174–79, 204; liberalism and, 165–74; masculinism of, 177, 205

Black Intellectuals. *See* African intellectuals

"Black is Beautiful campaign," 177, 191–92, 206

Bleek, Wilhelm, 217 n.3

Body. *See* Racial difference; Sexual difference

Boers, 40, 52

Borges, Jorge Luis, 20

Bourdieu, Pierre, 9, 22

Breytenbach, Breyten, 14, 61, 63, 82, 129, 131–47, 150–58, 187, 194, 204, 205; *Dog Heart,* 51, 145–46; and Louw, 138–46, 236 n.13; *Mouroir,* 154; other-making in, 140; *A Season in Paradise,* 52; trial and testimony of, 61, 76, 138–41; *The True Confessions of an Albino Terrorist,* 131–37, 145, 146–47, 151–58, 205; "A View from the Outside," 138, 141–45, 151

Breytenbach, Jan, 136

Breytenbach, Yolande, 63, 138, 153–54

Brink, André P., 61, 63; *Kennis van die aand,* 117–18

Broederbond. *See* Afrikaner Broederbond

Die Burger, 142, 144

Bushmen (San), 23, 217 n.3

Buthelezi, Gatsha, 165

Butler, Guy, 170

Capécia, Mayotte, 180

Cape Colony, 43; franchise in, 48

Carnegie Commission of Investigation on the Poor White Question in South Africa, 87, 134, 202, 203

Censorship, 61, 87, 118, 136–37, 152–55

Centre for Applied Legal Studies (CALS), 197–200

Césaire, Aimé, 180, 184, 187

Christianity, 27, 34, 51, 65, 120, 123, 128, 173. *See also* Mission schools

Cilliers, Sarel, 53–54

Cleaver, Eldridge, 181

Cloete, Stuart, 73

Coetzee, J. M., 45, 133–34, 189, 190; *Boyhood: Scenes from Provincial Life,* 189; *Giving Offense: Essays on Censorship,* 136, 137, 152–55

Colonialism, 190. *See also* Imperialism, British

Coloureds, 63, 91, 137, 145–46, 204

Complicity, ix, 1–2, 101, 106–7; acknowledgment and negotiation of, 8, 135, 156, 164, 176, 181, 189–90; acting in, 11, 12, 201; basis for responsibility, x, 26; Black Consciousness and, 164–66, 174–79; conceptual analysis by Kutz, 215–16 n.19; foldedness in human-being, 5, 8, 11, 15, 17, 22, 73, 75, 90–91, 95, 97, 103, 118, 125, 130, 132, 134, 136, 138, 156, 174, 200, 209–11; general and narrow senses of, 8, 10, 16, 21, 101, 107, 118–19, 157, 180–81, 200–201, 210; marginal figures and, 22, 101; Truth and Reconciliation Commission and, ix, 2–4, 8, 9, 11, 16, 17, 135, 204. *See also* Intellectual; Responsibility

Constitution of the Republic of South Africa, 38, 119

Couzens, Tim, 53

Cradock Four, 199

Crisis: in Louw, 75, 81; in Husserl, 228 n.39; in Valéry, 75, 228 n.39

Cronin, Jeremy, 150

Cronjé, Geoffrey, 14, 64–65, 76, 82, 133–34, 189, 203; Commission of Enquiry in regard to Undesirable Publications, 155; *Regverdige rasse-apartheid,* 76–77, 140

Cronwright-Schreiner, S. C., 36, 39, 219 n.16

Customary law, 65, 93, 208. *See also* Indirect rule

Degenaar, Johan, 61, 74, 77

De Klerk, F. W., 193

De Klerk, Willem, 139

de Man, Paul, x, 231 n.13

Derrida, Jacques, x; autobiography, 116; complicity, 8–11, 201; dissemination, 221 n.25; "Force of

Law," 49, 117; *Given Time,* 112–13; hospitality, 157; iterability, 16; justice and law, 49; "The Laws of Reflection," 169; *Of Grammatology,* 9, 78; *Of Spirit: Heidegger and the Question,* 8–11, 19, 201; *The Other Heading,* 66, 201; *Le problème de la genèse dans la philosophie de Husserl,* 9; "Racism's Last Word," 213 n.1; "Signature Event Context," 16, 221 n.25; *Specters of Marx,* 17, 136, 200; trace, 78, 160

Dhlomo, Herbert, 216 n.27

Dhlomo, R. R. R., 94

Disembodiedness, 27, 29, 33, 182

Dispropriation, 41, 49, 56. *See also* Phonetic script; Technics; Translation

Dostoyevsky, Fyodor, 7, 73, 152

Dreyfus, Alred, 4–5, 6, 21, 42, 47, 172

Drum, 14, 94, 95–96, 97, 99, 108, 121, 205

Du Bois, W. E. B., 42, 221 n.24

Du Plessis, Otto, 58

Durban Declaration on AIDS, 224 n.13

Dutch Reformed Church, 13

Du Toit, André, 61

Ellis, Havelock, 28, 35

Emerson, Ralph Waldo, 34, 219 n.15

English, 40–41, 65, 70, 107–10, 137, 143, 147, 150, 195

Europe(an): cultural identity of, 66; invocation by Louw, 57, 65–66, 85, 91; meaning for Afrikaner cultural identity, 59; racial meaning in South Africa, 59–60, 65

Evolutionary theory, 35; racism and, 39

Fanon, Frantz, 7, 15, 42, 74, 106, 107, 167, 172, 189, 190, 193, 205; *Black Skin, White Masks,* 179–88; *The Wretched of the Earth,* 192

Feminism, 25, 27, 38, 198, 200, 206

Fick, Johan, 238 n.8
Fischer, Bram, 216 n.25
Foucault, Michel, 4, 90, 111; *The Use of Pleasure,* 26–27, 28, 30, 33
Francophone Africa: colonial policy of assimilation in, 94
Freedom Charter, 101
Freire, Paulo, 173
Freud, Sigmund, 101–2, 103, 231 n.10
Funeral rites, 17, 119, 198, 200, 209

Geist: in Heidegger, 8–11
Gemeentelijke Universiteit of Amsterdam, 83
Gerdener, G. B. A. 222–23 n.1
Gerhart, Gail, 239 n.19
Gĩkũyũ, 137, 147–50
Girard, René, 152
Glissant, Édouard, 146
Gordimer, Nadine, 7, 14, 22, 74, 110, 187, 232 n.23; *The Black Interpreters,* 103, 107; *The Lying Days,* 171; "Speak Out: The Necessity for Protest," 170–71; *A World of Strangers,* 238 n.17
Gramsci, Antonio: "The Intellectuals," 7–8
Great Trek, 53, 145, 228 n.42
Group of 63, 146

Habermas, Jürgen, 4–5, 201
Hegel, G. W. F., 166, 185–86, 187, 241 n.2
Heidegger, Martin, x, 136; *Being and Time,* 80; *Inder-Welt-Sein* and *Sein bei* in, 80, 189; "The Self-Assertion of the German University," 9
Hellenism: and British imperialism, 38–39; at Oxford, 25, 28, 39; in Schreiner, 25, 37, 38–40. *See also* Homoeroticism
Hertzog, J. B. M., 55

Hoernlé, R. F. A., 14, 62, 64–65, 118, 203; *South African Native Policy and the Liberal Spirit,* 67–69, 77, 88–89. *See also* Liberalism; Multi-nationalism
Homoeroticism, 25, 31, 36–37. *See also* Hellenism
Hospitality, 50, 113, 119, 124–30, 157, 166, 174, 201
Hove, Chenjerai, 97
Die Huisgenoot, 74, 87, 223 n.7
Human rights, 8, 38
Hybridity, 52, 82, 95, 136, 137, 140, 144–46, 157–58, 204

Imperialism, British, 38–39, 40, 44, 48; Afrikaner resistance to, 70, 72, 90–91, 150, 202, 203
Indaba, 124, 128
Indirect rule, 12, 93–95. *See also* Customary law
Intellectual: advocate, 5, 42–43, 129; critical conscience, 71; figure of responsibility in complicity, 1–2, 4–12, 14, 18, 19, 135, 157, 164, 176, 198; and intellectualist in Louw, 78; standing for justice, 44–45. *See also* Advocacy; African intellectuals; Afrikaans intellectuals; Anglo–South African intellectuals; Complicity; Intellecual Life; Radical white intellectuals; Responsibility
Intellectual life: access of Blacks to, 23, 40, 100–101, 107, 114, 115; access of women to, 23, 27–38. *See also* Disembodiedness; Philosophy; Racial difference; Sexual difference
Interpreting, 21; in courtroom, 42, 48–49

Jakobson, Roman, 216 n.29
Jaspers, Karl: concept of "metaphysical guilt," 6, 42, 171

Loyalty, x, 8, 138, 142. See also *Lojale verset*

Macaulay, Thomas Babington, 45
Makgoba, William, 195
Malan, D. F., 58, 83, 108, 175
Malcolm X, 181
Mamdani, Mahmood, 12–14
Mandela, Nelson, 140, 167, 216 n.23
Mandela, Winnie, 207
Manganyi, N. Chabani, 14; *Being-Black-in-the-World,* 188–92
Marais, Ben, 59
Marx, Karl, 173, 187
Matabele, 40, 52
Maughan-Brown, David, 111–12
Mauss, Marcel, 112
Mbeki, Thabo, 119, 224 n.13
Memory, 120, 121, 127–29; and commemoration, 199
Miller, J. Hillis, 113, 232 n.21
Mimetic rivalry and violence, 133, 136, 149, 241 n.35
Miscegenation: Plaatje on, 52; Schreiner on, 51. *See also* Cronjé, Geoffrey
Mission schools, 13, 96, 216 n.23
Modisane, Bloke, 14, 16, 22, 175, 181, 204; *Blame Me on History,* 96–116, 129, 177, 205; "The Dignity of Begging," 55, 98–100, 101, 110–16; "The Situation," 102–3, 105, 109–10, 111. *See also* "Situation," figure of
Modisane, Joseph, 104
Mofolo, Thomas, 116
Moroka (Chief), 53–54
Moroka, Dr., 59
Mourning, 97, 103, 200, 210. *See also* Funeral rites
Mphahlele, Ezekiel: *The African Image,* 93–98, 121; "Mrs. Plum," 240 n.32
Mqhayi, S. E. K., 116

Mtintso, Thenjiwe, 207–9
Multinationalism. *See* Louw, N. P. van Wyk: multinationalism in
Mzilikazi, 40, 52, 220 n.21

Nakasa, Nat, 94, 96, 97
National Party, 13, 55, 57, 58, 83, 93, 108
National Socialism, ix; Heidegger and, 8–11; Louw and, 225 n.25
Natives' Land Act, 43, 53–54, 83
Natives Representative Council, 89
Naude, Beyers, 170
Ndebele, Njabulo S., 48, 62, 63, 118, 146, 150, 166, 192–96; "The English Language and Social Change in South Africa," 195; *Fools,* 193
Négritude, 93–95, 129, 168, 184–87, 193
New Testament, 127
Ngũgĩ wa Thiong'o, 15, 122, 137, 169; *Detained: A Writer's Prison Diary,* 147–51
Nietzsche, Friedrich, 215 n.17
Nkosi, Lewis, 108–9
Nongqawuse, 123
Norval, Aletta J., 74, 226 n.33
Ntsikana, 122
NUSAS (National Union of South African Students), 166, 167
Nxumalo, Henry, 97

Okhela, 135, 139
Okri, Ben, 97
Olivier, Gerrit, 61
Opposition, 8, 164, 176; and complicity, 9–10, 15. *See also* *Lojale verset;* Resistance
Ossewatrek of 1938, 59, 78

Pan Africanist Congress, 103
Parasitism, 112–14
Paton, Alan, 14, 95, 170, 232 n.23